# Prentice Hall
# GRAMMAR and COMPOSITION

## SERIES CONSULTANTS

### Grade 6
Joleen Johnson
Curriculum Writer, Office of
Secondary Instruction
San Bernardino City Unified Schools
San Bernardino, California

### Grade 7
Ellen G. Manhire
English Consultant Coordinator
Fresno, California

### Grade 8
Elizabeth A. Nace
Supervisor, Language Arts
Akron, Ohio

### Grade 9
Jerry Reynolds
Supervisor, Language Arts
Rochester, Minnesota

### Grade 10
Marlene Corbett
Chairperson, Department of English
Charlotte, North Carolina

### Grade 11
Gilbert Hunt
Chairperson, Department of English
Manchester, Connecticut

### Grade 12
Margherite LaPota
Curriculum Specialist
Tulsa, Oklahoma

## CRITIC READERS

Sheila Bridges
J.L. Wilkinson Middle School
Middleburg, FL

John Elias
Wilkes-Barre Area School District
Wilkes-Barre, PA

Linda Fiddler
Pulaski County Schools
Little Rock, AR

Beverly J. Follendorf
Sweetwater Union High School
San Diego, CA

Jeri B. Jackson
Mt. Gap Middle School
Huntsville, AL

Druscilla L. Jones
Fayette County Public Schools
Lexington, KY

Wilbert J. Lindwall
San Diego City Schools
San Diego, CA

George Comer
Gary Public Schools
Gary, IN

Gloria A. Peirsol-Marino
Lockhart Junior High School
Orlando, FL

Starlyn M. Norman
Howard Junior High School
Orlando, FL

Dora H. Patterson
Meadowbrook Junior High School
Orlando, FL

Margaret A. Reed
Minneapolis Public Schools
Minneapolis, MN

Kathleen A. Sherman
Carroll High School
Fort Wayne, IN

Annette R. Van Dusen
Oklahoma City Public Schools
Oklahoma City, OK

Mary Ann Weathers
Shelby City Schools
Shelby, NC

# Prentice Hall
# GRAMMAR AND COMPOSITION

SERIES AUTHORS

**Gary Forlini**    **Senior Author**
Pelham High School, Pelham, New York

**Mary Beth Bauer**    Harris County Department of Education,
Houston, Texas

**Lawrence Biener**    Locust Valley Junior-Senior High School,
Locust Valley, New York

**Linda Capo**    Pelham Junior High School,
Pelham, New York

**Karen Moore Kenyon**    Saratoga High School,
Saratoga, California

**Darla H. Shaw**    Ridgefield School System,
Ridgefield, Connecticut

**Zenobia Verner**    University of Houston,
Houston, Texas

 **PRENTICE HALL**
Englewood Cliffs, New Jersey
Needham, Massachusetts

**SUPPLEMENTARY MATERIALS**

Annotated Teacher's Edition
Teacher's Resource Book
Computer Exercise Bank
Writing Model Transparencies

Acknowledgments: page 719

PRENTICE HALL **Grammar and Composition**
*Fourth Edition*

ISBN 0-13-711813-9

20   19   18   17   16   15   14   13

**PRENTICE HALL**
A Division of Simon & Schuster
Englewood Cliffs, New Jersey 07632

# Contents

## Grammar    Usage    Mechanics

# III   Mechanics

## Composition and Allied Skills

# IV Composition–The Writer's Techniques

# V Composition–Forms and Process of Writing

14

# Grammar

# **1**

# **Nouns**

An artist paints with colors; a writer paints with words. Just as an artist begins with basic colors, a writer begins with basic kinds of words. These words are called the *parts of speech*. The eight parts of speech are *nouns, pronouns, verbs, adjectives, adverbs, prepositions, conjunctions,* and *interjections*. In the next eight chapters, you will learn about all of them.

## 1.1 The Noun

A *noun* is a naming word. Words such as *friend, sky, boat, love, courage,* and *Seattle* are nouns. They help people name what they are thinking or talking about.

**A noun is the name of a person, place, or thing.**

In English most nouns fall into three main groups.

### People, Places, and Things

The nouns in the chart are grouped under three main headings. You may know most of the nouns under the first two headings. You may not have realized that all of the words in the third group are nouns.

| People | |
|---|---|
| mechanic | Americans |
| Dr. Robinson | leader |

| Places | |
|---|---|
| Lake Mead | motel |
| classroom | Bunker Hill |

| Things | |
|---|---|

**Living and Nonliving Things That You Can See**

| bumblebee | motorcycle |
|---|---|
| petunia | notebook |

**Ideas and Things That You Cannot Usually See**

| strength | willingness |
|---|---|
| honesty | patience |

**EXERCISE A: Classifying Nouns.** The words in the following list are all nouns. Make three columns on your paper as shown in the example. Place each word in the correct column.

EXAMPLE:   window

| People | Places | Things |
|---|---|---|
| | | window |

| | | |
|---|---|---|
| 1. pillow | 8. map | 15. magazine |
| 2. happiness | 9. giraffe | 16. carelessness |
| 3. teacher | 10. sister | 17. hotel |
| 4. lungs | 11. sadness | 18. success |
| 5. tulip | 12. bald eagle | 19. beach |
| 6. beauty | 13. growth | 20. counselor |
| 7. string bean | 14. theater | |

**DEVELOPING WRITING SKILLS: Writing Sentences with Nouns.** Use the following instructions to write five sentences of your own. Underline the nouns you use.

EXAMPLE:  Write a sentence using a noun that names an idea
you cannot usually see.

We have always admired your <u>courage</u>.

1. Write a sentence using two nouns that name family members.
2. Write a sentence using a noun that names a living thing that you can see.
3. Write a sentence using a noun that names an idea you cannot usually see.
4. Write a sentence using a noun that names a nonliving thing that you can see.
5. Write a sentence using nouns that name two or more cities or states you would like to visit.

# 1.2 Different Kinds of Nouns

Some nouns belong to special groups. There are *collective nouns, compound nouns,* and *common* and *proper nouns*. Most of them are easy to recognize.

## Collective Nouns

A few nouns name groups of people or things. A *flock* of sparrows, for example, is a group of birds. An *audience* is a group of people. These nouns are called *collective nouns*.

**A collective noun is a noun that names a group of individual people or things.**

The following are common collective nouns.

| COLLECTIVE NOUNS | | |
|---|---|---|
| club | herd | army |
| troop | orchestra | committee |
| class | team | group |

**22**

**EXERCISE A: Recognizing Collective Nouns.** Each of the following groups of words contains one collective noun. Write each collective noun on your paper.

EXAMPLE:  noise    crowd    flower

crowd

1. vegetable    radio    family
2. jury    sailboat    happiness
3. freedom    squad    plant
4. crew    skyscraper    elephant
5. finger    assembly    newspaper

## Compound Nouns

Sometimes two words are used together to form a new word with a different meaning. You know, for example, the two separate words *station* and *wagon*. When they are used together, however, as in "Uncle Zeke owns a *station wagon*," the words *station wagon* mean "a car with space in the back for loading things." Together, the words take on a special meaning. A noun such as *station wagon* is said to be *compound*.

**A compound noun is a noun made up of two or more words.**

*Compound nouns* can be written in one of three ways. Some are written as separate words, others as hyphenated words, and still others as combined words.

| COMPOUND NOUNS | | |
|---|---|---|
| **Separate Words** | **Hyphenated Words** | **Combined Words** |
| post office | bull's-eye | flagship |
| junior high school | daughter in-law | railroad |
| Golden Gate Bridge | left-hander | doorknob |

**EXERCISE B: Identifying Compound Nouns.** Each of the following sentences has one or more compound nouns. Copy the sentences onto your paper and underline each compound noun.

EXAMPLE   The scouts hoisted their pennant up the <u>flagpole</u>.

1. In a desert both people and animals search for water holes.
2. The dining room in our hotel is quite near the swimming pool.
3. This new typewriter belongs to my father-in-law.
4. She has pictures of a wolf spider, a horned beetle, and a praying mantis.
5. Our teams excel in football and basketball.

**EXERCISE C: Finding the Correct Form of Compound Nouns.** Use a dictionary to find the correct spelling of each of the following compound nouns. Write the correct form on your paper.

EXAMPLE:   fire-drill      fire drill      firedrill

           fire drill

1. postmaster      post-master      post master
2. side-line      side line      sideline
3. son in law      soninlaw      son-in-law
4. base ball      baseball      base-ball
5. fire place      fire-place      fireplace

## Common and Proper Nouns

All nouns—even if they are collective or compound—can be classified as either *common nouns* or *proper nouns*.

**A common noun names any one of a class of people, places, or things.**

**A proper noun names a specific person, place, or thing.**

Common nouns are not capitalized, except at the beginning of a sentence or in a title. Proper nouns are always capitalized.

| Common Nouns | Proper Nouns |
|---|---|
| writer | May Swenson |
| state | Colorado |
| document | Declaration of Independence |

**EXERCISE D: Identifying Common and Proper Nouns.** Copy each of the following nouns onto your paper. Place a *C* after each common noun and a *P* after each proper noun. Then for each common noun, write a corresponding proper noun. For each proper noun, write a corresponding common noun.

EXAMPLE:   city

            city    C    Seattle

1. street
2. Chevette
3. Los Angeles
4. general
5. Jane Austen
6. Lassie
7. song
8. mayor
9. Hank Aaron
10. river

**DEVELOPING WRITING SKILLS: Writing Sentences with Different Types of Nouns.** Write five sentences of your own, each using the kind of noun that fits the description given in the following list. Underline these nouns.

EXAMPLE:   collective noun

            A <u>flock</u> of noisy geese flew overhead making sounds
            that sounded similar to dogs barking.

1. collective noun
2. compound noun that is hyphenated
3. three common nouns and two proper nouns
4. compound noun that is two separate words
5. compound noun that is a combined word

**25**

# Skills Review and Writing Workshop

## Nouns

### CHECKING YOUR SKILLS
Write the two nouns in each sentence.

(1) The Alhambra is a beautiful walled construction. (2) It overlooks Granada from a flat-topped hill. (3) From the city below, you see only sheer walls. (4) Once inside, however, you are surrounded by a group of Moorish palaces. (5) Each castle opens onto a courtyard. (6) You can see flowers and reflecting pools. (7) These small gardens hold their own delights. (8) The fragrance of blossoms pleases you. (9) You are soothed by water murmuring softly from fountains. (10) Truly, the place is like a paradise.

### USING GRAMMAR SKILLS IN WRITING
### Writing a Magazine Article
Specific nouns in a description of a place help readers see the place in their mind's eye. Imagine that you are writing about a special place for a magazine read by people who like to travel. Follow the steps below to write a description that is both interesting and accurate.

**Prewriting:** Choose a place that seems unusual to you. List at least three reasons that make it interesting to visit. Note details that would make it interesting to other people.

**Writing:** Begin with a sentence telling why the place is special. Continue with the details that back up your first sentence. Conclude by telling what you like best about the place.

**Revising:** Change any nouns that are overused or need to be made more specific. Check to make sure that each sentence is clear. After revising your description, proofread carefully.

# Pronouns

While there are thousands of nouns in English, there are fewer than one hundred *pronouns*—words such as *she, their, this, who,* and *what.* Although pronouns are not as colorful or exciting as nouns, they do have important uses in sentences. This chapter will help you learn to identify different types of pronouns.

## The Pronoun 2.1

*Pronouns* play a very important role in sentences.

**A pronoun is a word that takes the place of a noun or group of words acting as a noun.**

Pronouns make it possible to avoid using the same noun over and over. Read the following examples.

WITHOUT
PRONOUNS:     The *astronauts* described how the *astronauts* opened the *astronauts'* capsule.

WITH PRONOUNS:   The *astronauts* described how *they* opened *their* capsule.

The pronouns *they* and *their* stand for the noun *astronauts* at the beginning of the sentence. Sometimes a pronoun takes the place of a noun in an earlier sentence.

EXAMPLE: Finally, the *actress* reappeared. *She* smiled and bowed to the audience.

The pronoun *she* in the second sentence takes the place of the noun *actress* in the first sentence.

Once in a while, a single pronoun takes the place of a whole group of words.

EXAMPLE: *How they rescued Kim* is amazing. *It* is a story that will be told again and again.

In this example the pronoun *it* in the second sentence takes the place of four words: *how they rescued Kim.*


## Antecedents of Pronouns

The word or group of words that a pronoun replaces is called an *antecedent.*

**An antecedent is the noun (or group of words acting as a noun) for which a pronoun stands.**

The word *antecedent* means "something going before." In most instances an antecedent does come before the pronoun and later takes its place.

EXAMPLES: ANTECEDENT / PRONOUN / PRONOUN
The *astronauts* described how *they* opened *their* capsule.

ANTECEDENT / PRONOUN
Finally, the *actress* reappeared. *She* smiled and bowed to the audience.

ANTECEDENT / PRONOUN
*How they rescued Kim* is amazing. *It* is a story that will be told again and again.

Sometimes, an antecedent will come after the pronoun.

EXAMPLE: PRONOUN / ANTECEDENT
Whenever *he* makes a long distance call, *Jim* speaks for only a few minutes.

**28**

Sometimes a pronoun will not have any antecedent.

EXAMPLE:   *Everyone* knows what the truth is.

The pronoun *everyone* does not have a specific antecedent because its meaning is clear without one.

**EXERCISE A:  Recognizing Antecedents.** Find the antecedent for each underlined pronoun in the following sentences and write it on your paper.

EXAMPLE:   Martha explained how <u>she</u> won the contest.

      Martha

1. Ted tried to explain why <u>he</u> didn't phone.
2. Will the treasurer give <u>her</u> report?
3. Although the apples were red, <u>they</u> tasted sour.
4. If <u>they</u> arrive in time, the boys will do the work.
5. Baking cookies for the party is not a good idea. <u>It</u> takes too much time.
6. The rattlesnake kills <u>its</u> victims with venom.
7. Maria agreed that <u>she</u> was wrong.
8. Have the boys brought <u>their</u> swimsuits?
9. As the steamboat rounded the bend, black smoke poured from <u>its</u> smokestack.
10. The policeman gave <u>his</u> version of the accident.

## Personal Pronouns

*Personal pronouns* are used far more often than other pronouns.

**Personal pronouns refer to (1) the person speaking, (2) the person spoken to, or (3) the person, place, or thing spoken about.**

Personal pronouns are either singular or plural. Depending on whom or what they refer to, they are called first-person, second-person, or third-person pronouns. Study the forms in the following chart.

| PERSONAL PRONOUNS | | |
|---|---|---|
| | **Singular** | **Plural** |
| **First Person** | I, me, my, mine | we, us, our, ours |
| **Second Person** | you, your, yours | you, your, yours |
| **Third Person** | he, him, his<br>she, her, hers<br>it, its | they, them, their,<br>theirs |

It is important to understand when each type of personal pronoun is used.

*First-person pronouns,* such as *I, me, we, us,* and *our,* are used by the person who is actually speaking to refer to himself or herself either as an individual or as a member of a group.

EXAMPLE:   *I* received *my* presents yesterday.

*Second-person pronouns,* such as *you, your,* and *yours,* are used when a person is speaking directly to another person.

EXAMPLE:   *Your* present was by far the nicest.

*Third-person pronouns,* such as *he, she, it,* or *they,* are used to refer to someone or something that may not even be present.

EXAMPLE:   Bill phoned last night from school. *He* said *he* was sending a beautiful present.

Notice in the chart of personal pronouns that third-person singular pronouns have the greatest variety of forms. *He, him,* and *his* are used to refer to males. *She, her,* and *hers* are used to refer to females. *It* and *its* are usually used to refer to things.

**30**

**EXERCISE B: Identifying Personal Pronouns.** Copy the underlined pronoun in each of the following sentences onto your paper. Identify the pronoun as *first person, second person,* or *third person.*

EXAMPLE: The teacher asked <u>him</u> a difficult question.

him    third person

1. <u>We</u> tried to reach the police all morning.
2. The judge of the contest said that <u>your</u> dance was the best.
3. The jaguar struck the rock and injured <u>its</u> front paw.
4. The first two sketches of steamboats are <u>mine</u>.
5. My aunt said that <u>she</u> papered the entire room in less than a day.
6. Alexander didn't follow the directions given to <u>him</u>.
7. A herd of bighorn sheep appeared, but <u>they</u> were frightened away by the airplane.
8. The doctor said that <u>I</u> can expect the hand to hurt for several days.
9. After some discussion the explorers chose <u>their</u> route through the mountains.
10. The violinist said <u>he</u> practices seven days a week.

**DEVELOPING WRITING SKILLS: Writing Sentences with Personal Pronouns.** Write a short, clear sentence using a personal pronoun that fits each of the descriptions given in the following list. You may, if you wish, consult the chart of personal pronouns on page 30.

EXAMPLE: Third person, singular, feminine

Mother described her experience to the family.

1. first person, plural
2. third person, plural
3. third person, singular, masculine
4. second person, plural
5. first person, singular

# 2.2 Other Kinds of Pronouns

Although you probably use personal pronouns more than you use other kinds of pronouns, you should also know about some of the other kinds. This section will tell you about those other kinds of pronouns—*demonstrative, interrogative,* and *indefinite pronouns.*

## Demonstrative Pronouns

*Demonstrative pronouns* call attention to particular people, places, and things.

**A demonstrative pronoun points out a specific person, place, or thing.**

There are two singular and two plural demonstrative pronouns.

| DEMONSTRATIVE PRONOUNS | | | |
|---|---|---|---|
| **Singular** | | **Plural** | |
| this | that | these | those |

A demonstrative pronoun generally comes at the beginning of a sentence, with its antecedent appearing somewhere later in the same sentence. However, sometimes the demonstrative pronoun will come after its antecedent.

BEFORE:   *That* has always been my favorite movie.

              *Those* are the girls on the volleyball team.

AFTER:    We saw a Gila monster and a monitor. *These* were the most interesting of the zoo's lizards.

              Of all her stories, *those* about witches and dragons are my favorites.

32

**EXERCISE A: Recognizing Demonstrative Pronouns.**
Each of the following sentences contains a demonstrative pronoun. On your paper write each demonstrative pronoun.

EXAMPLE:  These are the highest grades I have ever received.

    These

1. This is the typewriter I hope to get for Christmas.
2. My uncle plays the bassoon. This is a very difficult instrument to play.
3. That seems to be the shortest route to the village.
4. Of all his excuses, these are the poorest.
5. This has been the happiest day of my life.
6. Yes, these are the oldest tombstones in Lexington's cemetery.
7. She said those are the most interesting fossils.
8. Ronald likes to display his models built from toothpicks. These are his pride and joy.
9. Isn't that a poster of one of Georgia O'Keeffe's paintings?
10. Before leaving for college, my sister gave me her jade necklace and silver pin. Those had always been her favorites.

# Interrogative Pronouns

To *interrogate* means to "ask questions."

**An interrogative pronoun is used to begin a question.**

All five interrogative pronouns begin with *w*.

| INTERROGATIVE PRONOUNS | | | | |
|---|---|---|---|---|
| what | which | who | whom | whose |

Most *interrogative pronouns* do not have antecedents. In the following examples, notice that only the second and the third pronouns have antecedents.

EXAMPLES:    Here is the refund check. *What* shall I do with it?

Which is the shortest way to the city?

Who is the pole-vaulter with the perfect record?

*Whom* does Bari want to see in the office?

This was found under the table. *Whose* can it be?

**EXERCISE B: Recognizing Interrogative Pronouns.** Each of the following items contains an interrogative pronoun. On your paper write each interrogative pronoun.

EXAMPLE:    What happened to the cookies I baked?

What

1. Whom did you send the package to?
2. That is beautiful. Whose is it?
3. She has two calculators. Which would you prefer to borrow?
4. Who is the actor with the high-pitched voice?
5. What is her occupation?
6. Who is coming to the party?
7. What should I say when I meet the Senator for the first time?
8. Which of the states has the largest deposits of coal?
9. With whom did you leave your telephone number and address?
10. Samantha has four albums by the Temptations. Which is the best?

## Indefinite Pronouns

*Indefinite pronouns* have many different forms.

**Indefinite pronouns refer to people, places, or things, often without specifying which ones.**

Notice in the following chart that a few indefinite pronouns can be either singular or plural, depending on use.

| INDEFINITE PRONOUNS | | | |
|---|---|---|---|
| **Singular** | | **Plural** | **Singular or Plural** |
| another | much | both | all |
| anybody | neither | few | any |
| anyone | nobody | many | more |
| anything | no one | others | most |
| each | nothing | several | none |
| either | one | | |
| everybody | other | | |
| everyone | somebody | | |
| everything | someone | | |
| little | something | | |

Indefinite pronouns often do not have antecedents. Sometimes, however, they do.

WITHOUT ANTECEDENTS:  *Everything* is ready for the trip.

*Few* are willing to wait until tomorrow

WITH ANTECEDENTS:  *Both* of the artists use watercolors.

As the animals paraded by, *several* seemed nervous.

**EXERCISE C: Recognizing Indefinite Pronouns.** Each of the following sentences contains at least one indefinite pronoun. On your paper write each indefinite pronoun.

EXAMPLE:  Each refused to speak to the other.

Each      other

1. Few in the class knew which nation colonized Angola.
2. Has everyone already had lunch?
3. Many of these insects burrow into the soil.
4. Neither cared for the concert, but both complimented the bandleader.
5. His excuse is that everyone arrived late.
6. In the field grew poison ivy and poison sumac; both are plants that can cause rashes.
7. Most can learn to use parallel bars after practicing for a while.
8. Our family knew none of their guests.
9. Most of the people I know would like to play the piano.
10. All of the poodles have been carefully trained.

**DEVELOPING WRITING SKILLS: Writing Sentences with Pronouns.** Write a short sentence or pair of sentences using a pronoun that fits each of the descriptions given in the following list. Underline the pronoun that you use.

EXAMPLE: demonstrative pronoun that comes after its antecedent

I picked out some library books. These seemed the most interesting to me.

1. demonstrative pronoun at the beginning of the sentence
2. demonstrative pronoun that comes after its antecedent
3. interrogative pronoun with an antecedent
4. interrogative pronoun without an antecedent
5. indefinite pronoun with an antecedent

# Skills Review and Writing Workshop

## Pronouns
### CHECKING YOUR SKILLS
Write the two pronouns in each sentence.

(1) On Wednesday Joel Hutter suggested that we organize a trivia contest for our homeroom. (2) Everybody asked who would be the judge. (3) Miss McGuire said that we could elect somebody or ask for a volunteer. (4) "My friend, Miss Duff, and her friend, Mr. Framis, just love trivia contests." (5) "Should I ask them?" (6) No one objected and several of the girls became really excited. (7) The twins asked Miss McGuire if she would like their trivia questions. (8) Then Miss McGuire asked which of us would like to volunteer questions. (9) Joel wanted us to make up our own. (10) Everybody thought that was a good idea.

### USING GRAMMAR SKILLS IN WRITING
### Writing a News Story
Pronouns add variety to writing. Imagine you are writing a story about your classmates for your school newspaper. Follow the steps below to write a news story.

**Prewriting:** Choose a community or school event that will interest your schoolmates. Then make notes. What happened? Who was involved? When and where did it happen? Outline events in the order in which they happened.

**Writing:** Begin with a statement that sums up your story and gets your readers' attention. Then tell the story as it happened, following your outline.

**Revising:** First look at your pronouns to make sure that the antecedents are clear. Then read the entire story to make other improvements. After revising, proofread carefully.

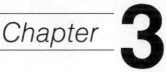

# Chapter 3

# Verbs

Every complete sentence has at least one *verb*. Verbs tell at what time something happens—in the present, in the past, or in the future. The two main types of verbs are *action verbs* and *linking verbs*. These verbs can also be used with *helping verbs*.

## 3.1 Action Verbs

Verbs such as *walk, chew, stop, fly, learn, open, do,* and *fix* all show some kind of action.

**An action verb tells what action someone or something is performing.**

EXAMPLES:    Father *broiled* our hamburgers.

The caterpillars *devoured* all the oak leaves.

The verb *broiled* explains what *father* did to the hamburgers. The verb *devoured* tells what the *caterpillars* did to the oak leaves. *Father* and *caterpillars,* the performers of the actions, are the *subjects* in these sentences. (See Chapter 9 for more about subjects.)

Some actions are easy to see. Some are not. Which of the following actions would you be able to see?

EXAMPLES:    The pitcher *throws* a fast ball.

I *believe* in justice.

Both *throws* and *believe* are action verbs, but they show different kinds of action. You can see a pitcher *throw* a ball. *Throwing* is a *visible* action. Also, you can see a person *broiling* a hamburger or a caterpillar *devouring* an oak leaf.

The verb *believe* also expresses an action, but it is a *mental* action, something you can not usually see. Compare the two two types of action verbs in the following chart.

| Visible Action | | Mental Action | |
|---|---|---|---|
| run | swim | remember | decide |
| rip | eat | understand | believe |
| bring | smile | expect | hope |
| tell | go | think | wonder |

**EXERCISE A: Identifying Kinds of Action Verbs.** Write the underlined action verb from each of the sentences. After each verb write *visible* or *mental* to identify the kind of action that the verb shows. Note that six are visible and four are mental.

EXAMPLE:    Marcia picked a bushel of apples from the tree.

picked        visible

1. My best friend chews her food thoroughly.
2. I wonder about my future all the time.
3. The fullback dropped the football in the end zone.
4. Four of us crowded into the back seat of the car.
5. We expect many people at the crafts fair.
6. The beetle scurried into a corner of the tent.
7. Like a great bird, the Concorde landed gracefully.
8. The hedgehog, a small mammal, eats insects.
9. I often worry about overpopulation.
10. I remember the day of the blackout very well.

**EXERCISE B: Recognizing Action Verbs.** Copy the following sentences onto your paper. Underline the action verb in each sentence.

EXAMPLE:   The plane from Madrid <u>arrived</u> three hours late.

1. The musician placed the piccolo in its case.
2. Bill sprinkled garlic onto the steaming bread.
3. This camera takes excellent pictures.
4. Years ago my grandmother baked her own pies for holidays.
5. My little brother waved the cowboy hat above his head.
6. The mayor cut the ribbon with a huge pair of scissors.
7. The ship struck the dock.
8. The fishermen occupied several villages near the river.
9. Darlene bought three albums this morning.
10. Flora plugged the leak in the water pipe with an old towel of hers.

**DEVELOPING WRITING SKILLS: Writing Sentences with Action Verbs.** Write ten original sentences, each using one of the following action verbs. Underline the verb in each sentence you write.

EXAMPLE:   grow

        She <u>grows</u> snap beans in the garden.

| | | |
|---|---|---|
| 1. sing | 5. touch | 9. drive |
| 2. ride | 6. watch | 10. ask |
| 3. plant | 7. swim | |
| 4. tell | 8. read | |

# 3.2 Linking Verbs

Some verbs do not show action. Instead, they *link* two parts of a sentence. A linking verb thus shows a relationship between other words in a sentence.

**A linking verb connects a noun or pronoun at or near the beginning of a sentence with a word at or near the end.**

Some of the most widely used verbs are *linking verbs*. The word after a linking verb usually identifies or describes a word in front of the verb.

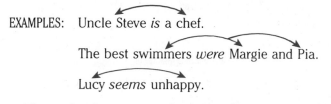

EXAMPLES:    Uncle Steve *is* a chef.

The best swimmers *were* Margie and Pia.

Lucy *seems* unhappy.

The verbs *is, were,* and *seems* all connect or link the words in front of them with the words after them. The verbs act almost like equal signs. *Chef* in the first sentence identifies *Uncle Steve*. *Margie* and *Pia* in the next sentence identify the *swimmers*. In the last sentence, *unhappy* describes *Lucy*.

## The Most Common Linking Verb

In English the most common linking verb is *be*. This verb has many forms.

| THE FORMS OF *BE* | | |
|---|---|---|
| am | can be | have been |
| are | could be | has been |
| is | may be | had been |
| was | might be | could have been |
| were | must be | may have been |
| am being | shall be | might have been |
| are being | should be | must have been |
| is being | will be | shall have been |
| was being | would be | should have been |
| were being | | will have been |
| | | would have been |

**EXERCISE A: Recognizing Forms of the Linking Verb Be.** Copy the following sentences. Underline the form of *be* in each one. Then draw a double- or triple-headed arrow connecting the words that are linked by the verb.

EXAMPLE: That dog is a collie.

1. Your next book will be *When the Legends Die*.
2. That purple jewel is an amethyst.
3. The keys have been rusty for some time now.
4. Her favorite colors are turquoise and tan.
5. Judy was the star of the show.
6. Carlos Cruz might be our next mayor.
7. The best play was *You're a Good Man, Charlie Brown*.
8. She should have been happy after winning.
9. Most snowflakes are delicately shaped hexagons.
10. I am always very hungry by lunch time.

## Other Linking Verbs

*Be* is the most commonly used linking verb, but there are some other important linking verbs you should know.

| OTHER LINKING VERBS | | |
|---|---|---|
| appear | look | sound |
| become | remain | stay |
| feel | seem | taste |
| grow | smell | turn |

These verbs are often used in the same way as *be* to link two parts of a sentence.

EXAMPLES: She later *became* a civil engineer.

The cream *tastes* sour.

The food *stayed* fresh and crisp.

42

**EXERCISE B: Identifying Other Linking Verbs.** Copy each of the following sentences onto your paper. Underline the linking verb in each one. Then draw a double- or triple-headed arrow connecting the words that are linked by the verb.

EXAMPLE: With the storm the road quickly <u>turned</u> muddy.

1. David appears hungry and tired.
2. His answer seemed wrong to me.
3. The two comics remained partners for thirty years.
4. The white, sandy beach looks inviting.
5. On this old record, the voices sound shrill and scratchy.
6. The apple pie smells delicious.
7. That quartz looks almost colorless.
8. Mary Ann became a fine lawyer.
9. For two years the house stayed empty.
10. This fabric feels rough to the touch.

# Action Verb or Linking Verb?

Many of the twelve verbs in the preceding chart can be used as either linking verbs or action verbs.

LINKING: The bread *smelled* stale. (*Smelled* links *bread* and *stale.*)

ACTION: Charles *smelled* the cake. (Charles is performing an action.)

LINKING: The Dutch bulbs *grow* tall. (*Grow* links *bulbs* and *tall.*)

ACTION: Annemarie *grows* tulips. (Annemarie is performing an action.)

To test whether a verb is a linking verb or an action verb, substitute *am,* or *are* for the verb. If the new verb links a word before it to a word after it and if the sentence still makes sense, then the original verb is a linking verb.

**43**

| Linking | Action |
|---------|--------|
| Tina *felt* weak | Tina *felt* the cloth. |
| (Tina *is* weak?) | (Tina *is* the cloth?) |
| Yes, it's a linking verb. | No, it's an action verb. |

**EXERCISE C: Distinguishing Between Action Verbs and Linking Verbs.** On your paper write the verb from each of the following sentences. After each action verb write *AV* and after each linking verb write *LV*.

EXAMPLE:  Suddenly a bright light appeared in the sky.

appeared     AV

1. The inspector sounded the alarm as a test.
2. During the drought the grass turned brown.
3. The room seems smaller now.
4. My brother grows tomatoes and scallions.
5. That robin appears at our bird feeder often.
6. The chocolate fudge tastes too sweet.
7. She stayed in Texas for two weeks.
8. Two years later my uncle became a judge.
9. The garage now looks clean.
10. Influenced by the bad weather, the animals turned skittish.

**DEVELOPING WRITING SKILLS: Writing Sentences with Linking Verbs.** Write ten sentences of your own, each using one of the following linking verbs. Underline the verbs and draw double-headed arrows connecting the words they link.

EXAMPLE:  seem

The lost children <u>seem</u> frightened.

1. became
2. was
3. remain
4. sound
5. look
6. appear
7. felt
8. grew
9. smell
10. turned

# Helping Verbs 3.3

Sometimes a verb that is in a sentence is made up of just one word. Often, however, a verb will be made up of several words. This type of verb is called a *verb phrase*. A verb phrase will have one, two, or three *helping verbs* before the key part of the verb.

**Helping verbs are added before another verb to make a verb phrase.**

The helping verbs in the following examples are italicized. Notice how they help to change the meaning of *put,* the key part of the verb.

EXAMPLES:  put

*had* put

*will* have put

*might* have put

*should have been* put

## Recognizing Helping Verbs

The various forms of *be* shown in the chart on page 41 are often used as helping verbs in front of other verbs. In the following chart, a number of different forms of *be* are used as helping verbs. All are italicized.

| SOME FORMS OF *BE* USED AS HELPING VERBS | |
| --- | --- |
| **Helping Verbs** | **Key Verbs** |
| *am* | growing |
| *has been* | warned |
| *was being* | told |
| *could have been* | reminded |
| *will have been* | waiting |

Some other common verbs are also used as helping verbs.

| OTHER HELPING VERBS | | | |
|---|---|---|---|
| do | have | shall | can |
| does | has | should | could |
| did | had | will | may |
| | | would | might |
| | | | must |

These additional helping verbs can be combined with different key verbs to form a variety of verb phrases. The following chart shows just a few of the many possible combinations that can be made.

| VERB PHRASES | |
|---|---|
| **Helping Verbs** | **Key Verbs** |
| *do* | remember |
| *has* | written |
| *would* | hope |
| *can* | believe |
| *may* | attempt |
| *must have* | thought |
| *should have* | grown |

**EXERCISE A: Supplying Helping Verbs.** Each of the following sentences contains one or more blanks. Write each sentence on your paper. Fill in each blank with a helping verb that makes sense in the sentence.

EXAMPLE:    Lars _____ _____ followed the path.

Lars should have followed the path.

1. Pasquale _____ win an important science award at graduation.

2. Judy _____ _____ taking medicine for her infection.
3. The team _____ _____ left for Boston by this time tomorrow.
4. He _____ ruined everything.
5. They _____ _____ taken better care of their tools.
6. My sister _____ read all of the Nancy Drew and Hardy Boys books.
7. I guess they thought we _____ not come anymore.
8. How _____ they travel to Mexico?
9. The city _____ planted a row of Norway maples along our street.
10. Our European visitors _____ _____ arrived this morning.

## Helping Verbs in Sentences

Words in a verb phrase can sometimes be separated by other words. Very often words such as *not, certainly,* and *seldom* come between a helping verb and the key part of the verb. In questions verbs of two or more words are frequently separated. In the following examples, the parts of each verb phrase are italicized.

WORDS TOGETHER: They *must have been taken* by taxi to the airport.

WORDS SEPARATED: Marie *has* certainly not *contacted* us.

He *had* carefully *kept* all the records.

*Can* they really *build* their own home?

**EXERCISE B: Finding Helping Verbs.** On your paper write the complete verb phrase from each of the following sentences. Include all the helping verbs, but do *not* include any of the words that may separate the parts of the verb phrase.

EXAMPLE: Have you walked the dogs yet?

Have walked

**47**

1. Government officials were quickly sent to the flood area.
2. Have they planted the vegetables in straight rows?
3. The new pupils should have been taken to meet the principal.
4. Who has been doing research on early polar flights?
5. We should have really taken more food along on the picnic.
6. The girls have not yet chosen a captain.
7. Have you remembered the famous campaign slogan about Tippecanoe?
8. They had not planned on a complete power failure.
9. Your mother could have certainly reached them by phone.
10. Does anyone in the room remember Patrick's last name?

**DEVELOPING WRITING SKILLS: Writing Sentences with Helping Verbs.** Write five sentences of your own, each using one of the following verb phrases. Underline all parts of the verb phrase. If you wish you can put the word *not* or some other word between parts of the verb phrase.

EXAMPLE:    would have written

      I thought she <u>would have written</u> me a letter by now.

1. have finished
2. must have taken
3. did arrive
4. could have been mistaken
5. should have left

# Skills Review and Writing Workshop

## Verbs

### CHECKING YOUR SKILLS

Write the verb or verb phrase in each sentence.

(1) Paul is running on skiis. (2) He is skiing cross-country. (3) With every step, he stabs his ski poles into the snow. (4) Then he pushes himself forward. (5) In this way, he can glide smoothly over the frosty surface. (6) Now hills are rising ahead of him. (7) Paul climbs them with a special herring-bone step. (8) At the top, he must rest. (9) Soon he will move down again onto flatter land. (10) New scenes and sights may lie ahead on this winter adventure.

### USING GRAMMAR SKILLS IN WRITING
### Writing a Sports Story

Good writers use vivid, precise verbs to bring their stories to life. Imagine that you are writing a description of an individual sport, such as swimming or hiking, for your school magazine. Follow the steps below.

**Prewriting:** Choose a sport that a person can carry out on his or her own. If possible, choose an individual sport that you yourself enjoy. In your mind's eye, watch the athlete going through the motions of the sport. List vivid verbs that come to mind to describe the athlete's movements and feelings.

**Writing:** Begin by showing the athlete in motion. Then follow the athlete through a series of typical actions, as in the paragraph above about the cross-country skiier.

**Revising:** First look at your verbs. Change any of them that could be made more vivid or accurate. Then read the entire description. Did you tell the actions in the sequence in which they happened? After you revise, proofread carefully.

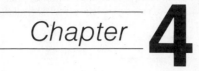

# Chapter 4

# Adjectives

How would you describe the weather on your last birthday? Was it *cold, damp,* and *blustery*? Was it *mild, dry,* and *sunny*? If your birthday comes in the summer, the best words might even be *hot* and *humid*.

All these words are *adjectives*. Used properly, they describe and sharpen the meaning of nouns and pronouns.

## 4.1 The Adjective

*Adjectives* are used with two other parts of speech.

**An adjective is used to describe a noun or a pronoun.**

### Adjectives as Modifiers

Adjectives *modify* nouns and pronouns. To *modify* means to "change slightly." Adjectives modify nouns and pronouns by slightly changing their meanings. For example, when you hear the noun *house,* a certain picture of a house may come into your mind. However, when you say "a small house," "a large wooden house," or "an old white Colonial house," the adjectives change the picture slightly.

Adjectives usually answer one of these four questions about the nouns and pronouns they modify: *What kind? Which one? How many? How much?*

| What Kind? | |
|---|---|
| *new* car | *striped* tie |
| **Which One?** | |
| *this* butterfly | *every* page |
| **How Many?** | |
| *one* hamburger | *many* cucumbers |
| **How Much?** | |
| *no* food | *little* rain |

When adjectives modify nouns, they usually come directly before the nouns. Occasionally they may come after.

BEFORE:   She saw *a bright, smiling* face.

AFTER:   The room, *narrow* and *dark,* frightened us.

Adjectives may also modify pronouns. When they do, they usually come after a linking verb. Occasionally they may come before.

AFTER:   They are *happy* and *talkative.*

BEFORE:   *Quiet* and *sullen,* he sat in a corner.

**EXERCISE A: Recognizing Adjectives and the Words They Modify.** Copy each of the following sentences onto your paper. Draw an arrow pointing from each underlined adjective to the noun or pronoun it modifies.

EXAMPLE:   He has not been <u>well</u> for <u>several</u> months.

**51**

1. A <u>loud</u>, <u>shrill</u> whistle pierced the air.
2. She is <u>beautiful</u> and <u>graceful</u>.
3. The desert, <u>smooth</u> and <u>white</u>, spread for miles before us.
4. We drove into the <u>noisy</u>, <u>crowded</u> intersection.
5. <u>Tall</u> and <u>slim</u>, he was the picture of health.
6. They are <u>unhappy</u> over the results of the poll.
7. We saw a <u>small</u>, <u>round</u>, <u>hairy</u> animal at the zoo.
8. I have <u>some</u> change, but we will need <u>more</u> money to get home.
9. In her <u>third</u> and <u>fourth</u> years, she broke the <u>swimming</u> records.
10. <u>That</u> man has <u>several</u> tickets to the game.

# Articles

Three common adjectives—*the, a,* and *an*—are known as *articles*. Articles stand in front of nouns, like other adjectives, and answer the question *Which one?*

The article *the* is called the *definite article.*

**The, the definite article, refers to a specific person, place, or thing.**

The word *the* notes one particular person, place, or thing.

EXAMPLES: *the* principal

*the* canoe

*the* only wool sweater

*A* and *an,* the other two articles, are called *indefinite articles.* These two articles are not as specific as *the.*

**A and an, the indefinite articles, refer to any single member in a group or class of people, places, or things.**

Indefinite articles point out a type of person, place, or thing, but they do not refer to a specific one.

EXAMPLES:   *a* principal (any principal)

*a* canoe (perhaps one of several)

*an* old sweater (any one of many)

You should also know when to use *a* and when to use *an*. *A* is used before consonant sounds. *An* is used before vowel sounds. Notice that you choose between *a* and *an* based on *sound*. The letter *h*, a consonant, may sound like either a consonant or a vowel. The letters *o* and *u* are also problems. They are vowels, but they sometimes sound like consonants.

| USING *A* AND *AN* | |
| --- | --- |
| ***A* with Consonant Sounds** | ***An* with Vowel Sounds** |
| a *y*ellow hat | an *e*lephant |
| a *h*appy time (*h* sound) | an *h*onest person (no *h* sound) |
| a *o*nce-over (*w* sound) | an *o*ld map (*o* sound) |
| a *u*nicorn (*y* sound) | an *u*ncle (*u* sound) |

**EXERCISE B: Distinguishing Between Definite and Indefinite Articles.** Write the article that will correctly complete each of the following sentences. The word in parentheses tells you which kind of article to use.

EXAMPLE:   __(Definite)__ ambulance raced up
__(indefinite)__ one-way street.

The ambulance raced up a one-way street.

1. Have you purchased __(definite)__ birthday cake yet?
2. __(Indefinite)__ older man stopped us in the street.
3. Our captain hit both __(indefinite)__ single and __(indefinite)__ home run.
4. __(Definite)__ oldest stamp in her collection is dated 1857.

5. He always takes either ___(indefinite)___ apple or ___(indefinite)___ banana to school.
6. The piano has ___(indefinite)___ ivory keyboard.
7. ___(Definite)___ President addressed ___(indefinite)___ joint session of Congress.
8. ___(Indefinite)___ audition notice for the show was posted by ___(definite)___ director.
9. Where are ___(definite)___ camera and ___(definite)___ film?
10. Tomorrow she will open ___(indefinite)___ account at ___(definite)___ bank.

## Nouns Used as Adjectives

Nouns can sometimes be used as adjectives. A noun used as an adjective usually comes directly before another noun and answers the question *What kind?* or *Which one?*

| Nouns | Used as Adjectives |
|---|---|
| shoe | a *shoe* salesperson (*What kind* of salesperson?) |
| wedding | the *wedding* day (*Which* day?) |

**EXERCISE C: Identifying Nouns Used as Adjectives.**
Write the noun used as an adjective from the following sentences. Next to it write the noun it modifies.

EXAMPLE:   A piano player entertained the guests.

      piano     player

1. Did you speak to the newspaper reporter?
2. My parents gave me a new tennis racket.
3. Please change the light bulb in the den.
4. The soldiers practiced under battle conditions.
5. In warm weather everyone works in shirt sleeves.
6. Were you able to repair the desk lamp?
7. Many good hotels still provide room service.

8. After dinner the whole family watched the television news.
9. Building stone walls helps him relax.
10. What does that highway sign say?

## Proper Adjectives

A *proper adjective* begins with a capital letter. There are two types of proper adjectives.

**A proper adjective is (1) a proper noun used as an adjective or (2) an adjective formed from a proper noun.**

A proper noun used as an adjective does *not* change its form. It is merely placed in front of another noun.

| Proper Nouns | Used as Proper Adjectives |
|---|---|
| Truman | the *Truman* library (*Which* library?) |
| Florida | *Florida* wetlands (*What kind* of wetlands?) |
| December | *December* weather (*What kind* of weather?) |

When an adjective is formed from a proper noun, the proper noun does change its form.

| Proper Nouns | Proper Adjectives Formed from Proper Nouns |
|---|---|
| America | *American* history (*What kind* of history?) |
| Victoria | *Victorian* ideas (*What kind* of ideas?) |

**EXERCISE D: Recognizing Proper Adjectives.** Find the proper adjective in each of the following sentences and write it on your paper. Then write the noun it modifies.

EXAMPLE:    Do all Shakespearean sonnets have fourteen lines?
            Shakespearean   sonnets

1. My sister played two Mozart symphonies.
2. The Austrian costumes at the fair were handmade.
3. The Easter holiday always reminds us of spring.
4. Has your Swiss watch been repaired?
5. A new Lincoln memorial has been dedicated in Springfield.
6. A well-known French fable was told.
7. Who would like to do a report on Elizabethan England?
8. Los Angeles smog affects the health of millions.
9. We read about the history of the American frontier.
10. I have pictures of the Mayan pyramids we visited last summer.

## Compound Adjectives

Adjectives, like nouns, can be *compound*.

**A compound adjective is made up of more than one word.**

Most *compound adjectives* are written as hyphenated words. Some are written as combined words, as in "a *runaway* horse." If you are unsure about how to write a compound adjective, look the word up in a dictionary.

| Hyphenated | Combined |
|---|---|
| a *well-known* actress | a *featherweight* boxer |
| a *full-time* job | a *fiberglass* wall |

**EXERCISE E: Recognizing Compound Adjectives.** In each of the following sentences, find the compound adjective and write it on your paper. Next to the adjective, write the noun it modifies.

EXAMPLE:   After the accident the oil-covered highway slowed traffic for hours.

          oil-covered     highway

1. They quickly chose the better-qualified candidate.
2. A farsighted person can usually read road signs.
3. Our hockey team scored two short-handed goals to win the game.
4. A huge hometown crowd turned out to welcome the hero.
5. Murphy likes to put on a know-it-all attitude.
6. Our teacher ordered thirty-five biology textbooks.
7. For her graduation party, my sister bought a bluish-green dress.
8. The volunteers smiled in spite of the heartbreaking news about the election.
9. The hit-and-run driver was given a heavy sentence.
10. A dark, shell-like covering protected the strange animal.

**DEVELOPING WRITING SKILLS: Writing Sentences with Adjectives.** Rewrite the following paragraph adding two or more adjectives to each sentence. Try to include nouns used as adjectives, proper adjectives, and compound adjectives in your sentences. Then underline the adjectives that you have added.

EXAMPLE:   The house has a garden.

          The <u>renovated</u> <u>Victorian</u> house has an <u>old-fashioned</u> <u>English</u> garden.

(1) One morning I sailed a raft to an island that was covered with trees and flowers. (2) No people were around, and I felt like an explorer discovering a continent. (3) Touring the west side of the island, I spotted the ruins of a fort that was overgrown with weeds. (4) I spent the rest of the day basking in the sunshine and swimming in the water. (5) At sunset, I wrapped myself in my jacket and headed back across the river toward home.

# 4.2 Pronouns Used as Adjectives

Like nouns, certain pronouns can be used as adjectives.

**A pronoun is used as an adjective if it modifies a noun.**

Among the pronouns that are sometimes used as adjectives are *personal, demonstrative,* and *interrogative pronouns.*

## Possessive Adjectives

The following personal pronouns are often called *possessive adjectives: my, your, his, her, its, our,* and *their.* These pronouns are considered adjectives because they are used before nouns and answer the question *Which one?* They are also pronouns because they have antecedents.

EXAMPLE:   Bobby fixed *his* bicycle.

*His* is an adjective because it modifies *bicycle.* At the same time, it is a pronoun because it stands for the antecedent *Bobby.*

**EXERCISE A: Identifying Possessive Adjectives.** In each of the following sentences, a possessive adjective is underlined. On your paper make three columns as shown in the example. Write the underlined word in the first column. Then write the noun it modifies in the second column and its antecedent in the third.

EXAMPLE:   The puppy was chasing its tail.

| Possessive Adjective | Noun Modified | Antecedent |
|---|---|---|
| its | tail | puppy |

1. Leslie finally reached her father at work.
2. After throwing off his sunglasses, the lifeguard dived into the ocean.

3. Each year, our maple loses <u>its</u> leaves early in October.
4. The astronauts kept <u>their</u> appointment with the reporters.
5. Andrea must be ready to meet <u>her</u> responsibilities as a member of the family.

## Demonstrative Adjectives

*This, that, these,* and *those,* the four demonstrative pronouns, are often used as *demonstrative adjectives*.

PRONOUN:   We saw *that.*

ADJECTIVE:   *That* car is a good buy.

PRONOUN:   Take *these.*

ADJECTIVE:   *These* tomatoes are overripe.

**EXERCISE B: Recognizing Demonstrative Adjectives.**
Copy the word *this, that, these,* or *those* in the following sentences. If it is used as a pronoun, write *pronoun* after it. If it is used as an adjective, write the noun it modifies after it.

EXAMPLE:   I read this last year.

        this     pronoun

1. Those bracelets are very expensive.
2. Can you imagine that?
3. I know this tunnel leads to daylight.
4. She found that novel hard to follow.
5. If you wish, you may have those.

## Interrogative Adjectives

*Which, what,* and *whose,* three of the interrogative pronouns, can be used as *interrogative adjectives*.

PRONOUN:   *Which* do you think he will choose?

ADJECTIVE:   *Which* prize do you think he will choose?

PRONOUN:   *Whose* can that be?

ADJECTIVE:   *Whose* umbrella can that be?

**EXERCISE C: Recognizing Interrogative Adjectives.** Find the word *which, what,* or *whose* in each of the following sentences, and copy it onto your paper. If it is used as a pronoun, write *pronoun* after it. If it is used as an adjective, write the noun it modifies after it.

EXAMPLE:   What do you want?

           What     pronoun

1. Which blouse did Connie finally buy?
2. What is his explanation for the mistake?
3. Whose mother will drive us to the game?
4. Which of us will pick up the speaker?
5. What kind of restaurant do you prefer?

**DEVELOPING WRITING SKILLS: Writing Sentences with Pronouns Used as Adjectives.** Write ten sentences of your own, each using one of the following words to modify a noun. Draw an arrow pointing from each adjective to the word it modifies.

EXAMPLE:   whose

        Whose shoes are these on the steps?

| | | | | |
|---|---|---|---|---|
| 1. what | 3. that | 5. these | 7. their | 9. his |
| 2. her | 4. our | 6. which | 8. this | 10. my |

# Skills Review and Writing Workshop

## Adjectives

### CHECKING YOUR SKILLS

Write the adjectives in each sentence.

(1) Lin-Po, the large panda, roams through Chinese forests. (2) Her body is heavy. (3) Indeed, she looks like a black-and-white bear. (4) Most experts, however, agree that she is not a real bear at all. (5) Instead, Lin-Po belongs to the familiar raccoon family. (6) Like most pandas, Lin-Po leads a very peaceful life. (7) She moves through tall trees, deciding which plants she will eat. (8) Feeding herself on bamboo shoots, she looks happy. (9) Few pandas remain in a natural environment. (10) Some people would want to take Lin-Po from her home to a zoo.

### USING GRAMMAR SKILLS IN WRITING
### Writing to Describe an Animal

Writers know that adjectives help make a description vivid. Imagine that you have been asked to describe a particular animal, perhaps your pet, for a friend who has never seen it. Follow the steps below to write a description.

**Prewriting:** Begin by making a list of details describing the animal's appearance and actions, using as many different adjectives as possible.

**Writing:** First write a sentence naming the animal and describing its appearance. Continue with details about the way it behaves, how it interacts with other animals, with people, and the place in which it lives. Conclude with a sentence that expresses your feelings about this animal.

**Revising:** Check your use of adjectives and improve any that could be more appropriate or exact. Change any overused adjectives, such as *pretty* or *nice*. After you have revised, proofread carefully.

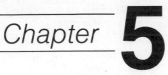

# Chapter 5

# Adverbs

*Adverbs*—words such as *carefully, often, seldom, finally, never, very,* and *soon*—play an important part in sentences. Like adjectives, adverbs are modifiers. Adjectives can modify two different parts of speech—nouns and pronouns. Adverbs, on the other hand, can modify three different parts of speech—verbs, adjectives, and other adverbs.

## 5.1 The Adverb

*Adverbs* can modify three different parts of speech.

**An adverb modifies a verb, an adjective, or another adverb.**

Although adverbs may modify adjectives and other adverbs, you will generally find that most adverbs modify verbs.

### Adverbs That Modify Verbs

An adverb that modifies a verb will answer one of these four questions: *Where? When? In what manner? To what extent?*

| ADVERBS THAT MODIFY VERBS | |
|---|---|
| **Where?** | |
| push *upward* | travels *everywhere* |
| fell *there* | go *outside* |
| **When?** | |
| arrived *yesterday* | *writes often* |
| comes *daily* | exhibits *yearly* |
| **In What Manner?** | |
| works *carefully* | chews *noisily* |
| speaks *well* | acted *willingly* |
| **To What Extent?** | |
| *hardly* ate | *almost* cried |
| *really* surprised | *partly* finished |

**EXERCISE A: Identifying How Adverbs Modify Verbs.**
Make four columns as shown. Decide which question each of
the underlined adverbs answers. Write each adverb in the appropriate column.

EXAMPLE:  Sally <u>carefully</u> wrapped the present.

| Where? | When? | In What Manner? | To What Extent? |
|---|---|---|---|
| | | carefully | |

1. They went through the motions <u>mechanically</u>.
2. In the confusion she <u>nearly</u> injured herself.
3. With much preparation they <u>eventually</u> left.
4. The applause ended, and the star <u>finally</u> appeared.
5. Six volunteers worked <u>cautiously</u> to free the child.
6. My aunt arrived <u>yesterday</u> from Washington.
7. Another skyscraper is being erected <u>nearby</u>.
8. Everyone on the team <u>now</u> practices diving.
9. After his long trip, Father was <u>scarcely</u> tired.
10. At the wedding people gathered <u>happily</u> around the bride.

**63**

## Adverbs That Modify Adjectives

An adverb modifying an adjective answers only one question: *To what extent?*

| ADVERBS THAT MODIFY ADJECTIVES |
|---|
| **To What Extent?** |
| *very* upset       *extremely* tall |
| *definitely* wrong     *not* hungry |

**EXERCISE B: Recognizing Adverbs That Modify Adjectives.** On your paper write the adverb from each of the following sentences. After each adverb write the adjective it modifies.

EXAMPLE:  Sean was almost late for his dental appointment.

almost    late

1. The afternoon sun was unusually pleasant.
2. We heard a very loud knock on the back door.
3. He was too short for the role.
4. The author was extremely upset by the poor sales of her book.
5. The owner of the store has been seriously ill for some time.
6. This fruit salad is quite tart.
7. The defendant was absolutely still as the foreman of the jury rose.
8. She is thoroughly adept at walking the high wire.
9. In his prediction my father was almost right.
10. In spite of her defeat, she was not sad at all.

## Adverbs That Modify Other Adverbs

Sometimes adverbs sharpen the meaning of other adverbs. An adverb modifying another adverb answers one question: *To what extent?* In the following chart, each example contains two adverbs. The first adverb in each modifies the second.

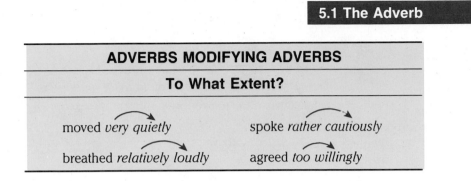

**ADVERBS MODIFYING ADVERBS**

**To What Extent?**

moved *very quietly*          spoke *rather cautiously*

breathed *relatively loudly*          agreed *too willingly*

**EXERCISE C: Recognizing Adverbs That Modify Other Adverbs.** In each of the following sentences, find the adverb that modifies another adverb by answering the question *To what extent?* Write this adverb on your paper. After this adverb write the adverb it modifies.

EXAMPLE:   The French visitors spoke too rapidly for me to understand them.

   too      rapidly

1. Time passed too slowly for the eager contestants.
2. Almost happily, the owner handed us the car keys.
3. The visitors were unusually well received by the mayor.
4. He was quite easily talked into changing his mind.
5. Debbie argued less loudly once she realized her error.
6. The movie ended rather suddenly.
7. The guest of honor arrived slightly late for the dinner.
8. This ring is entirely too expensive.
9. After receiving a ticket, my brother drove more slowly.
10. Do you promise to visit us relatively soon?

**DEVELOPING WRITING SKILLS: Writing Sentences with Adverbs.** Write five sentences of your own, each using an adverb that fits a description given below. Draw an arrow pointing from the adverb to the word it modifies.

EXAMPLE:   Modifies an adjective and answers *To what extent?*

   He rode in an extremely reckless manner.

**65**

1. modifies a verb and answers the question *Where?*
2. modifies a verb and answers the question *When?*
3. modifies a verb and answers the question *In what manner?*
4. modifies an adjective and answers the question *To what extent?*
5. modifies an adverb and answers the question *To what extent?*

# 5.2 Adverbs Used in Sentences

Adverbs can be located in almost any part of a sentence.

## Finding Adverbs in Sentences

Some of the possible locations of adverbs are in the chart. Arrows point to the words that the adverbs modify.

| LOCATION OF ADVERBS IN SENTENCES | |
|---|---|
| **Location** | **Example** |
| **At the Beginning of a Sentence** | *Silently,* she approached the farm. |
| **At the End of a Sentence** | She approached the farm *silently.* |
| **Before a Verb** | She *silently* approached the farm. |
| **After a Verb** | She traveled *silently* to the farm. |
| **Between Parts of a Verb Phrase** | She had *silently* traveled to the farm. |
| **Before an Adjective** | Her father was *always* quiet. |
| **Before Another Adverb** | Her father spoke *rather* quietly. |

**EXERCISE A: Locating Adverbs in Sentences.** Each of the following sentences contains one or two adverbs. Copy the sentences onto your paper and underline each adverb. Then draw arrows pointing from the adverbs to the words they modify.

EXAMPLE:   She has never forgotten his consistently smiling face.

1. From 1831 to 1836, Charles Darwin sailed slowly from one part of the world to another.
2. The timid dog seldom approached strangers.
3. The chef had deliberately told us to let the soup cool.
4. On Tuesday, Marie was rather sad.
5. He rather vaguely explained his reasons for leaving.
6. Cautiously, the veterinarian edged toward the huge goat on the table.
7. She has almost completed the first act of her play.
8. In *Great Expectations* Estella often teases Pip.
9. In anger he totally stopped trying.
10. American farmers efficiently produce a variety of fruits and vegetables.

# Adverb or Adjective?

Depending on the words they modify, some words can be either adverbs or adjectives. You can always tell the difference by seeing what part of speech a word modifies. As an adjective it will modify a noun or pronoun. As an adverb it will modify a verb, an adjective, or another adverb.

ADVERB MODIFYING VERB:   He works *hard*.

ADJECTIVE MODIFYING NOUN.   She enjoys *hard* work.

You should know also that although many words ending in -*ly* are adverbs, some are not. Several adjectives also end in -*ly*. These adjectives are formed by adding -*ly* to nouns.

| Nouns | Adjectives with *-ly* Endings |
| --- | --- |
| a famous *king* | a *kingly* feast |
| a true *friend* | a *friendly* person |
| a frightening *ghost* | the *ghostly* sight |

**EXERCISE B: Distinguishing Between Adverbs and Adjectives.** Indicate whether the underlined word in each of the following sentences is an *adverb* or an *adjective*.

EXAMPLE:   This is your <u>last</u> chance.

adjective

1. I am certain you have made a <u>timely</u> choice.
2. In stories a witch is generally a <u>homely</u> woman.
3. A new model was <u>recently</u> delivered.
4. <u>Daily</u> exercise is part of a good health program.
5. This was the actor's <u>first</u> appearance.
6. I finished <u>early</u> in the day.
7. After the play she received a dozen <u>lovely</u> roses.
8. Most of all I remember his <u>kindly</u> way.
9. The leader feels she is only <u>partly</u> responsible for our getting lost.
10. Carlene runs in the park <u>daily</u>.

**DEVELOPING WRITING SKILLS: Writing Sentences with Adverbs.** Write ten sentences of your own, each using one of the adverbs in the following list. Draw an arrow pointing from the adverb to the word that the adverb modifies.

EXAMPLE:   almost

Jamie almost learned to water-ski.

| | | |
| --- | --- | --- |
| 1. suddenly | 5. already | 9. badly |
| 2. regularly | 6. hardly | 10. somewhat |
| 3. often | 7. quickly | |
| 4. greatly | 8. soon | |

# Skills Review and Writing Workshop

## Adverbs

### CHECKING YOUR SKILLS
Write the two adverbs in each sentence.

(1) First, the dancer gently places two swords on the ground. (2) He crosses them very carefully. (3) The swords now form an X, with the blades widely separated. (4) The dancer begins to dance slowly, stepping gracefully over the blades. (5) He skips lightly, lifting his knees high. (6) He hops quickly, prancing in a strongly accented rhythm. (7) Bounding still faster, he whirls and leaps. (8) He whirls back again. (9) His feet just barely miss the crossed blades. (10) Standing proudly, he suddenly bows, ending the sword dance.

### USING GRAMMAR SKILLS IN WRITING
### Writing a Magazine Article
Professional writers know that adverbs help to make action clearer to the reader. Imagine you are writing a description of a dance for a school or class magazine. Follow the steps below.

**Prewriting:** Choose a dance that you know how to do, or one that you have watched carefully. List the movements of the dance in order, paying special attention to how and when each movement is executed.

**Writing:** Write the movements in order. Use enough specific adverbs so the reader can see the movements clearly. Do not omit any details.

**Revising:** First look at your adverbs and change any that are overworked or could be more accurate. Then read the entire description, looking for other improvements you can make. Correct any spelling or grammatical errors. After you have revised, proofread carefully.

# Prepositions

This chapter will introduce *prepositions* and describe how they are used to relate words to each other.

## 6.1 The Preposition

*Prepositions* show relationships within a sentence.

**A preposition relates the noun or pronoun following it to another word in the sentence.**

You should learn to recognize prepositions on sight.

| FIFTY COMMON PREPOSITIONS | | | | |
|---|---|---|---|---|
| about | behind | during | off | to |
| above | below | except | on | toward |
| across | beneath | for | onto | under |
| after | beside | from | opposite | underneath |
| against | besides | in | out | until |
| along | between | inside | outside | up |
| among | beyond | into | over | upon |
| around | but | like | past | with |
| at | by | near | since | within |
| before | down | of | through | without |

Prepositions consisting of more than one word are called *compound prepositions*.

| COMPOUND PREPOSITIONS | | |
|---|---|---|
| according to | by means of | instead of |
| ahead of | in addition to | next to |
| aside from | in back of | on account of |
| as of | in front of | on top of |
| because of | in place of | out of |

Prepositions have different meanings. Using a particular preposition affects the way other words in a sentence relate to one another. In the following sentence, for example, notice how each preposition changes the relationship between *passed* and *City Hall*.

EXAMPLE:   The parade *passed* $\begin{cases} \text{near} \\ \text{by} \\ \text{in front of} \\ \text{behind} \\ \text{opposite} \end{cases}$ *City Hall*.

**EXERCISE A: Recognizing Prepositions.** Find the preposition in each of the following sentences and write it on your paper. Then rewrite the sentence using a different preposition.

EXAMPLE:   My sister walked near the park.

near   My sister walked into the park.

1. The ticket holders waited patiently outside the theater.
2. A new dining room was built beside the old one.
3. The telephone book is under the table.
4. She placed the flower pots along the windowsill.
5. How did you get through the traffic jam?
6. The stamp show begins during winter vacation.
7. A housing development has been built across the river.

8. Let's pick the strawberries near the fence.
9. The doctor's office is around the corner.
10. Opposite the old statue, you will see the library.

## EXERCISE B: Recognizing Compound Prepositions.

Find the compound preposition in each of the following sentences and write it on your paper. Then rewrite the sentence using a different one-word or compound preposition.

EXAMPLE:   The ski chalet is on top of the mountain.

on top of   The ski chalet is on the mountain.

1. The broken lawnmower is in back of the barn.
2. In front of the entrance is a large warning notice.
3. The new highway passes next to the foothills.
4. In addition to the application, you must include a reference.
5. A very slow bus was ahead of our car.
6. Father bought me new clothes instead of a birthstone ring.
7. On account of the storm, the soccer game was canceled.
8. You will find the world atlas on top of the gray file cabinet.
9. She swam in front of the lifeguard stand.
10. We were all late because of his tardiness.

## DEVELOPING WRITING SKILLS: Writing Sentences with Prepositions.

Write ten sentences of your own, each using one of the prepositions in the following list.

EXAMPLE:   in

They had to be in Dallas by ten o'clock.

| | |
|---|---|
| 1. with | 6. toward |
| 2. between | 7. against |
| 3. as of | 8. next to |
| 4. in place of | 9. in back of |
| 5. according to | 10. through |

**72**

# Prepositions Used in Sentences 6.2

A preposition is never used by itself in a sentence.

**A preposition in a sentence is always part of a prepositional phrase.**

## Prepositional Phrases

A *prepositional phrase* is simply a group of words that begins with a preposition and ends with a noun or pronoun. The noun or pronoun following the preposition is called the *object of the preposition*.

Some prepositional phrases contain just two words—the preposition and its object. Others are longer because they contain modifiers.

| PREPOSITIONAL PHRASES | |
|---|---|
| **Prepositions** | **Objects of Prepositions** |
| *of* | *bread* |
| *near* | *us* |
| *from* | the *window* |
| *in* | their *class* |
| *during* | the long Presidential *campaign* |
| *in place of* | the old broken *chair* |

A prepositional phrase, regardless of its length, must have two parts: a preposition and an object of the preposition. The object of the preposition will generally be the first noun or pronoun following the preposition.

**EXERCISE A: Identifying Prepositional Phrases.** On your paper write the prepositional phrase appearing in each of the following sentences. Underline the preposition and circle the object of the preposition.

EXAMPLE:   The pigeon cage is on the roof.

on the (roof)

1. What do you expect to buy in the village?
2. The climbing party approached the Rockies by means of the Platte River.
3. This novel is a romantic tale of the Old South.
4. In the morning the cattle train continued its journey.
5. The trunk in the attic contains Grandma's old dresses.
6. Behind the door is the boiler room.
7. The sailboat turned and headed into the sun.
8. Between us, Glenn and I finished the apple pie.
9. The children were riding on top of a tired, old donkey.
10. The newspaper reporter stationed herself in front of the grandstand.

## Preposition or Adverb?

Some words can be used either as prepositions or as adverbs. When a word is used as a preposition, it begins a prepositional phrase and is followed by the object of the preposition. If the word has no object, it will generally be used as an adverb.

PREPOSITION:   The cherry orchard was *outside* the house.

ADVERB:   For privacy the two girls stepped *outside*.

PREPOSITION:   I found the wallet *behind* my bed.

ADVERB:   A group of children lagged *behind*.

**EXERCISE B: Distinguishing Between Prepositions and Adverbs.** In each of the following pairs of sentences, one sentence contains a word used as a preposition and the other contains the same word used as an adverb. Find the word that appears in both sentences. If the word acts as a preposition,

**74**

write the prepositional phrase on your paper. If the word acts as an adverb, write *adverb*.

EXAMPLE:   The gas station is down the road.

She examined the vase and then put it down.

down the road      adverb

1. Aunt Stacy told us about her army experiences.
   Tired as he was, he walked about for a few more minutes.
2. She tried to call us before but couldn't get us.
   He runs several miles each morning before breakfast.
3. The rowboat was found underneath the bridge.
   To repair the car, they crawled underneath.
4. "Come along," said my aunt.
   The surveyors walked along the creek.
5. Deer will sometimes come near.
   Near the old library is a Civil War statue.

**DEVELOPING WRITING SKILLS: Writing Sentences with Prepositional Phrases.** Write ten sentences of your own, each containing a prepositional phrase that begins with one of the prepositions listed below. Underline the preposition and circle the object of the preposition.

EXAMPLE:   inside

I searched <u>inside</u> my (closet) to find my favorite sweater.

1. above
2. after
3. beside
4. during
5. from

6. into
7. onto
8. outside
9. through
10. with

# Skills Review and Writing Workshop

## Prepositions

### CHECKING YOUR SKILLS

Identify the prepositional phrases in each sentence.

(1) In bowling, the ten pins are set in a triangle. (2) The number one pin is in front; the others stand behind in rows. (3) Pins numbered seven to ten are at the very back. (4) In spite of your skill, you may sometimes knock down all the pins except the ten pin. (5) To hit the ten pin, move to the extreme left of the alley. (6) The ten pin is at the extreme right corner in the back. (7) Throw the ball diagonally across the alley to hit the pin in the middle. (8) Do not throw it too far toward the gutter or it will drop off the alley. (9) Aim toward the middle of the pin. (10) Be careful not to slide over the foul line onto the alley.

### USING GRAMMAR SKILLS IN WRITING
### Writing an Explanation

Prepositions help writers to make directions and explanations clear. Imagine you are writing an article for a "how-to" book explaining a board game or other kind of recreational activity. Follow the steps below.

**Prewriting:** Choose an activity that you know well enough to teach to someone else. Go through the activity in your mind, making notes as you go. List the main points and outline the steps in learning the activity chronologically.

**Writing:** Begin to write with a statement about any background material that the reader must know. Then start your explanation of the activity at the beginning and go through to the end, following your outline.

**Revising:** Read your explanation to make sure your prepositional phrases are clear, and that your explanation can be easily followed. After you have revised, proofread carefully.

# 7

# Conjunctions and Interjections

The last two parts of speech are *conjunctions* and *interjections*, but conjunctions are more important.

## The Conjunction 7.1

*Conjunctions* are connecting words such as *and* or *but*.

**A conjunction connects words or groups of words.**

There are three types of conjunctions: *coordinating conjunctions, correlative conjunctions,* and *subordinating conjunctions*. This section discusses the first two kinds. The third is discussed in Section 11.2.

## Coordinating Conjunctions

*Coordinating conjunctions* connect similar words, groups of words, or even entire sentences.

| COORDINATING CONJUNCTIONS | | | | | | |
|---|---|---|---|---|---|---|
| but | and | nor | for | so | or | yet |

**77**

The coordinating conjunctions are circled in the following examples. The words connected by the conjunctions are italicized.

CONNECTING NOUNS: The *farmhouse* (and) the *cornfields* were flooded by the storm.

CONNECTING VERBS: She *will win* (or) *lose* the gold medal with this dive.

CONNECTING ADJECTIVES: A *blue* (or) *green* car will follow the van.

CONNECTING PREPOSITIONAL PHRASES: The bells ring *at nine o'clock* (and) *at noon.*

CONNECTING TWO SENTENCES: *My uncle wanted to fish,* (but) *my father wanted to swim.*

**EXERCISE A: Recognizing Coordinating Conjunctions.**
Copy the following sentences onto your paper, and circle the coordinating conjunction in each. Then underline the words or groups of words connected by the conjunction.

EXAMPLE: He likes to draw pictures of <u>lions</u> (and) <u>tigers</u>.

1. Andrew and Jane live far apart.
2. I have to take my medicine before breakfast or before dinner.
3. What is the connection between lightning and thunder?
4. My family is looking for a large yet inexpensive house.
5. I will be late getting home, for I have to make several stops.
6. Wind and rain lashed the Florida coastline.
7. I would like to bake cookies, but I am missing a few ingredients.
8. In the morning and in the evening, traffic backs up at this light.
9. The dancer was thin but strong.
10. You have a choice of cotton, wool, or polyester.

# Correlative Conjunctions

*Correlative conjunctions* always come in pairs, such as *whether . . . or* and *not only . . . but also*. There are five such pairs you should learn.

| CORRELATIVE CONJUNCTIONS | | |
|---|---|---|
| both . . . and | neither . . . nor | whether . . . or |
| either . . . or | not only . . . but also· | |

Like coordinating conjunctions, correlative conjunctions connect *similar* kinds of words or groups of words.

CONNECTING NOUNS:  (Either) the small *van* (or) the *bus* will pick us up.

CONNECTING PRONOUNS:  (Neither) *he* (nor) *she* is to be blamed.

CONNECTING VERBS:  Every morning she (both) *runs* (and) *swims*.

CONNECTING PREPOSITIONAL PHRASES:  She'll come—(whether) *by train* (or) *by plane*, I can't say.

CONNECTING TWO SENTENCES:  (Not only) *can they sing,* (but) *they can* (also) *tap-dance.*

**EXERCISE B: Recognizing Correlative Conjunctions.**
Copy the following sentences onto your paper and circle the correlative conjunction in each. Then underline the two words or groups of words connected by the conjunction.

EXAMPLE:   He lost (not only) his watch (but also) his wallet.

1. She will pay her tuition either by check or by money order.
2. Both Anne and Barbara volunteered to decorate the hall.
3. I will either buy or make her birthday card.
4. Not only were the rebels short on men, but they were also short on supplies.

5. She asked whether football or baseball was my favorite sport.
6. Neither flowers nor candy seems an appropriate gift.
7. The girls invited both Manuel and Pat to the dance.
8. Not only will they attend, but they will also bring five guests.
9. We expect them either in the evening or in the early morning hours.
10. That afternoon Robert was neither swimming nor diving.

**EXERCISE C: Writing Sentences Using Conjunctions.**
On your paper fill in the blanks in each of the following items with words that will make each sentence complete. Use as many words as you need to complete your ideas, but keep the conjunctions in the positions shown.

EXAMPLE:   I will be here whether _____ or _____ .

I will be here whether you win or you lose.

1. Either _____ or _____ .
2. I wonder whether _____ or _____ .
3. Not only _____ , but _____ also _____ .
4. Yesterday, _____ and _____ .
5. Neither _____ nor _____ .

**DEVELOPING WRITING SKILLS: Writing Original Sentences with Conjunctions.** Write ten sentences of your own, each using one of the following conjunctions.

EXAMPLE:   nor

Perry didn't want advice, nor did she want help.

1. but
2. both . . . and
3. or
4. and
5. whether . . . or

6. either . . . or
7. yet
8. not only . . . but also
9. for
10. neither . . . nor

**80**

# The Interjection 7.2

The *interjection* is the part of speech that is used least often of all.

**An interjection expresses feeling or emotion.**

Interjections are useful in expressing many different kinds of feelings and emotions.

SURPRISE:   *Oh,* we did not expect you today.

JOY:   *Goodness!* How good it is to see you.

PAIN:   *Ouch!* I stubbed my toe.

HESITATION:   I can't explain, *uh*, exactly how it happened.

IMPATIENCE:   *Tsk!* I think we've waited long enough.

**EXERCISE:   Recognizing Interjections.** Rewrite each of the following sentences using an appropriate interjection in place of the feeling shown in parentheses.

EXAMPLE:   __(Disappointment), __ we lost again.

          Aw, we lost again.

1. __(Joy)!__ I'm so glad you're here.
2. __(Impatience),__ you're never ready on time.
3. __(Pain)!__ Does that sting.
4. __(Hesitation),__ I don't know what to say.
5. __(Surprise),__ I can't believe you said that.

**DEVELOPING WRITING SKILLS: Using Interjections in Sentences.** Write five sentences of your own, each using one of the following interjections. Use commas or exclamation marks as punctuation.

EXAMPLE:   darn

          Darn! It's been raining ever since we arrived.

   1. whew      2. shucks      3. well      4. ouch      5. oh

**81**

# Skills Review and Writing Workshop

## Conjunctions and Interjections

### CHECKING YOUR SKILLS

Write the conjunctions and interjections in each sentence of the fable below.

(1) A mouse and a dog met on a path, and the dog barred the mouse's way. (2) Oh, how upset the mouse became, for the dog looked ferocious. (3) Unable to hide, the mouse didn't know whether to run or to fight. (4) Deciding to be friendly, the mouse not only smiled but also swept off his hat. (5) Well, the dog smiled and swept off his hat in return. (6) Meanwhile, a cat, who was nearby, saw the mouse and decided to snatch him away, but the mouse was too fast for her. (7) He scampered—whew!—between the dog's paws so the cat could not catch him. (8) The dog then told the cat either to leave quietly or he would bite her nose. (9) Not only did the cat leave but she left in a twinkling. (10) Moral: Be courteous to all, for you can never tell when you may need a friend.

### USING GRAMMAR SKILLS IN WRITING
### Writing a Fable

Conjunctions help writing to flow smoothly, and interjections can be used effectively for emphasis. Write a fable following the steps below to make your fable clear and amusing.

**Prewriting:** Start by writing down the moral or lesson of your fable. Then choose two animal characters. Outline the steps you need to go through to reach the moral.

**Writing:** Begin the fable by having the animals meet. Continue with dialogue and action. At the end of the story, state the moral, which explains what the story means.

**Revising:** Read your fable, to be sure you have used conjunctions correctly. After you have revised, proofread carefully.

# Reviewing Parts of Speech

The eight parts of speech are the building blocks of sentences. If you can identify the parts of speech, you can understand how a sentence is put together.

This chapter will look at the way all the parts of speech are used together in sentences.

## Determining Parts of Speech 8.1

The same word is not always the same part of speech. See how the word *down* is used as four different parts of speech in the following sentences.

AS A NOUN:   The team lined up for the second *down*.

AS A VERB:   He can *down* a quart of milk in one minute.

AS AN ADVERB:   She often drives *down* from the city.

AS A PREPOSITION:   The horse galloped *down* the lane.

While it is possible sometimes to guess a word's part of speech, the best way to determine the part of speech of a word is to study the sentence carefully.

**The part of speech of a word is determined by the way it is used in a sentence.**

The way to determine a word's part of speech is to study its relationship to the other words in the sentence. The following set of charts will help you review the parts of speech as they are used in sentences.

**Nouns.** A noun names a person, place, or thing.

| Part of Speech | Question to Ask Yourself | Examples |
|---|---|---|
| Noun | Does the word name a person, place, or thing? | *Lila* ate *breakfast.* The *school* is near the *highway.* |

**Pronouns.** A pronoun takes the place of a noun.

| Part of Speech | Question to Ask Yourself | Examples |
|---|---|---|
| Pronoun | Does the word take the place of a noun? | *He* asked for *them.* *Everyone* says *that!* |

**Verbs.** Verbs show action or link words.

| Part of Speech | Questions to Ask Youself | Examples |
|---|---|---|
| Verb | Does the word tell what someone or something did? | I *broke* the dish. |
|  | Does the word link the noun or pronoun before it with a noun or adjective that follows? | He *is* the judge. She *looks* happy. |

**Adjectives.** Adjectives modify nouns or pronouns.

| Part of Speech | Questions to Ask Yourself | Examples |
| --- | --- | --- |
| Adjectives | Does the word tell what kind, which one, how many, or how much? | *Three tall* and *angry* men appeared. |

**Adverbs.** An adverb modifies a verb, an adjective, or another adverb.

| Part of Speech | Questions to Ask Yourself | Examples |
| --- | --- | --- |
| Adverb | Does the word tell where, when, in what manner, or to what extent? | *There* she is. Do that *now*. She smiled *shyly*. |

**Prepositions.** A preposition relates a noun or pronoun following it to another word in the sentence.

| Part of Speech | Question to Ask Yourself | Examples |
| --- | --- | --- |
| Preposition | Is the word part of a phrase that ends in a noun or a pronoun? | Leave *at* dusk. They finished the cake *between* them. |

**Conjunctions and Interjections.** A conjunction connects words or groups of words. An interjection expresses emotion.

| Part of Speech | Questions to Ask Yourself | Examples |
| --- | --- | --- |
| Conjunction | Does the word connect other words? | Tom *or* Bill won. He *and* I did it. |

| Interjection | Does the word express feeling or emotion? | *Golly!* What a surprise. |

Practice using the questions in the middle columns of the charts. Try using the questions to decide the parts of speech of the two italicized words in this example.

EXAMPLE:   The *snow-filled* highway stalled drivers *along* the entire route.

At first glance the italicized word *snow-filled* might look like a noun. But notice that *highway*, the word after *snow-filled*, is a noun. *Snow-filled* seems to describe the word *highway*. Checking the chart on adjectives, you see that adjectives answer the question *What kind?* Since *snow-filled* does tell *what kind* of highway, it is an adjective.

The second italicized word, *along*, looks like an adverb or a preposition. Checking the chart on prepositions, you see that *along* fits the description of a word in a phrase that ends with a noun—in this case *route*. Thus *along* is not an adverb; it must be a preposition.

Use the chart now to find the parts of speech of *stalled*, *drivers*, and *entire*. With practice you will grow familiar with the questions and find it easy to identify all the parts of speech.

**EXERCISE A: Identifying Nouns, Pronouns, Verbs, and Adjectives.** Identify the underlined word in each of the following sentences as a *noun, pronoun, verb,* or *adjective.*

EXAMPLE:   She had an <u>outside</u> chance of winning the game.   adjective.

1. The <u>entire</u> wall collapsed in minutes.
2. The detective <u>questioned</u> all the suspects.
3. <u>Eclipses</u> do not occur very often.
4. The doctor spoke to <u>everyone</u> who knew the sick child.

5. <u>Finish</u> your math homework first.
6. She always uses a <u>calculator</u>.
7. This museum has an exhibit of <u>Roman</u> coins.
8. Did Mother find <u>the</u> train ticket?
9. Most of us <u>need</u> warmth and love.
10. In the <u>morning</u> the tourists left.

**EXERCISE B: Identifying Adjectives, Adverbs, Prepositions, and Conjunctions.** On your paper identify the underlined word in each of the following sentences as an *adjective, adverb, preposition,* or *conjunction.*

EXAMPLE:   The bus drove <u>past</u> without stopping.   adverb

1. The damaged train crept <u>along</u>.
2. Rescuers walked <u>along</u> the track.
3. Rain <u>and</u> sleet struck the windshield.
4. Later the old man walked <u>past</u>.
5. That is now <u>past</u> history.
6. Two speeding cars drove <u>past</u> the light.
7. The baby is small <u>yet</u> sturdy.
8. <u>Underneath</u> the table is a stack of newspapers.
9. Look <u>underneath</u> for the shovel.
10. Instead of helping the medicine had a <u>bad</u> effect.

**DEVELOPING WRITING SKILLS: Using Words as Different Parts of Speech.** Each of the words in the following list can be used as at least two different parts of speech. Write two sentences for each word, using the word as a different part of speech each time.

EXAMPLE:   snow

The snow quickly turned to slush.

It should snow for about six hours.

1. about     2. rule     3. that     4. ice     5. more

# Skills Review and Writing Workshop

## Reviewing Parts of Speech

### CHECKING YOUR SKILLS

Write the part of speech of each of the underlined words.

(1) A child <u>can</u> <u>load</u> a 35 mm camera. (2) To open <u>it</u>, <u>she</u> pushes a button. (3) She then inserts the fresh <u>spool</u> of <u>film</u> into the empty spool space. (4) That leaves a tail <u>or</u> leader of film sticking out <u>and</u> ready to be pulled. (5) She pulls the leader <u>of</u> film <u>across</u> the sprockets. (6) She <u>then</u> inserts the edge of the film <u>gently</u> into the slots in the empty spool. (7) Pulling the film <u>tightly</u>, she <u>quickly</u> makes certain it is in place. (8) <u>Presto</u>! She now <u>closes</u> the camera. (9) An <u>intelligent</u> child has just loaded a <u>35 mm</u> camera. (10) <u>What</u> could be <u>easier</u>?

### USING GRAMMAR SKILLS IN WRITING
#### Writing a Movie Review

A writer knows that using the parts of speech correctly makes writing clear and easy to read. Imagine you are writing a brief review of a movie for your hometown newspaper. Follow the steps below to write a review that will make your readers either want to go to see it or avoid it.

**Prewriting:** Choose a movie that you either strongly liked or disliked. List at least three reasons to support your view. Was the plot interesting or not? Were the characters believable? What special effects did the filmmaker use?

**Writing:** Begin writing with a sentence that names the movie and states your opinion of it. Then add your supporting reasons. Place the most important one last, since readers are most likely to remember the last reason you give. Conclude by making a recommendation for or against the movie.

**Revising:** Read the entire review, and improve any words or phrases that could be made clearer or more interesting. After you have finished revising, proofread carefully.

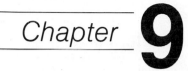
# Basic Sentence Parts and Patterns

The eight parts of speech are the building blocks of language. Whenever you speak and write, you use these basic units to express ideas. Patterns of words that communicate ideas are called *sentences*.

Not every pattern of words is a sentence. For example, the pattern "Walked John dog his" is not a sentence because it does not communicate an idea. The same words in a different pattern do form a sentence when you say, "John walked his dog."

This chapter will introduce you to the basic sentence patterns and describe how nouns, pronouns, verbs, and adjectives play key roles in sentences.

## The Basic Sentence 9.1

All sentences, in order to be sentences, must have two things in common.

# The Two Basic Parts of a Sentence

Every sentence, regardless of its length, must have two basic parts.

**A sentence must contain a subject and a verb.**

A sentence must have both. If one part is missing, what is left is not a sentence. Remember this as you study each of the two parts.

**The Subject.** A sentence must have a *subject.* Subjects are usually found at the beginning or near the beginning of a sentence. Most subjects are nouns or pronouns.

**The subject of a sentence is the word or group of words that answers the question *Who?* or *What?* before the verb.**

Each subject is underlined in the following examples. The verbs are labeled.

EXAMPLES:   The <u>road</u> is uneven.

<u>Siggy</u> broke the dish.

<u>She</u> knows our phone number.

The noun *road* is the subject in the first sentence. It tells *what* is uneven. In the next sentence, the subject is *Siggy.* It tells *who* broke the dish. The pronoun *she,* the subject in the final sentence, also tells *who: Who* knows our phone number? *She* knows.

Some subjects are not this easy to find. Some are more than one word. Others are not found at the beginning of their sentences. In some sentences the subject is understood rather than stated. But one rule is always true. Every subject answers the question *Who?* or *What?* before a verb.

**The Verb.** As one of the basic parts of a sentence, the verb tells something about a subject.

**The verb in a sentence tells what the subject does, what is done to the subject, or what the condition of the subject is.**

The verbs are underlined twice in the following examples. The subjects are labeled.

EXAMPLES:    Dori <u>framed</u> the picture herself.
<sub>S</sub>

The machine <u>was broken</u> by constant use.
<sub>S</sub>

He <u>seems</u> tired.
<sub>S</sub>

*Framed,* the verb in the first example, tells what the subject *Dori* did. The verb *was broken* explains what was done to the subject *machine. Seems,* a linking verb, tells something about the condition of the subject *he* by linking the subject to *tired.*

**EXERCISE A: Recognizing Subjects and Verbs.** Copy each of the following sentences onto your paper. Underline the subject once and the verb twice.

EXAMPLE:    The new <u>antenna</u> <u>gives</u> us better reception.

1. Our school offers a recreation program.
2. An eagle soared above the valley at dusk.
3. My old hammer disappeared from the drawer.
4. We visited Fisherman's Wharf in San Francisco.
5. Her sunburn caused her great discomfort.
6. The Parthenon is being eroded by air pollution.
7. The antique train chugged along the track.
8. Rossini wrote the opera *William Tell.*
9. This yellow ribbon comes in three widths.
10. The farmhouse is built entirely of stone.

## Using Subjects and Verbs to Express Complete Thoughts

Every good sentence must express a *complete thought.*

**A group of words with a subject and verb expresses a complete thought if it can stand by itself and still make sense.**

How can you tell if a group of words is *incomplete?* You can hear that something is missing. Consider this group of words.

INCOMPLETE THOUGHT: The donkey in the pasture.

"What about the donkey?" a reader would ask. "What did it do, or what was done to it?" By itself the group of words makes no sense because important words are missing, especially a verb. Using *donkey* as a subject, turn this incomplete thought into a sentence by adding a verb and words that help express a complete thought. The chart shows a few of the possibilities.

---

### COMPLETE THOUGHTS

       S                  V
The <u>donkey</u> in the pasture <u>was grazing</u> peacefully.

       S                  V
The <u>donkey</u> in the pasture <u>was being chased</u> by an angry dachshund.

       S             V
The <u>donkey</u> in the pasture <u>is</u> my favorite pet.

---

These examples are complete sentences because they meet all of the basic requirements: Each has a *subject* and a *verb* and expresses a *complete thought.*

An incomplete thought may lack both a subject and verb.

INCOMPLETE THOUGHT: At the foot of the mountain.

This incomplete thought contains two prepositional phrases. In this case the phrases can become a sentence only after *both* a subject and a verb are added to them.

                                      S      V
COMPLETE THOUGHT: The <u>explorers</u> <u>camped</u> at the foot of the mountain.

With a subject and verb added, this group of words now makes sense. It can stand by itself as a sentence.

In grammar incomplete thoughts are often called *fragments.* (See Section 12.1 for additional help in recognizing fragments and avoiding them in your writing.)

**EXERCISE B: Correcting Incomplete Thoughts.** None of the following groups of words expresses a complete thought. On your paper correct each one by adding whatever word or words are needed to make a sentence.

EXAMPLE:   The sailors from the ship.

The sailors from the ship spent their leave touring the city.

1. At the top of the stairs.
2. The girl in the yellow dress.
3. Grew in the desert.
4. Two visitors from Hartford.
5. Between you and me.

**EXERCISE C: Recognizing Sentences.** Only five of the following ten items are sentences. The rest are incomplete thoughts. If a group of words is a sentence, write *sentence* on your paper. If a group of words expresses an incomplete thought, add whatever words are needed to make a sentence. Then underline the subject once and the verb twice in each new sentence.

EXAMPLE:   A single rose on the bush.

A single <u>rose</u> <u>bloomed</u> on the bush.

1. Rain pelted the travelers.
2. The pastry shop in town.
3. The new coach of the basketball team.
4. Decided to stay in the park.
5. Music is my only hobby.

**93**

6. The schooner had three tall masts.
7. In the center of the town near the statue.
8. The telephone booth in the train station.
9. The whispers grew louder.
10. The atlas lists every river in North America.

**DEVELOPING WRITING SKILLS:** Writing Sentences.
Write five sentences using each of the nouns listed below as subject of a sentence. Then write five sentences using each of the listed verbs. Underline the subject once and the verb twice in the ten sentences.

EXAMPLE:  starfish

A <u>starfish</u> <u>washed up</u> on the shore.

| *Nouns* | *Verbs* |
|---|---|
| 1. wallet | 6. rescued |
| 2. mystery | 7. simmered |
| 3. project | 8. shivered |
| 4. breakfast | 9. encountered |
| 5. chimney | 10. hurried |

# 9.2 Complete Subjects and Predicates

Have you ever seen tiles laid on a floor? First a line is drawn down the center of the room. One tile is placed to the left of the line, and another is placed to the right. Then more tiles are added in the same way: one to the left, one to the right.

Imagine that the first tile on the left is a subject and the first tile on the right is a verb. You would then have a subject and a verb separated by a vertical line as shown in the example.

EXAMPLE:  <u>Ships</u> | <u>collided</u>.

Now in the same way that you would add a few more tiles if you were tiling a floor, add a few more words.

EXAMPLE:  Two <u>ships</u> | <u>collided</u> in the harbor.

**94**

At this point, you could add still more words.

EXAMPLE:  Two <u>ships</u> from Italy | <u>collided</u> in the harbor.

The center line is important in laying tiles. It is just as important in dividing a sentence into two parts. All the words to the left of the line in the preceding examples are part of the *complete subject.* (The word *ships,* on the other hand, is often called the *simple subject.*)

**The complete subject of a sentence consists of the subject and any words related to it.**

As you can see in the first of the preceding examples, the complete subject may be just one word, the subject itself. The complete subject may also be several words, as the last example shows.

All the words to the right of the line in the preceding examples are part of the *complete predicate.* (The word *collided* or a verb phrase such as *had collided,* on the other hand, is often called the *simple predicate.*)

**The complete predicate of a sentence consists of the verb and any words related to it.**

As the examples show, a complete predicate may be just the verb itself, or it may be the verb and several other words.

**EXERCISE: Recognizing Complete Subjects and Predicates.** Copy each of the following sentences onto your paper. Underline the subject once and the verb twice. Then draw a vertical line between the complete subject and the complete predicate.

EXAMPLE:  The <u>player</u> with the red hair | <u>is</u> the captain.

1. A tall stranger appeared on the stage.
2. This painting by Velázquez is extremely valuable.
3. The ship's watertight doors close automatically.

4. The smiling governor shook hands with all her guests.
5. Fire spread through the entire forest.
6. The people in the stands and on the field applauded loudly.
7. Our newly elected mayor took the oath of office.
8. This small engraving is a masterpiece of its type.
9. Costa Brava is an area of seaside resorts in Spain.
10. The fresh vegetables cooked rapidly in the wok.

**DEVELOPING WRITING SKILLS: Developing Complete Subjects and Predicates.** The first word in each of the following items is a noun or pronoun that can be used as a subject. The second word is a verb. Develop each item into a complete subject and predicate by adding details to the subject and verb.

EXAMPLE:   storm   swept

A violent storm swept across the lake.

1. story   begins
2. path   leads
3. bus   rumbled

4. each   is
5. sister   decided

# 9.3 Compound Subjects and Compound Verbs

Some sentences have more than one subject. Some have more than one verb.

## Compound Subjects

A sentence containing more than one subject is said to have a *compound subject.*

**A compound subject is two or more subjects that have the same verb and are joined by a conjunction such as *and* or *or.***

In the examples in the chart, the parts of the compound subjects are underlined once. The verbs are underlined twice.

| **SENTENCES WITH COMPOUND SUBJECTS** |
|---|
| Kim and Laurie are close friends. |
| She or I will prepare lunch. |
| Charlotte, Raleigh, and Durham are cities in North Carolina. |

**EXERCISE A: Recognizing Compound Subjects.** Each of the following sentences contains a compound subject. Copy the sentences onto your paper and underline the subjects that make up each compound subject.

EXAMPLE:   June and Ken moved to California.

1. Lou and Tony are working at the supermarket.
2. During the storm the teacher and the class waited under an awning.
3. A bus or train can be used to reach the museum.
4. Austria and Hungary were once united.
5. Lettuce, tomatoes, and cucumbers are the chief ingredients in his salad.
6. Bruckner and Mahler are two of the greatest Romantic composers.
7. Early that morning, my brother and sister left for school.
8. Ferns, insects, and toothed birds appeared in the Jurassic Period.
9. Instead of waiting for a taxi, Lou and Beth walked home.
10. Arthritis and diabetes are common diseases.

## Compound Verbs

Just as sentences can have compound subjects, they can have *compound verbs.* Compound verbs are also joined by conjunctions.

**A compound verb is two or more verbs that have the same subject and are joined by a conjunction such as *and* or *or*.**

In the following chart, the parts of the compound verbs are underlined twice. The subjects are underlined once.

| SENTENCES WITH COMPOUND VERBS |
| --- |
| Uncle Will sings or whistles all the time. |
| The Muellers travel often and visit many countries. |
| The dog turned three times, settled into the blanket, and fell asleep. |

Sometimes a sentence will have both a compound subject and a compound verb.

EXAMPLE:   The house and the garden face the lake and are protected by hedges.

**EXERCISE B: Recognizing Compound Verbs.** Each of the following sentences contains a compound verb. Copy the sentences onto your paper and underline the verbs that make up each compound verb.

EXAMPLE:   Jane Austen began a final book but died before its completion.

1. Arnie walks or takes the bus to school.
2. Dad planted a Japanese maple twenty years ago and has cherished it ever since.
3. My friends often go to the movies and have a pizza afterward.
4. The architect surveyed the land, asked questions, and began to draw her plans.
5. Later, Lucy washed her hair and settled down with a book.
6. My brother tripped on the curb and injured his ankle.

7. Sally got the signal from the third-base coach and hit a perfect bunt.
8. Francis Scott Key watched the bombardment of Fort McHenry in 1814 and was inspired to write "The Star-Spangled Banner."
9. The campers packed their gear and left the park.
10. I listened to the opera and fell asleep.

**EXERCISE C: Recognizing Compound Subjects and Compound Verbs.** Each of the following sentences contains a compound subject, a compound verb, or both. On your paper write the compound subjects and the compound verbs. Then label each compound subject and compound verb as in the example.

EXAMPLE:  The boy in the navy coat and the boy in the green blazer are teammates.

boy, boy   compound subject

1. Adobe bricks and other artifacts were found in the ruins.
2. The trip began in New Guinea and continued with stops in Australia and New Zealand.
3. Lisa and Sandy both draw and paint well.
4. Richard picked two quarts of red and black currants and made sherbet from them.
5. Crackerjacks, pretzels, and popcorn are American favorites.
6. Rodgers and Hammerstein wrote shows together but also worked with other partners.
7. The snakes escaped from the cage and slithered away.
8. Haiti and Martinique are both countries in the Caribbean.
9. The dripping ice sculpture trembled, shook once, and collapsed in a heap.
10. Prize livestock and homemade foods were at the fair.

**DEVELOPING WRITING SKILLS: Developing Sentences with Compound Subjects and Compound Verbs.** The items on the following page contain either a single subject with a compound verb or a compound subject with a single verb. Expand these parts into fully developed sentences by adding whatever words are necessary. Write the complete sentences on your paper. Remember to begin each sentence with a capital letter and to end it with an appropriate punctuation mark.

EXAMPLE:   rain   flooded, destroyed

> The rain flooded the valley and destroyed the crops.

1. books, records   were sold
2. teacher   showed, explained
3. apples, peaches   are used
4. scouts   walked, drove
5. chairs, tables, rugs   were ruined
6. actors   sing, dance
7. road   forks, continues
8. father, mother, brother   arrived
9. butterflies, moths   are
10. rescue party   climbed, reached

# 9.4  Special Problems with Subjects

In most sentences in English, the subject comes before the verb. This pattern is called *normal word order.* As long as the subject comes before the verb, the sentence is in normal word order, regardless of whether the subject and verb come near the beginning of the sentence, in the middle, or near the end.

NORMAL WORD ORDER:   A canoe glided down the stream.

At the first traffic light, we made a left turn.

As part of her physical fitness program, she swims daily.

100

Not all sentences are in normal word order. In some, the verb comes before the subject. In others, such as questions, the subject can appear between parts of a verb phrase. In still others the subject may seem to be missing altogether.

Finding subjects in sentences that are not in normal word order can be a problem. This section will give you practice in finding these difficult subjects.

## Subjects in Orders and Directions

*Stop! Finish your homework now.* These sentences and others that give orders or directions do not have subjects in front of their verbs. In fact, the subjects in such cases are not stated at all.

**In sentences that give orders or directions, the subject is understood to be *you*.**

The following chart lists examples of sentences that give orders or directions. The verbs are underlined twice. At the right the same sentences are repeated with the understood subjects in parentheses.

| Orders or Directions | With Understood *You* Added |
|---|---|
| <u>Wait</u> a moment. | (You) <u>Wait</u> a moment. |
| After reading the directions, <u>take</u> out the kit. | After reading the directions, (you) <u>take</u> out the kit. |
| Boys, <u>line</u> up in squads. | Boys, (you) <u>line</u> up in squads. |

**EXERCISE A: Recognizing Subjects That Give Orders or Directions.** On your paper write the subject of each of the sentences on the following page. Seven of the ten sentences give orders or directions. The other three are ordinary sentences in normal word order.

EXAMPLE:   Tom, help me milk the cows.

(you)

1. Remove the cassette carefully.
2. Sylvia, give the dog a bath.
3. You should take only one piece of pie.
4. Check the windows and the doors for leaks.
5. After finishing your homework, help Father.
6. A blanket of snow gently covered the lawn.
7. Tom, pile these boxes against the wall.
8. Stop the traffic!
9. The dictionary had been misplaced for a week.
10. Soldiers, take your posts immediately.

## Subjects in Questions

When the subject comes after the verb, a sentence is said to be in *inverted word order.* Inverted word order is found perhaps most often in questions.

**In questions the subject often follows the verb.**

Some questions in inverted word order begin with the words *what, which, whom, whose, when, where, why,* and *how.* Others begin with the verb itself or with a helping verb.

EXAMPLES:   How <u>are</u> the <u>kittens</u> today?

How <u>did</u> the <u>doctor</u> <u>say</u>?

<u>Were</u> the <u>labels</u> ready?

<u>Did</u> <u>she</u> <u>bring</u> her camera with her?

All of the preceding examples are in inverted word order. Notice in the first and third sentences that the entire verb comes before the subject. In the second and fourth sentences, however, a helping verb comes first. The subject is located between the parts of a verb phrase.

If you ever have trouble finding the subject in a question, use this trick: Change the question into a statement. The subject will then appear in normal word order, in front of the verb.

**102**

| Questions | Reworded as Statements |
|---|---|
| How <u>are</u> the <u>pups</u> today? | The <u>pups</u> <u>are</u> how today. |
| What <u>did</u> the <u>doctor</u> <u>say</u>? | The <u>doctor</u> <u>did say</u> what. |
| <u>Were</u> the <u>labels</u> ready? | The <u>labels</u> <u>were</u> ready. |
| <u>Did</u> <u>she</u> <u>bring</u> her camera with her? | <u>She</u> <u>did bring</u> her camera with her. |

Not every question is in inverted word order. Some are in normal word order, with the subject before the verb.

EXAMPLES:   Who <u>has</u> the camera?

Whose <u>story</u> <u>won</u> the writing contest?

**EXERCISE B: Finding the Subjects in Questions.** Copy the following sentences onto your paper. Underline the subject in each. Note that three of the sentences are in normal word order.

EXAMPLE:   How did <u>you</u> lose your shoes?

1. Where is the encyclopedia?
2. Have they visited the town hall yet?
3. Which rooms will be redecorated?
4. Whose science project finally won?
5. Are blueberries in season now?
6. What will you do with these packages?
7. Who planned last year's picnic?
8. How should I draw the solid bars on this graph?
9. Have the judges reached a decision?
10. When will we read Poe's short stories?

## Subjects in Sentences Beginning with *There* or *Here*

A sentence beginning with *there* or *here* is usually in inverted word order.

***There* or *here* is never the subject of a sentence.**

*There* has two uses in a sentence. First, it can be used simply as a sentence starter.

SENTENCE STARTERS:  There $\overset{V}{\underline{are}}$ three $\overset{S}{\underline{birds}}$ in that cage.

There $\overset{V}{\underline{is}}$ just one important $\overset{S}{\underline{rule}}$.

*There* can also be used as an adverb at the beginning of a sentence. *Here* can be used in the same way. As adverbs, *there* and *here* point out where.

ADVERBS:  There $\overset{V}{\underline{goes}}$ the football $\overset{S}{\underline{team}}$.

Here $\overset{V}{\underline{is}}$ the $\overset{S}{\underline{recipe}}$ for enchiladas.

Remember that sentences beginning with *there* and *here* will almost always be in inverted word order. Again, if you have trouble finding the subject, reword the sentence. The subject will then appear near the beginning.

| Sentences Beginning with *There* or *Here* | Reworded with Subjects Before Verbs |
|---|---|
| There <u>are</u> two <u>sandwiches</u> in your lunchbox. | Two <u>sandwiches</u> <u>are</u> in your lunchbox. |
| Here <u>is</u> the <u>telephone</u>. | The <u>telephone</u> <u>is</u> here. |

**EXERCISE C: Finding the Subject in Sentences Beginning with *There* and *Here*.** Copy the following sentences onto your paper. Underline the subject in each.

EXAMPLE:  There is no <u>excuse</u> for such sloppiness.

1. Here comes the express bus now.
2. There was another phone call for you an hour ago.
3. There have been three strikes in less than five years.

4. Here is some strawberry shortcake for dessert.
5. There goes the last train to the city.
6. There is an exciting new play on Broadway.
7. Here are the tickets to the hockey game.
8. There in the valley are the Mayan ruins.
9. There, smiling proudly, stands the winner of the ribbon.
10. Here is the money for your haircut.

**DEVELOPING WRITING SKILLS: Writing Sentences with Subjects in Various Positions.** Write five sentences of your own according to the following directions. Underline the subject in each sentence.

EXAMPLE:   Use *Did* to begin a question.

Did <u>you</u> return my library books?

1. Use *Are* to begin a question.
2. Use *Here* to begin a sentence.
3. Use *Which* to begin a question.
4. Use *Choose* to begin an order.
5. Use *There* to begin a sentence.

# Direct Objects 9.5

In Section 9.1 a *complete thought* was defined as a group of words that contains a subject and a verb and that can stand by itself and still make sense. Sometimes just a subject and a verb by themselves will express a complete thought. The following sentences, for example, do express complete thoughts.

EXAMPLES:   <u>Rain</u> <u>fell</u>.          <u>Birds</u> <u>sang</u>.

Often, however, a subject and verb alone will *not* express a complete thought.

EXAMPLES:   <u>Tracy</u> <u>wrapped</u>.     <u>That</u> <u>is</u>.     <u>He</u> <u>seems</u>.

**105**

These sentences need other words to complete the thoughts begun by the subjects and verbs. These other words are *complements.*

**A complement is a word or group of words that completes the meaning of a subject and verb.**

Complements usually appear right after the verb or very close to it. Most complements are nouns, pronouns, or adjectives. In the examples, the complements are labeled and boxed.

EXAMPLES:
COMPLEMENT
Tracy wrapped the present.

COMPLEMENT
That is a problem.

COMPLEMENT
He seems sick.

The next three sections describe three types of complements: *direct objects, indirect objects,* and *subject complements.* This section focuses on direct objects.

## The Direct Object

*Direct objects* follow action verbs.

**A direct object is a noun or pronoun that receives the action of a verb.**

You can find a direct object by asking *What?* or *Whom?* after an action verb.

EXAMPLES:
DO
My older brother grew a beard.
(Grew *what? Answer:* beard)

DO
The mayor rewarded the detective.
(Rewarded *whom? Answer:* detective)

*Beard* and *detective* are the direct objects of the verbs in the examples. In the first sentence, *beard* answers the question

**106**

*Grew what? Rewarded* in the second sentence answers the question *Rewarded whom?*

Like subjects and verbs, direct objects can be compound. That is, one verb can have two or more direct objects.

EXAMPLES:   At the fair I bought a book and a scarf
DO      DO

(Bought *what? Answer:* book, scarf)

The principal chose Marie, Stella, and Nina.
DO     DO       DO

(Chose *whom? Answer:* Marie, Stella, Nina)

**EXERCISE A: Recognizing Direct Objects.** Each of the following sentences contains a direct object. Copy the sentences onto your paper and underline each direct object.

EXAMPLE:   She tapped the <u>window</u> gently.

1. The visitor rang the bell twice.
2. Beethoven wrote only one opera.
3. She ate spaghetti for lunch.
4. My mother reads at least two books a month.
5. Phillis Wheatley wrote poetry about her life as a slave.
6. This morning Father skipped breakfast.
7. This tree produces hazelnuts.
8. She wrote original music for the show.
9. The steamer blew its whistle during the storm.
10. The kitchen clock uses only batteries.

**EXERCISE B: Recognizing Compound Direct Objects.** Each of the sentences on the following page contains a compound direct object. On your paper write only the nouns or pronouns that make up each compound direct object.

EXAMPLE:   We saw several yaks, tigers, and lions at the zoo.

        yaks   tigers   lions

1. My family visited Toronto and Ottawa.
2. Marge helped him and me with our homework.
3. He bakes delicious breads, cookies, and cakes.
4. My older sister teaches biology and chemistry at school.
5. We found Bill and her at the lake.
6. I will read *The Pearl* and *Death Be Not Proud* this summer.
7. Yesterday Martha got a vaccination and a checkup.
8. We can choose ice cream, fruit, or pie for dessert.
9. Barbara is touring Colombia and Panama this month.
10. Did the workers receive any praise or rewards?

## Direct Object, Adverb, or Object of a Preposition?

A direct object is not the only kind of word that can follow an action verb. If you learn to recognize the other kinds of words as well, you will be able to find the direct objects more easily.

**A direct object is never an adverb or the noun or pronoun at the end of a prepositional phrase.**

Compare the following three examples. The first has a direct object after the verb. The second has an adverb after the verb, and the third has a prepositional phrase.

WITH A DIRECT OBJECT: Tim left his room. *(DO over "left")*

WITH AN ADVERB: Tim left happily. *(ADV over "left")*

WITH A PREPOSITIONAL PHRASE: Tim left in the morning. *(PREP PHRASE over "in the morning")*

The first sentence consists of a subject, an action verb, and a direct object. *Room* answers the question *What?* The second sentence consists of a subject, an action verb, and an adverb. The adverb tells *in what manner* Tim left. The third sentence consists of a subject, an action verb, and a prepositional phrase. *Morning* is the object of the preposition *in*.

Many sentences will have a number of different words after the verb. Notice, for example, how it is possible to combine the three sentences just discussed into this pattern: Subject + Action Verb + Direct Object + Adverb + Prepositional Phrase.

EXAMPLE: <u>Tim</u> <u>left</u> his room happily in the morning.
        S    V     DO    ADV   PREP PHRASE

In this longer sentence, you can still tell that *room* is the direct object by asking *What?* after the verb.

**EXERCISE C: Distinguishing Between Direct Objects, Adverbs, and Objects of Prepositions.** Copy each of the following sentences onto your paper. Underline each direct object. Circle any adverbs or prepositional phrases. Not every sentence has all three.

EXAMPLE:   He dropped the <u>snake</u> (quickly) (into the sack.)

1. She touched the rabbit in the cage.
2. I asked my father often about the surprise.
3. Merri put the stamp on the letter.
4. Richard reminded Al repeatedly about the rehearsal.
5. He took his daughter with him to England.

## Direct Objects in Questions

In normal word order, a direct object follows a verb. In questions, which are often in inverted word order, the position of a direct object often changes as well.

**A direct object in a question will sometimes be found near the beginning of the sentence, before the verb.**

In the chart on the following page, questions are paired with sentences reworded in normal word order. Compare the positions of the direct objects in each.

| Questions | Sentences with Normal Word Order |
|---|---|
| DO<br>What <u>has she taken</u> from you? | DO<br><u>She has taken</u> what from you. |
| DO<br>Which T-shirt <u>do you like</u>? | DO<br>You <u>do like</u> which T-shirt. |
| DO<br>Whom <u>did you meet</u> in the cafeteria? | DO<br>You <u>did meet</u> whom in the cafeteria. |

In each of the three questions, the direct object appears in front of the verb instead of after it. If you find it hard to locate the direct object in a question, put the sentence into normal word order. Then the direct object will be found in its normal position after the verb.

**EXERCISE D:  Finding Direct Objects in Questions.** Copy each of the sentences and underline each direct object.

EXAMPLE:  <u>What</u> should we take with us to the picnic?

1. Whom did your sister invite to the party?
2. Which coat will you wear tonight?
3. What will you do with the twenty dollars?
4. What shall I buy?
5. Which groups will they audition for the dance?
6. Whom has Julie chosen as co-captain?
7. Whose radio did they borrow yesterday?
8. What effect did the aspirin have on the pain?
9. Which windows did the sonic boom break?
10. Which story will she read to us this evening?

**DEVELOPING WRITING SKILLS:  Writing Sentences with Direct Objects.** Write five sentences of your own, one for each of the following patterns. You may add any additional words or details as long as you keep the assigned pattern.

EXAMPLE:    direct object + helping verb + subject + verb

What did you just say?

1. subject + action verb + direct object
2. adjective + direct object + helping verb + subject + verb
3. subject + action verb + direct object + adverb
4. subject + action verb + direct object + prepositional phrase
5. subject + action verb + direct object + adverb + prepositional phrase

# Indirect Objects 9.6

Sentences with direct objects may also have another kind of complement, called an *indirect object.*

## The Indirect Object

An *indirect object* is only found in a sentence that has a direct object.

**An indirect object is a noun or pronoun that comes after an action verb and before a direct object. It names the person or thing that something is given to or done for.**

Always look for the direct object first in a sentence. Then look for an indirect object before it. An indirect object answers the question *To or for whom?* or *To or for what?* after an action verb.

EXAMPLES:    Lucy told him the news.
(Told *to whom? Answer:* him)

I gave each paper a number.
(Gave *to what? Answer:* paper)

*Him,* the indirect object in the first example, answers the question *To whom did Lucy tell the news? Paper,* the indirect object in the second example, answers the question *To what did I give a number?*

Most sentences with indirect objects will follow the same pattern: Subject + Action Verb + Indirect Object + Direct Object. An indirect object will almost always come between the verb and the direct object.

Like direct objects, indirect objects can be compound. The verb can be followed by two or more indirect objects.

EXAMPLE: He <u>gave</u> Chuck and Steve their desserts.

(Gave *to whom? Answer:* Chuck, Steve)

**EXERCISE A: Recognizing Indirect Objects.** Each of the following sentences contains a direct object and an indirect object. Copy the sentences onto your paper and underline each indirect object.

EXAMPLE: I sent <u>her</u> flowers for her birthday.

1. Yesterday Mother bought me a new dress.
2. After two meetings we finally gave our club a name.
3. Senator Lawton gave Mary the award.
4. Can he really get the boys tickets for the game?
5. I can show you the stamp album now.
6. Our teacher sent the principal an invitation.
7. I will draw her a map of directions to the restaurant.
8. The President sent Congress an important message.
9. Can you lend me a dollar?
10. The entire class wrote our representative a letter.

**EXERCISE B: Recognizing Compound Indirect Objects.** Each of the following sentences contains a compound indirect object. On your paper write only the nouns or pronouns that make up each compound indirect object.

EXAMPLE: Have you told your brother and sister the news?

brother    sister

**112**

1. Our parents brought Rafael and Maria souvenirs from Venice, Italy.
2. Our teacher gave Jimmy and her a pass to the dean.
3. Did you tell your mother and your father the whole story?
4. Ask the doctor and the nurse that question.
5. Give each flower and plant some fertilizer.
6. Dana wrote Brian and Matthew a letter.
7. Will you show Max and Gail those strange stones?
8. In the morning Mollie told Willy and Jeff the news.
9. I am selling Mark and John my coin collection.
10. Why don't you lend Ellie and Sue your tapes?

## Indirect Object or Object of a Preposition?

Sometimes an indirect object is confused with the object of a preposition.

**An indirect object never follows the preposition *to* or *for* in a sentence.**

Compare the positions of the words after the verbs in the following examples.

EXAMPLES:  Bill <u>gave</u> |them| a |map.|
                       IO        DO

Bill <u>gave</u> a |map| to them.
                  DO

*Them* in the first example is an indirect object. It comes between the verb and the direct object. In the second example, there is no indirect object. Instead, *them* follows the direct object and is the object of the prepositional phrase *to them*.

**EXERCISE C: Distinguishing Between Indirect Objects and Objects of Prepositions.** The sentences on the following page contain either an indirect object or an object of a preposition. Copy each sentence onto your paper. Underline each indirect object. Circle each object of a preposition.

**113**

EXAMPLE:    Mel gave his <u>dog</u> a bone.

1. The boys will show us the lake.
2. I found the keys for them.
3. Every Saturday Pete makes pizza for his family.
4. Certainly, I will tell her the answer.
5. I gave my ring to my younger sister.
6. Have you given the instructions to them yet?
7. She promised him another chance.
8. They are preparing a picnic basket for themselves.
9. Why don't you buy Amy a soda?
10. Terry happily delivered the package to them.

**DEVELOPING WRITING SKILLS:  Writing Sentences with Indirect Objects.** Write five sentences of your own according to the following directions.

EXAMPLE:    Write a sentence using *me* as an indirect object.

She gave me the last piece of paper in her notebook.

1. Write a sentence using *them* as an indirect object.
2. Write a sentence with a compound indirect object connected by *and.*
3. Change *her,* the object of the preposition in the following sentence, into an indirect object: I gave the message to *her.*
4. Write a sentence using *girls* as an indirect object.
5. Write a sentence with a compound indirect object connected by *or.*

# 9.7  Subject Complements

Action verbs can be followed by direct objects and indirect objects. Linking verbs can be followed by another kind of complement, called a *subject complement.*

**A subject complement is a noun, pronoun, or adjective that follows a linking verb and tells something about the subject.**

**114**

Nouns and pronouns used as subject complements are called *predicate nouns* and *predicate pronouns*. Adjectives used as subject complements are called *predicate adjectives*.

## Predicate Nouns and Pronouns

Nouns and pronouns used as subject complements follow linking verbs.

**A predicate noun or predicate pronoun follows a linking verb and renames or identifies the subject of the sentence.**

*Predicate nouns* and *pronouns* are not hard to find and identify. The first thing to notice is whether a sentence contains a linking verb such as *is, are, was, were,* or *will be.* A linking verb acts like an equal sign between the subject and the noun or pronoun. Both the subject and the noun or pronoun will refer to the same person, place, or thing. Study the examples in the following chart. The predicate nouns and pronouns are boxed and labeled.

| PREDICATE NOUNS AND PRONOUNS | |
|---|---|
| **Sentences** | **Relationships** |
| PN<br>Barbara is a talented artist. | Barbara = artist |
| Before World War II, Gdansk was<br>PN<br>Danzig. | Gdansk = Danzig |
| PRED PRON<br>The leader will be he. | leader = he |

The verbs in these examples are all forms of the linking verb *be.* (See Section 3.2 for lists of the forms of *be* and other linking verbs.)

Like other complements a predicate noun or predicate pronoun is never the object of a preposition. In the following sentence, *superstars* is not a predicate noun. It is the object of the proposition *of.*

EXAMPLE:  <u>O.J. Simpson</u> <u>was</u> [one] of football's superstars.
                                    PRED PRON        OBJ OF PREP

**EXERCISE A: Recognizing Predicate Nouns and Pronouns.** Copy the following sentences onto your paper and underline each predicate noun or predicate pronoun.

EXAMPLE:  The largest continent is <u>Asia</u>.

1. The losers will be they.
2. *The City Boy* is the title of a book by Herman Wouk.
3. This should be the correct address.
4. The capital of Turkey is Ankara.
5. In Greek mythology Athena was the goddess of wisdom.
6. One plant with supposedly magical powers is the mandrake.
7. A little knowledge is a dangerous thing.
8. The Amazon has always been the most famous river in South America.
9. Lichens are primitive plants.
10. The name of those fruit flies is drosophila.

## Predicate Adjectives

A linking verb may also be followed by a *predicate adjective.*

**A predicate adjective follows a linking verb and describes the subject of the sentence.**

Since a predicate adjective comes after a linking verb, it is considered part of the complete predicate of a sentence. In spite of this, a predicate adjective does *not* modify the words in the predicate. Instead, the predicate adjective describes the subject of the sentence.

**116**

| PREDICATE ADJECTIVES | |
|---|---|
| **Sentences** | **Relationships** |
| PA<br>Her story seems strange to us. | strange story |
| PA<br>Clipper ships were graceful. | graceful clipper ships |

**EXERCISE B: Recognizing Predicate Adjectives.** Copy the sentences and underline each predicate adjective.

EXAMPLE:   The milk tasted sour.

1. The new recipe for chili looks interesting.
2. St. Stephen's Cathedral in Vienna is absolutely majestic.
3. The sky became dark before the storm.
4. Of all the girls, she is the most athletic.
5. Because of the weather, the flight will be hazardous.
6. After winning, he was dizzy with excitement.
7. The sound from that speaker seems tinny.
8. The valley is particularly peaceful in the spring.
9. That roast duck smells delicious.
10. The climate there is unusually mild all year round.

## Compound Subject Complements

Like other sentence parts, subject complements can be compound. That is, a linking verb may be followed by two or more predicate nouns, pronouns, or adjectives.

EXAMPLES:   The co-captains are Nancy and Melissa.

The two musicians were Maureen and he.

The living room looks warm and cozy.

**117**

**EXERCISE C: Recognizing Compound Subject Complements.** Copy the following sentences onto your paper and underline each part of each subject complement.

EXAMPLE:  The best grain is either <u>wheat</u> or <u>rye</u>.

1. After the ice storm, the path was smooth and slick.
2. That woman is both a talented musician and a lyricist.
3. The main course is either beef or veal.
4. Two Spanish cities on the sea are Barcelona and Cádiz.
5. This time the desert appeared vast and treacherous.
6. The saxophonists in the band are Luis and she.
7. The colors of the banner will be orange, green, and purple.
8. The trip up the coast was neither smooth nor scenic.
9. Over the years the statue has turned old and gray.
10. Lincoln was a fine writer and storyteller.


**DEVELOPING WRITING SKILLS: Writing Sentences with Subject Complements.** Write ten sentences of your own, each using one of the following subjects and verbs. Include the type of subject complement given in parentheses. Add whatever additional details you think are needed.

EXAMPLE:  flowers   are   (compound predicate nouns)

My favorite flowers are carnations and roses.

1. cheerleaders   are   (compound predicate nouns)
2. cupcakes   look   (predicate adjective)
3. dog   is   (predicate noun)
4. roads   were   (compound predicate adjectives)
5. musicians   are   (compound predicate pronouns)
6. stew   smells   (predicate adjective)
7. friends   are   (compound predicate nouns)
8. Nashville   is   (predicate noun)
9. guides   will   be   (predicate noun and predicate pronoun)
10. voice   sounds   (compound predicate adjectives)

**118**

# The Four Functions 9.8 of Sentences

Sentences can be classified according to what they do. The four types of sentences in English are *declarative, interrogative, imperative,* and *exclamatory.*

*Declarative sentences* are the most common type. They are used to "declare" or state facts.

**A declarative sentence states an idea and ends with a period.**

DECLARATIVE:   In many Asian countries, rice is harvested by hand.

In *Interrogative* means "asking." An *interrogative sentence* is a question.

**An interrogative sentence asks a question and ends with a question mark.**

INTERROGATIVE:   Whose wallet is this?

In what country is Kabul?

The word *imperative* is related to the word *emperor,* a person who gives commands. *Imperative sentences* are like emperors: They give commands.

**An imperative sentence gives an order or a direction and ends with either a period or an exclamation mark.**

Most imperative sentences start with a verb. In this type of imperative sentence, the subject is understood to be *you.*

IMPERATIVE:   Follow the directions carefully.

Wait for me!

Notice the punctuation at the end of these examples. In the first sentence, the period suggests that a mild command is

**119**

being given in an ordinary tone of voice. The exclamation mark at the end of the last sentence suggests a strong command, one given in a loud voice.

To *exclaim* means to "shout out." *Exclamatory sentences* are used to "shout out" emotions such as happiness, fear, delight, and anger.

**An exclamatory sentence conveys strong emotion and ends with an exclamation mark.**

EXCLAMATORY:   She's not telling the truth!

What an outrage that is!

**EXERCISE: Identifying the Four Types of Sentences.** Read each of the following sentences carefully and identify it as *declarative, interrogative, imperative,* or *exclamatory.* After each answer write the appropriate punctuation mark for that sentence.

EXAMPLE:   Do you want to go to the movies

interrogative   ?

1. The lynx can be found in North America and Asia
2. Remove your shoes, please
3. Which topic will you choose for the report
4. Watch out for spiders
5. Will you agree to sing
6. Proper care of your teeth is important
7. In Roman legend Remus is the twin brother of Romulus
8. Give us the names now
9. What a terrible movie we saw
10. Are you ready to go

**DEVELOPING WRITING SKILLS: Writing Sentences with Different Uses.** Write five sentences of your own according to the directions given for each of the following items.

**120**

EXAMPLE:   Write an imperative sentence that does not end with
a period.

Watch out!

1. Write a question beginning with *Who.*
2. Write an exclamatory sentence expressing happiness.
3. Write a declarative sentence about Emily Dickinson.
4. Write an imperative sentence that begins with the verb
*Finish.*
5. Write a declarative sentence about your state.

# Diagraming Basic 9.9 Sentence Parts

Sentences can be diagramed to show how their basic parts
are related. In a diagram each word is positioned to show its
use in the sentence. This section will show you how to diagram the basic parts of sentences.

## Subjects and Verbs

In a diagram the subject and the verb are placed on a horizontal line, separated by a vertical line. The subject is placed
to the left. The verb is placed to the right.

EXAMPLE:   Snow fell.

| **Snow** | **fell** |

Names and compound nouns are diagramed in the same
way as *snow.* Verb phrases are diagramed in the same way as
*fell.*

EXAMPLE:   Robert Stone has been selected.

| **Robert Stone** | **has been selected** |

**121**

**EXERCISE A: Diagraming Subjects and Verbs.** Each of the following sentences contains a subject and a verb. Diagram each sentence, using the preceding examples as models.

1. Rhonda phoned.
2. Smoke was rising.
3. Mick Bradley has arrived.
4. Everyone has been chosen.
5. Skyscrapers sway.

## Adjectives, Adverbs, and Conjunctions

In addition to a subject and verb, many sentences contain adjectives, adverbs, and conjunctions. These parts of speech are added to a diagram in the following ways.

**Adding Adjectives.** An adjective is placed on a slanted line directly below the noun or pronoun it describes.

EXAMPLE:

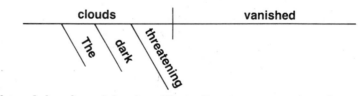

ADJ ADJ      ADJ      S      V
The dark, threatening clouds vanished.

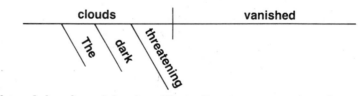

**Adding Adverbs.** Adverbs, like adjectives, are placed on slanted lines. They are placed directly under the verbs, adjectives, or adverbs they modify.

EXAMPLE:

ADJ   S      V    ADV  ADV
My mother drove very slowly.

**122**

**Adding Conjunctions.** Conjunctions are placed on dotted lines drawn between the words they connect.

EXAMPLE:
The tired *but* friendly traveler smiled warmly *and* gratefully.

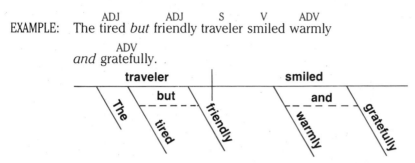

**EXERCISE B: Diagraming Sentences with Modifiers and Conjunctions.** Diagram each sentence.

1. The red bus stopped suddenly.
2. A tall and excited stranger appeared.
3. Our new doctor listened very carefully.
4. The large but swift ship glided effortlessly and gracefully.
5. She spoke carefully but eloquently.

# Compound Subjects and Verbs

To diagram a sentence with either a compound subject or a compound verb, you must split the main horizontal line.

**Compound Subjects.** Each part of a compound subject is diagramed on a separate horizontal line. The conjunction that connects the subjects is placed on a dotted vertical line, as shown in the following example.

EXAMPLE:
Red flags and blue banners appeared.

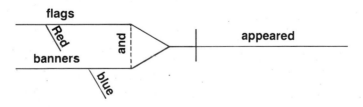

**Compound Verbs.** The diagram for a compound verb is similar to the diagram for a compound subject.

EXAMPLE:
$$\overset{S}{\text{Anne}} \overset{V}{\text{writes}} \text{clearly and} \overset{V}{\text{draws}} \text{well.}$$

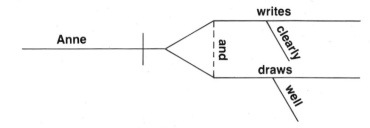

**EXERCISE C: Diagraming Compound Subjects and Compound Verbs.** Diagram the following sentences.

1. Coffee and cake were provided.
2. Tom calls daily and writes occasionally.
3. A white horse and a beautiful gold carriage were hired.
4. Students, parents, and teachers applauded happily.
5. The new school band assembled, waited, and finally marched.

## Orders

Diagrams for sentences that give orders follow a pattern similar to those you already know. The understood subject *you* is in the regular subject position, but in parentheses.

EXAMPLE:   Go today.

**EXERCISE D: Diagraming Orders.** Diagram the following sentences, placing the understood subjects correctly.

1. Read slowly.
2. Look closely.
3. Choose very carefully.
4. Try harder!
5. Stand up now!

## Complements

The three kinds of complements—direct objects, indirect objects, and subject complements—are all diagramed in different ways.

**Direct Objects.** A direct object is placed on the same horizontal line as the subject and verb. The direct object follows the verb and is separated from it by a short vertical line.

EXAMPLE:
$$\text{S} \quad \text{V} \quad \text{DO}$$
Steven bought a notebook.

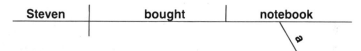

**Indirect Objects.** An indirect object is the only complement that is not placed on the main horizontal line. It is placed instead on a short horizontal line extending from a slanted line directly below the verb.

EXAMPLE:
$$\text{S} \quad \text{V} \quad \text{IO} \quad \text{DO}$$
Mother gave her a message.

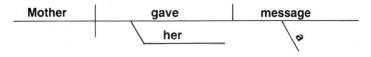

**Subject Complements.** The subject complements—predicate nouns, predicate pronouns, and predicate adjectives—follow linking verbs. Like direct objects, they are placed on the same horizontal line as the subject and verb. They are positioned after the verb and separated from it by a *slanted* line that points back to the subject.

EXAMPLE:
$$\text{S} \quad \text{V} \quad \text{PN}$$
Fred was our last representative.

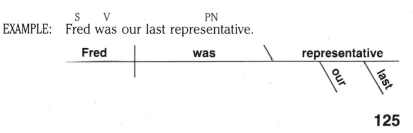

EXAMPLE:
S V PA
Fred is very talkative.

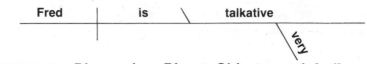

## EXERCISE E: Diagraming Direct Objects and Indirect Objects. Diagram the following sentences.

1. The girls opened the carton.
2. I gave them the news.
3. They told us several scary stories.
4. The boys bought themselves new sneakers.
5. The troop leader gave us a difficult assignment.

## EXERCISE F: Diagraming Subject Complements. Diagram the following sentences.

1. Dom is a fine swimmer.
2. The room is attractive.
3. That woman was once a powerful politician.
4. The redecorated kitchen looks absolutely sensational.
5. Alaska is the largest state.

## DEVELOPING WRITING SKILLS: Writing and Diagraming Sentences. Use the following instructions to write five sentences of your own. Then correctly diagram each sentence.

EXAMPLE: Write a sentence that contains a compound verb.

The dog yawned lazily and stretched.

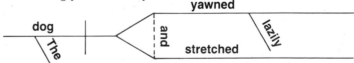

1. Write a sentence that contains a compound subject.
2. Write a sentence that contains two adjectives connected by *and.*
3. Write a sentence that gives an order.
4. Write a sentence that contains a subject complement.
5. Write a sentence that contains a direct object.

**126**

# Skills Review and Writing Workshop

## Basic Sentence Parts and Patterns

### CHECKING YOUR SKILLS

Write what parts of the sentence the underlined words represent.

(1) John Klinger, an irritable old man, <u>moved to a house on our mill pond</u>. (2) <u>The huge house</u> was much too big for him. (3) He <u>built</u> a fence around it and <u>chased</u> all the neighborhood children away. (4) Then he <u>befriended</u> a dog. (5) <u>He and the dog</u> became <u>inseparable</u>. (6) Soon John seemed <u>different</u>. (7) He was no longer a <u>grouch</u> but appeared <u>happy and content</u>. (8) The dog gave <u>him</u> affection. (9) John had wanted <u>affection and a friend</u> all along. (10) <u>What</u> did he gain by being so unfriendly to the neighbors?

### USING GRAMMAR SKILLS IN WRITING
### Writing a Biographical Sketch

A biographical sketch gives the reader a quick, clear view of an individual's personality. Imagine you are writing a brief biographical sketch for your school magazine. Follow the steps below.

**Prewriting:** Choose someone you know and think of how the person's actions and behavior express his or her personality. List details that develop and support your ideas about the person.

**Writing:** Begin writing by identifying the person and giving your main impression. Following your list, add descriptive details about the person and the person's actions that develop your idea of his or her personality. Conclude with a sentence that sums up your impressions.

**Revising:** Reread your sketch, and improve your sentence structure to make your writing more varied and interesting. When you have revised, proofread carefully.

**127**

# 10

# Phrases

Section 3.3 explained how a verb can be used with one or more helping verbs to form a verb phrase, such as *might have known.* In a sentence a verb phrase acts as *one* verb, as in "He *might have known* the intruder."

A verb phrase is only one of several kinds of phrases. All of these *phrases* have certain things in common.

**A phrase is a group of words that functions in a sentence as a single part of speech. Phrases do *not* contain a subject and verb.**

There are four other important kinds of phrases: *prepositional phrases* (introduced in Section 6.2), *appositive phrases, participial phrases,* and *infinitive phrases.* Each kind of phrase has different uses in sentences.

## 10.1 Prepositional Phrases

By itself a *prepositional phrase* is made up of at least two parts: a preposition and a noun or pronoun that is the object of the preposition.

EXAMPLE: PREP OBJ
near airports

The object of the preposition may be modified by one or more adjectives.

EXAMPLE:   <sup style="font-size:small"></sup>
PREP ADJ ADJ OBJ
near busy urban airports

The object may also be compound.

EXAMPLE:   
PREP            OBJ     OBJ
near busy urban highways and airports

No matter how long a prepositional phrase is or how many different parts of speech it contains, a prepositional phrase always acts in a sentence as if it were a one-word adjective or adverb.

## Phrases That Act as Adjectives

A prepositional phrase that acts as an adjective in a sentence is called an *adjective phrase.*

**An adjective phrase is a prepositional phrase that modifies a noun or pronoun by telling what kind or which one.**

One-word adjectives modify nouns or pronouns. Adjective phrases modify the same parts of speech. However, instead of coming before the noun or pronoun, an adjective phrase usually comes after it.

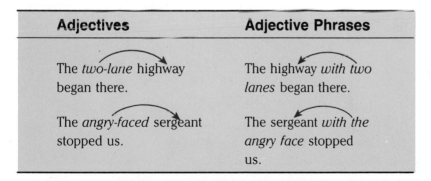

| Adjectives | Adjective Phrases |
| --- | --- |
| The *two-lane* highway began there. | The highway *with two lanes* began there. |
| The *angry-faced* sergeant stopped us. | The sergeant *with the angry face* stopped us. |

Adjective phrases answer the same questions as one-word adjectives do. *What kind* of highway began there? *Which* sergeant stopped us?

**129**

An adjective phrase can modify almost any noun or pronoun in a sentence.

MODIFYING A SUBJECT:   Each *of the captains* waved.

MODIFYING A DIRECT OBJECT:   He enjoys meals *without salt.*

MODIFYING A PREDICATE NOUN:   She is a woman *of great strength.*

When two adjective phrases appear in a row, the second phrase may modify the object of the preposition in the first phrase or both phrases may modify the same word.

MODIFYING THE OBJECT
OF A PREPOSITION:   The gas station *near the entrance to the highway* sells diesel fuel.

MODIFYING THE SAME WORD:   The box *of cookies in the pantry* is almost empty.

**EXERCISE A: Identifying Adjective Phrases.** Each of the following sentences contains at least one prepositional phrase used as an adjective. Copy the sentences onto your paper. Underline each adjective phrase and draw an arrow pointing from it to the word it modifies.

EXAMPLE:   Noise <u>from aircraft</u> may damage houses <u>near busy urban airports</u>.

1. He drank a whole quart of milk.
2. My aunt is the president of the charity.
3. Grandfather told a story about Maine.
4. The stamp on that envelope is extremely rare.
5. The city of Damascus is several thousand years old.
6. A visitor from Italy showed slides of Rome and Florence.
7. Is this the road to the exhibit?
8. The box of nails in the cellar spilled all over.

9. The dot in the center of the map is Lake Zaragosa.
10. The room in the back of the house is mine.

## Phrases That Act as Adverbs

One-word adverbs modify verbs, adjectives, and other adverbs. A prepositional phrase that acts as an adverb modifies the same parts of speech.

**An adverb phrase is a prepositional phrase that modifies a verb, adjective, or adverb. Adverb phrases point out where, when, in what manner, or to what extent.**

*Adverb phrases* are used in the same way as one-word adverbs, but because they are longer they sometimes provide more precise details.

| Adverbs | Adverb Phrases |
|---|---|
| Bring your paper *here.* | Bring your paper *to the desk.* |
| The parade began *early.* | The parade began *at exactly eleven o'clock.* |

Both *here* and *to the desk* in the first pair of examples answer the question *Bring where? Early* and *at exactly eleven o'clock* in the second pair answer the question *Began when?*

Adverb phrases can modify verbs, adjectives, and adverbs.

MODIFYING A VERB:  Father often talks *in a loud voice.*
(Talks *in what manner?*)

MODIFYING AN ADJECTIVE:  Joel was late *for rehearsal.*
(Late *in what manner?*)

MODIFYING AN ADVERB:  Jane finished earlier *in the week.*
(Earlier *to what extent?*)

**131**

Adverb phrases, unlike adjective phrases, are not always located near the words they modify in a sentence. Like one-word adverbs they can appear in almost any position in a sentence.

EXAMPLES: *After the raging storm,* the relieved crew opened the hatches.

Ellen packed her belongings *in a large canvas bag.*

Two or more adverb phrases can also be located in different parts of the sentence and still modify the same word.

EXAMPLE: *In the morning* we walked *to the village.*

**EXERCISE B: Identifying Adverb Phrases.** Each of the sentences contains at least one prepositional phrase used as an adverb. Copy the sentences. Underline each adverb phrase and draw an arrow from it to the word it modifies.

EXAMPLE: By chance they always lived near busy urban airports.

1. The trout stream winds through the forest.
2. Alice was early with her science report.
3. At dawn they prepared for the rescue attempt.
4. She seems happy with her new job.
5. At the hotel the visitor learned about the delay.
6. The astronauts arrived late for the test run.
7. In a well-prepared speech, Larissa explained her decision.
8. We piled flowers and other decorations near the station wagon.
9. From the doctor's office, she drove to the library.
10. Our coach is happy about our victory.

**DEVELOPING WRITING SKILLS: Writing Sentences with Prepositional Phrases.** Write ten sentences, each using one of the prepositional phrases as an adjective or adverb according to the instructions in parentheses. Underline each phrase and draw an arrow from it to the word it modifies.

EXAMPLE:    through the city   (as an adverb phrase)

The river flows <u>through the city</u>.

1. in the afternoon   (as an adverb phrase)
2. on the hanger   (as an adjective phrase)
3. in the white shoes ·  (as an adjective phrase)
4. to the museum director   (as an adverb phrase)
5. near cool waters   (as an adverb phrase)
6. in her beautiful letter   (as an adverb phrase)
7. on the road map   (as an adjective phrase)
8. in spite of their protests   (as an adverb phrase)
9. of mystery stories   (as an adjective phrase)
10. with one last effort   (as an adverb phrase)

# Appositives in Phrases 10.2

*Appositives* are nouns or pronouns placed directly after other nouns or pronouns to give additional information about these words.

**An appositive is a noun or pronoun placed after another noun or pronoun to identify, rename, or explain the preceding word.**

Note the way appositives are used in the chart.

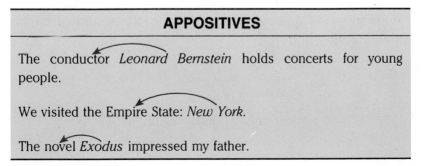

| APPOSITIVES |
|---|
| The conductor *Leonard Bernstein* holds concerts for young people. |
| We visited the Empire State: *New York.* |
| The novel *Exodus* impressed my father. |

**133**

An appositive can be expanded into a phrase by adding modifiers to it.

**An appositive phrase is a noun or pronoun with modifiers. It stands next to a noun or pronoun and adds information or details.**

The modifiers in the phrase are usually adjectives or adjective phrases.

---

### APPOSITIVE PHRASES

---

Willa Cather, *an American novelist,* wrote *My Antonia.*

Lisbon, *a thriving port in Portugal,* has often been the scene of espionage.

The shopping center—*a network of cars, shops, and people*—provides many jobs.

---

Appositives and appositive phrases can be compound.

EXAMPLES:   Two fruits, *strawberries* and *cantaloupe,* are the dessert's main ingredients.

The two settings, *a city in England* and *a city in Russia,* are contrasted in the book.

**EXERCISE A: Identifying Appositives and Appositive Phrases.** Copy the following sentences onto your paper. Underline each appositive or appositive phrase and draw an arrow pointing from it to the word it renames.

EXAMPLE:   The winner, <u>one of five semifinalists</u>, will be announced tomorrow.

1. The singer Marilyn Horne has a magnificent mezzo-soprano voice.
2. He owns just one car, a Dodge.

**134**

3. Her home, an old Victorian mansion, was destroyed in the fire.
4. Stephen Crane's poem "A Learned Man" is among my favorites.
5. Houston, a city of opportunity, has attracted many newcomers.
6. The composer Mozart wrote many pieces while still a child.
7. Her shoes, brown and white Indian moccasins, were handmade.
8. We were introduced to the leading man—a tall, strange, scowling person.
9. The desserts—chocolate pudding, peach pie, and fruit salad—are all delicious.
10. The English writer Virginia Woolf had a sister who was a respected painter.

**DEVELOPING WRITING SKILLS: Writing Sentences with Appositives.** Write ten sentences of your own, each using one of the following words or phrases as an appositive.

EXAMPLE:   an American writer

Pearl Buck, an American writer, spent many years in China.

1. my favorite city
2. an exciting group
3. a beautiful sight
4. the coach
5. a green vegetable
6. a street in town
7. our math teacher
8. a yellow flower
9. the family next door
10. an American hero

# Participles in Phrases 10.3

To understand the next two kinds of phrases, you must learn about *verbals*. A *verbal* is any verb that is used in a sentence not as a verb but as another part of speech. The verbals discussed in the next two sections are *participles* and *infinitives*.

Participles are used as adjectives. Infinitives are used as nouns, adjectives, or adverbs.

Though they are used as nouns, adjectives, or adverbs, verbals keep certain characteristics of verbs. They can be modified by an adverb or an adverb phrase. They can also be followed by a complement, such as a direct object. A verbal used with a modifier or a complement is called a *verbal phrase.*

This section explains participles, the first kind of verbal, and shows how they can be used in phrases.

## Participles

*Participles* are verb forms with two basic uses. When they are used with helping verbs, they are verbs. When they are used alone to modify nouns or pronouns, they become adjectives.

**A participle is a form of verb that is often used as an adjective.**

There are two kinds of participles: *present participles* and *past participles.* Each kind can be recognized by its ending. All present participles end in *-ing.*

EXAMPLES:  talking   doing   eating   wanting

Most past participles, on the other hand, end either in *-ed* or in *-d.*

EXAMPLES:  opened   jumped   played   moved

Other past participles end in *-n, -t, -en,* or some other irregular ending. (See Section 13.1 for a list of irregular past participles.)

EXAMPLES:  grown   felt   bought   eaten   held

In the chart on the following page, both present and past participles are used in sentences as adjectives.

**136**

| Present Participles | Past Participles |
|---|---|
| A *walking* tour was arranged. | The *cooked* food won't spoil. |
| *Playing,* she grabbed his hand. | He was by then, of course, a *grown* man. |

Participles, like other adjectives, answer such questions as *What kind?* or *Which one?*

**EXERCISE A: Identifying Present and Past Participles.** Write the participle from each sentence. Then write the word that the participle modifies.

EXAMPLE: I learned much from the growing baby.

      growing   baby

1. The burning logs were soon only embers.
2. The detective examined the marked bill.
3. What is the asking price for this vase?
4. The sheriff said the outlaw is a marked man.
5. The broken lamp can be repaired.
6. This is a frightening turn of events.
7. The spoiled cheese has turned green.
8. The pitcher was applauded by the cheering crowd.
9. Charlotte, a growing city, offers a rich past as well.
10. After the tournament she became a well-known athlete.

## Participial Phrases

A participle can be expanded into a *participial phrase* by adding a complement or modifiers.

**A participial phrase is a present or past participle that is modified by an adverb or adverb phrase or that has a complement. The entire phrase acts as an adjective in a sentence.**

**137**

Participles can be expanded in many different ways as shown in the chart.

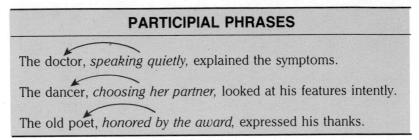

| PARTICIPIAL PHRASES |
|---|
| The doctor, *speaking quietly,* explained the symptoms. |
| The dancer, *choosing her partner,* looked at his features intently. |
| The old poet, *honored by the award,* expressed his thanks. |

The first participial phrase is formed by adding the adverb *quietly* to the participle *speaking.* The second is formed by adding the direct object *partner.* The third is formed by adding the adverb phrase *by the award.*

In each of the examples in the chart, the participial phrase is located after the noun it modifies. Each phrase could also be placed at the beginning of the sentence.

EXAMPLE: *Honored by the award,* the old poet expressed his thanks.

**EXERCISE B: Recognizing Participial Phrases.** Each of the following sentences contains a participial phrase. Copy the sentences onto your paper. Underline each participial phrase and draw an arrow pointing from it to the word it modifies.

EXAMPLE: On the table I saw several packages <u>wrapped in gold paper.</u>

1. The girl smiling shyly is my cousin from Florida.
2. Troubled by the news, Glenn phoned his parents.
3. Mrs. Grant, waiting for the right moment, whisked the fly out the window.
4. He found the ring hidden in a trunk.
5. Gliding swiftly, the canoe approached the rapids.

6. The *Twentieth Century Limited*, redecorated for the occasion, began its last run.
7. Noted for its mountains, Banff National Park is a popular resort.
8. I spoke to the runner holding his side in pain.
9. Greeting the guests, the mayor shook dozens of hands.
10. The ancient mammals, frozen for centuries in ice, were well preserved.

**DEVELOPING WRITING SKILLS: Writing Sentences with Participial Phrases.** Write ten sentences each using one of the participial phrases. Underline the participial phrase and draw an arrow pointing from it to the word it modifies.

EXAMPLE:  standing on a ladder

Standing on a ladder, the painter could reach the ceiling.

1. shivering in the cold air
2. examining the contract closely
3. holding a colorful bouquet of flowers
4. entering the room
5. responding to the question
6. caught in the storm
7. frightened by the movie
8. having finished her work
9. soaring through the air
10. changed into a frog

# Infinitives in Phrases 10.4

*Infinitives* can be used as three different parts of speech.

**An infinitive is the form of a verb that comes after the word *to* and acts as a noun, adjective, or adverb.**

# Uses of Infinitives

When it is used as a noun, an infinitive can be a subject, direct object, predicate noun, object of a preposition, or appositive.

| INFINITIVES USED AS NOUNS | |
|---|---|
| Subject | To *hear* is an ability we take for granted. |
| Direct Object | She quickly learned *to whistle.* |
| Predicate Noun | His ambition has always been *to write.* |
| Object of a Preposition | Justin wanted nothing except *to rest.* |
| Appositive | Her desire, *to paint,* was soon realized. |

Infinitives are also used as adjectives and adverbs. When used this way, they answer the usual questions for adjectives and adverbs.

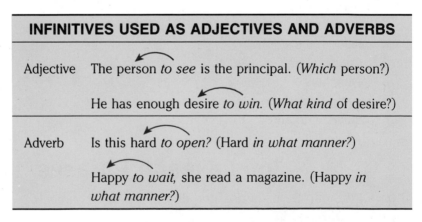

| INFINITIVES USED AS ADJECTIVES AND ADVERBS | |
|---|---|
| Adjective | The person *to see* is the principal. (*Which* person?) |
| | He has enough desire *to win.* (*What kind* of desire?) |
| Adverb | Is this hard *to open?* (Hard *in what manner?*) |
| | Happy *to wait,* she read a magazine. (Happy *in what manner?*) |

**EXERCISE A: Identifying Infinitives.** Find the infinitive in each of the following sentences and write it on your paper.

EXAMPLE: The ship is ready to sail.

to sail

1. My story is hard to describe.
2. As soon as he is old enough, he will want to drive.
3. All citizens should exercise their right to vote.
4. After the operation she hopes to improve.
5. A pleasant resort to visit is Hermosa Beach.
6. Her dream for many years was to dance.
7. George Hepplewhite, the cabinetmaker, always wanted to design.
8. Are the boys and girls ready to go?
9. A challenging game to try is chess.
10. We had no choice except to agree.

## Infinitive Phrases

Like participles, infinitives can be used with other words to form phrases.

**An infinitive phrase is an infinitive with modifiers or a complement, all acting together as a single part of speech.**

Infinitives can be turned into phrases in many different ways.

| INFINITIVE PHRASES | |
|---|---|
| Infinitive with Adverbs | You must try *to speak less rapidly.* |
| Infinitive with Adverb Phrase | *To swim across the English Channel* was her main ambition. |
| Infinitive with Direct Object | She wanted *to cross the street.* |

**EXERCISE B: Identifying Infinitive Phrases.** Write each infinitive phrase from the sentences on the following page.

EXAMPLE:   I wanted to write a letter to the President.

  to write a letter to the President

1. My father hoped to open a new business.
2. She finally decided to leave before dinner.
3. Somehow they expected to reach the other side.
4. George Mason helped to prepare the Bill of Rights.
5. While still in her teens, Queen Victoria began to rule the British Empire.
6. Sometimes it is hard to eat slowly.
7. The general's plan to capture the city backfired.
8. To write about the Civil War will require much research.
9. She has enough desire to try again.
10. The court official moved quickly to bring the prisoner into the courtroom.

**DEVELOPING WRITING SKILLS: Writing Sentences with Infinitive Phrases.** Write ten sentences, each using an infinitive phrase according to the directions in parentheses.

EXAMPLE:   to finish the assignment   (as an adverb after the adverb *rapidly*)

  We worked rapidly to finish the assignment.

1. to win the race   (as the direct object of the verb *want*)
2. to sing for the guests   (as an adverb after the adjective *happy*)
3. To present his plan   (as the subject at the beginning of a sentence)
4. to collect British stamps   (as a predicate noun after the verb *is*)
5. to go slowly   (as the direct object of the verb *plan*)
6. to bake the bread in an open-hearth stove   (as a predicate noun after the verb *was*)
7. to close the cabinet carefully   (as the direct object of the verb *remember*)
8. to get attention   (as the direct object of the verb *try*)

**142**

9. to find on the map   (as an adverb after the adjective *easy*)
10. To ask for help   (as the subject at the beginning of a sentence)

# Diagraming Prepositional 10.5 Phrases and Appositives

Diagraming subjects, verbs, complements, and modifiers was explained in Section 9.9. Before you study the following diagrams, you may want to review that section.

## Prepositional Phrases

The diagram for a prepositional phrase is drawn under the word it modifies. The diagram starts with a slanted line for the preposition and continues with a horizontal line for the object of the preposition. Adjectives that modify the object are placed below it on slanted lines.

PREPOSITIONAL PHRASE:   PREP on   OBJ OF PREP a cold morning

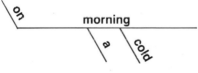

**Adjective Phrases.** An adjective phrase is placed directly under the noun or pronoun that the phrase modifies.

EXAMPLE:   A teacher *from our school* spoke briefly.

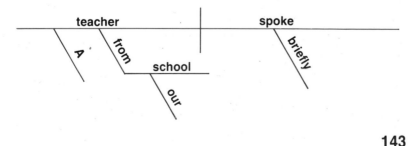

**143**

**Adverb Phrases.** The diagram for an adverb phrase is also placed directly under the word it modifies.

EXAMPLE:  His family fled *to the country.*

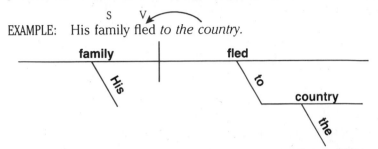

**EXERCISE A: Diagraming Prepositional Phrases.** Each of the following sentences contains one prepositional phrase. Diagram the sentences, using the preceding examples as models.

1. She is a singer of great talent.
2. The room in the hotel was very warm.
3. This is the top to the plastic container.
4. They arrived after midnight.
5. The senator reached the city in the late afternoon.

## Appositives

To diagram an appositive, place it in parentheses next to the noun or pronoun it renames. Any adjectives or adjective phrases that modify the appositive are placed below it.

EXAMPLE:  Bill spoke about Countee Cullen, *an American poet.*

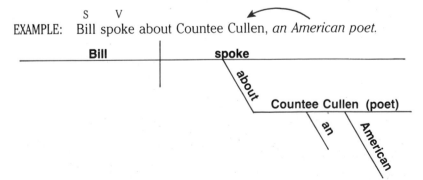

144

EXAMPLE: Albany, *the capital of New York,* is a river city.

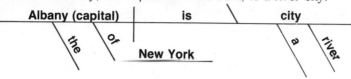

**EXERCISE B: Diagraming Appositive Phrases.** Diagram these sentences, each having an appositive phrase.

1. Leslie, a friend of mine, phoned yesterday.
2. Alex sent me a postcard from Lagos, the capital of Nigeria.
3. You will like *White Fang*, a story about a dog.
4. Chris Evert Lloyd, winner of many matches, will be there.
5. Mother traveled to Istanbul, a city in Turkey.

**DEVELOPING WRITING SKILLS: Writing and Diagraming Sentences with Prepositional Phrases and Appositives.** Write ten sentences, each using a prepositional phrase or an appositive from the lists below. Correctly diagram each sentence.

EXAMPLE: appositive—a world-famous violinist

Malcolm Tine, a world-famous violinist, will perform a concert Saturday.

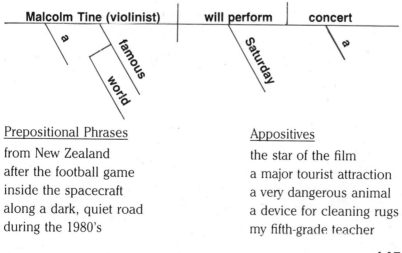

Prepositional Phrases

from New Zealand
after the football game
inside the spacecraft
along a dark, quiet road
during the 1980's

Appositives

the star of the film
a major tourist attraction
a very dangerous animal
a device for cleaning rugs
my fifth-grade teacher

**145**

# Skills Review and Writing Workshop

## Phrases

### CHECKING YOUR SKILLS

Write the *adjective phrase, adverb phrase, appositive phrase, participial phrase,* or *infinitive phrase* for each underlined phrase below.

(1) Cortés, <u>leader of the Spanish force in Mexico</u>, approached Montezuma's capital. (2) He came <u>with 400 Spaniards and 4,000 Indian allies</u>. (3) <u>Near Lake Chalco</u>, they were met. (4) Montezuma had sent nobles <u>to greet them</u>. (5) The Spaniards continued marching, <u>reaching Texcoco lake</u>. (6) <u>From the shore</u>, they could see the raised highways. (7) These long highways <u>of stone</u> were amazing. (8) They ran <u>for more than five miles</u>. (9) They could hold eight horsemen, <u>riding abreast</u>. (10) The Spaniards, <u>pushing forward</u>, feared a trap.

### USING GRAMMAR SKILLS IN WRITING
### Writing About an Event

Sometimes the bare facts of an event have to be expanded if your readers are to understand its meaning or importance. Follow the steps below to tell your classmates about an event in history.

**Prewriting:** Choose an interesting event you have read about in your history book. Write a brief outline of the event's main features. Next, list details to make the event come alive for your readers.

**Writing:** Describe the event in the order in which it happened. Add details by expanding your sentences with phrases to give your readers a clear idea of the event.

**Revising:** Reread your report to make sure your phrases are near the words they modify, and make improvements. After you have revised, proofread carefully.

# 11

# Clauses

This chapter will deal with another important group of words, the *clause*.

**A clause is a group of words with its own subject and verb.**

There are two basic types of clauses, and there is an important difference between them. The first kind is called an *independent clause*.

**An independent clause has a subject and a verb and can stand by itself as a complete sentence.**

Independent clauses can be short or long. What is important is that the clause express a complete thought and be able to stand by itself as a sentence.

INDEPENDENT
CLAUSES:

$$\overset{S}{\text{The}} \overset{V}{\text{bus arrived.}}$$

$$\text{In the morning } \overset{S}{\text{we}} \overset{V}{\text{began to explore the beach.}}$$

$$\overset{S}{\text{Marie Curie, a scientist, }} \overset{V}{\text{discovered radium.}}$$

The second type of clause is called a *subordinate clause.* This type of clause also contains a subject and a verb but differs from an independent clause in this way: By itself it does *not* express a complete thought.

**A subordinate clause has a subject and a verb but cannot stand by itself as a sentence. It is only part of a sentence.**

Read the following examples. Do *these* clauses express complete thoughts? The answer this time should be *no.*

SUBORDINATE CLAUSES:   after she finished her report

when the trunk was found in the attic

As you can see, each subordinate clause does have a subject and a verb. But in each case something is missing; more information is needed. Consider the first clause again. *After she finished her report,* what happened? Was she pleased? Was she disappointed? The thought is not complete; questions remain in the reader's mind.

Why is the thought in a subordinate clause *not* complete? Part of the answer can be found in the first word of each clause. Such words as *after* and *when* will often make a clause *dependent* on another idea. To make a complete thought from a subordinate clause, it is necessary to add an independent clause. In the following examples, the subordinate clauses are italicized; the independent clauses are not. Notice how the two kinds of clauses work together to express one complete thought.

EXAMPLES:   *After she finished her report,* Debbie felt relieved.

The mystery was solved *when the trunk was found in the attic.*

This chapter will show you how to combine subordinate clauses with independent clauses to make complete sentences. It will also explain how subordinate clauses can be used within sentences as adjectives and as adverbs.

# Adjective Clauses 11.1

A subordinate clause will sometimes act as an adjective in a sentence.

**An adjective clause is a subordinate clause that modifies a noun or pronoun.**

Like one-word adjectives and adjective phrases, an *adjective clause* answers the questions *What kind?* or *Which one?*

## Recognizing Adjective Clauses

Most adjective clauses begin with the words *that, which, who, whom,* and *whose.* Sometimes an adjective clause begins with an adverb, such as *since, where,* or *when.*

The adjective clauses in the following chart are italicized. The arrow in each sentence points from the adjective clause to the word in the independent clause that the adjective clause modifies. Notice also that the adjective clauses come right after the words they modify.

| ADJECTIVE CLAUSES |
| --- |
| She bought an expensive watch *that was made in Japan. (What kind* of watch?) |
| That radio, *which was made fifty years ago,* still works. (*Which* radio?) |
| This is the girl *who won the music prize.* (*Which* girl?) |

The person *whom we mean to invite* is Senator Jackson. (*Which* person?)

The book *whose title I can't remember* was written by Alcott. (*Which* book?)

In the week *since he left*, several things have changed. (*Which* week?)

He remembers a time *when he swam in that lake*. (*What kind* of time?)

Adjective clauses, as the chart on page 149 and above shows, can modify nouns or pronouns in any part of a sentence.

**EXERCISE: Identifying Adjective Clauses.** Copy the following sentences and underline the adjective clause in each.

EXAMPLE: The lake <u>where we swim</u> is a hundred feet deep in the center.

1. He is the pitcher whom we saw the last time.
2. *Kabloona,* which describes a Frenchman living among the Eskimos, was written by Gontran De Poncins.
3. A *tsunami* is a huge wave that is caused by an earthquake or volcanic eruption.
4. Is this the teacher who also makes silver jewelry?
5. In her talk the ambassador described Luxembourg, which has changed greatly.
6. The man whom you want lives across the street and three houses down.
7. A movie that I will never forget is *Zorba the Greek.*
8. The house where she lived is now a historic site.
9. This is the travel agent who offers trips to China.
10. The girl whose pen I used is my sister Elizabeth's best friend.

**150**

**DEVELOPING WRITING SKILLS:** **Writing Sentences with Adjective Clauses.** Follow the instructions to write ten sentences that contain adjective clauses. Underline each adjective clause.

EXAMPLE:    Write a sentence with a clause that begins *whom we chose*

The player <u>whom we chose as team captain</u> is the best athlete on the squad.

1. Write a sentence with a clause that begins *who always forgets.*
2. Write a sentence with a clause that begins *whom I visited recently.*
3. Write a sentence with a clause that begins *whose main job was.*
4. Write a sentence with a clause that begins *that George and I saw.*
5. Write a sentence with a clause that begins *that costs.*
6. Write a sentence with a clause that begins *which is calculated.*
7. Write a sentence with a clause that begins *which occurred recently.*
8. Write a sentence with a clause that begins *when my father left.*
9. Write a sentence with a clause that begins *where the children enjoyed.*
10. Write a sentence with a clause that begins *since the flood occurred.*

# Adverb Clauses 11.2

Subordinate clauses can also be used as adverbs.

**An adverb clause is a subordinate clause that modifies a verb, an adjective, or an adverb.**

Adverb clauses can answer any of the following questions about the words they modify: *Where? When? In what manner? To what extent? Under what condition?* or *Why?*

## Recognizing Adverb Clauses

Adverb clauses begin with *subordinating conjunctions.* The following chart lists a number of common subordinating conjunctions.

| COMMON SUBORDINATING CONJUNCTIONS | | |
|---|---|---|
| after | even though | unless |
| although | if | until |
| as | in order that | when |
| as if | since | whenever |
| as long as | so that | where |
| because | than | wherever |
| before | though | while |

A subordinating conjunction always comes *before* the adverb clause. The conjunction will usually appear in one of two places—either at the beginning of the sentence or in the middle, connecting two clauses.

EXAMPLES:
ADVERB CLAUSE      INDEPENDENT CLAUSE
Since you expect to be late, I will prepare dinner.

INDEPENDENT CLAUSE          ADVERB CLAUSE
I will prepare dinner since you expect to be late.

In addition to beginning an adverb clause, a subordinating conjunction connects the adverb clause to another word in the sentence. Study the examples in the following chart. The adverb clauses are italicized. The arrows point to the words that the clauses modify. Notice that each clause answers one of the questions for adverb clauses.

**152**

## ADVERB CLAUSES

| | |
|---|---|
| Modifying Verbs | Put the package *wherever you find room.* (Put *where?*) |
| | The parade will begin *when the train stops.* (Will begin *when?*) |
| | Leo spoke *as if he were frightened.* (Spoke *in what manner?*) |
| | I will have some lemonade *if you do too.* (Will have *under what condition?*) |
| Modifying an Adjective | I am tired *because I have been chopping wood all day.* (Tired *why?*) |
| Modifying an Adverb | She knows more *than the other engineers do.* (More *to what extent?*) |

Note that most of the adverb clauses in the chart modify verbs. Although adverb clauses can modify three different parts of speech, they usually modify verbs.

Note also that when an adverb clause begins a sentence, the clause is followed by a comma.

EXAMPLE: *When the rain stops,* the game will continue.

**EXERCISE: Identifying Adverb Clauses.** Copy the sentences onto your paper and underline each adverb clause.

EXAMPLE: <u>Before we left on vacation</u>, we put the dog in a kennel.

1. If the book is delivered in time, I will use it for my report.
2. Mike writes to his aunt at least twice a month even though she seldom answers.

**153**

3. I will return whenever you need me.
4. Grandma ran for mayor when the incumbent retired.
5. When Fred Astaire started his career, he danced with his sister Adele.
6. Our principal is busier than I have ever seen her.
7. A storm developed after we reached the turnpike.
8. Winston Churchill was better read than most of the other world leaders of his time were.
9. They drove to the park although it was very close.
10. Fortunately, my brother runs faster than I do.

**DEVELOPING WRITING SKILLS: Using Adverb Clauses in Sentences.** Combine each of the pairs of sentences into a single sentence by making one of them an adverb clause. Write the new sentences and underline the adverb clause. If necessary, refer to the list of subordinating conjunctions on page 152.

EXAMPLE:  I will work on my hobby. You want to sleep.

I will work on my hobby <u>if you want to sleep</u>.

1. Bob was late to the show. He missed part of the first act.
2. The lookout saw the danger. The ship still struck the iceberg.
3. They picked two bushels of blueberries. They fell asleep.
4. The traffic light suddenly flashed red. We tried to stop the car.
5. You want to see the play. Why don't you write away for tickets?

# 11.3 Classifying Sentences by Structure

All sentences can be classified according to the number and kinds of clauses they contain. The four basic types of sentence structures are *simple, compound, complex,* and *compound-complex.*

# The Simple Sentence

The *simple sentence* is the most common type of sentence structure.

### A simple sentence consists of a single independent clause.

Simple sentences vary in length. Some are quite short; others can be several lines in length. All simple sentences, however, contain just one subject and one verb. They may also contain adjectives, adverbs, complements, and phrases in different combinations.

Simple sentences can also have various compound parts. They can have a compound subject, a compound verb, or both. Sometimes they will also have other compound elements, such as a compound direct object or a compound phrase.

All of the following sentences are simple sentences. The subjects are underlined once and the verbs are underlined twice.

ONE SUBJECT AND VERB:   The <u>bell</u> <u>rang</u>.

COMPOUND SUBJECT:   <u>You</u> and <u>I</u> <u>need</u> some help.

COMPOUND VERB:   The <u>door</u> <u>squeaked</u> and <u>rattled</u>.

COMPOUND SUBJECT AND VERB:   My <u>mother</u> and <u>father</u> <u>said</u> goodbye and <u>left</u> on vacation.

COMPOUND DIRECT OBJECT:   <u>He</u> <u>opened</u> the letter<sup>DO</sup> and the box<sup>DO</sup>.

COMPOUND PREPOSITIONAL PHRASES:   <u>She</u> <u>walked</u> to the market<sup>PREP PHRASE</sup> and to the station<sup>PREP PHRASE</sup>.

What does a simple sentence not have? First, a simple sentence never has a subordinate clause. Second, it never has more than one independent clause.

**EXERCISE A: Recognizing Simple Sentences.** The following are simple sentences. Copy each one onto your paper and underline the subject once and the verb twice. Notice that some of the subjects and verbs are compound.

EXAMPLE:  Jan opened the envelope and read the letter aloud.

1. Rick and I caught trout under the bridge.
2. The trail left the forest and wound its way up the steep mountain.
3. According to the Bible, Ichabod was born at the hour of the capture of the Ark.
4. Spinach, kale, beans, and peas are all relatively inexpensive.
5. The empty wagon struck the fence and then crashed into the tree.

## The Compound Sentence

A *compound sentence* is made up of more than one simple sentence.

**A compound sentence consists of two or more independent clauses.**

In most compound sentences, the independent clauses are joined by a comma and a coordinating conjunction *(and, but, for, nor, or, so,* or *yet)*. Another example of how the independent clauses in a compound sentence may be connected is with a semicolon (;).

EXAMPLES:  I planned to go to the hockey game, but I could not get tickets.

Dorothy writes children's books; she also illustrates them.

Notice in both of the preceding examples that there are two separate and complete independent clauses, each with its own

**156**

subject and verb. Like simple sentences, compound sentences never contain subordinate clauses.

**EXERCISE B: Recognizing Compound Sentences.** The following are compound sentences. Copy each onto your paper. Underline the subject once and the verb twice in each independent clause.

EXAMPLE: <u>Kathleen</u> <u>folded</u> the letters, and <u>Jane</u> <u>sealed</u> the envelopes.

1. James must remember to bring the lantern, or we will have no light in the cabin.
2. The capital of Louisiana is Baton Rouge; other important cities are Shreveport, Lake Charles, and New Orleans.
3. The southern magnolia has huge white flowers; the northern variety has smaller, somewhat pinkish flowers.
4. She is interested in space exploration, so she reads every article and book on the subject.
5. The night sky was clear, but we did not see a single shooting star.

## The Complex Sentence

*Complex sentences* contain subordinate clauses.

**A complex sentence consists of one independent clause and one or more subordinate clauses.**

In a complex sentence, the independent clause is often called the *main clause.* The main clause has its own subject and verb, as does each subordinate clause.

EXAMPLES:
       MAIN CLAUSE        SUBORDINATE CLAUSE
    <u>This</u> <u>is</u> the street|that <u>he</u> <u>describes</u> in the book|.

           SUBORDINATE CLAUSE      MAIN CLAUSE
   |Because <u>she</u> <u>can</u> <u>speak</u> Spanish well,| <u>we</u> <u>can</u> <u>understand</u> her|.

The preceding two examples are both complex sentences. Each has a main clause and a subordinate clause. In the first, the subordinate clause is an adjective clause. In the second, the subordinate clause is an adverb clause.

In the next example, the complex sentence is more complicated because the main clause is split by an adjective clause.

EXAMPLE:   Andrea, who plays basketball, won a trophy

The two parts of the independent clause form one main clause: *Andrea won a trophy.*

**EXERCISE C: Recognizing Complex Sentences.** The following are complex sentences. Copy each onto your paper. Underline the subject once and the verb twice in each clause. Then put parentheses around each subordinate clause.

EXAMPLE:   <u>Alan</u> <u>is</u> smarter (than <u>we</u> <u>realized</u>).

1. The main road was closed after the bridge collapsed.
2. The actress whom I admire the most is Carol Burnett.
3. We continued our vacation trip when the dense fog lifted.
4. If you are not happy with their work, you can wallpaper the room yourself.
5. The cactus will grow if you do not overwater it.

## The Compound-Complex Sentence

The last type of sentence structure is the *compound-complex sentence.* As the name suggests, this structure is a combination of a compound sentence and a complex sentence.

**A compound-complex sentence consists of two or more independent clauses and one or more subordinate clauses.**

The example on the following page contains two independent and two subordinate clauses.

**158**

EXAMPLE:

INDEPENDENT CLAUSE   SUBORDINATE CLAUSE
|Mr. Martin was the teacher||whom I liked best|,

INDEPENDENT CLAUSE   SUBORDINATE CLAUSE
|but he no longer teaches||since he became ill|.

**EXERCISE D: Recognizing Compound-Complex Sentences.** The following are compound-complex sentences. Copy each onto your paper. Underline the subject once and the verb twice in each clause. Then put parentheses around each subordinate clause.

EXAMPLE:   The mountains are now barren, but the valleys remain fertile (because they are irrigated).

1. If she can pack quickly she can leave with me, but I must leave exactly in an hour.
2. The roads were closed after the storm struck, and they are still dangerous now.
3. After we fell asleep, raccoons invaded our campsite, but we awoke and chased them away.
4. I will help you if I can, yet I know little about making jelly.
5. Sarah called home because she was late for dinner, but no one answered.

**EXERCISE E: Identifying the Structure of Sentences.** On your paper identify the structure of each of the following sentences as *simple, compound, complex,* or *compound-complex.*

EXAMPLE:   We waited at the curb so that we could see the President.

   complex

1. After two days of rain, the sun finally appeared.
2. Since he learned to cook, he has made one rich dish after another.
3. He will need a day of rest after he returns from Spain.

**159**

4. Draw a map, and I will try to follow it.
5. Where have you put our movie reels?
6. The ship that we visited in the harbor is a French destroyer from World War II.
7. I will plant the tulips, or Jessie will plant them.
8. The phone stopped ringing before I could answer it.
9. Circe, according to Greek legend, changed the companions of Odysseus into pigs.
10. Tanya dives better than I do, but I can swim faster.

**DEVELOPING WRITING SKILLS: Writing Sentences with Different Structures.** Write five sentences of your own according to the following instructions.

EXAMPLE:   Write a complex sentence beginning with an adverb clause.

Since you didn't call me, I decided to go to the movies alone.

1. Write a simple sentence with a compound subject connected by *and*.
2. Write a compound sentence connected by the conjunction *or*.
3. Write a complex sentence in which an adverb clause follows the main clause.
4. Write a complex sentence in which an adjective clause comes right after the subject of the main clause.
5. Write a compound-complex sentence containing an adverb clause.

# 11.4 Diagraming Clauses

Diagrams for the different parts of simple sentences are shown in preceding sections. This section will show you how to diagram compound and complex sentences.

**160**

## Compound Sentences

A compound sentence consists of two or more independent clauses. Each clause in a compound sentence is diagramed on a separate horizontal line, one above the other. The clauses are joined at the verbs with a dotted line in the shape of a step. Place the conjunction or semicolon on the horizontal part of the step.

```
            S     V           DO              S     V
EXAMPLE:   Jeff  fixed  the  toaster,  and  then  he  began  his

           DO
           homework.
```

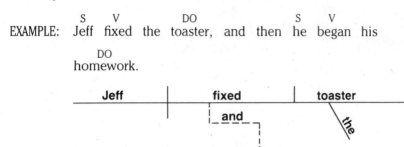

**EXERCISE A: Diagraming Compound Sentences.** Diagram each of the following compound sentences, using the preceding example as a model.

1. She enjoys all foods, but her husband is a vegetarian.
2. Agatha Christie wrote mystery stories; many of them are now famous.
3. He bought an expensive coin, but it was a forgery.
4. Hammurabi was a Babylonian king; he enacted a famous code of laws.
5. She has read many mysteries, but she dislikes spy stories.

## Complex Sentences

A complex sentence contains one independent clause and one or more subordinate clauses. In diagraming a complex sentence, each clause is placed on its own horizontal line.

**161**

**Adjective Clauses.** An adjective clause is placed on a separate horizontal line underneath the independent clause, with a dotted line connecting the two clauses. This line connects the noun or pronoun modified in the independent clause with the pronoun that begins the adjective clause.

EXAMPLE:  She is the pupil *who won the speech contest.*

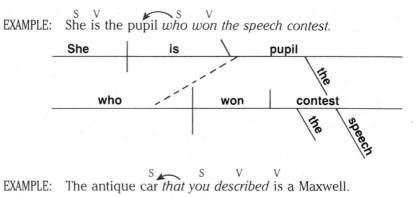

EXAMPLE:  The antique car *that you described* is a Maxwell.

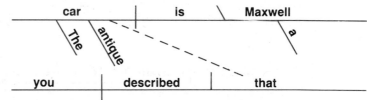

**Adverb Clauses.** Like an adjective clause, an adverb clause is placed on a separate horizontal line underneath the independent clause. A dotted line connects the modified verb, adverb, or adjective in the independent clause with the verb in the adverb clause. The subordinating conjunction that begins the adverb clause is written on the dotted line.

EXAMPLE:  I have known him *since he was a boy.*

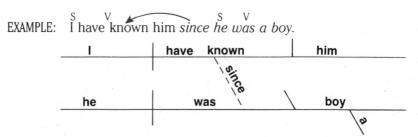

**162**

**EXERCISE B: Diagraming Subordinate Clauses.** Each of the following complex sentences contains either an adjective clause or an adverb clause. Diagram each sentence.

1. Squids, which have ten arms, often swim in large groups.
2. If you buy a ticket now, you will get a discount.
3. Here is the book that you wanted.
4. The bus left the station before the storm began.
5. If you come on the trip, you certainly will enjoy the scenery.

**DEVELOPING WRITING SKILLS: Writing and Diagraming Compound and Complex Sentences.** Use the following instructions to write five sentences of your own. Then correctly diagram each sentence.

EXAMPLE:  Write a complex sentence in which an adjective clause modifies the subject of the main clause.

The house that we rented overlooks the beach.

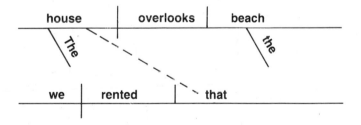

1. Write a compound sentence connected by the conjunction *but.*
2. Write a compound sentence connected with a semicolon.
3. Write a complex sentence in which an adjective clause modifies a direct object in the main clause.
4. Write a complex sentence beginning with an adverb clause.
5. Write a complex sentence in which an adverb clause follows the main clause.

**163**

# Skills Review and Writing Workshop

## Clauses

### CHECKING YOUR SKILLS

Write whether each of the underlined clauses below is an *independent, adjective,* or *adverb* clause.

(1) <u>When the trumpeter began to play</u>, the sounds of the orchestra faded into the background. (2) The trombones moaned softly, and <u>their groaning provided a base for the soaring melody</u>. (3) The saxophone joined the trumpet <u>because the trumpet alone could not express the deep lament</u>. (4) The piano, <u>which had been plunking along in the background</u>, suddenly began sending off sparks of melody. (5) Then, the singer, <u>who had been sulking against the piano</u>, drew a deep breath and drowned the audience in sound.

### USING GRAMMAR SKILLS IN WRITING
### Writing a Brief Description

Writers use such words as *when, but, because, that, which,* and *who* to show how one thought relates to another. Imagine you are writing a brief description of a happy moment for your autobiography. Follow the steps below to write a description that is both accurate and clear.

**Prewriting:** For your description, choose a brief moment that made you happy. Then make notes of details. List events in chronological order.

**Writing:** Write directly from your notes. Take care to construct your sentences using words such as *when, because,* and *who* to show the exact relationship between details and events. Use clauses to make your word picture clear.

**Revising:** Look at the entire description, and check your sentence structure to improve clarity and accuracy. After you have revised, proofread carefully.

**164**

*Chapter* **12**

# Avoiding Sentence Errors

Being able to recognize the parts of sentences can help you avoid certain errors in your writing.

## Avoiding Fragments 12.1

Some groups of words, even though they have a capital at the beginning and a period at the end, are not complete sentences. They are *fragments.*

**A fragment is a group of words that does not express a complete thought.**

A fragment is only *part* of a sentence.

### Recognizing Fragments

A sentence always has a subject *and* a verb. A fragment does not. It can be a group of words with no subject. It can be a group of words that includes a possible subject but no verb. It can be a group of words with a possible subject and only part of a possible verb. It can even be a subordinate clause standing alone.

## FRAGMENTS

In the early evening.
Felt happy and relaxed.
The sign in the corridor.
The train coming around the bend.
When she first smiled.

You will usually be able to tell if a group of words expresses a complete thought. One trick is to read the words aloud. This will help you hear whether or not some part is missing.

In the following chart, words have been added to the preceding fragments to make complete sentences. Read each italicized fragment; then read the complete sentence. Can you hear the difference?

## COMPLETE SENTENCES

The flight arrived *in the early evening.*
I *felt happy and relaxed.*
*The sign in the corridor* is surprising.
*The train* was *coming around the bend.*
*When she first smiled,* the whole world seemed to light up.

Each of the preceding examples needed one or more new parts. The first needed both a subject and a verb. The second needed only a subject. The third became complete when a verb and an adjective were added. The fourth became complete when a helping verb was added. The final example needed a complete independent clause to go with the subordinate clause.

**EXERCISE A: Recognizing Sentence Fragments.** Each of the following groups is either a sentence or a fragment. Write *F* if it is a fragment and *S* if it is a complete sentence.

**166**

EXAMPLE:    Firefighters climbing ladders.    F

1. Near the new traffic light.
2. A car jumping the curb.
3. The motor turned over.
4. Tried all day to contact them.
5. Since she speaks Spanish well.
6. The roof of the old auditorium.
7. Everyone accepted the decision.
8. At the bottom of the well.
9. Finished my shopping for the holidays.
10. Unless they answer by tomorrow.
11. The bicycle in front of the store.
12. The governor standing on the new platform.
13. The man suffering from the heat.
14. In hot weather a cold drink often helps.
15. Completed the project in an hour.
16. Since the new shopping mall opened.
17. A summer home near a lake.
18. She is very stubborn.
19. If I save fifty dollars.
20. Hoping to hear from you soon.

## Phrase Fragments

A phrase by itself is a fragment. It cannot stand alone because it does not have a subject and verb.

**A phrase should not be capitalized and punctuated as if it were a sentence.**

Three types of phrases—prepositional, participial, and infinitive—are often mistaken for sentences. A *phrase fragment* can be changed into a sentence in either of two ways.

The first way is to try adding the phrase fragment to a nearby sentence. The example on the following page shows a prepositional phrase following a complete sentence.

FRAGMENT:   The explorers left for the Arctic. *On the morning of March 4.*

You can correct this fragment simply by attaching it to the preceding sentence.

ADDED TO NEARBY SENTENCE:   The explorers left for the Arctic *on the morning of March 4.*

You can correct other fragments simply by attaching them to the beginning of a sentence. The participial phrase fragment in the next example can easily be corrected in this manner.

FRAGMENT:   *Arriving at the airport.* The prince and princess were greeted by cheers.

ADDED TO NEARBY SENTENCE:   *Arriving at the airport,* the prince and princess were greeted by cheers.

Sometimes, however, you may not be able to correct a phrase fragment by adding it to a nearby sentence. Then you will need to use the second way to change a phrase fragment into a sentence: Correct the fragment by adding to the phrase whatever is needed to make it a complete sentence. Often this method requires adding a subject and a verb.

| CHANGING PHRASE FRAGMENTS INTO SENTENCES ||
| **Phrase Fragments** | **Complete Sentences** |
| --- | --- |
| Near the old creek. | The treasure was found *near the old creek.* |
| Touching his hand. | *Touching his hand,* she asked for her father's advice. |
| To type well. | Sam learned *to type well.* |

There are, of course, many ways of adding words to phrase fragments in order to make them into sentences. If your teacher points out a phrase fragment in your writing, first try adding it to a nearby sentence. If that does not work, then turn the fragment into a sentence by adding words to it.

**EXERCISE B: Changing Phrase Fragments into Sentences.** Use each of the following phrase fragments in a sentence. You may use the phrase at the beginning, at the end, or in any other position in the sentence. Check to see that each of your sentences contains a subject and verb.

EXAMPLE:   In the morning after breakfast.

Sheri took·the dog to the kennel in the morning after breakfast.

1. On the telephone
2. To think clearly.
3. Getting tired.
4. On time to class.
5. Found on the beach.
6. Waiting at school.
7. Drinking cold milk.
8. On last night's news.
9. At breakfast.
10. Stung by a bee.

## Clause Fragments

All clauses have subjects and verbs, but some cannot stand alone as sentences.

**A subordinate clause should not be capitalized and punctuated as if it were a sentence.**

Subordinate clauses do not express complete thoughts. Although a subordinate adjective or adverb clause has a subject and verb, it cannot stand by itself as a sentence. (See Sections 11.1 and 11.2 for more information about subordinate clauses and the words that begin them.)

Like phrase fragments, *clause fragments* can usually be corrected in either of two ways: by attaching the fragment to a nearby sentence or by adding whatever words are needed to make the fragment into a sentence.

Notice how the following clause fragments are corrected by using the first method.

FRAGMENT:   The class enjoyed the poem. *That I recited to them as part of my oral report.*

ADDED TO NEARBY SENTENCE:   The class enjoyed the poem *that I recited to them as part of my oral report.*

FRAGMENT:   I'll play the game. *As long as you play it too.*

ADDED TO NEARBY SENTENCE:   I'll play the game *as long as you play it too.*

To change a clause fragment into a sentence by the second method, you must add an independent clause to the fragment.

| CHANGING CLAUSE FRAGMENTS INTO SENTENCES ||
| --- | --- |
| **Clause Fragments** | **Complete Sentences** |
| That you described. | I found the necklace *that you described.* |
| | The necklace *that you described* has been found. |
| When he knocked. | I opened the door *when he knocked.* |
| | *When he knocked,* I opened the door. |

**EXERCISE C: Changing Clause Fragments into Sentences.** Use each of the clause fragments in a sentence. See that each sentence contains an independent clause.

EXAMPLE:   That she wanted to use.

I lent her the hammer that she wanted to use.

**170**

1. If you write to me soon.
2. Who knows the combination to the lock.
3. That he told us.
4. Whom they described to the police.
5. Although she doesn't speak French too well.
6. When the river flooded the valley.
7. Who was born in 1976.
8. Because he waited too long.
9. Whose hat I found.
10. When the rain ended.

**EXERCISE D: Correcting Fragments.** Using your answers from Exercise A, correct each fragment you marked with an *F* by rewriting it as a complete sentence.

EXAMPLE:  Beside the post office.

  The town erected a statue of their late mayor beside the post office.

**EXERCISE E: Changing Fragments into Sentences.** Decide what is missing in each fragment, and then rewrite it as a complete sentence.

EXAMPLE:  In the spring of the year.

  In the spring of the year, the trees blossom.

1. At the top of the flagpole.
2. While she was raking the leaves in the back yard.
3. The room behind the kitchen.
4. Grinding his teeth in pain.
5. That you found last week in the attic.
6. In the morning or evening.
7. Frightened by the strange noises.
8. To listen to my records.
9. Whom you met in the market.
10. Two quarts of milk and a pound of butter.

**DEVELOPING WRITING SKILLS: Correcting Fragments in a Paragraph.** There are five fragments in the following paragraph. Rewrite the entire paragraph, correcting each fragment. You may correct a fragment by attaching it to a nearby sentence or by adding words to it to form a new sentence.

EXAMPLE:    The need for a national mint.

The need for a national mint was recognized soon after this country was founded.

(1) In 1793 a national mint was established. (2) In Philadelphia. (3) Silver coins were minted there for the first time in 1794. (4) Gold coins in 1795. (5) The original staff consisted of eleven office workers. (6) Nineteen in the coinage department and seven at the furnace. (7) There are six mints. (8) Now in operation. (9) Another mint was supposed to have been built in Oregon. (10) Destroyed by fire. (11) It was never completed.

# 12.2 Correcting Run-ons

A fragment is an incomplete sentence. A *run-on,* on the other hand, is an overcrowded sentence—one that has too much information.

**A run-on is two or more complete sentences that are not properly joined or separated.**

Run-ons are usually the result of haste. Learn to check your sentences carefully to see where one sentence ends and the next one begins.

## Two Kinds of Run-ons

There are two kinds of run-ons. One kind is made up of two sentences run together without any punctuation between them. The other consists of two or more sentences separated only by a comma.

| RUN-ONS | |
|---|---|
| **With No Punctuation** | **With Only a Comma** |
| I use our library often the reference section is my favorite part. | The Florida Keys are a chain of small islands, they are located off the southern tip of Florida. |

A good way to distinguish between a run-on and a sentence is to read the words aloud. Your ear will tell you whether you have one or two complete thoughts.

**EXERCISE A: Recognizing Run-ons.** On your paper write *S* if the item is a sentence and *RO* if the item is a run-on.

EXAMPLE: At fifteen John Keats began studying medicine, at twenty-one he was encouraged to work as a poet.  RO

1. On my last trip, I visited Platt National Park in Oklahoma I also spent some time at the Mesa Verde National Park in Colorado.
2. There are many famous horses in mythology, probably the most famous is the wooden horse of Troy.
3. After overcoming many problems, he finally finished staining the cabinet.
4. Saint Genevieve is the patron saint of Paris she is supposed to have prevented Attila the Hun from attacking that city.
5. The commuter railroads seem to have little trouble on weekends they run into problems with heavy passenger loads on weekdays.
6. The heart is a muscular, cone-shaped organ that maintains the circulation of the blood.
7. Some people prefer active sports, others like to watch sports on television.
8. Havana is the capital of Cuba it is also the chief port of the West Indies.

**173**

9. In 1926 Amy Lowell won the Pulitzer Prize for her poetry.
10. The side wall of the building collapsed, the next day the rest of the building was torn down.

## Three Ways to Correct Run-ons

There are three easy ways to correct a run-on.

**Using End Marks.** *End marks* are periods, question marks, and exclamation marks.

### Use an end mark to separate a run-on into two sentences.

Properly used, an end mark splits a run-on into two shorter but complete sentences. Which end mark you use depends upon the function of the sentence.

RUN-ON: In his search for a northeast passage to the Orient, Marco Polo finally reached northern China he named the country he found Cathay.

CORRECTED SENTENCES: In his search for a northeast passage to the Orient, Marco Polo finally reached northern China. He named the country he found Cathay.

RUN-ON: Have you found my watch, I lost it yesterday.

CORRECTED SENTENCES: Have you found my watch? I lost it yesterday.

**Using Commas and Coordinating Conjunctions.** Sometimes the two parts of a run-on are related and should stay in the same sentence. In that case the run-on can be changed into a compound sentence.

### Use a comma and a coordinating conjunction to combine two independent clauses into a compound sentence.

The five coordinating conjunctions used most often are *and, but, or, for,* and *nor.* To separate the two clauses properly, it is necessary to use both a comma and a coordinating conjunction. A comma by itself is not enough.

RUN-ON: My mother and father go shopping on Saturdays, I stay home and clean.

CORRECTED SENTENCE: My mother and father go shopping on Saturdays, and I stay home and clean.

RUN-ON: I want to go to the circus, I haven't any money.

CORRECTED SENTENCE: I want to go to the circus, but I haven't any money.

**Using Semicolons.** You can sometimes use a semicolon to punctuate the two parts of a run-on.

**Use a semicolon to connect two closely related ideas.**

Do not overuse the semicolon. Remember, semicolons should be used only when the ideas in both parts of the sentence are closely related.

RUN-ON: The first train to the city leaves at 6:05, the express doesn't leave until an hour later.

CORRECTED SENTENCE: The first train to the city leaves at 6:05; the express doesn't leave until an hour later.

**EXERCISE B: Correcting Run-ons.** Rewrite each of the following run-ons using any of the three methods described in this section. Use each method at least four times.

EXAMPLE: Tell the truth, it is easier than lying.

Tell the truth. It is easier than lying.

1. I had a terrible day at school, I lost my lunch and stained my shirt with dye during science.
2. An old saying says that a new broom sweeps clean our new coach may thus make a lot of changes.

**175**

3. Do you know who was the last President of the United States to serve two full terms, President Jimmy Carter served only one term.

4. Nancy loves humorous poems, her favorites are Carroll's "Jabberwocky" and Nash's "The Panther."

5. Finish your homework, then clean your desk.

6. My mother and aunt collect porcelain my brother and I collect coins.

7. Histamines cause itching, some people take antihistamines for relief.

8. Benito Juarez is a national hero in Mexico he helped defeat the French and drive them from his land.

9. Crops are damaged by a variety of pests, spraying with special insecticides sometimes helps.

10. A silver jubilee celebrates an event that occurred twenty-five years before, Queen Elizabeth II celebrated her silver jubilee in 1977.

11. First remove the shells from the nuts, then chop the nuts into small bits.

12. Have you read "The Man Without a Country" by Edward Everett Hale, I will never forget poor Philip Nolan.

13. Kyoto has a population of more than a million residents it is the third most populous city in Japan and its leading cultural center.

14. I just finished reading *Little Men* by Louisa May Alcott, she is also the author of *Little Women.*

15. The apartment is vacant it will be painted before the new tenants move in.

16. Pasteurization kills bacteria by heating liquids rapidly and then cooling them, this process helps make milk safe for drinking.

17. After many years she returned to the house in the country in which she lived as a child, it was shabby and run down.

18. Edgar Allan Poe was an orphan he was given a home and educated by John Allan.

**176**

19. Our roof was damaged we needed several days to repair it.
20. The French writer George Sand was a woman, her real name was Aurore Dupin.

**DEVELOPING WRITING SKILLS: Correcting Run-ons in a Composition.** Three of the sentences in the paragraph are run-ons. Rewrite the entire paragraph, correcting each run-on. Do not use the same method to correct all the run-ons.

EXAMPLE: Baseball has long been popular in the United States, a similar game was played even in colonial days.

Baseball has long been popular in the United States. A similar game was played even in colonial days.

(1) The history of baseball goes back much further than Abner Doubleday and Cooperstown, New York. (2) In this country a form of baseball was played even before Washington's time the origin of the game was probably the English game of rounders. (3) Experts agree that a game with a bat, a ball, and bases was played during the early part of the nineteenth century. (4) In New England the game was called town ball, Oliver Wendell Holmes reported playing the game at Harvard College in the 1820's. (5) The original playing field was a square rather than a diamond the batter stood halfway between home plate and first base. (6) The game was not invented by Abner Doubleday, and the first game was not played in Cooperstown. (7) In fact, baseball was probably first played in and around New York City.

# Correcting Misplaced Modifiers 12.3

A phrase or clause that acts as an adjective or adverb should be placed close to the word it modifies. Otherwise the meaning of the sentence may be unclear.

**A modifier should be placed as close as possible to the word it modifies.**

177

# Misplaced Modifiers

A modifier placed too far away from the word it modifies is called a *misplaced modifier*. Because they are misplaced, such phrases and clauses seem to modify the wrong word in a sentence.

MISPLACED MODIFIER: We rented a boat at the lake *with an outboard motor.*

The misplaced modifier is the phrase *with an outboard motor.* In the sentence it sounds as though the lake has an outboard motor. The sentence needs to be reworded slightly to put the modifer closer to *boat.*

CORRECTED SENTENCE: At the lake we rented a boat *with an outboard motor.*

Here is a somewhat different type of misplaced modifier.

MISPLACED MODIFIER: *Walking toward the house,* the tree on the lawn looked beautiful.

In this sentence *walking toward the house* should modify a person. Instead, it incorrectly modifies *tree.* How could the tree be walking toward the house? The sentence needs to be rewritten to include the name of the person who is actually doing the walking.

CORRECTED SENTENCE: *Walking toward the house,* Elizabeth admired the beautiful tree on the lawn.

**EXERCISE A: Recognizing Misplaced Modifiers.** Some of the sentences on the followig page are correct, but most of them contain a misplaced modifier. Read each sentence carefully and check the placement of the modifiers. If the sentence is correct, write *C* on your paper. If the sentence contains a misplaced modifier, write *MM.*

EXAMPLE:   My brother Richard bought a loaf of bread at the local supermarket that had turned green with mold.   MM

1. Crossing the street, the curb was very high.
2. She bought a jacket from the catalog with large patch pockets.
3. Traveling in Spain, the roof of their house collapsed.
4. A beautiful car with whitewalls and a vinyl roof appeared in our driveway.
5. Seth found a book in the local library about prehistoric animals.
6. Reaching the top of the hill, the town could be clearly seen.
7. Worried about her mother, April called home three times.
8. Bring the package to me with the green cord.
9. Two girls in red bathing suits swam near the dock.
10. Father bought a key chain for my sister with a whistle.

## Revising Sentences with Misplaced Modifiers

Among the most common misplaced modifiers are prepositional phrases, participial phrases, and adjective clauses. All are corrected in the same way—by placing the modifier as close as possible to the word it modifies.

First consider a misplaced prepositional phrase. This error usually occurs in a sentence with two or more prepositional phrases in a row.

MISPLACED:   Uncle Max built a house near the lake *with a private dock.*

The misplaced modifier should be moved closer to *house.*

CORRECTED:   Near the lake Uncle Max built a house *with a private dock.*

**179**

Participial phrases are sometimes used at the beginning of sentences. When such a phrase is used this way, it must be followed immediately by a word that it can logically modify.

MISPLACED:   *Flying over the mountains,* an electrical storm endangered our safety.

What is flying over the mountains? The sentence needs to be rewritten to put a word such as *plane* next to the modifier.

CORRECTED:   *Flying over the mountains,* our plane was endangered by an electrical storm.

A misplaced adjective clause should also be moved closer to the word it modifies. In the following sentence, the clause is so far away from *ring* that it seems to modify *months* or *searching.* The sentence needs to be rearranged.

MISPLACED:   I found the ring after several months of

searching *that my grandmother gave me.*

CORRECTED:   After several months of searching, I found the

ring *that my grandmother gave me.*

**EXERCISE B: Correcting Misplaced Modifiers.** Rewrite the sentences on the following page to eliminate the misplaced modifiers. In each rewritten sentence, underline the modifier that was misplaced in the original. Then draw an arrow pointing from the modifier to the word it modifies.

EXAMPLE:   My brother Richard bought a loaf of bread at the local supermarket that had turned green with mold.

At the local supermarket, my brother Richard

bought a loaf of bread <u>that had turned green with mold</u>.

**180**

1. The dress had already been purchased that she wanted.
2. Reaching the park, my aunt was waiting on a bench.
3. Uncle Ron bought a hat at the bazaar with a green feather.
4. I read the story when I got home with the surprise ending.
5. Told to move along, the hissing of the crowd increased.
6. The famous actor arrived late whom everyone hoped to see.
7. Walking rather slowly toward the station, the train was almost missed.
8. Tudor Castle was destroyed by a terrible fire built in 1512.
9. I received a new television from my mother with remote controls.
10. The soldiers finally caught the man after a long chase who was spying on them.


**DEVELOPING WRITING SKILLS: Placing Modifiers Correctly in Sentences.** Write ten sentences of your own, each containing one of the modifiers in the following list. Make sure that you place the modifiers correctly in your sentences.

EXAMPLE:   walking through the town

Walking through the town, the couple visited several tourist attractions.

1. with a broken arm
2. recovering from her illness
3. caught in the downpour
4. located nearby
5. feeling depressed
6. trying to save money
7. which needed repairs
8. that I had lost
9. inside the auditorium
10. standing on the corner

# Skills Review and Writing Workshop

## Avoiding Sentence Errors

### CHECKING YOUR SKILLS

Rewrite the following paragraph, correcting all fragments, run-ons, and misplaced modifiers.

(1) Eskimos use the principle of capturing warm air. (2) To heat their houses. (3) They build their houses with an entrance passage that slopes upward, this passage opens into the living quarters. (4) Through a trap door. (5) The living quarters are small, there are no openings above the level of the entrance. (6) The air is warmed by body heat and rises but cannot escape. (7) In this way. (8) Capturing warm air, their houses are heated. (9) When the houses are small and the roof is thick enough. (10) The Eskimos with little or no fire are able to live.

### USING GRAMMAR SKILLS IN WRITING
### Writing an Explanation

Writers know that sentences must be clear and thoughts must be complete. This is particularly important when you tell about how something works. Follow the steps below to write a clear explanation for your classmates.

**Prewriting:** Choose a process with which you are familiar, for example, how to make something, or the steps to take when applying for a job. Make notes about details. List the order in which things happen. Assume that your audience does not know as much about this process as you do.

**Writing:** Begin writing by telling what your explanation will be about. Then give the important details of the process in the order in which they happen.

**Revising:** Make sure your explanation contains no fragments, run-ons, or misplaced modifiers. Then make sure that each step follows clearly from the one before. After revising, proofread carefully.

# UNIT II

# *Usage*

# 13

# Levels of Usage

The way a word or expression is normally used in speaking or writing is known as usage. Usage varies according to time and place. Correct usage is language suitable for the occasion.

Standard English is the form that is used by most educated people. Nonstandard English is any dialect or form of language used by a particular social, regional, or ethnic group. It also includes slang. This chapter is concerned with Standard English.

## 13.1 Two Levels of Standard English

Standard English may be formal or informal. Formal English is used whenever a writer wants to discuss an important subject in a serious way. Formal English is more precise than informal English. Informal English resembles conversation and is used in casual writing.

### Formal English

Public speeches, business letters, wedding announcements, and most school reports are written in formal English.

**Formal English uses traditional standards of correctness. It often has complex sentence structures and uses a wide vocabulary.**

The chart below gives suggestions for writing formal English.

---

### WRITING FORMAL ENGLISH

1. Do not use contractions. For example, use *it is* instead of *it's* and *do not* instead of *don't*.

2. Slang is never used. Words such as *guy* are not acceptable.

3. Do not use the pronoun *you* in a general way to mean "a person." Use a noun or the pronoun *one* instead.

3. Use correct grammatical structure and precise wording. A sentence that sounds like everyday conversation is probably not formal English.

---

The sentence below is an example of formal English.

EXAMPLE:   What the brain does by itself is infinitely more fascinating and complex than any response it can make to chemical stimulation.—Ursula K. LeGuin

**EXERCISE A: Recognizing Formal English.** In each sentence below, choose the more formal of the pair of words or phrases shown in parentheses.

EXAMPLE:   (You can't, One cannot) enter here.

One cannot

1. Nearly half of our class (failed, flunked) the test.
2. (I've, I have) decided to take biology next year.
3. (You never know, One never knows) how it will turn out.
4. The storekeeper told the children to (leave, go away).
5. Hundreds of people (attended, showed up for) the game.
6. Most of the (kids, students) went to the class picnic.
7. (I have, I've) always been good at math.
8. (She's, She is) our new science teacher.
9. (You'd, One would) expect warm weather in spring.
10. They were (going to, off to) the country the next day.

# Informal English

Most conversations are held in informal English. Friendly letters, casual notes, and many newspaper and magazine articles are written in informal English.

**Informal English is conversational in tone. It uses a smaller vocabulary and shorter sentences than formal English.**

Informal English is just as correct as formal English, but is more like the language used in everyday life. The grammatical structure can be more relaxed, and many words and phrases that are not acceptable in formal English may be used in informal English.

The chart lists suggestions for writing informal English.

| WRITING INFORMAL ENGLISH |
|---|
| 1. Contractions are acceptable in informal English. |
| 2. Popular expressions, specialized vocabulary such as sports terms, and words and phrases used in friendly conversations are acceptable if they are not overused. |
| 3. The pronoun *you* may be used in a general way. |
| 4. Sentences can be looser and more conversational, more humorous, or more personal. Most of the words used are ordinary, everyday ones. |

The example below is written in informal English. Notice the use of contractions and the relaxed grammatical structure.

EXAMPLE:   It was one of those accidents that couldn't possibly happen; we'd had one of our rare eclipses by Earth's shadow that night; part of the air purifier had frozen up, and the single alarm in the circuit had failed to go off. Half a million dollars' worth of chemical and electronic engineering had let us down completely.—Arthur C. Clarke

**186**

**EXERCISE B: Recognizing Informal English.** One sentence in each pair below uses formal English; the other uses informal English. Label each sentence *formal* or *informal.*

EXAMPLE: a. I can't imagine why they did that.

    b. I cannot imagine why they did that.

    a. informal b. formal

1. a. Ellen enjoys sports very much.
   b. Ellen is really crazy about sports.
2. a. You can save money by vacationing in the off-season.
   b. One can save money by vacationing in the off-season.
3. a. My friend Joe is a great cook.
   b. My friend Joe is an excellent cook.
4. a. Some of the kids stayed around after school.
   b. Some of the students remained after school.
5. a. You can't predict when the volcano will blow up again.
   b. One cannot predict when the volcano will erupt again.
6. a. You'd have to be a genius to fix that contraption.
   b. Only an expert could repair that machine.
7. a. A lot of people think whales are pretty smart.
   b. Many people consider whales intelligent.
8. a. My brother's car was a total wreck after the crash last Friday.
   b. My brother's car was destroyed in the accident last Friday.
9. a. We all contributed money for my father's present.
   b. We all chipped in for my dad's present.
10. a. No reasonable person would believe that story.
    b. You'd have to be crazy to fall for that yarn.

**DEVELOPING WRITING SKILLS: Writing Formal and Informal English.** Write five sentences of your own in formal English, using the suggestions on page 185 as a guide. Then change your five sentences into informal English, using the suggestions on page 186.

# Skills Review and Writing Workshop

## Levels of Usage

### CHECKING YOUR SKILLS

Rewrite the following paragraph using formal English.

(1) Last night I went to the movies with my friend Joe. (2) My mom wanted me to let my kid sister come along, but I got out of it. (3) I told her Sis would be scared of all the snakes in the flick. (4) The evening was a flop. (5) First of all, we showed up late and missed the first scene. (6) We had to sit in the balcony; there weren't any seats downstairs. (7) Someone in the row behind us was talking his head off. (8) Someone in front of us was unwrapping candy bars so we couldn't hear. (9) Finally, the projector quit. (10) Don't ask me what the picture's about; I draw a blank.

### USING USAGE SKILLS IN WRITING
### Writing an Essay

Imagine that you are running for student council president. Your school newspaper has asked each candidate to write a formal essay explaining why she or he would make the best president. You are going to write about your qualifications following the steps below.

**Prewriting:** Make a list of things that you would like to change. Select two of these and make notes on possible solutions for each.

**Writing:** In formal English, write an introductory paragraph that states the purpose of your essay and mentions the problems that you will discuss and the reasons you would make the best president. Then write one body paragraph about each problem and your ideas about solutions. Then, write a concluding paragraph.

**Revising:** Revise your essay, making sure it is written in formal English. After you have revised, proofread carefully.

# 14

# Using Verbs

*Usage* refers to the way a word or expression is used in a sentence. The rules in this and the following chapters are those of standard English. You will probably be expected to apply these rules in most of the writing and speaking you do in school.

Verb usage is an area that causes many problems. Since verbs have many forms and uses, you may find yourself occasionally making mistakes with them. This chapter will help you learn to use them correctly in your speaking and writing.

## The Four Principal 14.1 Parts of Verbs

Verbs have different forms to express time. The form of the verb *walk* in the sentence "They *walk* very fast" expresses action in the present. In "They *walked* too far," the form of the verb shows that the action happened in the past. In "They *will walk* home," the verb expresses action in the future. These forms of verbs are known as *tenses.* To use the tenses of a verb correctly, you must know the *principal parts* of the verb.

**A verb has four principal parts: the *present*, the *present participle*, the *past*, and the *past participle*.**

Here, for example, are the four principal parts of the verb *walk.*

| THE FOUR PRINCIPAL PARTS OF *WALK* | | | |
|---|---|---|---|
| **Present** | **Present Participle** | **Past** | **Past Participle** |
| walk | (am) walking | walked | (have) walked |

The first principal part, called the present, is the form of the verb that is listed in a dictionary. Notice also the helping verbs in parentheses before the second and fourth principal parts. These two principal parts must be combined with helping verbs before they can be used as verbs in sentences. The result will always be a verb phrase.

Here are four sentences, each using one of the principal parts of the verb *walk.*

EXAMPLES:   He *walks* as if he were in a hurry.

June *was walking* behind us a minute ago.

They *walked* to the park.

We *have walked* three miles.

The way the last two principal parts of a verb are formed shows whether the verb is *regular* or *irregular.*

## Regular Verbs

Most verbs are *regular.*

**The past and past participle of a regular verb are formed by adding *-ed* or *-d* to the present form.**

To form the past and past participle of a regular verb such as *talk* or *look,* you simply add *-ed* to the present. With regular verbs that already end in *e*—verbs such as *move* and *charge*—you simply add *-d* to the present.

**190**

| PRINCIPAL PARTS OF REGULAR VERBS | | | |
|---|---|---|---|
| **Present** | **Present Participle** | **Past** | **Past Participle** |
| talk | (am) talking | talked | (have) talked |
| look | (am) looking | looked | (have) looked |
| move | (am) moving | moved | (have) moved |
| charge | (am) charging | charged | (have) charged |

**EXERCISE A: Recognizing the Principal Parts of Regular Verbs.** The verb or verb phrase in each of the following sentences is underlined. Identify the principal part used to form each verb.

EXAMPLE:  Ginny is painting a portrait of her sister.

present participle

1. Chris filled the flower pot with pebbles and soil.
2. We are visiting the state legislature tomorrow.
3. Roberto will join the photography club next fall.
4. Has Denise mentioned her vacation plans to you?
5. Hot meals always taste better on a cold day.
6. I had climbed the hill too late for the fireworks.
7. The lifeguards cleaned the pool every day last summer.
8. Why was Steve dancing down the hill?
9. I have not typed my essay yet.
10. Kate is planning a surprise party for her brother.

**EXERCISE B: Using the Principal Parts of Regular Verbs.** Copy each of the following sentences onto your paper, writing the correct form of the verb given in parentheses.

EXAMPLE:  They have ___(look)___ everywhere for the missing piece.

They have looked everywhere for the missing piece.

1. After the long train ride yesterday, we ___(sigh)___ in relief.

**191**

2. Before he left, Kevin __(ask)__ Jane to visit him soon.
3. Tracy __(march)__ in the parade last Thursday.
4. We have __(complain)__ about the noise, repeatedly.
5. Last week, the boys __(roll)__ Easter eggs across the lawn.
6. I am __(play)__ that sonata in the music recital.
7. Had you __(notice)__ him before he stood up?
8. After I __(polish)__ the floor last week, I never wanted to see another piece of wood.
9. Last winter the wind __(knock)__ down the old tree.
10. Rodney and Meg will __(start)__ their geography project.

## Irregular Verbs

Although most verbs are regular, many very common verbs are *irregular*. These are the verbs that tend to cause the most problems.

**The past and past participle of an irregular verb are *not* formed by adding -*ed* or -*d* to the present form.**

The third and fourth principal parts of irregular verbs are formed in various ways. They must, therefore, be memorized. The following charts show the most common of these verbs.

| IRREGULAR VERBS WITH THE SAME PAST AND PAST PARTICIPLE | | | |
|---|---|---|---|
| **Present** | **Present Participle** | **Past** | **Past Participle** |
| bring | (am) bringing | brought | (have) brought |
| build | (am) building | built | (have) built |
| buy | (am) buying | bought | (have) bought |
| catch | (am) catching | caught | (have) caught |
| fight | (am) fighting | fought | (have) fought |
| find | (am) finding | found | (have) found |
| get | (am) getting | got | (have) got *or* (have) gotten |

| | | | |
|---|---|---|---|
| hold | (am) holding | held | (have) held |
| lay | (am) laying | laid | (have) laid |
| lead | (am) leading | led | (have) led |
| lose | (am) losing | lost | (have) lost |
| pay | (am) paying | paid | (have) paid |
| say | (am) saying | said | (have) said |
| sit | (am) sitting | sat | (have) sat |
| spin | (am) spinning | spun | (have) spun |
| stick | (am) sticking | stuck | (have) stuck |
| swing | (am) swinging | swung | (have) swung |
| teach | (am) teaching | taught | (have) taught |

## IRREGULAR VERBS WITH THE SAME PRESENT, PAST, AND PAST PARTICIPLE

| Present | Present Participle | Past | Past Participle |
|---|---|---|---|
| bid | (am) bidding | bid | (have) bid |
| burst | (am) bursting | burst | (have) burst |
| cost | (am) costing | cost | (have) cost |
| hurt | (am) hurting | hurt | (have) hurt |
| put | (am) putting | put | (have) put |
| set | (am) setting | set | (have) set |

## IRREGULAR VERBS THAT CHANGE IN OTHER WAYS

| Present | Present Participle | Past | Past Participle |
|---|---|---|---|
| arise | (am) arising | arose | (have) arisen |
| be | (am) being | was | (have) been |
| begin | (am) beginning | began | (have) begun |
| blow | (am) blowing | blew | (have) blown |
| break | (am) breaking | broke | (have) broken |
| choose | (am) choosing | chose | (have) chosen |
| come | (am) coming | came | (have) come |

| | | | |
|---|---|---|---|
| do | (am) doing | did | (have) done |
| draw | (am) drawing | drew | (have) drawn |
| drink | (am) drinking | drank | (have) drunk |
| drive | (am) driving | drove | (have) driven |
| eat | (am) eating | ate | (have) eaten |
| fall | (am) falling | fell | (have) fallen |
| fly | (am) flying | flew | (have) flown |
| freeze | (am) freezing | froze | (have) frozen |
| give | (am) giving | gave | (have) given |
| go | (am) going | went | (have) gone |
| grow | (am) growing | grew | (have) grown |
| know | (am) knowing | knew | (have) known |
| lie | (am) lying | lay | (have) lain |
| ride | (am) riding | rode | (have) ridden |
| ring | (am) ringing | rang | (have) rung |
| rise | (am) rising | rose | (have) risen |
| run | (am) running | ran | (have) run |
| see | (am) seeing | saw | (have) seen |
| shake | (am) shaking | shook | (have) shaken |
| sing | (am) singing | sang | (have) sung |
| sink | (am) sinking | sank | (have) sunk |
| speak | (am) speaking | spoke | (have) spoken |
| spring | (am) springing | sprang | (have) sprung |
| swear | (am) swearing | swore | (have) sworn |
| swim | (am) swimming | swam | (have) swum |
| take | (am) taking | took | (have) taken |
| tear | (am) tearing | tore | (have) torn |
| throw | (am) throwing | threw | (have) thrown |
| wear | (am) wearing | wore | (have) worn |
| write | (am) writing | wrote | (have) written |

Check a dictionary whenever you are in doubt about the correct form of an irregular verb.

**194**

**EXERCISE C: Completing the Principal Parts of Irregular Verbs.** Without looking back at the charts, write the missing principal parts for the following irregular verbs on your paper.

| EXAMPLE: | Present | Present Participle | Past | Past Participle |
|---|---|---|---|---|
| | _____ | _____ | began | _____ |
| | begin | beginning | began | begun |

| | Present | Present Participle | Past | Past Participle |
|---|---|---|---|---|
| 1. | teach | _____ | _____ | _____ |
| 2. | _____ | _____ | cost | _____ |
| 3. | _____ | giving | _____ | _____ |
| 4. | _____ | _____ | _____ | worn |
| 5. | _____ | catching | _____ | _____ |
| 6. | fly | _____ | _____ | _____ |
| 7. | _____ | _____ | _____ | burst |
| 8. | _____ | _____ | went | _____ |
| 9. | _____ | paying | _____ | _____ |
| 10. | shake | _____ | _____ | _____ |
| 11. | _____ | _____ | lost | _____ |
| 12. | _____ | _____ | _____ | lain |
| 13. | _____ | swearing | _____ | _____ |
| 14. | say | _____ | _____ | _____ |
| 15. | _____ | _____ | found | _____ |
| 16. | _____ | _____ | _____ | frozen |
| 17. | _____ | _____ | got | _____ |
| 18. | ride | _____ | _____ | _____ |
| 19. | _____ | springing | _____ | _____ |
| 20. | _____ | _____ | _____ | put |
| 21. | _____ | growing | _____ | _____ |
| 22. | sink | _____ | _____ | _____ |
| 23. | _____ | _____ | _____ | broken |
| 24. | _____ | _____ | fought | _____ |
| 25. | _____ | leading | _____ | _____ |

**EXERCISE D: Using the Past of Irregular Verbs.** For each of the following sentences, choose the correct verb from the choices in parentheses and write it on your paper.

EXAMPLE:  I (built, builded) a scale model of the Golden Gate Bridge.

built

1. The pages of the magazine (sticked, stuck) together.
2. Mother (bid, bidded) thirty dollars for that old lamp.
3. The geese (flew, flied) across the autumn sky.
4. I (growed, grew) these vegetables myself.
5. Greg covered himself with suntan oil and (lied, lay) down on the blanket.
6. The old sailor (spinned, spun) many fantastic yarns about his adventures at sea.
7. Josie's comment (hurt, hurted) Nick, but he tried not to show it.
8. The lantern (swinged, swung) high above our heads.
9. I (caught, catched) the ball without difficulty.
10. The sun (set, setted) over the ocean in a blazing red ball.

**EXERCISE E: Using the Past Participle of Irregular Verbs.** For each of the following sentences, choose the correct verb from the choices in parentheses.

EXAMPLE:  Charlayne has never (flew, flown) in an airplane.

flown

1. Have you ever (went, gone) to a major league baseball game?
2. Ted had already (ate, eaten) dinner when he was invited to the cookout.
3. Gina did well for someone who has never (ridden, rode) a horse before.
4. If I had (known, knew) you were coming, I would have prepared lunch.

**196**

5. Betsy has already (drank, drunk) the entire pitcher of iced tea.
6. During the tour Dorrie could have (took, taken) several dozen photographs.
7. We can't go skating until the lake has completely (frozen, froze) over.
8. Garrett has often (spoke, spoken) to me about his ant farm.
9. I did not know that he had (wrote, written) an article about Jamaica.
10. Which candidate has (run, ran) most often for the Presidency?

**EXERCISE F: Supplying the Correct Principal Part of Irregular Verbs.** Copy each of the following sentences onto your paper, writing the correct past or past participle form of the verb given in parentheses.

EXAMPLE:   You should have __(bring)__ your radio with you.

You should have brought your radio with you.

1. After a spectacular career as a chef, my uncle __(lay)__ down his tall hat and favorite spoon and retired.
2. We always thought that he should have __(buy)__ his own restaurant.
3. Jay __(drive)__ into the parking lot and announced that we were already late.
4. Emily has always __(rise)__ early to exercise before going to school.
5. The snow __(fall)__ all day, creating drifts that were taller than we were.
6. I could not have __(sit)__ still for one more speech.
7. The bells of the old town hall had not __(ring)__ for years.
8. Dara __(give)__ her old tennis racket to her little brother.
9. While exploring, the boy had __(tear)__ a hole in his new jacket.
10. Last night I __(eat)__ raw fish for the first time.

11. Ernest has ___(sing)___ at family weddings often.
12. Once you have ___(choose)___ your subject, your research paper will begin to take shape.
13. Phil ___(throw)___ a cover over the bird cage and ran out.
14. The wind ___(blow)___ the clothes in the basket of laundry all over the yard.
15. Molly ___(burst)___ into laughter when she saw us.
16. Has everybody ___(pay)___ for the trip?
17. The model sailboat has ___(sink)___ without a trace.
18. The chimpanzee ___(shake)___ the rag doll and scolded it.
19. Hansel looked at Gretel and said, "I'm afraid we have ___(lose)___ our way."
20. Just then, Annemarie ___(see)___ a little house in the clearing.

**DEVELOPING WRITING SKILLS: Using the Principal Parts of Verbs.** Write a paragraph about a funny or interesting experience you have had. Use at least five of the verbs in the following list.

EXAMPLE:   break

I will never forget the day I broke my sister's new tennis racket.

| | | | | |
|---|---|---|---|---|
| 1. come | 3. do | 5. know | 7. see | 9. begin |
| 2. speak | 4. help | 6. run | 8. take | 10. ask |

# 14.2  The Six Tenses of Verbs

In English verbs have six *tenses*.

**A tense is a form of a verb that shows when something happens or when something exists.**

Each of the six tenses has a *basic* form and a *progressive* form. This section will explain the basic forms. The next section will explain the progressive forms.

# The Basic Forms of the Six Tenses

The chart shows the *basic* forms of the six tenses, using *begin* as an example. The first column gives the name of each tense. The third column gives the principal part needed to form each tense. Only three of the four principal parts are used in the basic forms: the present, the past, and the past participle.

| BASIC FORMS OF THE SIX TENSES OF *BEGIN* | | |
|---|---|---|
| **Tense** | **Basic Form** | **Principal Part Used** |
| Present | I begin | The Present |
| Past | I began | The Past |
| Future | I will begin | The Present |
| Present Perfect | I have begun | The Past Participle |
| Past Perfect | I had begun | The Past Participle |
| Future Perfect | I will have begun | The Past Participle |

Study the chart carefully. First learn the names of the tenses. Then learn the principal parts needed to form them. Notice also that only the last four tenses need helping verbs.

**EXERCISE A: Identifying the Basic Forms of Verbs.** The verb in each of the following sentences is underlined. Identify the tense of each verb.

EXAMPLE: Our elegant sand castle <u>has</u> partly <u>collapsed</u>.

      present perfect

1. I <u>had wondered</u> why you wrote that strange letter.
2. Lawrence <u>will drive</u> to Pasadena with his family next week.
3. My sisters always <u>hold</u> on to the railing at the skating rink.
4. By the end of the next lap, she <u>will have swum</u> one whole mile today.
5. Jeanne <u>has visited</u> Japan but not China.
6. Mrs. Vronsky's parrots <u>sing</u> arias from operas.

**199**

7. I <u>listened</u> to them sing last week.
8. Franklin <u>had underlined</u> every misspelled word in his composition.
9. What <u>will</u> you <u>do</u> with your snowshoes in Florida?
10. I <u>have</u> never <u>met</u> anyone as shy as Chuck.

## Conjugating the Basic Forms of Verbs

*Conjugating* verbs can help you become familiar with the many forms of verbs.

**A conjugation is a list of the singular and plural forms of a verb in a particular tense.**

Each tense in a conjugation has six forms that correspond to the first-, second-, and third-person forms of the personal pronouns. (See Section 2.1 for a review of the personal pronouns.)

To conjugate any verb, begin by listing its principal parts.

| PRINCIPAL PARTS OF *HIDE* | | | |
|---|---|---|---|
| **Present** | **Present Participle** | **Past** | **Past Participle** |
| hide | hiding | hid | hidden |

The following conjugation of *hide* shows all of the basic forms of this verb in the six tenses.

| CONJUGATION OF THE BASIC FORMS OF *HIDE* | | |
|---|---|---|
| | **Singular** | **Plural** |
| Present | I hide<br>you hide<br>he, she, it hides | we hide<br>you hide<br>they hide |
| Past | I hid<br>you hid<br>he, she, it hid | we hid<br>you hid<br>they hid |

| Future | I will hide<br>you will hide<br>he, she, it will hide | we will hide<br>you will hide<br>they will hide |
| --- | --- | --- |
| Present Perfect | I have hidden<br>you have hidden<br>he, she, it has hidden | we have hidden<br>you have hidden<br>they have hidden |
| Past Perfect | I had hidden<br>you had hidden<br>he, she, it had hidden | we had hidden<br>you had hidden<br>they had hidden |
| Future Perfect | I will have hidden<br>you will have hidden<br>he, she, it will have hidden | we will have hidden<br>you will have hidden<br>they will have hidden |

An important verb to learn to conjugate is the verb *be*. It is both the most common and the most irregular verb. The following charts list the principal parts and all the basic forms of *be* in the six tenses.

| PRINCIPAL PARTS OF *BE* | | | |
| --- | --- | --- | --- |
| **Present** | **Present Participle** | **Past** | **Past Participle** |
| be | being | was | been |

| CONJUGATION OF THE BASIC FORMS OF *BE* | | |
| --- | --- | --- |
| | **Singular** | **Plural** |
| Present | I am<br>you are<br>he, she, it is | we are<br>you are<br>they are |

| Past | I was | we were |
| | you were | you were |
| | he, she, it was | they were |
| Future | I will be | we will be |
| | you will be | you will be |
| | he, she, it will be | they will be |
| Present Perfect | I have been | we have been |
| | you have been | you have been |
| | he, she, it has been | they have been |
| Past Perfect | I had been | we had been |
| | you had been | you had been |
| | he, she, it had been | they had been |
| Future Perfect | I will have been | we will have been |
| | you will have been | you will have been |
| | he, she, it will have been | they will have been |

**EXERCISE B: Conjugating the Basic Forms of Verbs.** On your paper conjugate each of the following verbs. The first two verbs are regular; the second two are irregular. Use the conjugation of *hide* on pages 200 and 201 as your model. Begin each conjugation by listing the principal parts of the verb.

1. ask    2. move    3. bring    4. begin

**EXERCISE C: Supplying the Correct Tense.** Copy each of the following sentences onto your paper, supplying the basic form of the verb as directed in parentheses.

EXAMPLE:    Diane (buy—past) theater tickets for Thursday.

Diane bought theater tickets for Thursday.

1. Martie (replace—future) the harsh overhead light with track lights.
2. I (start—present perfect) to read this book about five times.
3. My father once (buy—past) a boa constrictor as a pet.
4. Angela often (imagine—present) that she lives in a different time and place.
5. She (want—past perfect) to invent a time-travel machine when she was younger.
6. They all (guess—future perfect) the ending by now.
7. That actor (be—present perfect) in the same play for the last four years.
8. The swimming pool (cost—past) more to build than the house.
9. Cora always (make—present) our costumes for Halloween.
10. We (see—past perfect) the dinosaur exhibit before it was opened to the public.

**DEVELOPING WRITING SKILLS: Using the Basic Form of the Six Tenses.** Write six sentences of your own for each of the following verbs. Use a different tense of the verb in each of your sentences.

EXAMPLE:  take

I take our dog out for a run every day.

I took a picture of the new building.

(and so on)

1. help        2. do        3. speak        4. be

# The Six Progressive 14.3 Forms of Verbs

Each of the six tenses introduced in Section 14.2 also has a progressive form. The present participle is used to make all six progressive forms.

# The Progressive Forms of the Six Tenses

The following chart shows the progressive forms of the six tenses, using as an example the verb *begin*.

| PROGRESSIVE FORMS OF THE SIX TENSES OF *BEGIN* | | |
| --- | --- | --- |
| **Tense** | **Progressive Form** | **Principal Part Used** |
| Present | I am beginning | |
| Past | I was beginning | |
| Future | I will be beginning | |
| Present Perfect | I have been beginning | The Present Participle |
| Past Perfect | I had been beginning | |
| Future Perfect | I will have been beginning | |

**EXERCISE A: Identifying the Progressive Forms of Verbs.**
Study the preceding chart. Then identify the tense of each of the following verbs.

EXAMPLE:   will have been waiting

   future perfect

1. has been going
2. is running
3. will be eating
4. had been exploring
5. was explaining
6. have been staying
7. are fixing
8. had been thinking
9. will be having
10. have been giving
11. were chopping
12. am agreeing
13. will have been taking
14. will be studying
15. have been competing
16. was working
17. is putting
18. had been paying
19. will have been making
20. have been sailing

## Conjugating the Progressive Forms of Verbs

Conjugating the progressive forms of any verb is easy if you know how to conjugate the basic forms of *be*.

**To conjugate the progressive forms of a verb, add the present participle of the verb to a conjugation of the basic forms of *be*.**

A complete conjugation of the basic forms of *be* is shown on pages 201 and 202. Compare that conjugation with the following conjugation of the progressive forms of *hide*.

| CONJUGATION OF PROGRESSIVE FORMS OF *HIDE* | | |
|---|---|---|
| | **Singular** | **Plural** |
| Present Progressive | I am hiding<br>you are hiding<br>he, she, it is hiding | we are hiding<br>you are hiding<br>they are hiding |
| Past Progressive | I am hiding<br>you were hiding<br>he, she, it was hiding | we were hiding<br>you were hiding<br>they were hiding |
| Future Progressive | I will be hiding<br>you will be hiding<br>he, she, it will be hiding | we will be hiding<br>you will be hiding<br>they will be hiding |
| Present Perfect Progressive | I had been hiding<br><br>you have been hiding<br>he, she, it has been hiding | we have been hiding<br>you have been hiding<br>they have been hiding |

| Past Perfect Progressive | I had been hiding | we had been hiding |
| | you had been hiding | you had been hiding |
| | he, she, it had been hiding | they had been hiding |
| Future Perfect Progressive | I will have been hiding | we will have been hiding |
| | you will have been hiding | you will have been hiding |
| | he, she, it will have been hiding | they will have been hiding |

**EXERCISE B: Conjugating the Progressive Forms of Verbs.** On your paper conjugate the following verbs in the progressive form. Use the chart on page 205 and above as your model.

   1. say      2. give

**EXERCISE C: Supplying the Correct Tense.** Copy each of the following sentences onto your paper, supplying the progressive form of the verb as directed in parentheses.

EXAMPLE:   Janine (try—past progressive) to tell you about the election.

          Janine was trying to tell you about the election.

   1. Otis (paint—present perfect progressive) houses all summer.
   2. I (cook—past progressive) when you called.
   3. Anita (design—future progressive) the yearbook cover.
   4. The Reeses (publish—future perfect progressive) our neighborhood newsletter for seven years next month.
   5. I (put—present progressive) Uncle Dal at the other end of the table.

**206**

6. Actually, I (think—past progressive) about my new records.
7. Renee (learn—past perfect progressive) Italian secretly for three months when her grandmother finally agreed to teach her.
8. The concert (start—future progressive) soon.
9. Carlos (keep—present perfect progressive) a diary since he was nine years old.
10. Jake (want—past perfect progressive) to live in the mountains for years before his family finally moved to Colorado last July.

**DEVELOPING WRITING SKILLS: Using the Progressive Forms of the Six Tenses.** Write six sentences of your own for each of the following verbs. Use a different tense in the progressive form in each sentence.

EXAMPLE:    take

He is taking us to the concert.

He was taking his time on the project.

(and so on)

1. see        2. have        3. hope        4. travel

# Glossary of Troublesome Verbs 14.4

Many people have problems with the verbs listed in this section. Some of the problems arise when the wrong principal part is used. Other problems are caused when the meanings of certain pairs of verbs are confused. As you read through the list, concentrate on those verbs that have caused you difficulty in the past. Then use the exercises to test your understanding. When you are writing and revising your compositions, refer to this section for help in checking your work.

**(1)** ***Ain't.*** *Ain't* is not correct English. Avoid using it in speaking and in writing.

INCORRECT:   This *ain't* the record I meant to buy.

CORRECT:   This *isn't* the record I meant to buy.

**(2)  Burst**   This irregular verb has the same form for three of its principal parts. The present, past, and past participle of *burst* are *burst*. *Bust* and *busted* are not correct. If you find you are using these incorrect forms, try replacing them with *break, broke,* or *broken.*

INCORRECT:   If you handle that balloon roughly, it *will bust.*

Tina *busted* open the eggs one by one.

He *has busted* the tape recorder.

CORRECT:   If you handle that balloon roughly, it *will burst.*

Tina *broke* open the eggs one by one.

He *has broken* the tape recorder.

**(3)  did, done**   *Done* is a past participle and can be used as a verb only with a helping verb such as *have* or *has.* If you find you are using *done* without a helping verb, try using *did* instead. Otherwise, add the helping verb before *done.*

INCORRECT:   I *done* all my exercises.

CORRECT:   I *did* all my exercises.

I *have done* all my exercises.

**(4)  drowned, drownded**   *Drown* is a regular verb. Its past and past participle are formed simply by adding *-ed* to the present form: *drown-+-ed. Drownded* is wrong. Do not add the extra *d* either in speaking or in writing.

INCORRECT:   When their ship split in half, the Viking warriors *drownded.*

CORRECT:   When their ship split in half, the Viking warriors *drowned.*

**208**

**(5)  gone, went**  *Gone* is the past participle of *go* and can be used as a verb only with a helping verb such as *have* or *has. Went* is the past of *go* and is never used with a helping verb.

INCORRECT:  The Martins *gone* on vacation.

Niva *has went* along with them.

CORRECT:  The Martins *have gone* on vacation.

The Martins *went* on vacation.

Niva *has gone* along with them.

Niva *went* along with them.

**(6)  have, of**  In conversation the words *have* and *of* sound very much alike. Be careful not to write *of* when you really mean the helping verb *have* or its contraction *'ve.*

INCORRECT:  He should *of* apologized.

CORRECT:  He should *have* apologized.

He *should've* apologized.

**(7)  lay, lie**  These verbs cause many problems because they look and sound almost alike and have similar meanings. The first step in learning to distinguish between *lay* and *lie* is to memorize their principal parts.

PRINCIPAL PARTS:  lay  laying  laid  laid

lie  lying  lay  lain

To avoid confusing these many different forms, the next step is to compare the meaning and use of the two verbs.

*Lay* usually means "to put (something) down" or "to place (something)." This verb is almost always followed by a direct object. In the examples on the following page, the direct objects are labeled.

EXAMPLES:  Don always *lays* his keys<sup>DO</sup> on the table in the hallway.

Mom and Dad *will be laying* new tiles<sup>DO</sup> in the kitchen.

Janet *laid* the plans<sup>DO</sup> out on the counter.

The engineers *have laid* the cement<sup>DO</sup> for the driveway.

*Lie* usually means "to rest in a reclining position." It also can mean "to be situated." *Lie* is never followed by a direct object. In the following examples, the words after the forms of the verb *lie* are adverbs and prepositional phrases, not direct objects.

EXAMPLES:  My father usually *lies* down after dinner.

The cat *is lying* on top of the television for warmth.

They did not realize it, but the solution to the mystery *lay* right before them.

The food *had lain* in the sun all afternoon.

When using *lay* and *lie,* pay special attention to one particular area of confusion: *Lay* is the present tense of *lay. Lay* is also the past tense of *lie.*

PRESENT TENSE OF LAY:  We always *lay* that blanket on the ground when we have a picnic.

PAST TENSE OF LIE:  Because I felt dizzy after the game, I *lay* down quickly.

**(8) *raise, rise***   *Raise* has several common meanings: "to lift (something) upward," "to build (something)," "to grow (something)," or "to increase (something)." Its principal parts are *raise, raising, raised,* and *raised. Raise* is usually followed by a direct object.

**210**

EXAMPLES:    *Raise* your arms^DO higher.

The city *is raising* a new theater^DO in the park.

Larry actually *raised* mushrooms^DO in his desk.

Grace's landlord *has raised* the rent^DO.

*Rise,* on the other hand, is not usually followed by a direct object. *Rise* means "to get up," "to go up," or "to be increased." Its principal parts are *rise, rising, rose,* and *risen. Rise* is usually followed by either an adverb or a prepositional phrase.

EXAMPLES:    The moon *will rise* at 8:00 p.m.

For a week I *was rising* before dawn.

The giant hot-air balloon *rose* for a moment and then collapsed.

Prices *have risen* steadily since 1970.

**(9) saw, seen**    *Seen* is a past participle and can be used as a verb only with a helping verb such as *have* or *has.* If you find you are using *seen* without a helping verb, try using *saw* instead. Otherwise, add the helping verb before *seen.*

INCORRECT:   We *seen* the three lion cubs at the zoo.
CORRECT:   We *saw* the three lion cubs at the zoo.

We *have seen* the three lion cubs at the zoo.

**(10) set, sit**    These verbs are often confused. The first step in learning to distinguish between *set* and *sit* is to learn their principal parts.

PRINCIPAL PARTS:   set    setting    set    set
sit    sitting    sat    sat

*Set* commonly means "to put (something) in a certain place." It is usually followed by a direct object.

EXAMPLES:  
DO
*Set* the lamp on top of the file cabinet.

DO
He *is setting* traps for the rats.

DO
Felix *set* the clock back an hour.

DO
Tom and my sister Lisa *have set* a date for their wedding.

*Sit* usually means "to be seated" or "to rest." In its usual meanings, *sit* is never followed by a direct object. In the following examples, the words following the verbs are adverbs and prepositional phrases.

EXAMPLES: The wizard's castle *sits* on that mountain.

The pigeons *have been sitting* atop that statue all day.

Valerie *sat* for a portrait.

The panther *has sat* in that tree for hours.

## EXERCISE A: Avoiding Problems with Troublesome Verbs

**1–5.** For each of the sentences, choose the correct verb from the choices in parentheses and write it on your paper.

EXAMPLE: (Ain't, Aren't) you ready to leave yet?

Aren't

1. He (did, done) the experiment four times before he got any results.
2. The heavy orchestration (drownded, drowned) out the singer's delicate voice.
3. The piñata (bust, burst) open, showering the children with dozens of toys.
4. Cyril (gone, has gone) ahead to save us a place at the movies.

**212**

5. After all, it (isn't, ain't) easy to find ten seats together on Saturday night.
6. Sally has turned in a hand-written essay because her typewriter is (busted, broken).
7. It seems as if everyone in this school (went, gone) to the same summer camp.
8. I don't like my spaghetti to be (drowned, drownded) in tomato sauce.
9. They (ain't, aren't) convinced that we need a new television set.
10. You (done, have done) a great job with the set for the variety show.

## EXERCISE B: Avoiding Problems with Troublesome Verbs

**6–10.** For each of the following sentences, choose the correct verb from the choices in parentheses and write it on your paper.

1. The Greens are (laying, lying) a new wood floor in their dining room.
2. Do you realize that you (could of, could've) won that race with more training?
3. I (seen, saw) a shooting star a second ago.
4. The assembly will (rise, raise) when the judge enters the courtroom.
5. Then everyone will (set, sit) down when she says, "Be seated."
6. Gil (has seen, seen) many strange plants on his various field trips.
7. A Druid shrine once (laid, lay) somewhere in these hills.
8. There is absolutely no need for you to (raise, rise) your voice.
9. Every morning Laurie (sets, sits) her parakeet on a special swing next to the dining-room table.
10. I should (of, have) looked him straight in the eye and said, "None of your business."

**213**

**EXERCISE C: Avoiding Problems with Troublesome Verbs**
**1–10.** For each of the following sentences, choose the correct verb from the choices in parentheses and write it on your paper.

1. My aunt always used to say, "I'll be there if the Lord is willing and the creeks don't (raise, rise)."
2. Maybe we should (have, of) turned left instead of right at that intersection.
3. I almost (drownded, drowned) in the wading pool in a freak accident last week.
4. Aside from embarrassing me, the experience really (did, done) me no harm.
5. The radio station had to shut down because its transmitter was (busted, broken).
6. The children (lay, laid) on their backs to look at the stars.
7. (Sit, Set) down and take a look at this puzzle.
8. He (ain't, isn't) finished peeling the potatoes yet.
9. Cassie (gone, went) to find a tow truck.
10. I (had seen, seen) one at that gas station we passed a few miles back.

**DEVELOPING WRITING SKILLS: Using Troublesome Verbs Correctly.** Write an original sentence for each of the following verbs.

EXAMPLE: sat

At the circus they sat in the front row, near the clowns.

| | | |
|---|---|---|
| 1. have | 5. set | 9. seen |
| 2. done | 6. burst | 10. gone |
| 3. isn't | 7. drowned | |
| 4. lie | 8. raise | |

# Skills Review and Writing Workshop

## Using Verbs

### CHECKING YOUR SKILLS

Rewrite the paragraph below, correcting all errors in verb usage.

(1) The cast members were not froze in terror on opening night. (2) They knowed that they had rose above being nervous. (3) First, two cast members busted their legs in a skiing accident. (4) Then the director catched the measles and was out for a week. (5) Two days before the show opened, the costume rental agency admitted that the costumes were still laying on a stage in a neighboring state! (6) The agency assured them, however, that an employee had went to pick the costumes up. (7) Yet it become clear that all these difficulties had drew the cast together. (8) On opening night they set down and went over their efforts. (9) They shaked hands and rose, determined to make the show a success. (10) When the show begun, the audience saw a confident cast.

### USING USAGE SKILLS IN WRITING
### Describing Action

Many experts say that an author's choice of verbs is crucial to successful writing, especially in descriptions of action. Follow the steps below to create a paragraph describing an action.

**Prewriting:** Focus on the preparation for some event, such as for a party or practicing for a game. List all the activities that went into the preparation.

**Writing:** In chronological order describe the activities that led up to the event. In the last sentence reveal the effect of these activities: Was the event successful?

**Revising:** First, check your verbs. Make sure they are all correct and specific. Then check for other improvements you can make. After you have revised, proofread carefully.

# 15

# Using Pronouns

Many pronouns change form according to use. Case is the relation between a pronoun's form and its use. This chapter will explain the three cases and show you how to use the various forms of pronouns correctly.

## 15.1 The Three Cases of Personal Pronouns

The personal pronouns listed on page 30 in Section 2.1 are presented in three groups. Pronouns in the first group refer to the person speaking; those in the second refer to the person spoken to; those in the third refer to the person, place, or thing spoken about. Pronouns can also be grouped according to three *cases.*

**English has three cases: *nominative, objective,* and *possessive.***

### The Three Cases

The personal pronouns are grouped in the following chart according to the three cases.

### THE USES OF PERSONAL PRONOUNS BY CASE

| Nominative Case | Use in Sentence |
|---|---|
| I, we<br>you<br>he, she, it, they | Subject of a Verb<br>Predicate Pronoun |

| Objective Case | Use in Sentence |
|---|---|
| me, us<br>you<br>him, her, it, them | Direct Object<br>Indirect Object<br>Object of a Preposition |

| Possessive Case | Use in Sentence |
|---|---|
| my, mine, our, ours<br>your, yours<br>his, her, hers, its, their,<br>theirs | To Show Ownership |

**EXERCISE A: Identifying Case.** On your paper identify the case of the personal pronouns that are underlined in the following sentences.

EXAMPLE:  Didn't Richard give her the directions?

> objective

1. After an hour of cleaning flounder, Winnie lost her taste for fish.
2. He dedicated the book to his chiildren.
3. Spring came at last; a month of rain came with it.
4. Show me the trick that you learned.
5. The last people in the auditorium were Ian and I.
6. Carlos saw her once again at the foot of the staircase.
7. At least the land is ours, no matter what happens to the house.
8. The twins stopped crying when Rolfie swung them both in the air.

9. <u>She</u> would like to learn how to ski down the intermediate slope.
10. Does any one of <u>you</u> know how to write a sonnet?

## The Nominative Case

Personal pronouns in the *nominative case* have two uses in sentences.

**Use the nominative case (1) for the subject of a verb and (2) for a predicate pronoun.**

In the following examples, notice that the predicate pronouns follow linking verbs.

SUBJECTS: *I* collect stamps.

*She* wrote a letter to the President.

PREDICATE PRONOUNS: It was *he* who saved the child.

The fastest runner is *she.*

**Case in Compound Subjects.** People seldom forget to use the nominative case when a personal pronoun is used by itself as a subject. No one but someone imitating Tarzan would say, "*Me* collect stamps." Problems sometimes occur, however, when the pronoun is part of a compound subject. When this happens, it is important to check that the pronoun is in the nominative case.

INCORRECT: Gina and *me* collect stamps.

*Me* and Gina collect stamps.

To make sure you are using the correct case of a personal pronoun in a compound subject, use just the pronoun with the verb in the sentence. In the preceding examples, "Me collect" clearly sounds wrong. The nominative case *I* is correct and should be used.

CORRECT: Gina and *I* collect stamps.

**218**

Notice in the corrected example that the pronoun *I* comes second in the compound subject. It is usually considered bad usage to put *I* first.

POOR:  *I,* Dennis, and Grace worked together.

BETTER:  Dennis, Grace, and *I* worked together.

**The Sound of Predicate Pronouns.**  In conversation and in informal writing, people often use the objective case for any personal pronoun after a linking verb. Many people think the objective case sounds better than the nominative case after a linking verb. In formal speaking and writing, however, you should still use the nominative case.

INFORMAL:  "Who is it?" "It's *me.*"

FORMAL:  The finalists in the contest are Dominico, Pam, and
   *I.*

**EXERCISE B: Using Personal Pronouns in the Nominative Case.** Complete each of the following sentences by writing an appropriate nominative pronoun on your paper. Then indicate how each pronoun is used in the sentence.

EXAMPLE:  _____ think that this photograph is best.

   We    subject

1. _____ cannot remember what happened.
2. It must be _____; no one else would arrive this late in the evening.
3. Willard and _____ will set up the tent.
4. The door creaked open, and a voice from outside said, "It is _____."
5. The maples are turning red; soon _____ will be losing their leaves.
6. When Bart's dog was sent to those groomers, _____ came back looking embarrassed and bald.
7. The person who did this is _____.

8. My contest entry was postmarked early, but _____ got lost in the mail.
9. When the wind blows this way, _____ can just hear the music.
10. The first people to speak after the announcement were Tony and _____.

## The Objective Case

Personal pronouns in the *objective case* have three uses.

**Use the objective case (1) for a direct object, (2) for an indirect object, and (3) for the object of a preposition.**

DIRECT OBJECTS:   Cate invited *me* to her party.

The dog chased *us* across the lawn.

INDIRECT OBJECTS:   Diego wrote *her* a letter.

I told *them* the story.

OBJECTS OF PREPOSITIONS:   Were they talking about *me?*

Give this message to *them.*

Mistakes with pronouns in the objective case usually happen only when the object is compound.

INCORRECT:   Cate invited Ron and *I* to her party.

Diego wrote his mother and *she* a letter.

Were they talking about Lois and *I?*

Again, to check whether the case of the personal pronoun is correct, use the pronoun by itself after the verb or preposition. In the preceding examples, "Cate invited I," "Diego wrote she," and "Were they talking about I" all sound wrong. Objective pronouns are needed.

CORRECT:   Cate invited Ron and *me* to her party.

Diego wrote his mother and *her* a letter.

Were they talking about Lois and *me?*

**EXERCISE C: Using Personal Pronouns in the Objective Case.** Complete each of the following sentences by writing an appropriate objective pronoun on your paper. Then indicate how each pronoun is used in the sentence.

EXAMPLE:   Why didn't Edwin invite _____ to this dinner?

   me   direct object

1. If Mark and Susie leave now, who will go with _____?
2. Teresa showed _____ the sealed envelope containing the secret formula.
3. This speech was drafted for _____ by a new member of the staff.
4. When you catch the brass ring, throw _____ at that large painted clown.
5. Unfortunately, John made a mistake and told _____ the plans for the surprise party.
6. The helicopter lifted Jo and _____ high up over the city.
7. The donation was a secret between Tracy and _____.
8. As the song went on and on, Kit made faces at _____.
9. The man in the ticket booth sold _____ four seats for the 9:30 show.
10. Chris hugged the baby girl and then set _____ down in the crib.

# The Possessive Case

Personal pronouns in the *possessive case* show possession in two ways.

**Use the possessive case of personal ponouns to show possession before nouns. Also use certain personal pronouns by themselves to show possession.**

BEFORE NOUNS:   The dog buried *its* bone.

   She hurt *my* feelings.

BY THEMSELVES:    Is this hat *yours* or *his?*

                        *Hers* was the most moving speech.

Notice that personal pronouns ending in -*s* are never written with an apostrophe.

INCORRECT:    *Our's* is the last house on the right.

                That book is *his',* not *her's.*

CORRECT:    *Ours* is the last house on the right.

             That book is *his,* not *hers.*

When the pronoun *it* ends with an apostrophe and an -*s,* it is not a possessive personal pronoun. Instead, it is a contraction that means *it is.*

CONTRACTION:    *It's* too late to help them now.

POSSESSIVE PRONOUN:    A snake sheds *its* skin as it grows.

### EXERCISE D: Using Personal Pronouns in the Possessive Case.

For each of the following sentences, choose the correct word from the choices in parentheses. Write the correct word for each sentence on your paper.

EXAMPLE:    Now that Kim has gone away to school, this room is all (yours, your's).

            yours

1. The dog eats (it's, its) food as if there were no tomorrow.
2. Kip has difficulty keeping (his', his) shoelaces tied.
3. The boat is (theirs, their's), but we can use it.
4. How many of these albums are (our's, ours)?
5. Rita said that some of the records are (hers, her's).
6. Every other poem in the literary magazine is (your's, yours)!
7. (Its, It's) my problem, not David's.
8. I wrote the melody, but the lyrics are (his', his).
9. I always forget which house is (your's, yours).
10. The thermometer reached (its, it's) highest point for the year today.

**EXERCISE E: Checking the Case of Personal Pronouns.**
Many of the underlined pronouns in the following sentences
are incorrect. On your paper identify each error and, after it,
write the form of the pronoun that should be used in formal
writing. For sentences without any errors, write *correct*.

EXAMPLE:    Here are <u>your</u> clothes and <u>your</u> books; this room
            must be <u>your's</u>.

            your's   yours

1. The singers in the opening number will be Patti, Maxine,
   and <u>me</u>.
2. Aunt Bertie trained the cat and changed <u>it's</u> habits.
3. When <u>our</u> grandmother arrived, the conductor helped <u>her</u>
   off the train.
4. The judges couldn't choose between <u>her</u> and <u>I</u>.
5. <u>You</u> will be happy to hear that the assignment is now <u>yours</u>.
6. Delia showed José and <u>I</u> the diagrams.
7. <u>Its</u> the first house on the left in that block.
8. It was <u>he</u> who ate <u>my</u> pie.
9. Elijah and Clarice could not believe that <u>their's</u> was the
   winning ticket.
10. Kevin, Larry, and <u>me</u> are studying together.

**DEVELOPING WRITING SKILLS: Using Pronouns Correctly.** Write five sentences of your own, each using one of the
following personal pronouns in the form indicated in
parentheses.

EXAMPLE:   we (as a subject)

           We were ahead by three when it began to rain.

1. you and I   (as predicate pronouns)
2. them   (as an indirect object)
3. its   (to show possession)
4. him and her   (after a preposition)
5. me   (as a direct object)

# Skills Review and Writing Workshop

## Using Pronouns

### CHECKING YOUR SKILLS

Rewrite the paragraph below, correcting errors in pronoun usage.

(1) "Can it be him?" the princess sobbed, looking at a frog wearing the prince's ring. (2) The frog just flicked it's tongue at a dragonfly. (3) "Him and me certainly have our problems," the princess mourned. (4) "Isn't there anyone who can help we?" (5) Just then a good witch appeared, waving hers magic wand. (6) "It's me who can help, my dear," she told the startled princess. (7) "You and him must hold hands." (8) The princess did as her was told, and a moment later the prince replaced the frog. (9) He looked at the witch adoringly and asked how him and the princess could repay her. (10) The witch took his' arm and said, "You and her can give each other up, and you can marry me instead."

### USING USAGE SKILLS IN WRITING
#### Writing a Spoof

One way to create humor is to "twist" a traditional scene or story. Follow the steps below to create your own spoof.

**Prewriting:** Choose a typical scene from a fairy tale, a romance, or an adventure story. First, write a list of the standard events of the scene. Then consider which ones to change in order to create an unexpected twist.

**Writing:** Write the events of the scene, blending the traditional with the changes you planned. Be sure the ending is a twist on the typical ending.

**Revising:** First, look at your pronouns to make sure they are all correct. Then check for other improvements you can make. After you have revised, proofread carefully.

**224**

# 16

# Making Words Agree

Subjects and verbs work together in sentences. For example, you would never say, *"I are* the winner!" or *"Am she* your best friend?" You would hear that something is wrong with these sentences. The problem is that the subjects and verbs do not *agree.*

In most of the sentences you speak and write, the subjects and verbs agree almost automatically. You would probably say, *"I am* the winner!" or *"Is she* your best friend?" In some sentences, however, you might be tempted to make a verb agree with a word that is not the subject. In such a case, check to find the real subject and make sure that it agrees with its verb. Pronouns and the words they stand for must also agree. This chapter will explain the rules of agreement and how to make parts of sentences work together correctly.

## Agreement Between Subjects and Verbs 16.1

Subject and verb *agreement* has one main rule.

**A subject must agree with its verb in number.**

The *number* of a word can be either *singular* or *plural*. Singular words indicate *one*. Plural words indicate *more than one*. Only nouns, pronouns, and verbs have number: They are either singular or plural.

## The Number of Nouns and Pronouns

Most of the time it is easy to tell whether a noun or pronoun is singular or plural. Compare, for example, the singular and plural forms of the nouns in the following chart.

| NOUNS | |
|---|---|
| **Singular** | **Plural** |
| friend | friends |
| box | boxes |
| knife | knives |
| mouse | mice |

Most nouns are made plural by adding *-s* or *-es* to the singular form (friend*s* and box*es*). Some nouns become plural in other ways (kni*ves* and m*ice*). (See Section 36.2 for more information about ways of making nouns plural.)

Chapter 2 listed the singular and plural forms of the various kinds of pronouns. For example, *I, he, she, it,* and *this* are singular. *We, they,* and *these* are plural. *You, who,* and *some* are either singular or plural.

Be sure you can recognize the number of nouns and pronouns. This skill will be very useful when you need to decide whether there is agreement among the words in a sentence.

**EXERCISE A: Recognizing the Number of Nouns and Pronouns.** On your paper indicate whether each of the following words is *singular* or *plural*.

EXAMPLE: children   plural

| | | | |
|---|---|---|---|
| 1. they | 6. oxen | 11. brain | 16. cousins |
| 2. I | 7. these | 12. this | 17. princess |
| 3. both | 8. river | 13. forest | 18. fireplace |
| 4. feet | 9. goose | 14. she | 19. automobile |
| 5. me | 10. it | 15. person | 20. knight |

# The Number of Verbs

Verbs have many forms to express time. Few of these forms cause problems in agreement because most of them can be used with either singular or plural subjects (I *hide*, we *hide*, he *began*, they *began*). Problems involving the number of verbs usually occur only with third-person forms of verbs in the present tense (she *wants*, they *want*) and with certain forms of the helping verb *be* (I *am*, we *are*).

Study the following chart, which shows the basic forms of two verbs in the present tense.

| SINGULAR AND PLURAL VERBS IN THE PRESENT TENSE | | |
|---|---|---|
| **Singular** | | **Plural** |
| **First and Second Person** | **Third Person** | **First, Second, and Third Person** |
| (I, you) hide | (he, she, it) hides | (we, you, they) hide |
| (I, you) begin | (he, she, it) begins | (we, you, they) begin |

Notice that the verb changes only in the third-person singular column, where an -*s* is added to the verb. Unlike nouns, which usually become *plural* when an -*s* is added, verbs become singular when an -*s* is added.

The helping verb *be* may also indicate whether a verb phrase is singular or plural. The following chart shows only those forms of *be* that are always singular. Learn to recognize them.

| FORMS OF THE HELPING VERB *BE* THAT ARE ALWAYS SINGULAR |
| --- |
| am     is     was     has been |

**EXERCISE B: Recognizing the Number of Verbs.** On your paper write the verb from the choices in parentheses that agrees in number with the pronoun. After each answer write whether the verb is singular or plural.

EXAMPLE:   they (meets, meet)

         meet   plural

1. he (say, says)
2. we (is, are)
3. it (was, were)
4. she (wait, waits)
5. I (is, am)

6. we (has, have)
7. he (has been, have been)
8. they (is, are)
9. it (is, are)
10. they (forgives, forgive)

## Agreement with Singular and Plural Subjects

To check for agreement between a subject and a verb, begin by determining the number of the subject. Then make sure the verb has the same number.

**A singular subject must have a singular verb.**

**A plural subject must have a plural verb.**

In the following examples, the subjects are underlined once and the verbs twice.

SINGULAR SUBJECT AND VERB:   Jeff always has a good time at the beach.

         She was here earlier today.

         A movie is being shown in the auditorium.

**228**

PLURAL SUBJECT AND VERB:   The <u>surfers</u> always <u>have</u> a good time at the beach.

They <u>were</u> here earlier today.

The <u>movies</u> <u>are being shown</u> in the auditorium.

All the subjects in the preceding examples stand next to or near their verbs. Often, however, a subject is separated from its verb by a prepositional phrase. In these cases it is important to remember that the object of a preposition is never the subject of a sentence.

**A prepositional phrase that comes between a subject and its verb does *not* affect subject-verb agreement.**

In the following examples, the subject is *arrival,* not *sports cars,* which is the object of the preposition *of.* Since *arrival* is singular, it cannot agree with the plural verb *have caused.*

INCORRECT:   The <u>arrival</u> of several new sports cars <u>have</u> <u>caused</u> much excitement at the showroom.

CORRECT:   The <u>arrival</u> of several new sports cars <u>has</u> <u>caused</u> much excitement at the showroom.

**EXERCISE C: Making Verbs Agree with Singular and Plural Subjects.** For each of the following sentences, choose the correct verb from the choices in parentheses and write it on your paper.

EXAMPLE:   The lines of this table (follows, follow) the style of the late Victorian period.

follow

1. The air (has, have) become stale since we shut the windows.
2. Moss usually (grows, grow) on the north side of trees.
3. The eggplants in our garden (is, are) particularly large this summer.

4. The children in this photograph (looks, look) uncomfortable.
5. The lace on these dresses (was, were) handmade.
6. The newspapers in this collection (dates, date) back to the Revolutionary War.
7. An acre of trees and meadows (surrounds, surround) the little church.
8. The numbers next to the lines on this map (indicates, indicate) the number of miles between each interchange.
9. The guests at the meeting (is, are) wearing name tags.
10. The handwriting in these bills and letters (seems, seem) to belong to the same person.

## Agreement with Compound Subjects

A compound subject is made up of two or more subjects joined by a conjunction such as *or, nor,* or *and.* (See Section 9.3 for information about finding compound subjects in sentences.) Several rules govern the way in which verbs must agree with compound subjects.

**Two or more singular subjects joined by *or* or *nor* must have a singular verb.**

In the following examples, the conjunction *or* joins two singular subjects. Although these two subjects are part of a compound subject, the verb must be singular.

INCORRECT:   Either the <u>telephone</u> or the <u>doorbell</u> <u>are ringing.</u>

CORRECT:   Either the <u>telephone</u> or the <u>doorbell</u> <u>is ringing</u>.

Problems often occur when the parts of a compound subject joined by *or* or *nor* are mixed in number.

**When singular and plural subjects are joined by *or* or *nor*, the verb must agree with the closest subject.**

In the following examples, notice how the verb depends on the subject that is closer to it.

**230**

SINGULAR SUBJECT CLOSER:   Neither the <u>nails</u> nor the <u>hammer</u> <u>is</u>
in the tool chest.

PLURAL SUBJECT CLOSER:   Neither the <u>hammer</u> nor the <u>nails</u> <u>are</u>
in the tool chest.

Compound subjects joined by *and* can cause still another problem.

**A compound subject joined by *and* is usually plural and must have a plural verb.**

*And* usually acts as a plus sign. Whether the parts of the compound subject are all singular, all plural, or mixed in number, they usually add up to a subject that takes a plural verb.

EXAMPLES:   The <u>dog</u> and <u>cat</u> <u>are fighting</u>.

The <u>dogs</u> and <u>cats</u> <u>are fighting</u>.

The <u>dogs</u> and the <u>cat</u> <u>are fighting</u>.

This rule has two exceptions. The first is this: If the parts of the compound subject taken together are thought of as a single thing, then the compound subject is considered singular and must have a singular verb.

SINGULAR COMPOUND SUBJECT:   <u>Bacon</u> and <u>eggs</u> <u>is</u> a very popular breakfast. (Bacon + eggs = one breakfast)

The other exception involves the words *every* and *each.* Either of these words before a compound subject indicates the need for a singular verb.

SINGULAR COMPOUND SUBJECT:   Every <u>tree</u> and <u>shrub</u> <u>has</u> <u>been</u> <u>pruned</u>.

**EXERCISE D: Making Verbs Agree with Compound Subjects Joined by *Or* and *Nor*.** For each of the sentences listed on the next page, choose the correct verb from the choices in parentheses and write it on your paper.

**231**

EXAMPLE:   Neither the twins nor their dog (has, have) managed
           to stay out of the swimming pool today.

           has

 1. Either Sam or Lena (drives, drive) the car here each day.
 2. I will go, even though neither Leslie nor Bill (is, are) going.
 3. Either potatoes or corn (tastes, taste) good with chicken.
 4. Neither the front door nor the windows (has been, have
    been) locked.
 5. Neither the texture nor the colors of this fabric (goes, go)
    . well with that hat.
 6. Neither the play nor the two movie versions (captures, cap-
    ture) the flavor of the original book.
 7. Neither the subway system nor the bus routes (serves,
    serve) that part of town.
 8. Neither Meg nor Elsa (wants, want) to go the museum.
 9. Neither greeting cards nor wrapping paper (is, are) sold in
    this store.
10. Either one book or a few articles (is, are) sufficient back-
    ground for this report.

## EXERCISE E: Making Verbs Agree with Compound Subjects Joined by *And*. Choose the correct verb from the choices in parentheses and write it on your paper.

EXAMPLE:   Every singer and dancer on this stage (knows, know)
           how much work the show needs.

           knows

 1. Pens and pencils (was, were) poised to write.
 2. Peanut butter and jelly (is, are) my favorite combination for
    sandwiches.
 3. The books and magazines on the shelf (was, were) out of
    order.
 4. Every boot, shoe, and belt in that store (is, are) made of
    leather.

5. Cherry pie and apple strudel (was, were) our choices.
6. A prince and princess always (lives, live) happily ever after.
7. Each folder and packet in the files (was, were) labeled.
8. Ducks and geese usually (stops, stop) at this park on their way south.
9. Every worker and manager in our plants (offers, offer) suggestions for improvements.
10. The shops and department stores in this mall (is, are) paying more rent this year than ever before.


**EXERCISE F: Checking to See If Subjects and Verbs Agree.** For each of the following sentences, choose the correct verb from the choices in parentheses and write it on your paper.

EXAMPLE:   Every cake and pie on these shelves (is, are) on sale.

          is

1. Neither Sal nor her sisters (has, have) seen the puppies.
2. Pork and beans (was, were) our favorite campfire food when we were younger.
3. The glass in the panes of these Colonial cabinets (comes, come) from England.
4. Each fruit and vegetable in these bins (was, were) grown on our own farm.
5. Either the Capitol or the White House (fits, fit) into our schedule.
6. Neither the flowers in this drawing nor the landscape in that one (looks, look) realistic.
7. This dress and that pair of jeans (costs, cost) more this year than they did last year.
8. Francine and Clare always (performs, perform) together in our variety shows.
9. Jeff (does, do) fine work.
10. The players on either football team (is, are) almost too muddy to tell apart.

**EXERCISE G: Correcting Errors in Subject and Verb Agreement.** In some of the sentences below, subjects and verbs do not agree in number. If a sentence is correct, write *correct*. If it is faulty, rewrite the sentence correctly.

EXAMPLE:   Neither the moon nor the stars is visible tonight.

Neither the moon nor the stars are visible tonight.

1. They understands what they need to do in order to win.
2. Strawberries, sour cream, and brown sugar is the ingredients in the dessert.
3. Neither the hurricane lamps nor the chandelier provide sufficient light for this room.
4. Each basketball uniform and sweat suit were embossed with the name of the school.
5. The typewriters in our main office come equipped with computer memories.

**DEVELOPING WRITING SKILLS: Writing Sentences with Singular, Plural, and Compound Subjects.** Use each of the following items as the subject of a sentence, along with a form of the verb *be.* Make sure that subject and verb agree in number. Underline the subject once and the verb twice.

EXAMPLE:   they

They are the musicians in the dance band.

1. she and I
2. the buildings in the city
3. the Congress and the President
4. every taxi and bus
5. either Chuck or Carol

# 16.2 Special Problems with Subject-Verb Agreement

Certain kinds of sentences are likely to cause special problems when you check for subject-verb agreement.

## Agreement in Sentences with Unusual Word Order

In most sentences the subject comes before the verb. Sometimes, however, this normal word order is turned around, or *inverted.* In sentences with inverted word order, you must look for the subject after the verb. (See Section 9.4 for more information about inverted word order.)

**When a subject comes after the verb, the subject and verb still must agree with each other in number.**

Sentences beginning with *there* or *here* are almost always in inverted word order. Look for the subject after the verb when you are checking for agreement. In the following sentences, the subjects are underlined once and the verbs, twice.

EXAMPLES:    There were several baby elephants at the zoo.

Here is the key to the back door.

The contractions *there's* and *here's* both contain the singular verb *is: there is* and *here is.* Take care not to use these contractions with plural subjects.

INCORRECT:   Here's the keys to the house.

CORRECT:   Here are the keys to the house.

Many questions are also in inverted word order. To check for agreement, find the subject and then make sure the subject agrees with the verb.

INCORRECT:   Where is the keys to the house?

CORRECT:   Where are the keys to the house?

**EXERCISE A: Checking Agreement in Sentences with Inverted Word Order.** On your paper write the subject from each of the following sentences. Choose the correct verb from the choices in parentheses and write it next to the subject.

EXAMPLE:   There (is, are) a few new rules in this pamphlet.

            rules   are

1. How (has, have) she learned my name?
2. Which records (has, have) Heather brought with her?
3. There (is, are) many reasons for building a new wing onto the school.
4. "Where (is, are) my three fiddlers?" cried Old King Cole.
5. How many times (has, have) Martin filled his plate?
6. Here (is, are) the stamps from Portugal.
7. The experts say there (is, are) hope for the economy next year.
8. Here in this room (lie, lies) the solution to the mystery.
9. Why (has, have) he called me so late in the evening?
10. There (was, were) three ducks on the lake.

## Agreement with Indefinite Pronouns

Indefinite pronouns used as subjects can also cause agreement problems.

**Many indefinite pronouns can agree with either a singular or a plural verb. The choice depends upon the meaning given to the pronoun.**

Turn back to the list of indefinite pronouns in Section 2.2. Notice that some of the pronouns are always singular. Singular pronouns include those ending in *-one (anyone, everyone, someone)*, those ending in *-body (anybody, everybody, somebody)*, and those that imply one *(each, either)*. Others are always plural: *both, few, many, others,* and *several.* Some can be either singular or plural: *all, any, more, most, none,* and *some.* Study the list carefully and learn to recognize the number of indefinite pronouns.

Here are examples showing indefinite pronouns from each of the three categories. Notice in the first group that the prepositional phrases between the subjects and verbs do not affect agreement between the subjects and verbs.

**236**

ALWAYS SINGULAR:  <u>Each</u> of the coins <u>is</u> silver.

<u>Everyone</u> in the first five rows <u>was delighted</u> by the play.

<u>Either</u> of those hats <u>is</u> warm.

ALWAYS PLURAL:  <u>Few</u> <u>have chosen</u> a topic yet.

<u>Many</u> <u>are waiting</u> until they finish reading the book.

<u>Several</u> <u>have</u> not <u>started</u> reading the book.

EITHER SINGULAR OR PLURAL:  <u>Some</u> of the milk <u>is</u> frozen.

<u>Some</u> of the desserts <u>are</u> frozen too.

With an indefinite pronoun that can be either singular or plural, the antecedent of the pronoun determines its number. In the last set of examples, the antecedent of *some* in the first sentence is *milk*. Since *milk* is singular, the verb is singular. In the second sentence, the antecedent of *some* is *desserts*, which is plural. The verb, therefore, is plural.

## EXERCISE B: Checking Agreement with Indefinite Pronouns.

For each of the following sentences, choose the correct verb from the choices in parentheses and write it on your paper.

EXAMPLE:  Most of the story (was, were) written from a child's point of view.

      was

1. Most of the students (has, have) spelled "encyclopedia" correctly.
2. Several of these performing dogs (was, were) trained abroad.
3. (Does, Do) any of the participants want to answer that question?
4. All of the tickets (was, were) sold before Wednesday.
5. Some of the concrete (has, have) not set yet.

6. Everyone (laughs, laugh) when Al puts on his insect costume.
7. All of the ice cream (has, have) melted.
8. Each of the rooms (represents, represent) a different period of American history.
9. Both of the contestants (has, have) brought good luck charms with them.
10. Some of these movies (was, were) first seen by your grandparents.

**EXERCISE C: Checking Special Problems in Agreement.** For each of the following sentences, choose the correct verb from the choices in parentheses and write it on your paper.

EXAMPLE:   Most of the breadcrumbs (was, were) blown away by the wind.

were

1. Each of the sliding doors (sticks, stick).
2. What (was, were) the minimum daily requirement for each team member?
3. All of the stamps (was, were) on the package.
4. (Hasn't, Haven't) they realized yet that we were joking?
5. Each of the kittens (has, have) white patches on its ears.
6. Here (is, are) your concert tickets.
7. Everyone (wants, want) some steamed clams.
8. How often (has, have) they traveled in the West?
9. There (is, are) many strong points in Stella's plan, but it is too expensive.
10. Most of the doors in this house (squeaks, squeak).

**DEVELOPING WRITING SKILLS: Writing Sentences With Subject and Verb Agreement.** Write ten sentences, each using one of the following subjects. Choose a verb from the list that agrees in number with the subject. Use the verb as a single verb of the sentence or as a helping verb.

EXAMPLE:   each of you      has

Each of you has been given a different assignment.

| Subjects | Verbs |
|----------|-------|
| 1. both of these books | is   are |
| 2. many of the parents | was   were |
| 3. most of the rooms | has   have |
| 4. some of this lettuce | don't   doesn't |
| 5. both of them | |
| 6. some of the news programs | |
| 7. all of his energy | |
| 8. one of the show dogs | |
| 9. they (Write a question beginning with *Where.*) | |
| 10. several people (Write an inverted-order sentence beginning with *There.*) | |

# Agreement Between Pronouns 16.3 and Antecedents

An antecedent is the word or words for which a pronoun stands. A pronoun's antecedent may be a noun, a group of words acting as a noun, or even another pronoun. This section will explain the ways in which pronouns must agree with their antecedents. If you are not sure that you can quickly recognize pronouns and antecedents, review Chapter 2 before continuing with this section.

## Making Personal Pronouns and Antecedents Agree

Personal pronouns should agree with their antecedents in two important ways.

**A personal pronoun must agree with its antecedent in both person and number.**

*Person* tells whether a pronoun refers to the person speaking (first person), the person spoken to (second person), or the person, place, or thing spoken about (third person). *Number* tells whether the pronoun is singular (referring to one) or plural (referring to more than one). Personal pronouns must agree with their antecedents in both person and number.

EXAMPLE:   I told *David* to bring a bathing suit with *him.*

In the example the pronoun *him* is third person and singular. It agrees with its antecedent *David,* which is also third person (the person spoken about) and singular.

**Avoiding Shifts in Person.** One kind of mistake in agreement occurs when a personal pronoun does not have the same person as its antecedent. This mistake usually involves the careless use of *you* (the second person pronoun) to refer to a noun in the third person.

INCORRECT:   *Stephanie* has learned Serbo-Croatian. This is the language *you* need to know when *you* go to Yugoslavia.

CORRECT:   *Stephanie* has learned Serbo-Croatian. This is the language *she* needs to know when *she* goes to Yugoslavia.

Whenever you use the word *you,* make sure it refers to the person you are speaking to or writing to and not to any other person.

**Avoiding Shifts in Number.** Making pronouns and antecedents agree in number may sometimes be a little more difficult. Problems may arise, for example, when the antecedent is a compound joined by *or* or *nor.*

**Use a singular personal pronoun to refer to two or more singular antecedents joined by *or* or *nor.***

**240**

Two or more singular subjects joined by *or* or *nor* must have a singular verb. In the same way, two or more singular antecedents joined by *or* or *nor* must have a singular pronoun.

INCORRECT:   Either *Jennie* or *Carol* will lend me *their* gloves.

CORRECT:   Either *Jennie* or *Carol* will lend me *her* gloves.

If a compound antecedent is joined by *and,* however, the pronoun should be plural.

EXAMPLE:   *Jennie* and *Carol* will lend us *their* gloves.

**EXERCISE A: Making Pronouns and Antecedents Agree.**
Rewrite each of the following sentences, filling in the blank with an appropriate pronoun.

EXAMPLE:   The children had left _____ toys all over the living room.

The children had left their toys all over the living room.

1. Lucy was hoping that _____ name would be chosen.
2. Bob and Chris planned _____ work carefully.
3. Each girl was asked to give _____ own opinion.
4. All pilots are likely to remember _____ first flights.
5. Either Katie or Jenny will ask _____ parents to drive us to the dance.
6. Each boy had to memorize _____ lines for the skit to be given that night.
7. Lisa learned to ski so that _____ could join the teen-agers on the slope.
8. Neither Jeremy nor Ian was willing to lend us _____ stereo.
9. Cathy and Linda wanted to try on _____ new uniforms immediately.
10. When they were young, Neil and Sally spent hours playing with _____ blocks.

**EXERCISE B: Avoiding Shifts in Person and Number.**
Each sentence contains a single error in pronoun-antecedent agreement. Rewrite each sentence correctly, underlining the pronoun that you have changed and its antecedent.

EXAMPLE:   Each member of the girls' swim team spends much of their free time practicing.

Each <u>member</u> of the girls' swim team spends much of <u>her</u> free time practicing.

1. Julio now knows that you can't play in the school band without practicing.
2. Either Curtis or Tim will bring their surfboard today.
3. Each fish in the aquarium acted as if they could not be bothered by our attention.
4. All students should know that you have to register today.
5. The puppies rolled over and kicked its legs.
6. Each stained-glass window had their own design.
7. Elsa is planning to exhibit her pottery at the artists' fair, where you can set up a display booth without charge.
8. Either Sandra or Audrey will be photographed in their cap and gown for the yearbook.
9. Al likes to visit Manhattan, where you can do a lot of sight-seeing without a car.
10. All reporters must turn in her stories before the deadline.

## Agreement Between Personal Pronouns and Indefinite Pronouns

Indefinite pronouns (listed in Section 2.2) are words such as *each, everybody, either,* and *one.* Pay special attention to the number of a personal pronoun when the antecedent is a singular indefinite pronoun.

**Use a singular personal pronoun when its antecedent is a singular indefinite pronoun.**

Do not be misled by a prepositional phrase that follows an indefinite pronoun. The personal pronoun must agree with the indefinite pronoun, not with the object of the preposition. In the two incorrect sentences below, the pronoun *their* mistakenly agrees with *cats* and *groups,* the two objects of prepositions.

| Incorrect | Correct |
|---|---|
| *One* of the cats has lost *their* collar. | *One* of the cats has lost *its* collar. |
| *Everyone* in the two groups expressed *their* opinion. | *Everyone* in the two groups expressed *his* opinion. |

**EXERCISE C: Making Personal Pronouns and Indefinite Pronouns Agree.** For each of the following sentences, choose the correct personal pronoun from the choices given in parentheses and write it on your paper.

EXAMPLE:  One of these peaches has a soft spot on (its, their) skin.

       its

1. Each of these letters contains a mistake in (its, their) heading.
2. We sold all of these paintings along with (its, their) frames.
3. Let each of the girls use (her, their) own microfilm reader.
4. Neither of the boys has chosen an easy poem for (his, their) recitation.
5. Some of the birds stay up north and take (its, their) chances with the winter weather.
6. Either of these puppies should be able to recognize (its, their) master.
7. Each of the Boy Scouts had brought (his, their) collection of patches to the jamboree.
8. Some of these stamps are valuable for (its, their) flaws.

9. Everyone in this room should be prepared to give (her, their) report.
10. Take any one of the books from these shelves and check through (its, their) index.

**EXERCISE D: Checking Agreement Between Pronouns and Antecedents.** Most of the following sentences contain errors in pronoun-antecedent agreement. Find the sentences with errors and rewrite them on your paper. Write *correct* for those sentences without faults.

EXAMPLE:   Lily found that painting wasn't difficult once you made your first mark on the blank canvas.

Lily found that painting wasn't difficult once she made her first mark on the blank canvas.

1. Each of these magazines has a subscription blank attached to their cover.
2. Jess believes that you should try to be a star in many different sports.
3. Neither Judy nor Carol has their own pair of skis and ski poles.
4. Not one of the dishes tasted as good as it had sounded in the waiter's description.
5. Several of the runners in the marathon finished his first five miles together.
6. Every lawn on the block where I live has their share of crabgrass.
7. All of the mail carriers wear pith helmets, which protect you from the heat.
8. Some of these people can trace their family trees back more than ten generations.
9. Each one of the boys on the school team has their own basketball.
10. Patsy forgot her bus schedule, which you really needed on the cross-country trip.

**DEVELOPING WRITING SKILLS: Writing Sentences with Pronouns and Antecedents.** Write ten sentences of your own, using personal pronouns that refer to the following listed antecedents. Make sure that the pronouns agree with their antecedents in person and number. In each sentence, draw an arrow from the pronoun to its antecedent.

EXAMPLES:    comedians

We asked the comedians to tell their jokes to the planning committee first.

each of the actresses

Each of the actresses brought her script to the meeting.

1. everyone
2. either Louise or Martha
3. passengers and drivers
4. label or tag
5. each runner

6. Danny or Ramon
7. each of the women
8. all of the men
9. some people
10. Janet

# Skills Review and Writing Workshop

## Making Words Agree

### CHECKING YOUR SKILLS

Rewrite the paragraph below, correcting all errors in agreement.

(1) As usual, my parents, brothers, and sister is arguing about our vacation. (2) Each of my two brothers has their own favorite place for fishing, while my sister is insisting on the beach. (3) Neither I nor my parents is excited about these ideas. (4) My father thinks that you should see someplace new; he wants to camp out in Alaska. (5) His idea is not popular since the rest of us is not that adventurous. (6) My mother wants to visit a city because you can do so much. (7) The only thing on my mind are lots of food (8) The argument have gone on for three hours without a decision. (9) Now our dog raises her head and howls, adding its voice to the commotion. (10) Not one of us believe that getting there is half the fun.

### USING USAGE SKILLS IN WRITING
### Writing About a Proverb

Proverbs are sayings that express a general truth, such as "Haste makes waste" and "Look before you leap." Write a paragraph about a proverb by following the steps listed below.

**Prewriting:** Choose a proverb. Take notes on what you believe the proverb means and on whether you agree or disagree with the proverb and why.

**Writing:** Begin by stating the proverb. Then explain what it means. Tell whether you agree or disagree with the proverb and explain why.

**Revising:** First, eliminate any problems in agreement. Then look for other improvements you can make. After you have revised, proofread carefully.

246

# Chapter 17

# Using Modifiers

Adjectives and adverbs can be used in comparing people, places, or things. The form an adjective or adverb has depends on the kind of comparison that is being made.

The following example shows how adjectives change form: "Loretta is a *kind* person. She is *kinder* than Al. She is the *kindest* person I know." Adverbs may change form as shown in this sentence: "A collie can run *fast,* a whippet can run *faster,* and a greyhound can run *fastest* of all." These different forms of adjectives and adverbs are known as *degrees of comparison*.

**Most adjectives and adverbs have three degrees of comparison: the *positive,* the *comparative,* and the *superlative* degree.**

The *positive* degree is used when no comparison is being made. This is the form listed in a dictionary. The *comparative* degree is used when two things are being compared. The *superlative* degree is used when three or more things are being compared.

The first three sections in this chapter will explain the three degrees of adjectives and adverbs and show you how they should be used in sentences. The fourth section will discuss certain troublesome adjectives and adverbs and give you a chance to practice using them.

# 17.1 Regular Adjectives and Adverbs

You may recall from Chapters 4 and 5 that adjectives and adverbs are modifiers. Adjectives can modify nouns or pronouns. Adverbs can modify verbs, adjectives, or other adverbs. These two parts of speech can be either *regular* or *irregular*. Luckily, most adjectives and adverbs in English are *regular*—that is, their comparative and superlative degrees are formed in predictable ways. How these degrees are formed depends on the number of syllables in the positive form.

## Modifiers with One or Two Syllables

The comparative and superlative degrees of most adjectives and adverbs of one or two syllables can be formed in either of two ways.

**Use -*er* or *more* to form the comparative degree and -*est* or *most* to form the superlative degree of most one- and two-syllable modifiers.**

Adding -*er* and -*est* is the most common method.

| COMPARATIVE AND SUPERLATIVE DEGREES FORMED WITH -*ER* AND -*EST* | | |
|---|---|---|
| **Positive** | **Comparative** | **Superlative** |
| fast | faster | fastest |
| tall | taller | tallest |
| narrow | narrower | narrowest |
| sunny | sunnier | sunniest |

*More* and *most* can also be used to form the comparative and superlative degrees of most one- and two-syllable modifiers. These words should not be used when they sound awkward, as in "A greyhound is *more fast* than a beagle."

Notice in the following chart that two of the examples from the preceding chart—*narrow* and *sunny*—can be used with *more* and *most*. *More* and *most* are also used to form the comparative and superlative degrees of most adverbs ending in *-ly* and of one- and two-syllable modifiers that would sound awkward with *-er* and *-est*.

| COMPARATIVE AND SUPERLATIVE DEGREES FORMED WITH *MORE* AND *MOST* | | |
|---|---|---|
| **Positive** | **Comparative** | **Superlative** |
| narrow | more narrow | most narrow |
| sunny | more sunny | most sunny |
| quickly | more quickly | most quickly |
| just | more just | most just |

Use *-er* and *-est* with the last two examples above. Notice how awkward they sound. If you are not sure which form to use, say the words aloud and it will become clear. Use whichever sounds better.

**EXERCISE A: Forming the Comparative and Superlative Degrees of One- and Two-Syllable Modifiers.** On your paper write the comparative and superlative degrees of the following modifiers. If the degrees can be formed in either way, write the *-er* and *-est* forms.

EXAMPLE:   gentle

        gentler     gentlest

| | | | | |
|---|---|---|---|---|
| 1. nervous | 3. painful | 5. quiet | 7. soft | 9. clear |
| 2. brightly | 4. slowly | 6. late | 8. young | 10. short |

# Modifiers with Three or More Syllables

When an adjective or an adverb has three or more syllables, its comparative and superlative degrees are easy to form.

**Use *more* and *most* to form the comparative and superlative degrees of all modifiers of three or more syllables.**

Never use *-er* or *-est* with modifiers of more than two syllables.

| DEGREES OF MODIFIERS WITH THREE OR MORE SYLLABLES | | |
|---|---|---|
| **Positive** | **Comparative** | **Superlative** |
| popular | more popular | most popular |
| affectionate | more affectionate | most affectionate |
| intelligently | more intelligently | most intelligently |

**EXERCISE B: Forming the Comparative and Superlative Degrees of Modifiers with More than Two Syllables.** On your paper write the comparative and superlative degrees of the following modifiers.

EXAMPLE:   beautiful

more beautiful     most beautiful

1. generous
2. unattractive
3. suddenly
4. capable
5. powerfully
6. envious
7. talented
8. secretly
9. delicate
10. comfortable

**DEVELOPING WRITING SKILLS: Forming the Comparative and Superlative Degrees of Regular Modifiers.** On your paper write two sentences for each of the following modifiers. Use the comparative degree in the first sentence and the superlative degree in the second.

EXAMPLE:   quickly

When the storm approached, Paula responded more quickly than Pete.

Dave, however, responded the most quickly, running immediately to close the windows.

| | | |
|---|---|---|
| 1. wisely | 5. gracefully | 9. funny |
| 2. fast | 6. pretty | 10 likable |
| 3. cold | 7. expensive | |
| 4. memorable | 8. boldly | |

# Irregular Adjectives and Adverbs 17.2

A few adjectives and adverbs are *irregular*. Their comparative and superlative degrees must be memorized.

**Learn the irregular comparative and superlative forms of certain adjectives and adverbs.**

The following chart lists the most common irregular modifiers.

| DEGREES OF IRREGULAR ADJECTIVES AND ADVERBS | | |
|---|---|---|
| **Positive** | **Comparative** | **Superlative** |
| bad | worse | worst |
| badly | worse | worst |
| far (distance) | farther | farthest |
| far (extent) | further | furthest |
| good | better | best |
| well | better | best |
| many | more | most |
| much | more | most |

**EXERCISE A: Recognizing the Degree of Irregular Modifiers.** On your paper indicate the degree of the underlined word in each of the following sentences.

EXAMPLE: Uncle Fred's collection of timepieces includes <u>many</u> official railroad clocks.

positive

1. Vinnie enjoyed Monkey Island <u>more</u> than any other part of the zoo.
2. How can Maureen sing as <u>well</u> as she does with a head cold?
3. The <u>worst</u> suggestion of all was that we paint the gym floor silver for the dance.
4. As I read <u>further</u>, I realized why the prime suspect couldn't have committed the crime.
5. Caroline's schoolwork has gotten <u>better</u> since she became interested in reading.
6. Although the rink was in <u>bad</u> condition, we managed to have a good time ice-skating.
7. I thought our team did <u>best</u> in the egg-tossing contest.
8. Juan had hiked the <u>farthest</u> when the competition ended.
9. Completing the reading list will look <u>good</u> on your record.
10. Which of you has eaten the <u>most</u> pudding?

**EXERCISE B: Using the Comparative and Superlative Degrees of Irregular Modifiers.** Copy each of the following sentences onto your paper, supplying the form of the modifier requested in parentheses.

EXAMPLE: The fog seems (bad—comparative) this morning.

worse

1. Sid ran (much—comparative) when he lived in the city.
2. The (bad—superlative) she can do is to disagree with you.
3. The piano sounds (good—comparative) since we removed the tennis ball from its strings.

4. Pluto is the (far—superlative) planet from the sun.
5. Terry plays softball even (badly—comparative) than I do.
6. I have written (many—comparative) stories this week than ever before.
7. My dog behaves (well—superlative) just after she has eaten.
8. What surprised me (much—comparative) was Sharon's ability to predict the outcome.
9. Our china and glassware fared the (badly—superlative) at the hands of the movers.
10. The (good—superlative) photograph caught Leroy while he was still standing on the inner tube.

**DEVELOPING WRITING SKILLS: Forming the Comparative and Superlative Degrees of Irregular Modifiers.** On your paper write two sentences for each of the following modifiers. Use the comparative degree in the first sentence and the superlative degree in the second.

EXAMPLE:    much

They earned more money mowing lawns than babysitting.

They earned the most money washing cars.

1. far        2. good        3. many        4. bad        5. well

# Using the Comparative and 17.3 Superlative Degrees

Try to remember the following rules when you use the comparative and superlative degrees.

**Use the comparative degree to compare *two* people, places, or things.**

**Use the superlative degree to compare *three or more* people, places, or things.**

You usually do not need to mention specific numbers when you are making a comparison. The wording of the rest of the sentence will generally make it clear whether you are comparing two items or more.

EXAMPLES:  The radio sounds *better* now.

Lorenzo makes the *best* pizzas in town.

In the first example, the comparative degree *better* clearly compares the radio's present sound to its past sound. In the second example, the superlative degree *best* compares Lorenzo's pizzas to all other pizzas in town.

When you use modifiers to compare just two items, take care not to use the superlative degree.

INCORRECT:  Of the two pizzas, this one was the *best*.

CORRECT:  Of the two pizzas, this one was *better*.

In addition, when you use modifiers in either the comparative or the superlative degree, take care not to make *double comparisons*. Do not use both *-er* and *more* to form the comparative degree or both *-est* and *most* to form the superlative degree. Use one or the other method, but not both. Moreover, never use *-er* and *-est* or *more* and *most* with an irregular modifier.

INCORRECT:  This assignment is *more easier* than I thought.

Salisbury Mills is the *most beautifullest* town in the county.

The blueberry pie turned out *worser* than it did the last time.

CORRECT:  This assignment is *easier* than I thought.

Salisbury Mills is the *most beautiful* town in the county.

The blueberry pie turned out *worse* than it did the last time.

**254**

**EXERCISE: Correcting Errors in Degree.** Several of the following sentences contain errors in degree. On your paper rewrite the incorrect sentences to correct them. Write *correct* if the sentence contains no errors.

EXAMPLE:    This ski jump is the highest of the two at Sunrise Lodge.

This ski jump is the higher of the two at Sunrise Lodge.

1. The jester realized more sooner than the rest of the court what the king meant.
2. Which of these two bushes has produced the most roses?
3. Gerri's secrets were safer with Joel than with her friend Kim.
4. I couldn't judge whose work was better—Dean's, Helen's, or Chrisanne's.
5. Yesterday had to be the most hottest day of the year.
6. Which one of your eyes is weakest?
7. Mr. Crespi grew more fonder of that wild rabbit as the summer went on.
8. Of all the sections of the test, I felt most comfortable with the essay question.
9. If I had to choose between beets and sauerkraut, I would say that I dislike beets most.
10. The most worst job Craig ever had to do involved counting bees in a hive.

**DEVELOPING WRITING SKILLS: Using the Comparative and Superlative Degrees.** For each of the modifiers on page 256, write two sentences. Use the comparative degree in the first sentence and the superlative degree in the second.

EXAMPLE:    spectacular

The sequel was more spectacular than the original.

The next movie may be the most spectacular of all.

| | | |
|---|---|---|
| 1. silly | 5. wonderful | 9. soft |
| 2. warm | 6. much | 10. colorful |
| 3. ambitious | 7. badly | |
| 4. suddenly | 8. lazy | |

# 17.4 Glossary of Troublesome Adjectives and Adverbs

Several common adjectives and adverbs cause problems for people, both in speaking and writing. As you read through the following list, note those words that have caused you problems in the past. Then use the exercises to test your understanding. When you are writing and revising your compositions, turn to this section to check your work.

**(1)  bad, badly**    *Bad* is an adjective. Use it after linking verbs, such as *are, appear, feel, look,* and *sound. Badly* is an adverb. Use it after action verbs, such as *act, behave, do,* and *perform.*

INCORRECT:   Jan looked *badly* after the operation.
$\overset{\text{LV}}{}$

I did *bad* on the test.
$\overset{\text{AV}}{}$

CORRECT:   Jan looked *bad* after the operation.
$\overset{\text{LV}}{}$

I did *badly* on the test.
$\overset{\text{AV}}{}$

**(2)  fewer, less**    Use the adjective *fewer* to answer the question "How many?" Use the adjective *less* to answer the question "How much?"

HOW MANY:   *fewer* calories    *fewer* chores

HOW MUCH:   *less* food    *less* work

**(3)  good, well**    *Good* is an adjective. *Well* can be either an adjective or an adverb, depending on meaning. A common mistake is the use of *good* after an action verb. Use the adverb *well* instead.

INCORRECT: The children next door have behaved good all day. <sup>AV</sup>

CORRECT: The children next door have behaved *well* all day. <sup>AV</sup>

As adjectives *good* and *well* have slightly different meanings which are often confused. *Well* usually refers simply to a person's or an animal's health.

EXAMPLES: Janet felt *good* after the hike.

The fresh bread smells *good*.

That puppy is not *well*.

**(4) *just*** When used as an adverb, *just* often means "no more than." When *just* has this meaning, place it in the sentence right before the word it logically modifies.

INCORRECT: Do you *just* want one baked potato with your steak?

CORRECT: Do you want *just* one baked potato with your steak?

**(5) *only*** The position of *only* in a sentence sometimes affects the sentence's entire meaning. Consider the meaning of these sentences.

EXAMPLES: *Only* she answered that question. (Nobody else answered that question.)

She *only* answered that question. (She did nothing else with the question.)

She answered *only* that question. (She answered that question and no other question.)

Mistakes involving *only* usually occur when it is placed in a sentence in a way that makes the meaning confusing.

UNCLEAR: *Only* take advice from me.

BETTER: Take advice *only* from me.

Whenever you use *only* in a sentence, make sure it gives a listener or reader your exact meaning.

**EXERCISE: Correcting Errors Caused by Troublesome Adjectives and Adverbs.** Most of the following sentences contain errors in the use of the modifiers discussed in this section. Identify the errors, and rewrite the sentences in which they appear. Write *correct* on your paper if a sentence contains no errors.

EXAMPLE:   There are less flowers in the garden now.

There are fewer flowers in the garden now.

1. Tony just reached the station one minute before the train pulled out.
2. Cheryl looks very well with short hair.
3. I only made two dozen cookies for the party.
4. There is fewer snow on the ground this winter than last.
5. He did not deserve to win because he played badly.
6. You talk good, but you write better.
7. The bee sting I received yesterday looks badly.
8. As the day went on, we saw less sky and more clouds overhead.
9. Cazzie just needs one more plant to make his botany project complete.
10. Only add a little water; otherwise, it will be impossible to mold the sand.
11. Less than a hundred students attended the game.
12. Governor Merlo handled the hecklers at the rally very well.
13. The jumpy defendant performed very bad on the witness stand.
14. We were given just two sandwiches apiece to last us all day.
15. Considering the obstacles we faced, I think we did pretty good.
16. Don't feel badly about the quiz; nobody in the class did good on it.
17. You need less potatoes and more flour to make this pastry successfully.

18. Shelly looked bad, but she sounded good when she sang.
19. Don't just dust the tops of the tables; dust their legs as well.
20. You only may compete once in this contest.

**DEVELOPING WRITING SKILLS:  Using Troublesome Adjectives and Adverbs Correctly.** On your paper write a sentence according to the directions in each of the following items.

EXAMPLE:　Use *good* with a linking verb.

The performance of the dolphins was especially good.

1. Use *bad* with a linking verb.
2. Use *well* as an adverb.
3. Use *less* to modify a noun.
4. Use *Only* at the beginning of a sentence.
5. Use *just* to mean "no more than."
6. Use *fewer* to modify a noun.
7. Use *good* as an adjective.
8. Use *badly* to describe an action.
9. Use *only* after a verb.
10. Use *well* as an adjective.

# Skills Review and Writing Workshop

## Using Modifiers

### CHECKING YOUR SKILLS

Rewrite the following paragraph, correcting all errors in adjective and adverb usage.

(1) I have attended both Edgel School and Hadley School, but I like Edgel best. (2) Hadley is smaller and offers less extracurricular opportunities. (3) In fact, Hadley only offers one activity: sports. (4) Even so Hadley does worst in sports than Edgel. (5) Hadley School just has a few activities while Edgel has a great many. (6) Furthermore, Edgel is more newer and more prettier than Hadley. (7) Many people just regard it as about the prettiest campus in the state. (8) Edgel also has fine buses, more clean and more efficient than Hadley's. (9) Finally, the lunches at Edgel taste well in comparison with Hadley's average meals. (10) I am glad I now attend Edgel, the best of the two schools.

### USING USAGE SKILLS IN WRITING:
### Writing a Paragraph of Contrast

Identifying differences—contrast—is an important writing and thinking skill. Follow the steps below to write a paragraph of contrast.

**Prewriting:** Choose two television shows of the same type, one you consider good, one bad. Prepare two columns, one for each show, and take notes on the points of contrast.

**Writing:** Name the two shows, and tell which one you consider superior. Then discuss each point of contrast, showing how one show is superior to or weaker than the other.

**Revising:** First, look at your adjectives and adverbs and make sure they are all correct. Then look for other improvements you can make. After you have revised, proofread carefully.

**260**

# Chapter 18

# Solving Special Problems

Many mistakes in speaking and in writing involve words and expressions that are considered wrong by most educated Americans. Other problems involve words that are easily confused because they are spelled almost alike. In the following sections, note those problems that occur in your speaking or writing.

## Double Negatives 18.1

Negative words, such as *nothing* and *not,* are used to deny something or to say *no.* At one time it was customary to use two or more negative words in one clause to add emphasis. Today only one negative word is needed to give a sentence a negative meaning.

### The Mistaken Use of Double Negatives

Some people mistakenly use *double negatives*—two negative words—when only one is called for.

**Do not write sentences with double negatives.**

The sentences on the left in the following chart contain double negatives. Notice on the right how each can be corrected in either of two ways.

| Double Negatives | Corrected Sentences |
|---|---|
| Silas did*n't* invite *nobody*. | Silas did*n't* invite anybody. Silas invited *nobody*. |
| I have*n't no* time now. | I have*n't* any time now. I have *no* time now. |
| She *never* told us *nothing* about her party. | She *never* told us anything about her party. She told us *nothing* about her party. |

**EXERCISE: Correcting Double Negatives.** The following sentences contain double negatives, which are underlined. Correct each sentence in *two* ways.

EXAMPLE:   I did<u>n't</u> see <u>no</u> airplanes.

I didn't see any airplanes.

I saw no airplanes.

1. That bicycle factory has<u>n't</u> made <u>nothing</u> for ten years.
2. The railroad tracks that run past our yard do<u>n't</u> lead <u>nowhere</u>.
3. Do<u>n't</u> eat <u>nothing</u> now, or you won't enjoy your dinner.
4. Lillian has<u>n't</u> <u>no</u> place to keep her model train set.
5. The Governor has<u>n't</u> shown <u>nobody</u> the speech he is delivering tonight.
6. Lonnie has<u>n't</u> played <u>no</u> music with an orchestra.
7. These sandals do<u>n't</u> have <u>no</u> straps.
8. There were<u>n't</u> <u>no</u> more seats on the bus after we got on.

9. I can't remember <u>nothing</u> about my dreams last night.

10. Sheila wouldn<u>'t</u> give me <u>none</u> of her crackers.

**DEVELOPING WRITING SKILLS: Writing Negative Sentences.** On your paper write ten negative sentences of your own, each using one of the following words.

EXAMPLE:   hasn't

The kitten hasn't touched the yarn yet.

| | | | | |
|---|---|---|---|---|
| 1. not | 3. no | 5. never | 7. haven't | 9. nothing |
| 2. none | 4. won't | 6. nobody | 8. doesn't | 10. nowhere |

# Fifteen Common Usage 18.2 Problems

This section contains fifteen common usage problems in alphabetical order. Some of the problems are expressions that you should avoid in both your speaking and your writing. Others are words that are often confused because of similar spelling or meaning.

As you read through the list, note the problems that may have caused you difficulty in the past. Then use the exercises for practice in recognizing and avoiding those problems.

Later, when you write and revise your compositions, this section can help you check your work. If you do not find the explanation of a problem in this section, check for it in the index at the back of the book.

**(1) accept, except**   Do not confuse the spelling of these words. *Accept,* a verb, means "to take (what is offered)" or "to agree to." *Except,* a preposition, means "leaving out" or "other than."

VERB:   She willingly *accepted* responsibility for the others.

PREPOSITION:   Everyone *except* him will be at the party.

**263**

**(2)** *advice, advise*    Do not confuse the spelling of these related words. *Advice,* a noun, means "an opinion." *Advise,* a verb, means "to give an opinion to."

NOUN:    My mother gave me *advice* about how to answer the letter.

VERB:    My mother *advised* me to accept the invitation to the dance.

**(3)** *affect, effect*    *Affect,* almost always a verb, means "to influence" or "to bring about a change in." *Effect,* usually a noun, means "result."

VERB:    The cold weather *affected* the delicate plants on our porch.

NOUN:    What *effect* did the Emancipation Proclamation have on the outcome of the Civil War?

**(4)** *at*    Do not use *at* after *where*.

INCORRECT:    Do you know *where* we're *at*?

CORRECT:    Do you know *where* we are?

**(5)** *because*    Do not use *because* after *the reason*. Eliminate one or the other.

INCORRECT:    *The reason* I am late is *because* the bus broke down.

CORRECT:    I am late *because* the bus broke down.

   *The reason* I am late is that the bus broke down.

**(6)** *beside, besides*    These two prepositions have different meanings and can not be interchanged. *Beside* means "at the side of" or "close to." *Besides* means "in addition to."

EXAMPLES:   We picnicked *beside* the lake.

   No one *besides* us was there.

**(7)** *different from, different than*    *Different from* is generally preferred over *different than*.

**264**

EXAMPLE:   The book's ending was *different from* what I had
hoped.

**(8)  farther, further**     *Farther* is usually used to refer to
distance. *Further* means "additional" or "to a greater degree or
extent."

EXAMPLES:   Haven't we walked much *farther* than a mile?

I need *further* advice.

When he began raising his voice, I listened no
*further*.

**(9)  in, into**     *In* refers to position. *Into* suggests motion.

POSITION:   The ruler is *in* the desk drawer.

MOTION:   Put the ruler *into* the top drawer.

**(10)  kind of, sort of**     Do not use *kind of* and *sort of* to
mean "rather" or "somewhat."

INCORRECT:   The new record that I brought home sounds *sort
of* scratchy.

CORRECT:   The new record that I brought home sounds *rather*
scratchy.

**(11)  like**     *Like*, a preposition, usually means "similar
to" or "in the same way as." It should be followed by an object. Do not use like before a subject and a verb. Use *as* or *that*
instead.

PREPOSITION:   The rubbing alcohol felt *like* ice on my feverish
skin.

INCORRECT:   The stew that I ordered doesn't taste *like* it should.

CORRECT:   The stew that I ordered doesn't taste *as* it should.

**(12)  that, which, who**     *That* can be used to refer to
either things or people. *Which* should be used to refer only to
things. *Who* should be used to refer only to people.

**265**

THINGS:  The dress *that* (or *which*) I designed won first prize.

PEOPLE:  The dancer *that* (or *who)* performed is my brother.

**(13) *their, there, they're*** Do not confuse the spelling of these three words. *Their,* possessive adjective, always modifies a noun. *There* is usually used either as a sentence starter or as an adverb. *They're* is a contraction for *they are.*

POSSESSIVE ADJECTIVE:  The team won all of *their* games.

SENTENCE STARTER:  *There* are no easy answers to the problem of prejudice.

ADVERB:  Move the chair over *there.*

CONTRACTION:  *They're* trying to set new track records.

**(14) *to, too, two*** Do not confuse the spelling of these words. *To,* a preposition, begins a prepositional phrase or an infinitive. *Too,* with two *o*'s, is an adverb and modifies adjectives and other adverbs. *Two* is a number.

PREPOSITION:  *to* the store       *to* Maine

INFINITIVE:  *to* meet       *to* see

ADVERB:  *too* sad       *too* quickly

NUMBER  *two* buttons       *two* apples

**(15) *when, where, why*** Do not use *when, where,* or *why* directly after a linking verb such as *is.* Reword the sentence.

INCORRECT:  In the evening *is when* I do my homework.

The gym *is where* our wrestling team practices.

To see Yellowstone National Park *is why* we came to Wyoming.

CORRECT:  I do my homework in the evening.

Our wrestling team practices in the gym.

We came to Wyoming to see Yellowstone National Park.

**266**

**EXERCISE A: Avoiding Usage Problems 1–5.** For each of the following sentences, choose the correct form from the choices in parentheses and write it on your paper.

EXAMPLE:   I can't (accept, except) this check for a million dollars.

accept

1. When I asked you for (advice, advise), I didn't expect a lecture.
2. Do you know where the public telephones (are, are at)?
3. Everyone (accept, except) Elsie burst out laughing at the burnt pancakes.
4. The reason I spoke up was (because, that) you were absolutely right.
5. Praise had an unusual (affect, effect) on the new puppy.
6. Marcie never forgot the day when her puzzle was (accepted, excepted) for the math club's newsletter.
7. The weather always (affects, effects) Zack's state of mind.
8. I have finally discovered where your secret hiding place (is, is at).
9. The Highway Patrol (advices, advises) motorists to stay off the roads today.
10. Gil's reason for leaving at nine was (because, that) he had an early class.

**EXERCISE B: Avoiding Usage Problems 6–10.** For each of the following sentences, choose the correct form from the choices in parentheses and write it on your paper.

1. You need to explain your idea (farther, further).
2. This parakeet is different (from, than) the others because it can already speak.
3. The decorations around their windows indicate that these buildings are (kind of, rather) old.
4. The Frisbees were (in, into) the trunk of the car.

5. Carol is the girl who just sat down (beside, besides) Nancy.
6. I was (sort of, rather) upset after I stepped on the bee.
7. This newspaper is entirely different (from, than) the way it used to be.
8. (Beside, Besides) visiting the Statute of Liberty, we're going to Radio City today.
9. I think the country store is (farther, further) than five miles away.
10. The young father tiptoed (in, into) the baby's room to close the window.

**EXERCISE C: Avoiding Usage Problems 11–15.** For each of the following sentences, choose the correct form from the choices in parentheses and write it on your paper.

1. This trunk is (the place where, where) I keep my old toys.
2. It takes (too, two) people to ride a seesaw.
3. In his skin-diving outfit, my father looked exactly (as, like) a frog.
4. The rabbit (that, whom) we saw had ears of different colors.
5. (There, They're) are two sets of twins in that family.
6. Late fall is (the time when, when) slightly sour apples taste best.
7. (As, Like) the twig is bent, so grows the tree.
8. The person (that, which) won the contest has not yet claimed the prize.
9. (Too, To) few people know how to do their own home repairs.
10. Their mother called to say that (their, they're) coming to the party.

**EXERCISE D: Avoiding Usage Problems 1–15.** For each of the following sentences, choose the correct forms from the choices in parentheses and write them on your paper.

**268**

1. If Amy had (accepted, excepted) my first request, I would not be asking her for (farther, further) help now.
2. (As, Like) you, (there, they're) going to the mountains this year.
3. Take my (advice, advise) and go (in, into) the storm shelter now.
4. This corner is (the place where, where) my cat prefers (too, to) sleep.
5. The student (which, who) wrote that poem has already published (too, two) stories.
6. One reason Keith runs is (because, that) jogging has a good (affect, effect) on his posture.
7. When I asked where the gas station (was, was at), she told me it was much (farther, further) down the road.
8. (Beside, Besides) the drums, (their, there) daughter Cindy plays the piano and xylophone.
9. The door was (kind of, rather) unusual because its knobs were different (from, than) the others in the house.
10. The towels were (to, too) close (to, too) the ocean.

## DEVELOPING WRITING SKILLS: Writing Sentences.

Write ten sentences of your own, using each of the following words.

EXAMPLES:  further

I'd like to discuss the theme of the movie further.

beside

Vera walked beside her brother as they crossed the intersection.

| | |
|---|---|
| 1. accept | 6. like (preposition) |
| 2. advice | 7. except |
| 3. beside | 8. advise |
| 4. further | 9. effect |
| 5. affect | 10. besides |

# Skills Review and Writing Workshop

## Solving Special Problems

### CHECKING YOUR SKILLS

Rewrite the following paragraph, correcting all errors in usage.

(1) I had a terrible time at the Halloween party I went too. (2) The only reason I went was because my friends were going. (3) But when we got there, I saw that my costume looked kind of silly. (4) I would not have minded accept everyone else's costumes were great. (5) I would have left as soon as we got there, but I couldn't get no ride home. (6) For a while I stood besides my friend Eric and watched the crowd of clowns, robots, and cowboys. (7) But when it was time to bob for apples, I joined in, putting my head further into the bucket than anyone else. (8) I ended up with the wettest head their. (9) I have only one piece of advise for people who plan to go to Halloween parties. (10) Be different than your friends—stay home!

### USING USAGE SKILLS IN WRITING
#### Writing a News Story

News stories answer the questions Who? What? Where? When? and Why? about an event. Follow the steps below to write a news story about an event you recently witnessed.

**Prewriting:** Answer the questions Who? What? Where? When? and Why? about the event. Make notes of your answers as well as of other colorful details.

**Writing:** Write a short news story describing the event. You can add interesting details to make your description of the facts more vivid.

**Revising:** First, check to make sure you have avoided double negatives and other special usage problems. Then, check for other ways to improve the news story. After you have revised, proofread carefully.

270

# *Mechanics*

# Chapter 19

# Using Capitals

*Capital letters* act as signals. Capitals help you to identify the beginning of a sentence and to recognize important words within a sentence. A sentence without capitals can be some-what confusing: *the slaterville art festival will show paintings by picasso from ann wilke's private collection.*

When capitals are added, the sentence is easier to under-stand: *The Slaterville Art Festival will show paintings by Picasso from Ann Wilke's private collection.*

The definition of capitalization is a simple one.

**To capitalize means to begin a word with a cap-ital letter.**

The six sections in this chapter explain rules that will help you capitalize correctly in your writing.

## 19.1 Capitals for Sentences and the Word *I*

Every sentence must begin with a capital letter. The word *I* must also be capitalized, every time you use it.

# Sentences

The first word in a sentence must begin with a capital.

**Capitalize the first word in declarative, interrogative, imperative, and exclamatory sentences.**

DECLARATIVE:   Several motorists were impatiently waiting for the light to change.

INTERROGATIVE:   Isn't anyone willing to listen?

IMPERATIVE:   Walk carefully on this slippery pavement.

EXCLAMATORY:   What an unusual day this is!

There are also situations, especially in informal writing, in which only a part of a sentence is written out. A capital letter is still required for the first word in each partial sentence.

EXAMPLES:   Where?   For how much?   Never!

**EXERCISE A: Using Capitals to Begin Sentences.** Copy the following items onto your paper, adding the missing capitals.

EXAMPLES:   why did you choose this restaurant?

Why did you choose this restaurant?

1. what an interesting plot that was!
2. sit up and listen carefully.
3. would you mind if we ask one more question before you leave?
4. which way should we turn? right? left?
5. show me the blueprint for your new home.
6. if anyone can change your opinion, he can.
7. why not? they owe you a favor.
8. today clothing fashions are determined by the individual.
9. my mother and father would like both of you to stay for dinner.
10. wow! these fireworks are spectacular!

## The Word *I*

The word *I* must be capitalized wherever it appears.

**Always capitalize the word *I*.**

EXAMPLE:   *I* watched the clock while *I* waited for you.

**EXERCISE B: Capitalizing the Word *I*.** Copy the following sentences, adding the missing capitals.

EXAMPLE:   she and i have never been friends.

She and I have never been friends.

1. i began to wonder what i should do next.
2. the child smiling into the camera is i.
3. i think i am going to be a little late.
4. he said i would be the candidate.
5. after that experience, i'll never swim there again.

**DEVELOPING WRITING SKILLS: Capitalizing Sentences and the Word *I*.** Write five sentences of your own that fit the following requirements. Be sure to capitalize correctly.

EXAMPLE:   A sentence including the word *I*

Jenny and I met at the zoo.

1. A sentence that ends with a question mark
2. A sentence that ends with a period
3. A sentence that ends with an exclamation mark
4. A sentence followed by a one-word question
5. A sentence using the word *I* twice

# 19.2 Capitals for Proper Nouns

An important use of capitals is to show that a word is a proper noun. It names a specific person, place, or thing.

**Capitalize all proper nouns.**

# Names of People

The name of a specific person is perhaps the most common kind of proper noun.

**Capitalize each part of a person's full name.**

EXAMPLES:   Cindy F. Broughton      L. T. Smart

**EXERCISE A: Using Capitals for Names.** Each of the following sentences contains one or more names that need to be capitalized. On your paper rewrite the names, adding the missing capitals.

EXAMPLE:   Many unusual ingredients show up in the omelets chris makes.

Chris

1. Our whole class has just finished reading a book by paul zindel.
2. I guessed correctly that jamie left the water running in the sink and that pete forgot to lock the door.
3. The scholarship awards were presented by anthony r. hughes.
4. We asked marcia to bring the pizza and jim to bring a tossed salad.
5. This newly built wing of the library will be dedicated to p. l. martinez.

# Geographical Places

The names of geographical places are also proper nouns.

**Capitalize geographical names.**

According to this rule, any place that can be found on a map should be capitalized. The following chart includes examples of different kinds of geographical names that need capital letters.

**275**

| GEOGRAPHICAL NAMES | |
|---|---|
| **Streets** | the Avenue of the Americas, Wildflower Drive |
| **Towns and Cities** | Freeville, Youngstown, Cairo |
| **Counties** | Dade County, Cook County |
| **States and Provinces** | Nebraska, Alberta |
| **Nations** | India, Spain, the United States of America |
| **Continents** | North America, Antarctica, Asia |
| **Valleys and Deserts** | Death Valley, the Kalahari Desert |
| **Mountains** | the Cascade Range, Pike's Peak, Mount Everest |
| **Sections of a Country** | the Gulf Coastal Plain, the Northeast, the South |
| **Islands** | Corsica, the Balearic Islands |
| **Scenic Spots** | the Grand Canyon, the Riviera |
| **Rivers and Falls** | the Danube, the Colorado River, Victoria Falls |
| **Lakes and Bays** | Lake Champlain, Bay of Biscay |
| **Seas and Oceans** | the Red Sea, the Arctic Ocean |

A *compass point*, such as south or northeast, is capitalized only when it names a specific geographical location. When a compass point refers to a direction, it is not capitalized.

EXAMPLES: The South is experiencing a serious drought.

Drive south for three miles and you will be there.

**EXERCISE B: Using Capitals for Geographical Names.**
Add the missing capitals to each geographical place name.

EXAMPLE: The capital of austria is vienna.

Austria   Vienna

**276**

1. We drove to mount rainier national park.
2. My favorite postcard shows the grand canyon.
3. The canary islands are west of africa in the atlantic ocean.
4. I watched a program about the everglades.
5. The iris is the state flower of tennessee.
6. We hope to visit australia and new zealand.
7. The matterhorn is one of the mountains in the alps.
8. Tracy lives in van nuys, orange county, california.
9. They are staying near lake winnipeg in manitoba.
10. The white sands desert resembles snowy hills.

## Other Proper Nouns

Other kinds of proper nouns also need capitals.

**Capitalize the names of specific events and periods of time.**

The following chart contains examples of events and periods of time that require capitalization.

| SPECIFIC EVENTS AND TIMES | |
| --- | --- |
| **Historical Periods** | the Age of Enlightenment, the Mesozoic Era, the Middle Ages |
| **Historical Events** | World War II, Boston Tea Party |
| **Documents** | the Declaration of Independence, the Treaty of Paris |
| **Days** | Wednesday, Saturday |
| **Months** | December, October |
| **Holidays** | Washington's Birthday, Thanksgiving Day, Labor Day |
| **Religious Days** | Christmas, Passover, Ramadan |
| **Special Events** | the Fiddlers' Convention, the New York Marathon |

The names of seasons are an exception to the rule. Seasons of the year, despite the fact that they name a specific time of year, are not capitalized.

EXAMPLES:   The most popular color this fall is rust.

This book is about a girl who travels in the summer.

Other proper nouns that need capitals are those that name specific groups.

**Capitalize the names of various organizations, government bodies, political parties, races, and nationalities, as well as the languages spoken by different groups.**

The proper nouns shown in the next chart are groups with which many people are familiar. All specific groups, however, must be capitalized, even if they are not well-known.

| SPECIFIC GROUPS | |
|---|---|
| **Clubs** | the Kiwanis Club |
| **Organizations** | the National Governors' Association |
| **Institutions** | the Massachusetts Institute of Technology |
| **Businesses** | the Chemstrand Corporation |
| **Government Bodies** | Congress, the Supreme Court, Parliament |
| **Political Parties** | the Democrats, the Republican Party |
| **Races** | Caucasian, Mongoloid |
| **Nationalities** | Chinese, German, Iranian, Argentinian |
| **Languages Spoken by Different Groups** | English, Spanish, Italian, Swahili, Dutch |

In order to show respect, you should also use capitals for the names of the religions of the world and other related words.

### Capitalize references to religions, deities, and religious scriptures.

The following chart presents a list of five of the world's major religions. Next to each religion examples of some of the related religious words that you must be sure to capitalize in your writing are given.

| RELIGIOUS REFERENCES | |
|---|---|
| **Christianity** | God, the Lord, the Father, the Son, the Holy Ghost, the Bible, books of the Bible (Genesis, Deuteronomy, Psalms, and so on) |
| **Judaism** | God, the Lord, the Father, the Prophets, the Torah, the Talmud, the Midrash |
| **Islam** | Allah, the Prophet, Mohammed, the Koran |
| **Hinduism** | Brahma, the Bhagavad-Gita, the Vedas |
| **Buddhism** | Buddha, Mahayana, Hinayana |

Note in the following examples, however, that the words *god* and *goddess* in references to ancient mythology are not capitalized.

EXAMPLES:   the god Jupiter      the goddess Juno

A final rule applies to proper nouns such as monuments, memorials, buildings, celestial bodies, awards, the names of specific vehicles, and trademarks.

### Capitalize the names of other special places and items.

The following chart gives examples of some of these other special places and items that you should capitalize in your writing.

| OTHER SPECIAL PLACES AND ITEMS | |
| --- | --- |
| **Monuments** | the Statue of Liberty |
| **Memorials** | the Winston Churchill Memorial |
| **Buildings** | the Houston Museum of Fine Arts, the Empire State Building |
| **Celestial Bodies** (except the earth, moon, and sun) | the Milky Way, Jupiter, Aries |
| **Awards** | the Newbery Award, the Nobel Peace Prize |
| **Air, Sea, Space, and Land Craft** | the *Spirit of St. Louis,* the *Monitor, Voyager 2,* a Mercury Cougar |
| **Trademarks** | Zenith, Nabisco Wheat Thins |

**EXERCISE C: Capitalizing Other Proper Nouns.** Each of the following sentences contains one or more proper nouns that need to be capitalized. On your paper rewrite the proper nouns, adding the missing capitals.

EXAMPLE:   Jane Addams won the nobel peace prize in 1931.

Nobel Peace Prize

1. Next saturday I plan to visit the prudential building.
2. The professor explained that islam requires its followers to fast during the holy month of ramadan.
3. In 1917 the british issued the balfour declaration, a statement of their policy in the middle east.
4. During the renaissance many forms of art flourished.
5. The caldecott medal is awarded annually for an illustrated children's book.
6. Mark, who knows both portuguese and spanish, said that the two languages are quite different from each other.
7. Jeff water-skied when he attended the university of hawaii.

8. The bill of rights is an essential part of the constitution of the united states.

9. This year our class will learn about the platforms of the two major political parties—the republicans and the democrats.

10. Stella's youngest brother just joined the little league, and his team will be playing the first friday in may.

11. Lucy interviewed one of the first men to work for the tennessee valley authority.

12. As an employee of general motors, Sal was well informed about new developments in car safety.

13. We stood quietly inside the lincoln memorial.

14. Every easter we enjoy watching the easter parade on television.

15. Last year my parents celebrated new year's eve by going for a ride on the staten island ferry.

16. Napoleon was defeated by the english at the battle of waterloo.

17. The highest court in our nation is the supreme court.

18. I prefer kellogg's rice krispies to any other cereal.

19. The last star in the handle of the little dipper is polaris.

20. Next Ben gave a clear description of grant's tomb.

**DEVELOPING WRITING SKILLS: Using Capitals for Proper Nouns.** Write ten sentences of your own, each containing a proper noun or nouns of the kind indicated in the following items. Be sure to capitalize correctly.

EXAMPLE:  A holiday

Halloween is Jack's favorite holiday.

1. An award
2. A trademark
3. A day of the week and a month
4. An institution
5. A special event
6. A ship
7. A religion and one of its holy writings
8. A nationality
9. A monument
10. A government body

# 19.3 Capitals for Proper Adjectives

When a proper noun or a form of a proper noun is used to describe another noun, it is a proper adjective. As a proper adjective, it will generally need a capital.

**Capitalize most proper adjectives.**

EXAMPLES:    Arabian stallion    Spanish rice

Senatorial candidate

Many proper adjectives are formed from the brand names of products.

**Capitalize brand names used as adjectives.**

EXAMPLES:    Kleenex tissue    Scott's grass seed

Red Devil paint

**EXERCISE: Using Capitals for Proper Adjectives.** On your paper write a meaningful proper adjective to complete each of the following phrases. Be sure to capitalize the phrases correctly.

EXAMPLE:    _____ fashions

French fashions

1. _____ shampoo       6. _____ margarine
2. _____ meatballs      7. _____ music
3. _____ imports        8. _____ television
4. _____ designer       9. _____ potatoes
5. _____ bread         10. _____ cameras

**DEVELOPING WRITING SKILLS: Using Capitals for Proper Adjectives.** Pretend that you have just finished shopping for groceries. Write a brief paragraph describing the contents of your shopping cart. Use at least five proper adjectives to describe the products that you have purchased, including at least three brand names.

# Capitals for Titles of People 19.4

Two major rules govern capitals in people's titles.

## Social and Professional Titles

One rule covers titles used before names and in direct address.

**Capitalize the title of a person when the title is followed by the person's name or when it is used in direct address.**

The following chart shows several common titles.

| TITLES OF PEOPLE | |
|---|---|
| **Social** | Mister, Madam or Madame, Miss, Sir |
| **Business** | Doctor, Professor, Superintendent |
| **Religious** | Reverend, Father, Rabbi, Bishop, Sister |
| **Military** | Private, Ensign, Captain, General, Admiral |
| **Government** | President, Secretary of State, Ambassador, Senator, Representative, Governor, Mayor |

The following examples show four titles in use.

BEFORE A NAME:  Detective O'Toole, Major Faulks, and Doctor Perkins have arrived.

DIRECT ADDRESS:  Look, Sergeant, the fingerprints match.

See Section 20.1 for information about capitalizing abbreviated social and professional titles.

**EXERCISE A: Using Capitals for Social and Professional Titles.** Each of the following sentences contains either a title before a name or a title used in direct address. Rewrite each title, adding the missing capital.

**283**

EXAMPLE:   The young recruit saluted sergeant Benjamin.

Sergeant

1. We asked captain Miller to speak to us.
2. During the meeting ambassador Bede spoke twice.
3. Ask professor Smedley when the papers are due.
4. During the war, Jim became lieutenant Harding.
5. At three o'clock sister Helen led the children outdoors.
6. The men have been pushed to the breaking point, colonel.
7. Our lawyer, attorney Black, explained the contract to us.
8. Quick, nurse, take this sample to the laboratory.
9. The cartoonist criticized the foreign policy of president Johnson.
10. Please, governor, tell us whether you intend to run again.

## Titles for Family Relationships

Another rule applies to titles for family relationships.

**Capitalize titles showing family relationships when the title is used with the person's name or in direct address. The title may also be capitalized in other situations when it refers to a specific person, except when the title comes after a possessive noun or pronoun.**

BEFORE A NAME:   We respect Uncle Frank's opinion.

DIRECT ADDRESS:   Be careful, Sal, or you will spill the paint.

REFERRING TO A SPECIFIC PERSON:   We haven't seen Grandmother in almost a year.

AFTER POSSESSIVES:   Alan's father is the team's captain.

No one knew my sister better.

Notice that the titles used in the last two examples are not capitalized because they are used after the possessive words *Alan's* and *my*.

**284**

**EXERCISE B: Using Capitals for Family Titles.** If a title in a sentence lacks a capital or if a title has been incorrectly capitalized, rewrite the title on your paper, correcting the error. If the sentence is correct, write *correct.*

EXAMPLE:  My sister and I wear the same size.

   correct

   1. Are we having meat loaf again, dad?
   2. Paul's Uncle gave us free swimming lessons.
   3. The children begged Grandfather Davis to come along.
   4. Naturally, uncle Glen wanted to show my brothers and me his new ranch.
   5. My Mother is always willing to listen to me.
   6. Last winter our Aunt was vacationing in the Alps.
   7. They finally decided that Mother McKee was not guilty.
   8. I told you, cousin Angela, that everyone liked the fudge.
   9. Why not ask your brother to lend you his bicycle?
  10. I'm sorry, son, but you will not be allowed to go.

**DEVELOPING WRITING SKILLS: Using Capitals for Titles of People.** Write ten sentences of your own, each including an example of the kind of title described in each item.

EXAMPLE:  A government title used before a name.

   Representative Rachel Tyler spoke to our class.

   1. A military title
   2. A family member's title used in direct address
   3. A social title used in direct address
   4. A business title used before a name
   5. A family member's title used after a possessive
   6. A government title used in direct address
   7. A business title used in direct address
   8. A family member's title used before a name
   9. A religious title
  10. A social title used before a name

# 19.5 Capitals for Titles of Things

Titles of certain things require capitals also.

## Written Works and Works of Art

The titles of different kinds of written works and works of art must always be capitalized.

**Capitalize the first word and all other important words in the titles of books, periodicals, poems, stories, plays, paintings, and other works of art.**

Each word in a title of this kind should begin with a capital except for the articles *(a, an, the)* and prepositions and conjunctions of fewer than five letters. Articles and short prepositions or conjunctions should be capitalized only when they are used as the first word in a title.

EXAMPLES: A Separate Peace

     U.S. News and World Report

     Young Woman with a Water Jug

     "The Man That Corrupted Hadleyburg"

**EXERCISE A: Using Capitals for Written Works and Works of Art.** Rewrite each of the following titles, adding the missing capitals. Use underlining and quotation marks as shown.

EXAMPLE: "of missing persons"

     "Of Missing Persons"

1. the heart is a lonely hunter
2. sports illustrated
3. "the monkey's paw"
4. joy in the morning
5. head of a woman
6. the gold of the gods
7. the man who came to dinner
8. "to a field mouse"
9. road and track
10. "to a waterfowl"

# School Courses

The titles of certain courses must also be capitalized.

**Capitalize the title of a course when the course is a language or when the course is followed by a number.**

EXAMPLES:    French        History 3A        Math 203

Language courses are always capitalized. Other courses are not capitalized when they are used in a general way.

EXAMPLE:    My morning classes include science and Latin.

**EXERCISE B: Using Capitals for Courses.** In each of the following sentences, choose the correctly written course title from the choices in parentheses and write it on your paper.

EXAMPLE:    Lisa is a student in my (algebra, Algebra) class.

        algebra

1. While studying (civics I, Civics I), I became interested in politics.
2. Few people in (physics, Physics) understood the work they were assigned.
3. After Pat finished her first year of (russian, Russian), she decided to study an easier language.
4. Next year Bert and I will be taking (geometry, Geometry).
5. In (spanish, Spanish) we are studying the conjugation of verbs.

**DEVELOPING WRITING SKILLS: Using Capitals for Titles of Things.** Write ten sentences, each including a specific example of the kind of title described in each item.

EXAMPLE:    A sculpture (underlined)

        Rodin's <u>The Thinker</u> is one of the most famous sculptures in the world.

1. A poem (in quotation marks)
2. A language course
3. A painting (underlined)
4. A math course
5. A book (underlined)
6. A history course followed by a number
7. A short story (in quotation marks)
8. A science course
9. A play (underlined)
10. A periodical (underlined)

# 19.6 Capitals in Letters

The following rule covers capitals used in letters.

**Capitalize the first word and all nouns in letter salutations and the first word in letter closings.**

SALUTATIONS:   Dear Ms. Goodwin,      Dearest Jane,
                          My dear Family,

CLOSINGS:   With love,      Sincerely,      Best wishes,

**EXERCISE: Using Capitals for Salutations and Closings in Letters.** On your paper rewrite each of the following letter parts, adding the missing capitals.

EXAMPLE:   dear uncle bill,

                   Dear Uncle Bill,

1. my dear kevin,          4. affectionately yours,
2. dearest friends,         5. yours truly,
3. dear gwen and brenda,

**DEVELOPING WRITING SKILLS: Using Capitals in Letters.** Write a short letter of one paragraph thanking a relative for a gift. Be sure to capitalize correctly throughout the letter.

# Skills Review and Writing Workshop

## Using Capitals

### CHECKING YOUR SKILLS

Rewrite the following paragraph, adding capital letters wherever they are needed.

(1) the classics society of hall high school plans a trip to italy and greece this winter. (2) mister dorado, the club advisor, will accompany the group. (3) on january 15, the group will leave from the john f. kennedy airport in new york. (4) they will arrive in athens the next day. (5) they will visit the sites of ancient sparta and thebes. (6) two days later, they will fly to milan. (7) later, in rome, those who wish can visit the colosseum. (8) next they will visit naples. (9) before leaving for home, they will attend a reception given by david orsini, president of the young travelers association. (10) on friday, they will arrive back in boston.

### USING MECHANICS SKILLS IN WRITING

#### Writing a News Release

Clubs and other groups often send news releases to their local newspapers. Follow the steps below to write a news release.

**Prewriting:** Choose a school or community event. List details about the event in order of importance and the names of the people that were involved in it. Note facts about the day, the time, and the place.

**Writing:** Begin with a summary of the event that tells *who*, *where*, *when*, and *how*. Then relate the details, beginning with the most important and ending with the least important.

**Revising:** Check your capitalization to make sure all proper names of people, places, and organizations begin with a capital letter. Check to be sure your facts are correct, and look for ways to improve your news release. After you have revised, proofread carefully.

# 20

# Using Abbreviations

*Abbreviations* are used to save time or space.

**To *abbreviate* means to shorten a word or phrase.**

Some abbreviations may be used in formal writing, such as essays and business letters. Others may be used only in informal writing, such as notes and lists.

## 20.1 Abbreviations of Titles of People

Titles may identify a person's social position, business, or profession. These titles are often abbreviated.

### Social Titles Before Names

The following rule applies to social titles.

**Abbreviations of social titles used before a proper name begin with a capital letter and end with a period. They can be used in any type of writing.**

The most common abbreviations of social titles are shown in the following examples.

SOCIAL TITLES:   Mr.     Mrs. or Mme. (Madame)

Messrs. (plural of Mr.)

Mmes. (plural of Mrs. and Mme.)

As you read the following sentences, notice that each abbreviation is followed by a proper name.

EXAMPLES:   The postman's name is Mr. Seymour Frank.

Mrs. Madison is their best salesperson.

NOTE ABOUT   *Miss* and the plural form *Misses* are social ti-
MISS AND *Ms.:*   tles used before names of single women. They
are not abbreviations and are not punctuated
with a period. The title *Ms.* can be used before
the name of a single or married woman. Although *Ms.* is not an abbreviation of another
word, it is followed by a period.

EXAMPLES:   Miss Clark is a friend of mine.

I talked briefly with Ms. Schmidt.

**EXERCISE A: Using Abbreviations of Social Titles Before Names.** Copy the following sentences adding the abbreviation of an appropriate social title or the titles *Miss* or *Ms.* before each name. Use at least four different titles.

EXAMPLE:   _____ Stephens is a very unusual neighbor.

Mr. Stephens is a very unusual neighbor.

1. No one was more reliable than _____ Solomon.
2. _____ Danforth and Simkins were proud of their company's good reputation.
3. She preferred to be called _____ Hawkins by her associates.
4. We asked _____ Haskin to explain.
5. Addressing the League of Women Voters were _____ Edith Fisher and Mary Hodges.

# Business and Professional Titles Before Names

Abbreviations of business and professional titles before names are used less often in formal writing.

**Abbreviations of other titles used before proper names also begin with a capital letter and end with a period. These abbreviations are used less often in formal writing.**

The following chart shows the abbreviations of the most common governmental, military, and professional titles.

| ABBREVIATIONS OF COMMON TITLES | | | | | |
|---|---|---|---|---|---|
| **Governmental** | | **Military** | | **Professional** | |
| Rep. | Representative | Pvt. | Private | Dr. | Doctor |
| Sen. | Senator | Sgt. | Sergeant | Atty. | Attorney |
| Gov. | Governor | Lt. | Lieutenant | Prof. | Professor |
| Treas. | Treasurer | Maj. | Major | Rev. | Reverend |
| Sec. | Secretary | Gen. | General | Fr. | Father |
| Pres. | President | Ens. | Ensign | Sr. | Sister |
| | | Adm. | Admiral | | |

These titles should usually be spelled out in formal writing, especially when only last names are used with them.

EXAMPLES:  Treasurer Montero presented the budget.

Lieutenant Johnson arrived this morning.

Professor Brown spoke to the class.

In certain cases, however, abbreviations of these titles may be used in formal writing. *Dr.*, like *Mr.* and *Mrs.*, may be used any time it accompanies a name. Common nonreligious titles may also be abbreviated if they are used with a first name or initials as well as a last name.

**292**

EXAMPLES:  Dr. Gordon has office hours this morning.

Sen. Bill Bradley of New Jersey voted in favor of the legislation.

**EXERCISE B: Using Abbreviations of Business and Professional Titles Before Names.** Copy the following sentences, using the abbreviated form of each of the titles.

EXAMPLE:  Private Jamie Peters hoped to become a sergeant.

Pvt. Jamie Peters hoped to become a sergeant.

1. Sergeant Chris Jackson saluted the officers.
2. Attorney Bruce Landon appeared in court.
3. The minutes of the last meeting were read by Secretary Caroline Nunez.
4. Ensign Barry Saunders has reported for duty.
5. The book was by Professor Kathleen Anderson.

## Titles After Names

Some abbreviations of social and professional titles appear after proper names.

**Abbreviations of titles after a name start with a capital letter and end with a period. They can be used in any type of writing.**

The following chart shows abbreviations of some common titles that are written after names.

| ABBREVIATIONS OF COMMON TITLES | |
|---|---|
| **Social** | **Professional** |
| Jr. Junior | D.D.S.  Doctor of Dental Surgery |
| Sr. Senior | M.D.   Doctor of Medicine |
| | Ph.D.  Doctor of Philosophy |
| | R.N.   Registered Nurse |

Notice in the following examples that when an abbreviation is written after a name, a comma is placed before and after the abbreviation. When the abbreviation is at the end of a sentence, only one comma is used.

EXAMPLES:   Mark Edwards, Sr., was elected.

I have an appointment with Elizabeth Green, D.D.S.

**EXERCISE C: Using Abbreviations of Titles After Names.** Copy the following sentences onto your paper, using the abbreviated form of each of the titles.

EXAMPLE:   My father is Robert Richardson, Senior.

My father is Robert Richardson, Sr.

1. The article was written by Sylvia Robinson, Doctor of Philosophy.
2. A. E. Randolph, Doctor of Medicine, recently opened an office in town.
3. Joseph Banks, Junior, practices the piano every day.
4. George Pawloski, Doctor of Dental Surgery, hired a new receptionist.
5. My cousin recommended E. L. Arnold, Registered Nurse.

**DEVELOPING WRITING SKILLS: Using Abbreviated Titles Correctly.** Write ten sentences of your own, each using the abbreviation of one of the titles described in the following items. Follow the rules for formal writing.

EXAMPLE:   A professor

Prof. A. L. Sawyer spoke to us about a special course.

1. A lawyer
2. A married woman
3. A governor
4. A doctor of philosophy
5. A medical doctor
6. A man
7. Two married women
8. A registered nurse
9. A senator
10. A secretary

# Abbreviations for Time and 20.2 Historical Dates

Abbreviations are also used for time and historical dates.

## Time

Abbreviations are often used to express time before noon and time after noon.

**For abbreviations of time before noon and after noon, either capital letters followed by periods or small letters followed by periods are acceptable. These abbreviations can be used in any type of writing.**

ABBREVIATIONS:   A.M. *or* a.m. (*ante meridiem*, before noon)

P.M. *or* p.m. (*post meridiem*, after noon)

These abbreviations should be used only with numerals.

WITH NUMERALS:   At exactly 9:15 A.M., the plane took off.

WITHOUT NUMERALS:   I will meet you at four o'clock in the afternoon.

**EXERCISE A: Using Abbreviations of Time.** From the words given in parentheses, choose the abbreviation or phrase that correctly expresses time in each of the following sentences and write it on your paper.

EXAMPLE:   They arrive promptly at nine (a.m., in the morning).

in the morning

1. At 4:30 (A.M., in the morning) the smoke detector awoke the sleeping family.
2. This turkey will be done at 1:30 (p.m., in the afternoon).
3. Every evening at precisely 9:00 (a.m., p.m.), Mr. Findley pours a cup of tea.

4. Report to your commanding officer before three o'clock (P.M., in the afternoon).

5. The cash register was unlocked at eight o'clock (a.m., in the morning).

## Dates

Another rule applies to abbreviations used for historical dates.

**Abbreviations for historical dates before and after the birth of Christ require capital letters followed by periods. They can be used in any type of writing.**

ABBREVIATIONS:   B.C. (before Christ)

A.D. (*anno Domini*, in the year of the Lord)

These abbreviations are generally used with numerals. B.C. must always follow the number. A.D. may be used either after or before the number.

EXAMPLES:   In 586 B.C. the Babylonians conquered Jerusalem for the second time.

Rome was almost completely destroyed by fire in 64 A.D.

A.D. 1066 marked the end of Saxon rule in England.

**EXERCISE B: Using Abbreviations of Historical Dates.** Copy the following sentences onto your paper, writing the abbreviated form for each historical date given in parentheses.

EXAMPLE:   Mary, Queen of Scots, was crowned in (1543 in the year of the Lord), the year after her birth.

Mary, Queen of Scots, was crowned in 1543 A.D., the year after her birth.

1. In (44 before Christ) Julius Caesar was assassinated.
2. St. Patrick arrived in Ireland in (432 in the year of the Lord).

**296**

3. Nefertiti was a ruler of Egypt from (1367–1350 before Christ).
4. King Edward III, who reigned from (1327–1377 in the year of the Lord), was one of England's best-liked monarchs.
5. In (451 in the year of the Lord) Gaul was invaded.

**DEVELOPING WRITING SKILLS: Using Abbreviations of Time and Dates.** Using the following information, write five sentences, each including an abbreviation of the indicated time or date.

EXAMPLE:    1588 in the year of the Lord (the Spanish Armada was defeated)

The Spanish Armada was defeated in 1588 A.D.

1. 1512 in the year of the Lord (Michelangelo finished painting the ceiling of the Sistine Chapel)
2. thirty minutes past two in the afternoon (a storm knocked out electric and telephone service)
3. about 2300 before Christ (the oldest known map was made)
4. six o'clock before noon (the alarm clock went off)
5. 1831 in the year of the Lord (Michael Faraday produced electricity)

# Geographical Abbreviations 20.3

Abbreviations of geographical terms are often used in informal writing, such as notes and lists. They are also used frequently in addressing envelopes.

**Abbreviations for geographical terms used before or after a proper noun begin with a capital letter and end with a period. They are seldom used in formal writing.**

The following chart shows some common geographical abbreviations.

## ABBREVIATIONS OF GEOGRAPHICAL TERMS

| Ave. | Avenue | Ft. | Fort | Prov. | Province |
|------|--------|-----|------|-------|----------|
| Bldg. | Building | Hwy. | Highway | Pt. | Point |
| Blk. | Block | Is. | Island | Rd. | Road |
| Blvd. | Boulevard | Mt. | Mountain | Rte. | Route |
| Co. | County | Natl. | National | Sq. | Square |
| Dist. | District | Pen. | Peninsula | St. | Street |
| Dr. | Drive | Pk. | Park, Peak | Terr. | Territory |

**Traditional abbreviations for states begin with a capital letter and end with a period. They are seldom used in formal writing.**

## TRADITIONAL ABBREVIATIONS FOR STATES

| Ala. | Alabama | Md. | Maryland | Ore. | Oregon |
|------|---------|-----|----------|------|--------|
| Alaska | Alaska | Mass. | Massachusetts | Pa. | Pennsylvania |
| Ariz. | Arizona | Mich. | Michigan | R.I. | Rhode Island |
| Ark. | Arkansas | Minn. | Minnesota | S.C. | South |
| Calif. | California | Miss. | Mississippi | | Carolina |
| Colo. | Colorado | Mo. | Missouri | S. Dak. | South |
| Conn. | Connecticut | Mont. | Montana | | Dakota |
| Del. | Delaware | Nebr. | Nebraska | Tenn. | Tennessee |
| Fla. | Florida | Nev. | Nevada | Tex. | Texas |
| Ga. | Georgia | N.H. | New | Utah | Utah |
| Hawaii | Hawaii | | Hampshire | Vt. | Vermont |
| Ida. | Idaho | N.J. | New Jersey | Va. | Virginia |
| Ill. | Illinois | N. Mex. | New Mexico | Wash. | Washington |
| Ind. | Indiana | N.Y. | New York | W. Va. | West |
| Iowa | Iowa | N.C. | North | | Virginia |
| Kans. | Kansas | | Carolina | Wis. | Wisconsin |
| Ky. | Kentucky | N. Dak. | North Dakota | Wyo. | Wyoming |
| La. | Louisiana | O. | Ohio | | |
| Me. | Maine | Okla. | Oklahoma | | |

In 1963 the Postal Service introduced a new set of abbreviations.

**The official Postal Service abbreviations for states require capital letters with no periods. They are generally not used in formal writing.**

Use the Postal Service abbreviations when you address envelopes.

## OFFICIAL POSTAL SERVICE ABBREVIATIONS

| | | | | | |
|---|---|---|---|---|---|
| AL | Alabama | MD | Maryland | OR | Oregon |
| AK | Alaska | MA | Massachusetts | PA | Pennsylvania |
| AZ | Arizona | MI | Michigan | RI | Rhode Island |
| AR | Arkansas | MN | Minnesota | SC | South |
| CA | California | MS | Mississippi | | Carolina |
| CO | Colorado | MO | Missouri | SD | South |
| CT | Connecticut | MT | Montana | | Dakota |
| DE | Delaware | NE | Nebraska | TN | Tennessee |
| FL | Florida | NV | Nevada | TX | Texas |
| GA | Georgia | NH | New | UT | Utah |
| HI | Hawaii | | Hampshire | VT | Vermont |
| ID | Idaho | NJ | New Jersey | VA | Virginia |
| IL | Illinois | NM | New Mexico | WA | Washington |
| IN | Indiana | NY | New York | WV | West |
| IA | Iowa | NC | North | | Virginia |
| KS | Kansas | | Carolina | WI | Wisconsin |
| KY | Kentucky | ND | North Dakota | WY | Wyoming |
| LA | Louisiana | OH | Ohio | | |
| ME | Maine | OK | Oklahoma | | |

NOTE ABOUT D.C.: The traditional abbreviation for the District of Columbia is D.C.; the Postal Service abbreviation is DC. Use the traditional abbreviation in formal writing whenever it follows the word *Washington*.

EXAMPLE:   We visited Washington, D.C., on our class trip.

**EXERCISE: Using Geographical Abbreviations.** Write the traditional abbreviation for each geograhical term given in parentheses in each of the sentences.

EXAMPLE:   The United States purchased the (Louisiana) (Territory) in 1803.

La.     Terr.

1. The White House is located at 1600 Pennsylvania (Avenue), Washington, (District of Columbia).
2. Go to the corner of Walnut (Street) and Bergen (Boulevard).
3. We visited Monhegan (Island) off the coast of (Maine).
4. My brother received his infantry training at (Fort) Benning, (Georgia).
5. We drove through Calgary, Alberta (Province), on the Trans-Canada (Highway).

**DEVELOPING WRITING SKILLS: Understanding Geographical Abbreviations.** Write five sentences, each using the word that one of the following abbreviations stands for.

EXAMPLE:   Is.

Long Island is part of the state of New York.

1. Pk.     2. Mt.     3. Fla.     4. TX     5. Rd.

# 20.4 Abbreviations of Measurements

Abbreviations of traditional and metric measurements may also be useful in your writing.

## Traditional Measurements

Abbreviations of traditional measurements are written according to the following rule.

**With traditional measurements use small letters and periods to form the abbreviations. These abbreviations are not used in formal writing except with numerals.**

The chart shows examples of traditional abbreviations. The abbreviation of *Fahrenheit* is an exception. A capital *F* is used. Notice that the plural forms are the same as the singular.

| TRADITIONAL MEASUREMENTS | | | | | |
|---|---|---|---|---|---|
| in. | inch(es) | tsp. | teaspoon(s) | pt. | pint(s) |
| ft. | foot; feet | tbsp. | tablespoon(s) | qt. | quart(s) |
| yd. | yard(s) | oz. | ounce(s) | gal. | gallon(s) |
| mi. | mile(s) | lb. | pound(s) | F. | Fahrenheit |

The following sentences show how the rule is applied.

WITHOUT NUMERALS:   My temperature was one hundred degrees Fahrenheit.

WITH NUMERALS:   My temperature was 100° F.

**EXERCISE A: Abbreviating Traditional Measurements.** Write the abbreviation for each of the following.

EXAMPLE:   ten yards

        10 yd.

1. four pints
2. six miles
3. one teaspoon
4. zero degrees Fahrenheit
5. three feet
6. twelve inches
7. two tablespoons
8. one pound
9. five gallons
10. seven ounces

## Metric Measurements

The abbreviations of metric measurements follow a different rule.

**With metric measurements use small letters and no periods to form the abbreviations. These abbreviations are not used in formal writing except with numerals.**

The abbreviations of *liter* and *Celsius* are exceptions to the rule. They are both written with capital letters.

| METRIC MEASUREMENTS | | |
|---|---|---|
| g   gram(s) | mm   millimeter(s) | L  liter |
| kg  kilogram(s) | cm   centimeter(s) | C  Celsius |
|  | m    meter(s) |  |
|  | km   kilometer(s) |  |

WITHOUT NUMERALS:   We rode our bicycles sixteen kilometers.

WITH NUMERALS:   We rode our bicycles 16 km.

**EXERCISE B: Abbreviating Metric Measurements.** Write the abbreviation for each of the following.

EXAMPLE:   one hundred centimeters

       100 cm

1. one liter
2. six grams
3. four liters
4. one kilogram
5. five millimeters
6. twenty degrees Celsius
7. one centimeter
8. eight meters
9. one kilometer
10. twenty kilometers

**DEVELOPING WRITING SKILLS: Using Abbreviations of Measurements.** On your paper write five sentences, each using the abbreviation of one of the following items.

EXAMPLE:   three tablespoons

      The recipe calls for 3 tbsp. of vinegar.

1. six miles
2. two liters
3. one gallon
4. three grams
5. four feet

# Skills Review and Writing Workshop

## Using Abbreviations

### CHECKING YOUR SKILLS

Rewrite the following paragraph, correcting each underlined term that is inappropriate in formal writing. If the term is appropriate, simply recopy it.

(1) Mr. and Mrs. R. Rice are inviting friends to a costume party on <u>Fri</u>. (2) It will begin at <u>7:00 p.m.</u> (3) Its theme will be "<u>Calif</u>. Here I Come." (4) Among the honored guests will be <u>Gov</u>. Leeds. (5) The party, according to Mr. Rice, will also honor <u>Ms</u>. Ko. (6) Paul Grout will take photos with his 35 <u>mm</u> camera. (7) Linda Sooney will sing while everyone consumes <u>gal</u>. of ice cream. (8) Jack Barnes will again describe his trip to <u>Wyo</u>. (9) The party is expected to end at one a.m. in the morning. (10) <u>Drs</u>. are asked to come without costume so they can be located quickly in an emergency.

### USING MECHANICS SKILLS IN WRITING
### Writing a Social Note

Abbreviations are useful to authors in informal writing. However, many abbreviations are out of place in more formal writing. Follow the steps below to write a polite social note.

**Prewriting:** Think of the purpose of your social note. Then write down the basic information.

**Writing:** Write directly from your notes. Underline any term that seems too formal. If that term is a title or relates to time, you can *usually* use an abbreviation. Otherwise, it is safer to use the fully spelled out form.

**Revising:** First look at your abbreviations. Eliminate all that seem awkward. Then read the entire note for accuracy. After you have revised, proofread carefully.

# Chapter 21

# Using Punctuation Marks

*Punctuation marks* tell readers to pause, to stop, or to read in a questioning or surprised tone. Punctuation marks also connect certain ideas with other ideas or set ideas apart.

**Punctuation is an accepted set of symbols used to give specific directions to the reader.**

The most common punctuation marks follow.

| COMMON PUNCTUATION MARKS | | | | | |
|---|---|---|---|---|---|
| period | . | comma | , | quotation marks | " " |
| question mark | ? | semicolon | ; | hyphen | - |
| exclamation mark | ! | colon | : | apostrophe | ' |

Learning to use punctuation marks correctly will help you improve your writing.

## 21.1 End Marks

Sentences, words, and phrases may all be concluded with one of the three types of *end marks*.

304

There are three end marks: the period (.), the question mark (?), and the exclamation mark (!). They usually indicate the end of a sentence.

## Uses of the Period

The end mark used most often is the *period.*

**Use a period to end a declarative sentence— that is, to end a statement of fact or opinion.**

STATEMENT OF FACT:   Woody Allen is a movie star.

STATEMENT OF OPINION:   I have always thought he was a talented actor.

In addition to punctuating declarative sentences, a period is also used to punctuate many imperative sentences.

**Use a period to end an imperative sentence— that is, to end a direction or command.**

DIRECTION:   First place the right end of the shoestring over the left.

COMMAND:   Listen carefully to the directions given by the policeman.

Finally, a period is used after most abbreviations.

**Use a period to end most abbreviations.**

As the preceding rule indicates, most abbreviations require the use of the period, although there are some exceptions. The examples below show some of the abbreviations that do require periods.

INITIALS:   R. F. Nordstrom

TITLES:   Mr.   Mrs.   Dr.   Sgt.   Jr.

PLACE NAMES:   Ave.   Rte.   Tex.   Fla.

Notice that when an abbreviation is located at the very end of a sentence, only one period is required.

EXAMPLE:   Be sure to include Jack Jenkins, Jr.

**EXERCISE A: Using the Period.** The following sentences do not have periods. Copy each of the sentences onto your paper, adding the missing periods.

EXAMPLE:   Mrs M L Richards arranged the benefit

Mrs. M. L. Richards arranged the benefit.

1. Smooth the wet plaster with your hands
2. Please ask Donald Palmer, Jr, for his opinion
3. Deliver this message to Mrs Allen quickly
4. Col J D Packard, a friend of ours, is stationed in California
5. Dr Jefferson's new assistant is Lee Tomas, R N

## Uses of the Question Mark

The *question mark* is most commonly used to end an interrogative sentence, a sentence that asks a question requiring an answer.

**Use a question mark to end an interrogative sentence—that is, to end a direct question.**

INTERROGATIVE SENTENCES:   Who turned in a paper with no name on it?

How much money is in our savings account?

Sometimes a single word or a phrase is used to ask a question. In this situation the word or phrase is punctuated with a question mark just as a complete sentence would be.

**Use a question mark to end an incomplete question in which the rest of the question is understood.**

EXAMPLES:   You said that the airplane landed. Where?

She wants to complete the assignment. But how?

**306**

**EXERCISE B: Using the Question Mark.** Each of the following items is missing one or more question marks. Copy each item, adding the missing question marks.

EXAMPLE:   Which desk is yours

Which desk is yours?

1. Where should I write my signature
2. Who called on the telephone When
3. How many people are needed to sign this petition
4. Was this dog ever taught to stay off the furniture
5. Why did these customers complain About what

## Uses of the Exclamation Mark

*Exclamation marks* are used to punctuate sentences that show strong feelings.

**Use an exclamation mark to end an exclamatory sentence—that is, to end a statement showing strong emotion.**

EXAMPLE:   You surprised me!

**Use an exclamation mark after an imperative sentence if the command is urgent and forceful.**

EXAMPLE:   Move away from the fire!

**Use an exclamation mark after an interjection expressing strong emotion.**

EXAMPLE:   Goodness! I forgot to bring my homework.

Too many exclamation marks can make your writing too emotional. Be sure to use them sparingly.

**EXERCISE C: Using the Exclamation Mark.** Each of the following items is missing one or more exclamation marks. Copy each item, adding the missing exclamation marks.

EXAMPLE: Stop Don't forget your money

Stop! Don't forget your money!

1. Hooray We finally won a game
2. Don't light a match
3. You're late again
4. Oh I have never been so furious at anyone else in my life
5. Say That was an unexpected move
6. Take your feet off the table now
7. What an amazing act of courage that was
8. Hey I remember the answer now
9. Wait for me
10. Quick Grab my hand

**DEVELOPING WRITING SKILLS: Using End Marks Correctly in Sentences.** On your paper write ten sentences of your own that meet the following requirements. Be sure to use the correct end mark after each sentence and after any other word or phrase within your sentences that requires one.

EXAMPLE: A one-word imperative sentence

Hurry!

1. An urgent command
2. A statement of opinion containing the abbreviation of a person's social title
3. A direct question
4. A mild command
5. An exclamatory sentence
6. A statement of opinion
7. An interjection expressing strong emotion followed by a statement of fact
8. A declarative sentence followed by an incomplete question
9. An interrogative sentence followed by an incomplete question
10. An imperative sentence containing a person's initials

# Commas That Separate 21.2 Basic Elements

While an end mark signals a full stop, a *comma* signals a brief pause. It may be used to *separate* basic elements in a sentence, or it may be used to set off elements added to a sentence.

Many people use more commas than are necessary, while others use fewer than they should. To avoid the overuse or underuse of commas, include a comma in your writing only when you know that a specific rule applies.

This section presents rules for commas that are used to *separate* basic elements of a sentence. Section 21.3 will help you use commas to set off added elements correctly.

## Commas with Compound Sentences

A compound sentence consists of two or more independent clauses—that is, groups of words that express complete thoughts—joined by one of the coordinating conjunctions *(and, but, for, nor, or, so,* and *yet).*

**Use a comma before the conjunction to separate two independent clauses in a compound sentence.**

Notice that each of the following sentences is compound because it is made up of more than one complete thought. In the first sentence, a comma and the conjunction *but* separate the independent clauses. In the second a comma and the conjunction *and* separate the independent clauses.

COMPOUND SENTENCES:   The coat was not practical, but I could not resist buying it.

Summer camp was almost over, and everyone felt somewhat sad about leaving each other.

**309**

Remember to use a comma before a conjunction only when there are complete thoughts on *both sides* of the conjunction. Do not use a comma when there is just a word, phrase, or subordinate clause on either side of the conjunction.

WORDS:   A *rug* or *mat* will help keep the floor of the cabin clean.

PHRASES:   Light was reflected *from the road* and *off the car's hood.*

SUBORDINATE CLAUSES:   Choose someone *who has experience* but *who can also follow directions.*

In some compound sentences, the independent clauses are very brief, and the meaning is clear. When this occurs, the comma before the conjunction may be omitted.

EXAMPLE:   Jonathan listened carefully but he heard nothing.

**EXERCISE A: Using Commas with Compound Sentences.** A comma has been left out of each of the following sentences. On your paper write the word before the comma, the comma, and the conjunction following the comma.

EXAMPLE:   The article was interesting but it did not have the information I needed.

interesting, but

1. I was foolish to have trusted you but I won't make the same mistake again.
2. Alexandra folded the clean laundry and I placed it in the basket.
3. The victims of the hurricane were stunned for they had lost everything.
4. There was no furniture in the tiny cabin nor was there any source of light.
5. He used the back of a spoon to make peaks in the frosting and she pressed grated coconut along the top and sides.

**310**

6. Jill missed the flight so we don't expect her to arrive tonight.
7. You can use this free ticket for yourself or you can give it to a friend.
8. No one answered the telephone and it finally stopped ringing.
9. Becky offered a reward for the return of her billfold but not a single person responded to her advertisement in the evening paper.
10. We expected the weather to turn colder yet the day was warm and sunny.

## Commas Between Items in a Series

When three or more similar items appear in a series, commas are needed to separate them.

**Use commas to separate three or more words, phrases, or clauses in a series.**

Notice in the following examples that the number of items in the series is one more than the number of commas needed. For example, in the first sentence, there are *three* items in the series, separated by *two* commas.

SERIES OF WORDS:   The beverages included *tomato juice, ginger ale,* and *iced tea.*

SERIES OF PHRASES:   Ceramic vases were placed *on the table, on the mantel,* and *on the window sill.*

SERIES OF CLAUSES:   We could not understand *why the accident happened, who caused it,* or *how everyone escaped injury.*

One exception to the rule for using commas in a series occurs when each item is separated from the others by a conjunction.

EXAMPLE:   My sister collects stamps and coins and bottle caps.

**311**

**EXERCISE B: Using Commas with Items in a Series.**
Copy the sentences, adding commas where they are needed.

EXAMPLE: Her favorite authors were Tolkien Asimov and Cather.

    Her favorite authors were Tolkien, Asimov, and Cather.

1. For exercise Robert lifted weights rode a bicycle and did push-ups.
2. Ann was scheduled to take English algebra earth science Spanish and gym.
3. Our small garden plot produced tomatoes lettuce radishes and zucchini.
4. Sharon swept the sidewalk raked the leaves and painted the mailbox.
5. After the movie I still didn't understand why the crime was committed who did it or whether the criminals were caught.
6. To get there you must walk past the large oak tree over the grassy knoll and along the gravel driveway.
7. To work here you must have a white uniform comfortable shoes a black apron and a white cap.
8. Do you want to bring pretzels salad or soda to the picnic?
9. The best time to go fishing is before dawn just at dawn or several hours before dusk.
10. We had to decide whom we should invite where we would have the reception and what food we would serve.

## Commas Between Adjectives

Sometimes adjectives need to be separated by commas.

### Use commas to separate adjectives of *equal rank.*

Two methods can be used to help decide whether two or more adjectives are of equal rank. First, if the word *and* can be placed between the adjectives without changing the meaning of the sentence, then the adjectives are of equal rank. Second, if the order of the adjectives can be changed, then they are equal.

Study the following examples. Then try both methods for deciding whether the adjectives are of equal rank.

EXAMPLES:  You have made a *simple, polite* request.

Disorganized, illogical, messy* papers must be rewritten.

If you tried both methods on these examples, you learned that the adjectives are of equal rank. Therefore, commas are needed to separate them. In other sentences, however, placing an *and* between the adjectives or changing their order would alter the meaning of the sentence.

**Do not use commas to separate adjectives that must stay in a specific order.**

Apply the two methods for determining whether the adjectives are of equal rank to the following examples.

EXAMPLES:  A *few hardy* plants were unaffected by the severe frost.

Some eager* birds woke me this morning with their chirping.

As you can see, the italicized adjectives in the examples cannot be separated by *and,* and their order cannot be changed without destroying the meaning of the sentences. Therefore, no commas should be added.

NOTE ABOUT COMMAS WITH ADJECTIVES: A comma should never be used to separate the last adjective in a series from the noun it modifies.

INCORRECT:  The frisky, young, dog ran to greet us.

CORRECT:  The frisky, young dog ran to greet us.

**313**

**EXERCISE C: Using Commas Between Adjectives.** In each of the following sentences, two or more adjectives have been underlined. Copy the adjectives onto your paper, adding commas only in those places where they are needed.

EXAMPLE:   <u>Many</u> <u>old</u> mansions have been made into apartment houses.

Many old

1. This <u>quiet</u> <u>obedient</u> dog is a pleasure to have around.
2. <u>Several</u> <u>shiny</u> spoons were placed to the right of each knife.
3. Mowing the lawn on such a <u>hazy</u> <u>hot</u> <u>humid</u> day was no fun.
4. We heard <u>four</u> <u>sharp</u> <u>trumpet</u> blasts signal the entrance of the royal visitors.
5. The <u>shabby</u> <u>frayed</u> coat hung limply from the child's slender body.

**DEVELOPING WRITING SKILLS: Using Commas That Separate Basic Elements in Your Writing.** Follow the directions below to write five sentences of your own. Be sure to use commas only where they are needed to separate basic elements in your sentences.

EXAMPLE:   Write a compound sentence using the conjunction *and.*

She pitched a fast ball, and the batter swung and missed.

1. Write a sentence containing a series of three prepositional phrases.
2. Write a sentence containing two adjectives of equal rank.
3. Write a sentence containing a series of three nouns.
4. Write a sentence containing two adjectives that must remain in a specific order.
5. Write a compound sentence using the conjunction *but* to join the independent clauses.

# Commas That Set Off 21.3 Added Elements

Commas are used not only to separate similar kinds of words and groups of words but also to *set off*—that is, set apart—certain parts of a sentence from the rest.

As you read the rules for commas used to set off added elements, remember that commas should be used in your writing only when a specific rule applies.

## Commas After Introductory Material

Sometimes a sentence begins with introductory material. Generally, the extra word or words are set off from the rest of the sentence by a comma.

**Use a comma after an introductory word, phrase, or clause.**

The following examples illustrate three types of introductory material.

| KINDS OF INTRODUCTORY MATERIAL | |
|---|---|
| **Introductory Words** | *Well,* I need a minute to decide. |
| | *Tom,* where are you? |
| | *Please,* put some clams in the chowder. |
| **Introductory Phrases** | *Within the cozy nest,* the baby rabbits slept soundly. |
| | *Frightened by the thunder,* the poodle ran under the bed. |
| | *To qualify for this job,* a person must earn no more than the minimum wage. |
| **Introductory Clauses** | *If Teresa asks for me,* tell her I will return. |
| | *Where there is good food and music,* there you will find Albert. |

When a prepositional phrase of only two or three words begins a sentence, a comma is generally not needed to set the phrase off.

EXAMPLE:    *During the night* we heard a loud racket.

### EXERCISE A: Using Commas with Introductory Material.
Each of the following sentences needs a comma to set off introductory material. On your paper write the introductory material, the comma, and the word following the comma.

EXAMPLE:    On our flight to Utah we ate a delicious lunch.

On our flight to Utah, we ate a delicious lunch.

1. Oh how can I win against such impossible odds?
2. Before three o'clock that afternoon a light rainfall began.
3. When the children saw the rainbow they began to talk excitedly of a pot of gold.
4. Surprised Oliver gazed in amazement at the people gathered to congratulate him.
5. Repaired the bicycle will last for several years.
6. Goodness no one could lift this rock without help.
7. To win a prize a person must throw all the rings over the peg.
8. Until the first of the year I will be living at the same address.
9. For many days and nights the small craft was lost at sea.
10. Even though Lynn had studied for the exam she thought the questions were difficult.

## Commas with Parenthetical Expressions

A *parenthetical expression* is a word or phrase that is not essential to the meaning of the sentence. These words or phrases generally add extra information to the basic sentence.

**316**

### Use commas to set off parenthetical expressions.

Parenthetical expressions are sometimes written at the beginning of a sentence as introductory material. These expressions may also be written in the middle of or at the end of a sentence. A parenthetical expression in the middle of a sentence needs a comma before it and a comma after it to set it off. If it is written at the end of the sentence, only one comma is needed.

Examples of parenthetical expressions are shown below.

| KINDS OF PARENTHETICAL EXPRESSIONS | |
|---|---|
| **Names of People Being Addressed** | Watch, *Frank*, while I show you how to shift the tractor into third gear.<br>Stop whispering, *Pamela and Dan.* |
| **Certain Adverbs** | You are, *therefore*, the person I would choose.<br>Your answer is incorrect, *however.* |
| **Common Expressions** | This tax benefit, *on the other hand*, will help small businesses.<br>His singing is off-key, *I believe.* |

### EXERCISE B: Using Commas with Parenthetical Expressions.

Copy each of the following sentences, adding commas as needed to set off the parenthetical expressions.

EXAMPLE:   Their garden however was untouched by the storm.

Their garden, however, was untouched by the storm.

1. Wait Ron and Hugh until the elevator doors open.
2. We nevertheless appreciated your help during the campaign.
3. Travel in this helium-filled balloon is not without hazards of course.

4. Write a one-page essay on the meaning of liberty Lois.
5. Maxine did succeed therefore in raising her grade.
6. Don't feed peanuts to the giraffe Elaine.
7. The truth in fact is just the opposite.
8. The praying mantis on the other hand kills many harmful insects.
9. Please Vic tell me which fork is used for salad.
10. This table I think should be placed near the door.

## Commas with Nonessential Expressions

Sometimes, it is difficult to decide when to set off material with commas. Knowing whether a word, phrase, or clause is *essential* or *nonessential* to the meaning of a sentence helps.

Essential material cannot be left out without changing the meaning of the sentence. Nonessential material, on the other hand, can be left out.

Do not set off essential material with commas. You should, however, use commas to set off nonessential material.

**Use commas to set off nonessential expressions.**

The following chart shows examples of essential and nonessential material. Notice that the number of commas depends on the position of the nonessential material. Notice also that each nonessential expression can be left out without changing the meaning of the sentence.

| APPOSITIVES AND APPOSITIVE PHRASES | |
|---|---|
| **Essential** | The American author *Louisa May Alcott* wrote *Little Women.* |
| **Nonessential** | Louisa May Alcott**,** *an American author***,** wrote *Little Women.* |
| | *Little Women* was written by Louisa May Alcott**,** *an American author.* |

| PARTICIPIAL PHRASES | |
|---|---|
| Essential | The puppy *barking frantically* is Asta. |
| Nonessential | Asta, *barking frantically*, chased a rabbit. |
| | A rabbit was chased by Asta, *barking frantically.* |
| **ADJECTIVE CLAUSES** | |
| Essential | The guest *who arrived late* missed dinner. |
| Nonessential | Bill, *who arrived late*, missed dinner. |
| | Dinner was missed by Bill, *who arrived late.* |

**EXERCISE C: Using Commas with Nonessential Expressions.** Read each of the following sentences carefully to determine whether the underlined expression is essential or nonessential. If the material is essential, write *E*. If it is nonessential, copy the sentence onto your paper, adding a comma or commas as needed.

EXAMPLE: Lee Taylor who lives in Miami is visiting us.

Lee Taylor, who lives in Miami, is visiting us.

1. The fan cheering loudest is my mother.
2. I have invited the Gordon brothers who live next door.
3. Lauren Edwards my cousin is visiting me.
4. The cousin who has been visiting me is going home.
5. I enjoyed reading the mystery stories written by Agatha Christie.
6. Did you see the boy running down the street?
7. Edna St. Vincent Millay the well-known poet wrote "Renascence" when she was only nineteen.
8. The Sierra Club was founded in 1892 by the explorer, naturalist, and writer John Muir.
9. In 1890 Congress influenced by John Muir established the first national parks in the United States.

10. In 1908 Muir Woods National Monument <u>a redwood forest</u> <u>near San Francisco</u> was named in his honor.

**DEVELOPING WRITING SKILLS: Using Commas to Set Off Added Elements.** On your paper, write five sentences of your own. Include in each of your sentences one of the following items. Use commas where they are needed to set off added elements.

EXAMPLE:   An introductory phrase

   During the last week of October, it was announced that we had won the contest.

1. An introductory clause
2. A common expression as a parenthetical expression
3. A nonessential adjective clause
4. A person's name used in direct address
5. A nonessential appositive

# 21.4 Special Uses of the Comma

Commas are also used to set off dates, geographical names, and other special material.

## Commas with Dates and Geographical Names

Commas are used to separate the different parts of some dates and geographical names. The following rule applies to dates consisting of several parts.

**When a date is made up of two or more parts, use a comma after each item except in the case of a month followed by a day.**

Notice in the following examples that commas are not used to set off a month followed by a numeral standing for a day.

Commas are used, however, to set off a day of the week followed by a month.

EXAMPLES:  On July 12, 1939, Aunt Rachel arrived in this country with just a few possessions.

Tuesday, March 18, was carefully circled on his calendar.

When a date contains only a month and a year, you can either use a comma to set them apart or not.

EXAMPLES:  I will graduate in June, 1987.

I will graduate in June 1987.

A similar rule covers geographical names.

**When a geographical name is made up of two or more parts, use a comma after each item.**

EXAMPLES:  They lived in Marietta, Georgia, for several years.

My friend Pedro was born in El Salto, Durango, Mexico.

**EXERCISE A: Using Commas with Dates and Geographical Names.** Copy each of the following sentences onto your paper, adding commas where they are needed.

EXAMPLE:  Their destination was Austin Texas.

Their destination was Austin, Texas.

1. We will be visiting Annapolis Maryland on May 20.
2. On July 20 1969 astronauts landed on the moon for the first time.
3. Anna expects her grandparents to arrive Friday April 3.
4. After traveling to Bryce Canyon Utah Karen drove to Canyonlands National Park Utah where she took pictures of the sandstone formations.
5. On October 17 1781 General Cornwallis surrendered in Yorktown Virginia.

**321**

## Other Uses of the Comma

Commas are also used in other situations. These situations include addresses, letter salutations and closings, numbers, and quotations. The following rule governs the use of commas in addresses.

**Use a comma after each item in an address made up of two or more parts.**

In the following example, commas are needed after the name, street, and city. Notice, however, that no comma separates the state from the ZIP code. Instead of using a comma, simply leave some extra space between the state and the ZIP code.

EXAMPLE:   She is corresponding with her friend Arlene Black-
           well, 32 Birdsong Avenue, Falmouth, Massa-
           chusetts  02540.

Notice, however, that when the same address is written on an envelope, most of the commas are eliminated.

EXAMPLE:   Arlene Blackwell
           32 Birdsong Avenue
           Falmouth, Massachusetts   02540

The next rule covers the use of commas in salutations and closings in letters.

**Use a comma after the salutation in a personal letter and after the closing in all letters.**

SALUTATIONS:   Dear Jim,      My dear Beth,

CLOSINGS:   With affection,      Sincerely,

Using commas according to the following rule makes it easier to read large numbers.

**With numbers of more than three digits, use a comma after every third digit, counting from the right.**

**322**

EXAMPLES:  2,532 bricks

a population of 1,860,421

82,471,908 grains of sand

NOTE ABOUT COMMAS WITH NUMBERS: No commas should be used with ZIP codes, telephone numbers, page numbers, or serial numbers.

ZIP CODE:  14878

TELEPHONE NUMBER:  (607) 555-1328

PAGE NUMBER:  on page 1817

SERIAL NUMBER:  402 36 4113

A final use of the comma is to show where a direct quotation begins and ends.

**Use commas to set off a direct quotation from the rest of a sentence.**

The placement of the commas depends upon the "he said/ she said" part of the sentence. As you study the following examples, notice the correct placement of the commas. (See Section 21.7 for more information about punctuating quotations.)

EXAMPLES:  Gordon murmured with a yawn, "This is a dull movie."

"I thought," Lydia said, "that you liked horror movies."

"This is the third time I've seen this one," Gordon replied.

**EXERCISE B: Using Commas in Other Situations.** Commas have been left out of the following items. Copy each item onto your paper, adding commas where they are needed.

EXAMPLE:  "My sister is studying to be a chemist" he said.

"My sister is studying to be a chemist," he said.

1. Beth answered dreamily "What was the question?"
2. My dear Jason        Affectionately
                           Susan
3. She said "Our new telephone number is (312) 555-0476."
4. "Coal is just one of many sources of energy" responded Chris.
5. This huge igloo is made of 3500 blocks of ice.
6. He told them "The serial number is 103 22 411."
7. Address the letter to Diane Freemont 104 Fairview Drive Richmond Virginia 23227.
8. The teacher said "You will find it on page 1324."
9. "I am eager" said Nan "to meet the new exchange student."
10. Mr. Frederick Clifford
    1490 Apple Orchard Street
    Covington Kentucky 41011

**DEVELOPING WRITING SKILLS: Using Commas in Special Situations.** Write five sentences of your own, each including one of the following items. Use commas where they are needed to set off material.

EXAMPLE:    A page number in a book

                The information you need is on page 1142.

1. The name of a city and a state
2. A direct quotation
3. The number 15423672
4. A date consisting of a month, day, and a year
5. An address consisting of a name, street, town or city, state, and ZIP code

# 21.5 The Semicolon

The *semicolon* looks like a period over a comma (;). In use the semicolon signals a less final pause than a period but a stronger separation than a comma.

Semicolons are used to join complete ideas within sentences and to avoid confusion in sentences already containing several commas.

## Semicolons Used to Join Independent Clauses

The following rule governs the use of semicolons with independent clauses.

**Use a semicolon to join independent clauses that are not already joined by the conjunctions *and, or, nor, for, but, so* or *yet.***

Each of the following examples shows an independent clause joined by a comma and a conjunction. Notice that no semicolons are used.

CLAUSES WITH COMMA:   Grate a small amount of cheese over the spaghetti, *but* don't smother it.

A severe snowstorm struck unexpectedly, *and* as a result, high drifts blocked many roads.

Notice, however, that when the comma and the conjunction are omitted from the sentence, a semicolon must be used in place of them.

CLAUSES WITH SEMICOLON:   Grate a small amount of cheese over the spaghetti; don't smother it.

A severe snowstorm struck unexpectedly; as a result, high drifts blocked many roads.

A semicolon should only be used when there is a close relationship between the two independent clauses. If the two clauses are not very closely related, they should be written as separate sentences with a period or other end mark to separate them.

INCORRECT: The uses of plastic are almost countless; aluminum is obtained from bauxite.

CORRECT: The uses of plastic are almost countless. Aluminum is obtained from bauxite.

**EXERCISE A: Using Semicolons to Join Independent Clauses.** Semicolons have been left out of the following sentences. Read each sentence and decide where a semicolon is required. On your paper write the word before each semicolon, the semicolon, and the word that follows it.

EXAMPLE: Becky is fascinated by sharks however, she has not yet met one close up.

sharks; however

1. Some cheeses are made from cow's milk others are made from goat's milk.
2. They decided not to go shopping instead, they went walking in the park.
3. This glass lens is concave the other is convex.
4. Ten goldfish swam in the pond their scales glinted in the sun.
5. This home used to be a one-room schoolhouse it was built over a century ago.

## Semicolons Used to Avoid Confusion

Sometimes, to avoid confusion, semicolons are used to separate items in a series.

**Consider the use of a semicolon to avoid confusion when items in a series already contain commas.**

When the items in a series already contain several commas, semicolons can be used to make a sentence easier to read. Semicolons are placed at the end of all but the last *complete* item in the series.

**326**

EXAMPLES:    The patient's room was brightened by many get-well cards, sent by friends and relatives; several bouquets of fresh flowers, arranged on tables; and colorful circus posters, tacked to the walls.

                The fans, cheering loudly; the band, playing a rousing march; and the cheerleaders, turning cartwheels, helped inspire the team to play well.

## EXERCISE B: Using Semicolons to Avoid Confusion.

Copy each sentence below, adding semicolons where they should be used.

EXAMPLE:    They received cards from Honolulu, Hawaii Phoenix, Arizona and Seattle, Washington.

                They received cards from Honolulu, Hawaii; Phoenix, Arizona; and Seattle, Washington.

1. We were served onion soup, topped with melted cheese homemade rye bread, covered with butter and fruit salad, made with six different kinds of fresh fruit.
2. The little girl was wearing a yellow raincoat, which was made of shiny vinyl a matching hat, which was tied neatly under her chin and red boots, which reached to her knees.
3. In less than a year, William had expanded the family to include a large woolly dog with a huge appetite two skinny, stray cats with unfriendly dispositions and a pair of cooing, fluttering pigeons.
4. The music was performed by Fred, who played the flute Samantha, who played the clarinet and Ella, who played the saxophone.
5. Richard, my cousin Donna, the girl next door and Liz, my best friend, went to the concert with me.

## DEVELOPING WRITING SKILLS: Using Semicolons in Your Own Writing.

Write two different sentences for each of the following items.

1. Use a semicolon to join two closely related, independent clauses.
2. Use a semicolon to separate a series of items already containing several commas.

# 21.6 The Colon

The *colon* looks like two periods, one above the other (:). This section explains how the colon can be used to introduce lists of items and in certain other special situations.

## The Colon as an Introductory Device

One major use of the colon is to introduce a list that follows an independent clause.

**Use a colon before a list of items following an independent clause.**

In the following example, the colon directs the reader's attention to the list directly following it. The words before the colon make up an independent clause because they express a complete idea.

EXAMPLE: Ann's doll collection included many different items: a cornhusk doll from Idaho, a dried-apple doll from Maine, a bride doll from Portugal, and a ballerina doll from the Soviet Union.

It is important to keep in mind that a colon should never be used directly after a verb or a preposition. Read the following three sentences carefully. The first sentence is incorrect because a colon directly follows the verb *were*. The second sentence is incorrect because the colon follows the preposition *about*. The third sentence is correct because the colon now follows a complete clause. Although the words *the following* hint that there is more to come, the clause is still complete.

INCORRECT:  Some of the features in the magazine were: an article on gardening, a column about antiques, and an essay on American humor.

               Some of the features in the magazine were about: gardening, antiques, and American humor.

CORRECT:   Some of the features in the magazine were the following: an article on gardening, a column about antiques, and an essay on American humor.

## EXERCISE A: Using Colons to Introduce Lists of Items.

Colons have been left out of each of the following sentences. On your paper write the word before the colon, the colon, and the word following the colon.

EXAMPLE:   The movie starred my favorite actors Paul Newman, Robert Redford, and Katherine Ross.

               actors: Paul

1. This company produces paper pulp used for the following products paper plates, party hats, streamers, and confetti.
2. The apartment consisted of many spacious rooms three bedrooms, an eat-in kitchen, two baths, and a living room.
3. Maryanne chose three poets to study Dickinson, Frost, and Sandburg.
4. A reliable medical encyclopedia should include certain information descriptions of major diseases, lists of their symptoms, and advice about when to consult a physician.
5. In this wallet are my life's savings six dollar bills, eight quarters, and two nickels.
6. We wanted to buy a home in the country to have these benefits room to expand, space to enjoy outdoor activities, and land for a vegetable garden.
7. Their birthdays were all in the summer June 30, July 15, and August 12.
8. Zack arrived at the beach armed with the following items a picnic basket, a rubber raft, a folding chair, and towels.

9. Indications of extreme stress may include the following rapid pulse, accelerated breathing, dizziness, or fatigue.
10. I will visit three countries Japan, China, and India.

## The Colon in Special Situations

The colon is also used to show time with numerals, to end salutations in business letters, and to signal important ideas.

**Use a colon in a number of special writing situations.**

The chart shows the use of the colon in special situations.

| SPECIAL USES OF THE COLON | |
|---|---|
| **Numbers Giving the Time** | 12:25 P.M.<br>3:00 a.m. |
| **Salutations in Business Letters** | Gentlemen:<br>Dear Ms. Brown: |
| **Labels Used to Signal Important Ideas** | Caution: High voltage<br>Warning: Trespassers will be prosecuted. |

**EXERCISE B: Using Colons in Special Situations.** Copy the items, adding the colon missing in each.

EXAMPLE:   700 a.m.

   7:00 a.m.

1. 630 p.m.
2. Caution Falling rocks
3. Dear Mmes. Jordon and Farnsworth
4. Gentlemen
5. Warning The Surgeon General has determined that cigarette smoking is dangerous to your health.

**330**

**DEVELOPING WRITING SKILLS: Using Colons in Your Own Writing.** Follow the instructions that are given below to write sentences of your own. Use colons as needed.

EXAMPLE: Write a salutation for a business letter.

Dear Miss Rivera:

1. Write a sentence containing a numeral that gives the time of day.
2. Write a list of items following an independent clause.
3. Write a sentence containing a list that does not require a colon.
4. Write a label followed by an important idea.

# Quotation Marks with 21.7 Direct Quotations

When you write research papers or essays, you may sometimes wish to use the exact words from a book to support your own ideas. When you write fiction, you may sometimes want your characters to speak in their own words to make the story more vivid and interesting. *Quotation marks* identify the exact spoken or written words of others that you are including in your writing. These punctuation marks are used in all kinds of writing situations.

Study this section carefully. It should help you use quotation marks with greater confidence in your own writing.

## Direct and Indirect Quotations

Before you can use quotation marks correctly, you must first be able to tell the difference between *direct* and *indirect* *quotations.*

**A direct quotation represents a person's exact speech or thoughts and is enclosed in quotation marks (" ").**

**331**

EXAMPLES:   Jenny said, "Tomorrow I am going mountain climbing."

"I hope lunch is ready," thought Martin.

Indirect quotations do not repeat the exact words a person said or thought. Instead, an indirect quotation paraphrases or explains what someone said or thought.

**An indirect quotation reports the general meaning of what a person said or thought and does not require quotation marks.**

EXAMPLES:   Jenny said that tomorrow she was going mountain climbing.

Martin hoped that lunch was ready.

**EXERCISE A: Distinguishing Between Direct and Indirect Quotations.** Read each of the following sentences carefully to determine whether it contains a direct quotation that requires quotation marks or an indirect quotation. If the sentence contains a direct quotation, write *D* next to the appropriate number on your paper. If it contains an indirect quotation, write *I*.

EXAMPLE:   She hoped that she would be chosen.

I

1. I guess I've lost my watch again, Chris moaned.
2. Termites have caused extensive damage to the house, explained the inspector.
3. Bill wondered if he should try out for the track team.
4. She said that each person was responsible for his or her own actions.
5. Let's leave now, suggested Barbara.
6. I wondered why all my pens had disappeared.
7. Carol thought that school would be cancelled because of the snow.
8. This situation is intolerable, Mike declared with a frown.

9. All day, I hoped that someone else would wash the dinner dishes tonight.
10. No one is listening to the stereo, Mother said.

## Direct Quotations with Introductory, Concluding, and Interrupting Expressions

Quotations are generally accompanied by expressions such as *he thought* or *she replied.* Expressions of this kind can introduce, conclude, or interrupt the quoted material. The following rule describes how to punctuate quotations with introductory expressions.

**When an introductory expression precedes a direct quotation, place a comma after the introductory expression and write the quotation as a full sentence.**

EXAMPLE:    Timothy told his friend, "I had a great time at camp."

Ginnie wondered, "Would I enjoy going to a summer camp?"

The second rule covers quotations that have concluding expressions.

**When a concluding expression follows a direct quotation, write the quotation as a full sentence ending with a comma, question mark, or exclamation mark inside the quotation mark. Then write the concluding expression.**

As you study the following examples, notice the different kinds of punctuation placed before the final quotation marks. In the first example, a comma signals a pause rather than a full stop. The final end mark is not used until the end of the concluding expression. In the last two examples, however, end

**333**

marks are necessary before the final quotation mark to signal a question or an exclamation.

EXAMPLES: "I think you would have fun at camp," Timothy said.

"What activities does the camp offer?" inquired Ginnie.

"It's everything anyone could want!" exclaimed Timothy enthusiastically.

Since concluding expressions are not complete sentences, they do not begin with capital letters. Notice also that the closing quotation marks are always placed outside the punctuation at the end of the direct quotations.

Interrupting expressions are governed by their own punctuation rule.

**When the direct quotation of one sentence is interrupted, end the first part of the direct quotation with a comma and a quotation mark. Place a comma after the interrupting expression, and then use a new set of quotation marks to enclose the rest of the quotation.**

Each of the following examples is *one* sentence. As you study them, notice the following details in each one: (1) the comma inside the quotation mark at the end of the first part of the quotation; (2) the small letter at the beginning of the interrupting expression; (3) the comma inserted after the interrupting expression; (4) the small letter at the beginning of the second part of the quotation; and (5) the end mark inside the last quotation mark.

EXAMPLES: "Since the camp is located on a lake," explained Timothy, "we can go swimming and boating and water-skiing."

"Do you think," interrupted Ginnie, "that I could learn to water-ski?"

**334**

Sometimes a quotation is made up of two sentences, with a complete sentence on each side of the interrupting expression. A final rule is needed for this situation.

**When two sentences in a direct quotation are separated by an interrupting expression, end the first quoted sentence with a comma, question mark, or exclamation mark and a quotation mark. Place a period after the interrupter, and then write the second quoted sentence as a full quotation.**

Read the following examples carefully and notice the following details: (1) the different kinds of punctuation at the end of the first quoted sentence; (2) the small letter at the beginning of the interrupting expression; (3) the period following the interrupting expression; (4) the capital at the beginning of the second quoted sentence; and (5) the end mark inside the last quotation mark.

EXAMPLES:   "First you must pass the swimming test," replied Timothy. "Then you can take water-skiing lessons."

"That's great!" said Ginnie. "Do they also teach canoeing?"

**EXERCISE B: Using Direct Quotations with Introductory, Concluding, and Interrupting Expressions.** The following direct quotations have not been correctly punctuated or capitalized. Copy each of the sentences onto your paper, making the necessary corrections.

EXAMPLE:   Where are the ski poles he asked

"Where are the ski poles?" he asked.

1. Why would you throw out these blue jeans asked Milly don't you know they're an important part of my wardrobe
2. I guess it's time said Laverne to return to work
3. Here laughed Lauren are the missing keys

**335**

4. Otters are among the most playful of animals Glenn explained
5. Stop the guard yelled this is private property
6. The secretary smiled icily and said you can't see her without an appointment
7. I can't decide whether to order the clams or the scallops said Shirley which is better
8. A lion Edna stated does not make a good pet
9. Delphene moaned I can't walk another mile without stopping to rest
10. The pen I borrowed from you leaked all over my shirt complained Arthur

## Quotation Marks with Other Punctuation Marks

You may sometimes find it hard to decide whether another punctuation mark should go inside or outside the quotation marks. If you study the three rules and the examples that follow, you should be able to make these decisions correctly.

The first rule covers commas and periods.

**Always place a comma or a period *inside* the final quotation mark.**

EXAMPLES:    "Today is my sixtieth birthday," Uncle Joe said.

He added , "It doesn't seem possible."

Two other rules cover question marks and exclamation marks. The first involves quoted questions and exclamations within sentences that are declarative.

**Place a question mark or exclamation mark *inside* the final quotation mark if the end mark is part of the quotation.**

In the following examples, notice that the sentences themselves are declarative. In the first example, however, the quoted material asks a question. In the second the quoted material shows strong emotion. In these cases, the end marks go with the quotations, inside the quotation marks.

EXAMPLES:  Janet asked, "Have you seen my pet toad**?**"

Her sister exclaimed, "No, and I don't want to**!**"

Remember that two end marks are not necessary. In the following examples, the quoted material requires a question mark, and the entire sentence appears to need a period. Since two final punctuation marks are never used, the period is dropped.

INCORRECT:  George thought, "Why am I listening to this**?**".

CORRECT:  George thought, "Why am I listening to this**?**"

In some situations the entire sentence requires a question mark or an exclamation mark. In these cases the placement of the final punctuation changes.

**Place a question mark or exclamation mark *outside* the final quotation mark if the end mark is part of the entire sentence, not part of the quotation.**

Both quotations in the following examples are declarative. The sentences themselves, however, are *not* declarative. The first sentence is a question; the second sentence is an exclamation.

EXAMPLES:  How can you say, "I don't like this"**?**

Don't ever say, "I can't"**!**


**EXERCISE C: Using End Marks with Direct Quotations.**
End marks have been left out of the following sentences. Read each sentence and decide if the missing punctuation goes inside or outside the quotation marks. Copy each sentence onto your paper, adding the missing end marks.

EXAMPLE:   He asked the lifeguard, "When can we swim"

He asked the lifeguard, "When can we swim?"

1. The director told us, "Do not run near the pool "
2. Karen shrieked, "We won the game "
3. Didn't you hear him say, "Tomorrow is a holiday "
4. Mona thought, "Shouldn't a lifeguard be on duty "
5. The small child cried, "I want that bear "
6. Did the park attendant say, "Please place your rubbish in the containers "
7. I was shocked to hear him say, "I won't answer you "
8. When did I last say, "That's a really tough job "
9. Angrily, he shouted, "You don't know anything about it "
10. Rosa asked, "Has the position been filled yet "

## Quotation Marks for Dialogue

A conversation between two or more people is called a *dialogue.*

**When writing dialogue, begin a new paragraph with each change of speaker.**

In the following example of dialogue, capitalization and punctuation are used as they would be for any quotations. Remember, however, to indent whenever a new speaker talks.

EXAMPLE:   "Why don't we go to Ontario for a vacation?" Grandfather asked.

Surprised, Danielle replied, "Why do you want to go to Ontario? Let's go somewhere else. I'd like to spend a few days fishing."

"You can't be serious!" exclaimed Grandfather. "Ontario has access to one third of the world's freshwater supply. We could fish for walleye, muskie, pike, trout, and bass."

"In that case," said Danielle, "maybe I should reconsider."

**338**

**EXERCISE D: Using Quotation Marks with Dialogue.** The following selection is an example of dialogue. However, it is missing some punctuation marks and indentations. Read the selection carefully and decide where punctuation marks and indentations are required. Then copy the paragraphs onto your paper, making the necessary changes. You should have four paragraphs when you finish.

(1) What exclaimed Andrea, pointing at a strange-looking object lying on the sand, is that? (2) Don't you know? asked Marty. (3) That's an empty horseshoe crab's shell. (4) I've never seen anything like it said Andrea. (5) Are horseshoe crabs good to eat? (6) No, they aren't replied Marty. (7) Perhaps that's why they aren't an endangered species. (8) In fact, these peculiar creatures have been in existence since the days of the dinosaurs.

**DEVELOPING WRITING SKILLS: Using Quotation Marks in Your Own Writing.** Choose one of the following topics or make up one of your own. Then write a dialogue between two or three people consisting of at least fifteen sentences. Use as many different quotation rules as possible, and remember to punctuate and indent correctly.

| | |
|---|---|
| A planning session | A request |
| A school lunch | A visit to a relative |
| A frightening experience | A surprise party |

# Underlining and Other Uses 21.8 of Quotation Marks

Certain titles and names should be *underlined* in your writing. Other titles should be enclosed in quotation marks. Quotation marks are used in all types of writing and printing. Underlining, however, is used only for handwritten or typed materials. Printed materials use italics instead of underlining.

UNDERLINING: <u>The Hobbit</u>

ITALICS: *The Hobbit*

This section first explains which kinds of titles and names require the use of underlining in all written or typed material. It then explains which kinds of titles require the use of quotation marks.

## Underlining

Long written works that are made up of several parts should be underlined whenever they are written or typed. For example, the title of a book that contains several chapters or units should be underlined.

**Underline the titles of long written works and the titles of publications that are published as a single work.**

The following chart shows some of the titles that are covered by this rule.

| WRITTEN WORKS THAT ARE UNDERLINED | |
|---|---|
| **Title of a Book** | <u>Black Beauty</u> |
| **Title of a Play** | <u>What Price Glory</u>? |
| **Title of a Long Poem** | <u>The Wasteland</u> |
| **Title of a Magazine** | <u>Popular Electronics</u> |
| **Title of a Newspaper** | the Miami <u>Herald</u> |
| | the Chicago <u>Tribune</u> |

The titles of other kinds of major works should also be underlined.

**Underline the titles of movies, television and radio series, and works of music and art.**

The following chart illustrates some of the titles covered by this rule.

| ARTISTIC WORKS THAT ARE UNDERLINED | |
|---|---|
| **Title of a Movie** | Revenge of the Pink Panther |
| **Title of a Television Series** | Little House on the Prairie |
| **Title of a Long Musical Work** | The Magic Flute |
| **Title of a Record Album** | Long Distance Voyager |
| **Title of a Painting** | The Passage of the Delaware |
| **Title of a Sculpture** | Bird in Space |

The names of individual planes, ships, space vehicles, trains, and cars are also underlined.

**Underline the names of Individual air, sea, space, and land craft.**

AIR:  the Hindenburg

SEA:  the Leonardo Da Vinci

SPACE:  the Voyager 2

LAND:  the Southwest Limited

**EXERCISE A: Underlining Titles and Names.** Each of the following sentences contains a title or a name that needs to be underlined. Write the items that require underlining on your paper and underline them.

EXAMPLE:  Enid Bagnold's novel National Velvet has been a classic for years.

National Velvet

1. Many of the articles in Popular Science can be understood by people with little scientific knowledge.
2. In 1847 Henry Wadsworth Longfellow's long narrative poem Evangeline was published.
3. Olivia Newton-John and John Travolta starred in Grease.
4. Their drama club will be presenting the play The Dark at the Top of the Stairs.

5. Each week the children looked forward to watching the television series The Wonderful World of Disney.
6. In 1976 Viking I landed on Mars.
7. I am reading Rumer Godden's novel An Episode of Sparrows.
8. The Hudson River was named for Henry Hudson who explored it in the Half Moon.
9. When we lived in Virginia, we had subscriptions to both Time and Newsweek.
10. John Singleton Copley, a famous American artist, painted Watson and the Shark.

## Quotation Marks

The titles of short written works and works that are part of longer works are generally enclosed in quotation marks.

**Use quotation marks around the titles of short written works.**

The following chart shows examples of the kinds of works that you should enclose in quotation marks.

| WRITTEN WORKS THAT TAKE QUOTATION MARKS | |
| --- | --- |
| **Title of a Short Story** | "The Richer, the Poorer" |
| **Chapter from a Book** | "Hazel's Decision" from Watership Down |
| **Title of a Short Poem** | "The Concord Hymn" |
| **Title of an Article** | "Windmills: Alternative Energy Sources" |

Titles of other short works are also enclosed in quotation marks.

**Use quotation marks around the titles of episodes in a series, songs, and parts of a long musical composition.**

| ARTISTIC WORKS THAT TAKE QUOTATION MARKS | |
|---|---|
| Title of an Episode | "The Nile" from <u>The Cousteau Odyssey</u> |
| Title of a Song | "The Best Things in Life Are Free" |
| Title of a Part of a Long Musical Work | "The Storm" from the <u>William Tell Overture</u> |

**EXERCISE B: Using Quotation Marks with Titles.** Each of the following sentences contains a title that needs quotation marks. Some of the sentences also contain titles that need underlining. Copy the titles onto your paper, either enclosing them in quotation marks or underlining them.

EXAMPLE: Her favorite patriotic song was Katharine Lee Bates' America the Beautiful.

"America the Beautiful"

1. If mysteries interest you, read Chapter 4, Some Who Escaped, in the book The Bermuda Triangle.
2. Jim used an article, The Lee Boyhood Home, from the magazine Colonial Homes as a source for his paper on General Robert E. Lee.
3. Paula, a collector of old songs, played School Days for us.
4. My favorite selection from the Peer Gynt Suite, Edvard Grieg's orchestral work, is In the Hall of the Mountain King.
5. Bob read Weekender Sloop, an article in Popular Science, and then built his own craft.
6. I understand the feeling expressed in Housecleaning, a poem by Nikki Giovanni.
7. A short story by Daphne du Maurier is The Split Second.
8. Irving Berlin's song Blue Skies was in the musical Betsy.
9. Did you watch the episode Myth and the Moundbuilders on the Odyssey series last night?

10. Walt Whitman speaks of the human soul in the short poem A Noiseless Patient Spider.

**DEVELOPING WRITING SKILLS: Using Underlining and Quotation Marks.** Write five sentences of your own, each including one of the following items. Be sure to punctuate and capitalize correctly.

EXAMPLE:   The title of a short story

Shirley Jackson's "Charles" reminds me of my own little brother.

1. A song title
2. The title of a short poem
3. The title of a book and one of its chapters
4. A movie title
5. The name of a magazine

# 21.9 The Hyphen

The *hyphen* is used to combine some numbers and some word parts and to show a connection between the syllables of words that are broken at the ends of lines.

## Hyphens for Numbers

Some compound numbers and fractions require the use of the hyphen. One rule applies to hyphens used with compound numbers.

**Use a hyphen when writing out the numbers *twenty-one* through *ninety-nine*.**

EXAMPLES:   Before she fell asleep, Tracy counted to *fifty-three.*

*We mailed seventy-seven* invitations to my brother's birthday party.

Another rule applies to hyphens used with fractions that modify nouns.

**Use a hyphen when writing fractions that are used as adjectives.**

EXAMPLE:    A *two-thirds* vote of approval was necessary.

When a fraction is used as a noun, however, no hyphen should be used.

EXAMPLE:    *Two thirds* of the members voted their approval.

**EXERCISE A: Using Hyphens with Numbers.** Read the following sentences carefully to decide where hyphens are needed. If words in a sentence need a hyphen, rewrite the words on your paper to make them correct. If a sentence does not have any missing hyphens, write *correct.*

EXAMPLE:    Three fourths of the students attended the game.

　　　　　　correct

1. Stephanie started her own business at the age of thirty three.
2. One third of the apartments are rented.
3. Our class has to read eighty five pages in this book by next Friday.
4. To be frank, your paper consists of one fifth fact and four fifths fiction.
5. There were more than one hundred different kinds of flavors to choose from.
6. This drink is made up of two thirds citrus juice and one third carbonated water.
7. One eighth of the student body attended the concert last night.
8. Uncle George moved to San Diego when he was twenty one.
9. A nine tenths majority has voted to pass the amendment.
10. Twenty two students attended the science seminar.

**345**

## Hyphens for Word Parts and Compound Words

Hyphens are also used to separate certain *prefixes* (which begin words) and *suffixes* (which end words). The next two rules below govern the use of hyphens with prefixes and suffixes.

**Use a hyphen after a prefix that is followed by a proper noun or adjective.**

EXAMPLES:    Our family plans to take our annual vacation in mid-July.

Pro-American marchers sang patriotic songs.

Three other prefixes and one suffix always require the use of hyphens.

**Use a hyphen in words with the prefixes *all-*, *ex-*, and *self-* and with the suffix *-elect*.**

EXAMPLES:    all-powerful          self-employed

ex-football player      president-elect

In many instances, compound words also require the use of hyphens.

**Use a hyphen to connect two or more nouns that are used as one word, unless the dictionary gives a different spelling.**

Compound nouns are written in several ways. Some are written as one word. Others are written as separate words. Still others require hyphens. Unless you are sure how a compound word is spelled, consult a dictionary.

ONE WORD:    groundhog      daylight

footstep      earthquake

SEPARATE WORDS:    seat belt          sweet potato

waiting room      time limit

WITH HYPHENS: son-in-law       secretary-treasurer

                 great-grandmother     six-year-olds

Compound modifiers follow a different rule.

**Use a hyphen to connect a compound modifier that comes before a noun.**

In a compound modifier, the hyphen shows that the first modifier describes the second modifier, not the noun.

EXAMPLES: *Mass-produced* items are usually cheaper than ones made by hand.

The seven *well-fed* puppies curled up together for a nap.

Sometimes a compound modifier comes after a noun. Generally, no hyphen is needed in this situation.

BEFORE: The *never-ending* noise of traffic passing beneath my window kept me awake.

AFTER: The noise of traffic passing beneath my window was *never ending*.

It is wise, however, to consult a dictionary when you use compound modifiers after nouns. If the dictionary spells the words with hyphens, the words should always be hyphenated.

EXAMPLES: My *happy-go-lucky* friend rarely frowns.

My friend is *happy-go-lucky*.

You should also remember a final rule when you write compound modifiers.

**Do not use a hyphen with a compound modifer that includes a word ending in -*ly* or in a compound proper adjective or a compound proper noun acting as a adjective.**

INCORRECT: poorly-written letter     South-American tourist

CORRECT: poorly written letter      South American tourist

**EXERCISE B: Using Hyphens with Word Parts and Compound Words.** Look at the following items and decide where hyphens are needed. If an item is correct as it is, write *correct* on your paper. If an item does need hyphenation, rewrite the item to make it correct.

EXAMPLE:   an old fashioned story

an old-fashioned story

1. A pre Columbian civilization
2. A mid April deadline
3. a well known speaker
4. a North American river
5. a senator elect
6. a self improvement course
7. an all important decision
8. a daughter in law
9. three four year olds
10. a carefully prepared report

## Rules for Dividing Words at the End of a Line

Hyphens serve a useful purpose when they are used to divide words at the ends of lines. They should not, however, be used more often than is necessary. Following are several rules that determine the way in which a word at the end of a line can be divided.

The first rule for dividing words at the end of a line is the most important rule for you to remember and use whenever you divide words.

**If a word must be divided, always divide it between syllables.**

EXAMPLE:   Maxine's conversation, usually quite monoto-
nous, is characterized by a frequent repeti-
tion of ideas.

**348**

In addition to the preceding rule, other details also affect word division. As the following example indicates, a hyphen used to divide a word should never be placed at the beginning of the second line. It must be placed at the end of the first.

INCORRECT: To make one large room, knock down this par
-tition.

CORRECT: To make one large room, knock down this par-
tition.

In addition, one-syllable words should never be divided, even if they seem long or sound like two-syllable words.

INCORRECT: fif-th      brow-se      stra-ight
CORRECT: fifth      browse      straight

When a one-syllable word does not fit at the end of a line, just leave the space and write the word, without a hyphen, on the next line.

If you are uncertain about the division of syllables in a specific word, consult a dictionary.

Another rule covers the division of words that have single-letter syllables.

**Do *not* divide a word so that a single letter stands alone.**

The following words are correctly broken into syllables. They should not, however, be divided at the end of a line.

INCORRECT: i-dle      a-lone      ink-y
CORRECT: idle      alone      inky

Proper nouns and proper adjectives also should never be divided.

**Do *not* divide proper nouns or proper adjectives.**

INCORRECT: Eliza-beth      Ger-many
CORRECT: Elizabeth      Germany

**349**

If a word is already hyphenated, follow a final rule.

**Divide a hyphenated word only after the existing hyphen.**

INCORRECT: The directions are self-ex-
planatory.

CORRECT: The directions are self-
explanatory.

**EXERCISE C: Using Hyphens to Divide Words.** Imagine that you have to decide either to hyphenate each of the following words at the end of a line or to write the complete word on the next line. If a word can be divided, write the part of the word that would appear at the end of the first line. If the word cannot be divided, write the complete word.

EXAMPLE: Anthony

Anthony

1. dirty
2. fight
3. better
4. Spanish
5. icicle
6. well-deserved
7. payment
8. stretch
9. abolish
10. restless

**DEVELOPING WRITING SKILLS: Using Hyphens in Your Own Writing.** Write ten sentences of your own, each including one of the following items.

EXAMPLE: The prefix *self-* followed by an adjective

The self-proclaimed leader failed to inspire the troops.

1. A hyphenated number
2. A hyphenated fraction
3. A prefix followed by a proper adjective
4. The prefix *ex-* followed by a noun
5. A hyphenated compound noun

**350**

6. A hyphenated compound modifier
7. A compound modifier that is not hyphenated
8. A fraction used as a noun
9. An already hyphenated word that is divided at the end of a line
10. A prefix followed by a proper noun

# The Apostrophe 21.10

The *apostrophe* (') is used mainly in two situations. The first situation is when a writer wants to show possession in nouns and pronouns. The second situation is when a writer wants to indicate missing letters in contractions.

## Apostrophes with Possessive Nouns

Use apostrophes with nouns to show ownership.

**Use an apostrophe and -*s* to show the posses-
sive case of most singular nouns.**

EXAMPLES:  The color of the *sky* becomes the *sky's* color.

The idea of *Mrs. Aldrich* becomes *Mrs. Aldrich's* idea.

The reed of the *clarinet* becomes the *clarinet's* reed.

Even when a singular noun already ends in -*s*, an apostrophe and -*s* can usually be added to show possession.

EXAMPLES:  The shape of the *lens* becomes the *lens's* shape.

The texture of the *moss* becomes the *moss's* texture.

The book report of *Tess* becomes *Tess's* book report.

Another rule applies to the possessive form of most plural nouns.

**351**

**Add just an apostrophe to show the possessive case of plural nouns ending in -s or.-es.**

EXAMPLES:    The flavor of the *strawberries* becomes the *strawberries'* flavor.

               The buzzing of the *bees* becomes the *bees'* buzzing.

Forming the possessive of plural nouns that do not already end in *-s* requires a different rule.

**Add an apostrophe and -s to show the possessive case of plural nouns that do *not* end in -s or -es.**

EXAMPLES:    The fur of the *mice* becomes the *mice's* fur.

               The work of the *men* becomes the *men's* work.

               The dream of the *children* becomes the *children's* dream.

The following two steps can help you decide where to place the apostrophe and whether an *-s* is needed when you form possessives. First, determine the owner of the quality or object involved. Ask yourself, "To whom does it belong?" Second, if the answer to this question is a singular noun, follow the rule for forming singular possessives. If the answer is a plural noun, follow the rules for forming plural possessives.

If you wish to use the phrase *the mountains beauty,* ask yourself, "To what does the beauty belong?" If the answer is "the mountain," then the possessive is singular: *the mountain's beauty.* If the answer is "the mountains," then the possessive is plural: *the mountains' beauty.*

**EXERCISE A: Using Apostrophes to Form Possessives of Nouns.** The first ten of the following nouns are singular. The last ten are plural. Make two columns on your paper, labeled as in the example. Then write the correct possessive form for each word in the appropriate column.

**352**

EXAMPLE:  friend

|  | Singular | Plural |
|---|---|---|
|  | friend's |  |

1. boss
2. piano
3. stove
4. butter
5. wind
6. Gus
7. wheel
8. bass
9. chimney
10. mouse
11. mice
12. homes
13. authors
14. women
15. sweaters
16. calves
17. oaks
18. cars
19. children
20. keys

## Apostrophes with Pronouns

Both indefinite pronouns and personal pronouns can indicate possession. Follow the next rule to form the possessive of indefinite pronouns.

**Use an apostrophe and -s with indefinite pronouns to show possession.**

EXAMPLES:  everybody's plans        each one's decision

somebody's book        one another's ideas

someone's seat        one's home

nobody's suggestion        another's problem

Possessive personal pronouns do not take an apostrophe or an -s.

**Do *not* use an apostrophe with possessive personal pronouns.**

The following personal pronouns show possession: *my, mine, your, yours, his, her, hers, its, our, ours, their,* and *theirs.* Notice that no apostrophes are used with them.

**353**

Some of these personal pronouns are generally used as adjectives.

EXAMPLES:   *Your* painting is unusual.

              Carrie broke *her* glasses.

Others can be used as subjects, objects, and subject complements.

EXAMPLES:   *Yours* is a good idea.

              Give me *mine.*

              This jacket is *his.*

Whatever the use, it is important to remember that an apostrophe should never be added to a personal pronoun to make it show possession.

**EXERCISE B: Using Apostrophes with Pronouns.** Rewrite each of the following sentences, replacing the blank or blanks with the possessive forms of appropriate indefinite pronouns or personal pronouns.

EXAMPLE:   They borrowed _____ jackets.

              They borrowed each other's jackets.

1. _____ is the red bicycle and _____ is the blue one.
2. _____ voice is unique.
3. Mr. Stanton told _____ class to bring _____ books daily.
4. Try not to listen to just _____ advice.
5. _____ baseball glove may not fit you.
6. The injured bird had lost _____ sense of direction.
7. We counted _____ vote before we wrote _____ new secretary's name on the board.
8. _____ opinion would be welcome.
9. _____ sister and _____ brother are playing tennis tonight.
10. _____ was a good idea, but _____ was even better.

**354**

# Apostrophes with Contractions

*Contractions* are shortened forms of words or phrases.

**Use an apostrophe in a contraction to indicate the position of a missing letter or letters.**

Contractions are often used in informal speaking and writing. For example, instead of saying, "I am ready," most people would probably say, "I'm ready."

The following chart shows some of the many contractions formed with verbs.

| COMMON CONTRACTIONS WITH VERBS | | |
|---|---|---|
| **Verb + *not*** | are not (aren't) <br> is not (isn't) <br> was not (wasn't) <br> were not (weren't) <br> cannot (can't) | could not (couldn't) <br> did not (didn't) <br> do not (don't) <br> should not (shouldn't) <br> would not (wouldn't) |
| **Pronoun + the Verb *will*** | I will (I'll) <br> you will (you'll) <br> he will (he'll) <br> she will (she'll) | we will (we'll) <br> they will (they'll) <br> who will (who'll) |
| **Pronoun or Noun + the Verb *be*** | I am (I'm) <br> you are (you're) <br> he is (he's) <br> she is (she's) <br> it is (it's) | we are (we're) <br> they are (they're) <br> who is (who's) <br> where is (where's) <br> Andy is (Andy's) |
| **Pronoun or Noun + the Verb *would*** | I would (I'd) <br> you would (you'd) <br> he would (he'd) <br> she would (she'd) | we would (we'd) <br> they would (they'd) <br> who would (who'd) <br> Penny would (Penny'd) |

Remember that you should avoid using contractions in formal speaking or writing.

INFORMAL: *What's* the solution?

FORMAL: *What is* the solution?

### EXERCISE C: Using Apostrophes with Contractions.
Each of the following sentences contains one or more word groups that can be written as contractions. On your paper write each of these word groups as a contraction.

EXAMPLE: They are leaving at five.

They're

1. Who would want a car that cannot go more than ten miles without breaking down?
2. I was not listening and did not hear your question.
3. Who will pick out Lee's birthday present?
4. Who is going to the dance?
5. Connie is feeling much better, and she will be released from the hospital tomorrow.
6. We will appoint one representative who will attend every meeting.
7. Where is the book that was on the top shelf?
8. Were you not about to say something?
9. We did not see Krista's picture in the school yearbook.
10. We could not decide whether we would go to the movies or just stay home.

## Special Uses of the Apostrophe

Four special kinds of plurals are formed with apostrophes. They are plurals of numbers, symbols, letters, and words used to name themselves.

EXAMPLES: three *4*'s and four *6*'s

two *?*'s

Don't confuse *m*'s with *n*'s.

You say too many *uh*'s.

**EXERCISE D: Recognizing Special Uses of the Apostrophe.** Write five sentences of your own, each using the plural for one of the following numbers, symbols, letters, or words. Be sure to underline as in the example and use apostrophes wherever they are needed.

EXAMPLE:   u

> Her <u>u</u>'s looked like <u>v</u>'s.

    1. !      2. i      3. maybe      4. 3      5. what

## DEVELOPING WRITING SKILLS: Using Apostrophes in Your Own Writing.

Write ten sentences of your own according to the instructions in each of the following items.

EXAMPLE:   Use the possessive form of the word *kitten*.

> The kitten's paws were very soft.

1. Use the possessive form of the word *apartments*.
2. Use the contraction for *they will*.
3. Use the possessive form of the indefinite pronoun *someone*.
4. Use the possessive form of the word *children*.
5. Use the possessive form of the word *glass*.
6. Use the contraction for *you would*.
7. Use the plural form of the letter *d*.
8. Use the possessive personal pronoun *their*.
9. Use the plural form of the number *6*.
10. Use the possessive form of the word *actress*.

# Skills Review and Writing Workshop

## Using Punctuation Marks

### CHECKING YOUR SKILLS

Rewrite the following paragraph, adding all the necessary punctuation.

(1) I heard Mrs Hart calling for me (2) Help she cried (3) I didnt know what was wrong but I ran to her aid (4) On top of her roof was a huge black cat it was the size of a German shepherd dog (5) I was on the way to the store she said Please go to the store for me while I try to get the animal off my roof (6) She gave me a list for the following items one pound of hamburger a dozen eggs and a loaf of bread (7) When I came back with the groceries the cat was on the sidewalk and Mrs Hart was petting it (8) Standing on the ground the cat seemed even bigger (9) Mrs Hart was carrying a book called How to Care for a Panther (10) Was I surprised

### USING MECHANICS SKILLS IN WRITING
### Writing an Eye-Witness Report

Incorrect punctuation makes a writer's report hard to follow. Follow the steps below to write a brief, correctly punctuated eye-witness report of a recent event.

**Prewriting:** An eye-witness report tells what you saw exactly as it happened. Write a quick outline of what happened, paying particular attention to chronological order.

**Writing:** Begin by setting the scene. Tell where you were, who else was there, and what time it was. Then relate the events as you saw them happen. Use vivid, accurate words that will catch and hold your readers' attention.

**Revising:** Read the entire report, making sure that none of the details are inaccurate or misleading, and that you have used punctuation marks correctly. After you have finished revising, proofread carefully.

# UNIT **IV**

# *Composition*
## *The Writer's Techniques*

# Chapter 22

# The Writing Process

Imagine that you were given the chance to watch your favorite author at work. What would you expect to see? Page after page flowing effortlessly, almost magically, from the writer's pen? A perfect chapter written all at once with no erasures and no changes? It would be nice if authors could work this way. In fact, they cannot.

Good writing is hardly ever created all at once. Instead, writers usually do a number of different things when they write. They spend some time thinking and planning, some time getting their ideas down on paper, and some time reworking and improving their writing. All of these different activities make up the steps of the writing process.

You can learn to follow the same steps professional writers do. The three steps of the writing process you will need to practice are called prewriting, writing, and revising.

## 22.1 Prewriting

Prewriting activities help you discover what you want to say. These activities include thinking of usable and appealing topics, selecting one of these topics and narrowing it down, considering your audience and purpose, determining your main idea and supporting information, and choosing a form for organizing and presenting your thoughts. As you can see, during the prewriting stage you will be making quite a number of decisions. Making these decisions will make the rest of the process easier.

## Exploring Topics

Sometimes, writing topics will be assigned to you. At other times you will be able to choose your own topic.

**To explore ideas for writing topics, think about your interests, experiences, and ideas.**

You may find it helpful to keep a list of writing topics. Use the activities below in order to help you build your list of topics.

**Putting Your Knowledge and Interests to Work.** Quite often, other people will be interested in the unique things you know. Do you have a special skill or hobby? Are you an expert in a particular subject? Are there topics you would like to learn more about? Use the chart below as a guide for identifying your personal fund of knowledge and interests.

---

### IDENTIFYING YOUR KNOWLEDGE AND INTERESTS

**Ask Yourself:** What topics do I know about?
What topics am I willing to find out about?

1. People: friends, relatives, neighbors, acquaintances, famous people
2. Places: home, school, outdoors, indoors, store, room, town, camp
3. Events—Past and Present: holidays, sad or happy days, firsts
4. Things: pets, machines, collections, tools, plants, flowers
5. Activities: hobbies, sports, community activities, studies, household chores

---

**Free Writing.** For five minutes, write quickly without stopping. Do not go back to fix anything. Just keep writing. If you get stuck, write the same work over and over again until a new thought comes. At the end of five minutes, read what you have written. Circle any surprising and interesting words, phrases, or sentences you might use later. Then write again for five minutes, continuing what you were writing or starting a new topic. Again, look for what is valuable and discard the rest. Try this process several times, each time sifting out the good parts of what you have written.

**Writing in a Journal.** Keep a daily journal in which you write down interesting things you see, read, or hear. Write down thoughts and new ideas. When you are looking for writing topics, reread your journal. Look for items to expand or develop.

**Using Novels, Stories, Newspapers, and Magazines.** There are a number of ways you can use written material to spark your writing. For example, you can imitate the form of a piece of writing. If you have read a story that is told mainly through the exchange of letters, try writing a story like that yourself. Or, try writing a follow-up to a story; borrow a character and write about his or her further adventures. For an adventuresome approach to newswriting, borrow a headline from a newspaper and then think of your own article to go with it. In addition, try writing an article similar to one you might find in your favorite magazine. Look at the topics covered in past issues of the magazine. See if you can update one of these topics or develop it your way.

**Brainstorming.** Get together with a friend or a group of people and brainstorm for writing ideas. Start with a general topic like sports and think of as many ideas as you can for writing about it. Accept all ideas without criticizing any of them. A variation of brainstorming can be a group of people who write their ideas on paper. After writing for a few moments, group members exchange papers. Each person reads the ideas on the new paper and continues brainstorming. Possibly one of your ideas someone reads will spark a new idea.

**Using Your Senses.** Use all your senses (sight, smell, touch, hearing, and taste) to explore a topic. A chart like the one below can be especially helpful when you write a description.

| USING THE SENSES |
|---|
| **Topic:  Description of a Supermarket** |
| Sight: shopping carts, children<br>Smell: fresh vegetables, spilled liquid<br>Touch: cantaloupe, tomatoes<br>Hearing: register, microphone<br>Taste: free samples |

As you use these techniques, you will discover a number of ideas for writing. Try exploring new topics. Writing will then be an adventure in finding out what you think about many things.

**EXERCISE A:  Working with Your Knowledge and Interests.** Make a chart like the one on page 361. Fill in each category with your own specific information. Then list a possible writing topic for each of the five categories.

EXAMPLE:  1. People: Uncle Joe, our new neighbor, Annie
Possible topic—How I met our new neighbor

**EXERCISE B:  Free Writing.** Write quickly for five minutes. Then, stop and read what you have written. Circle interesting items. Try this several times, using the same or different topics.

**EXERCISE C:  Writing in a Journal.** Every day for one week, write about the same topic. Then select and list the best ideas you have about this topic.

**EXERCISE D: Brainstorming.** With a small group, brainstorm for a list of topics related to the general topic *computers*.

**EXERCISE E: Using Your Senses.** To explore a particular location, make a list of items in that location that appeal to the five senses—sight, smell, touch, hearing, and taste.

## Selecting and Narrowing a Topic

Once you discover an interesting topic, you may find that it is too large to handle in one paper.

**Choose a topic that you can effectively cover in the assigned amount of space.**

The way to deal with a large topic is to subdivide it. Cut it into pieces small enough to handle. Then select one manageable portion to write about.

Clustering is one technique for dividing large, general topics into smaller ones. Examine the following cluster for the topic *newspaper*.

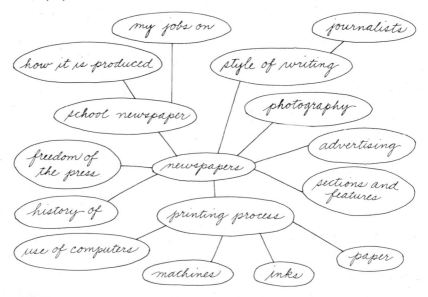

**EXERCISE F: Choosing and Narrowing a Topic.** Use clustering to divide a general topic into smaller topics. Use one of the following general topics: *travel, baseball, animals, heroes,* or *art.*

## Considering Your Audience and Purpose

Knowing who your audience is and what your purpose is makes writing easier.

**Determine your audience and your purpose before you begin writing.**

Your audience is made up of the people who will read your writing. Often, your audience will be a teacher or classmates.

Your purpose for writing will also influence your writing. Are you trying to inform, to persuade, or to entertain your audience?

The chart below gives examples of narrow writing topics. For each topic the purpose and audience are listed.

| Topic | Audience | Purpose |
|---|---|---|
| How to submit articles | Whole school | To inform |
| Reasons for advertising in the school paper | Local businesses | To persuade |
| Anecdotes from the newsroom | Classmates | To entertain |

**EXERCISE G: Considering Audience and Purpose.** Make a chart with three columns labeled *Topic, Audience,* and *Purpose.* Then list three small topics related to the larger topic *animals.* Fill in an audience and a purpose for each.

EXAMPLE:

| Topic | Audience | Purpose |
|---|---|---|
| How to train a dog | Classmates | To explain |

## Developing Main Ideas
## and Supporting Information

What if you had to condense all the material you plan to write about into one sentence? That sentence would contain your most important or *main idea*.

**State a main idea. Then gather and organize supporting information to develop it effectively.**

When you state your main idea, you are completing an important planning step. With your main idea in mind, you can then select supporting information—the kind of information that will explain your main idea.

Following is an example of a main idea statement that was developed from the general topic of newspapers.

MAIN IDEA:    I had several different assignments when I worked
                          on our class newspaper.

To support this main idea, the writer would need information telling about the assignments he or she had handled when working on the class newspaper. Techniques such as brainstorming and free writing could help to gather this information.

Here is a list of supporting information for the main idea.

—arranging and reporting interviews
—holding contests
—preparing an ongoing feature
—making puzzles and games
—working with volunteers
—writing a column about computers
—answering letters to the newspaper

The information you gather to support your main idea can be organized in a number of ways. The particular method you choose will depend on your audience and purpose. The following chart shows a few of the many ways of organizing material.

| ORGANIZATION OF SUPPORTING INFORMATION | |
|---|---|
| Chronological order | Information listed in the order in which it happened in time |
| Order of importance | Information arranged from least to most important, or visa versa |
| Comparison and contrast | Information arranged according to similarities and differences among items |
| Developmental | Information arranged so that one point leads logically to the next |

Once you have chosen the method for organizing your writing, look over your list of information. Add and subtract items from the list and then number them in the order you have chosen.

**EXERCISE H: Developing a Main Idea and Support.** Write a main idea, a list of supporting information, and a method of organization for one of your topics from Exercise G on page 365.

**EXERCISE I: Using the Prewriting Steps.** Practice the prewriting stage of the writing process by choosing your own topic. Then, use whatever methods you wish to narrow that topic down so that you can write a short paper about it. Next, decide on who your audience will be and determine what your purpose is. Write a main idea and make notes about the topic. Then, choose a method of organizing your paper and number your notes according to the method you chose. Add or subtract any ideas that will improve your work.

**DEVELOPING WRITING SKILLS: Prewriting.** Choose another general topic and follow all the steps of the prewriting stage to create an outline for a short paper.

# 22.2 Writing

Once you have completed the prewriting steps, you are ready to write. Even though you are prepared, do not expect to compose a perfect paper on the first try.

## Writing the First Draft

When you plunge into writing your first draft, move along as quickly as you can.

**Translate your prewriting notes into sentences and paragraphs without worrying about punctuation, spelling, grammar, or fine-tuning.**

As you write, you may make discoveries. One idea may remind you of another. This is not only natural, it is fortunate. It means your mind is actively working. The important point is this: You do not have to follow your list or any of your plans exactly the way you made them. Plans are, after all, only plans. Think of your writing plans as flexible, elastic, and even disposable.

When your first draft is complete, you have made a major accomplishment. Now you have something you can work on. You can examine your ideas, your word choices, and your sentences. You can make improvements. One draft may lead to another. Each change you make should bring your writing closer to the way you want it to be.

**EXERCISE: Writing a First Draft.** Using your plans from Exercise I on page 367, write a first draft of a short paper.

**DEVELOPING WRITING SKILLS: Preparing a First Draft.** Use the plans you made when you completed the Developing Writing Skills on page 367 to write the first draft of a short paper.

# Revising 22.3

The revising step is as important as prewriting and writing are. Revising means looking at your paper carefully and critically.

## Revising for Sense

Start the revising step by being sure your paper makes sense. To revise your paper for sense put yourself in the reader's position. Try to imagine you have never seen your paper before when revising.

**Read your paper critically to make sure that all the ideas support your purpose and that they are presented logically and connected clearly.**

Asking yourself the questions in the following chart can help you revise your paper for sense.

| REVISING FOR SENSE |
| --- |
| 1. Have I clearly stated my topic? |
| 2. Will the main idea be clear to my readers? |
| 3. Is there enough supporting information? |
| 4. Are the ideas presented in a logical order? |
| 5. Are the connections between the ideas clear and logical? |

**EXERCISE A: Revising for Sense.** Using the chart on this page, revise the following paragraph, making sure that it makes sense.

Her real name was Elizabeth Cochrane. She chose the name Nelly Bly from a song title. When she wrote newspaper stories, she used the name Nelly Bly. She was eighteen when she began to work as a reporter on the Pittsburgh *Dispatch*. She also

**369**

learned and wrote about how police treated women prisoners by pretending to be a thief and being arrested. Later, she arranged to be put in a mental hospital as a patient so that she could write about conditions there. She traveled around the world in 72 days, 6 hours, and 11 minutes. In 1889, she was sent by the newspaper the New York *World* to travel around the world faster than the hero of the novel *Around the World in Eighty Days* did.

**EXERCISE B: Revising Your Paper.** Use the checklist on page 369 to revise the paper you wrote for the Exercise on page 368.

## Editing for Word Choice and Sentences

The second stage in revising is often called *editing*. This process involves checking your choice of words and your sentences.

**Read your paper several times, making sure that every word is the best possible one to express your thoughts and that the sentences are clear and varied.**

The chart below lists questions to ask yourself as you edit.

| EDITING WORDS AND SENTENCES |
|---|
| 1. Does each word mean exactly what I want to say? |
| 2. Does the language sound right for the intended audience? |
| 3. Is the meaning of each sentence clear? |
| 4. Have I used a variety of sentence lengths and structures? |

Notice how revising the draft on the following page has improved it. The writer has chosen vivid words and has varied the length of the sentences. You may want to read both versions aloud to make the differences clear.

**370**

At one time or another, I have done most of the jobs at the
*started my career*
Gazette, our class newspaper. I ~~began~~ at the Gazette as a
*feature*
₍ₐ₎ reporter. ~~of features~~. For three ~~whole~~ editions, I wrote "The

Interview of the Week" column. I interviewed important members
*the principal, and*
of the staff: the head of the cafeteria,₍ₐ₎ the baseball coach.
*mastering      and beginning to feel comfortable*
Just as I was ~~getting used~~ to this job, I was switched to

"Contests." For one week I ran a contest to see who could write
*witty*
the funniest joke. I presented a prize to the winner--a₍ₐ₎ fourth
*our*
grader. Then I joined a group that answered mail written to₍ₐ₎
*fictional advice columnist,   unusual   not-so-serious   Later,*
"Dear Blabby." We gave₍ₐ₎ advice for some₍ₐ₎ ~~funny~~ problems.₍ₐ₎ I moved
*everywhere            my*
on to the photography crew. I took pictures ~~all over~~, including₍ₐ₎
*favorite place,          at the Gazette has been a good one.*
the kindergarten. I think my experience₍ₐ₎ ~~was good~~. I have
*to work*
learned to work under the pressure of a deadline and₍ₐ₎ as part of
*Most of all, I enjoy      ing my          so that others can share it.*
a team. ~~It is great to~~ hav₍ₐ₎ ~~your~~ writing published₍ₐ₎

## EXERCISE C: Editing. Edit the following passage for word choice and types of sentences.

Edward R. Murrow was a famous radio newscaster. He broadcast news about the bombing of London during World War II. People in the United States could hear bombs exploding in the background. Murrow was the host of a television program called *See It Now* from 1951 to 1958. Historical events were presented as though they were taking place at the time of the program. He was the host of a television program called *Person to Person* from 1953 to 1959. He interviewed famous people in their homes. He was the director of the U.S. Information Agency from 1961 to 1964.

## EXERCISE D: Editing Your Paper. Use the checklist on page 370 to edit the paper you wrote for the Exercise on page 368.

## Proofreading and Publishing

Proofreading is the last step in the writing process.

**Proofreading involves making final corrections in spelling, capitalization, punctuation, and grammar.**

When you proofread, do not change the ideas. When you have finished proofreading and correcting your paper, recopy it neatly, if necessary.

Your finished work can be published or shared in a number of different ways. Publishing may mean handing the final version of your paper to your teacher. Sometimes, you may share your work with your classmates or relatives or friends. You could send your best work to a school newspaper or magazine.

**EXERCISE E: Proofreading.** Proofread the following.

(1) Sunday, I woud like to operate a television camera. (2) Shooting pictures of a newscaster conducting an interveiw in a studio does not intrest me, however. (3) I would rather take pictures right wear the news is happening, as it is happenning of course, that means I would have to work under difficult conditions. (4) Bad weather and dangerous situations would make getting good pictures a challenge. (5) because I have always enjoyed facing challenges, I think operating a news camera would be a rewarding and interesting profetion for me.

**EXERCISE F: Proofreading Your Writing.** Proofread the paper you wrote for the Exercise on page 368. If necessary, recopy your paper. Share it with your teacher or classmates.

**DEVELOPING WRITING SKILLS: Revising, Editing, and Proofreading Your Writing.** Revise, edit, and proofread the paper you wrote for Developing Writing Skills on page 368. Share it with your classmates.

# Writing Workshop: The Writing Process

## ASSIGNMENT 1

**Topic**   Animal Behavior

**Form and Purpose**   An essay that describes and explains an aspect of animal behavior

**Audience**   Animal lovers

**Length**   Three to five paragraphs

**Focus**   After narrowing the topic to a specific animal and an aspect of its behavior, write a thesis statement. Then support your thesis with facts, details, and examples.

**Sources**   Books, encyclopedias, magazines, museums

**Prewriting**   Choose several types of animals that interest you, and research their behaviors. Narrow your topic to a single animal. Then write a thesis statement and prepare an outline.

**Writing**   Follow your outline as you write a first draft. Include footnotes if you use information from other sources.

**Revising**   The checklists on pages 369 and 370 will help you revise, edit, and proofread your essay.

# Chapter 23

# Improving Your Use of Words

This chapter will help you choose words that will make your writing clearer and more interesting and help you avoid expressions that weaken your writing.

## 23.1 Using Precise Words

Every sentence that you write has a message for your reader. Whether or not the reader understands the message will often depend on the words you use.

### Choosing Action Words

Some verbs are action verbs—*laugh, slide, twist, think*—and some verbs are linking verbs—*is, appear, seem.* Strong writing generally includes action verbs.

**Use action verbs to express your ideas vividly and forcefully.**

Linking verbs can be used successfully in many sentences, but you should avoid relying on linking verbs when you can use action verbs to make your ideas clearer or more direct. In the following chart, note how the sentences with action verbs get the same ideas across more directly.

| With Linking Verbs | With Action Verbs |
|---|---|
| My cousin *is* a teacher at the art school. | My cousin *teaches* at the art school. |
| The children finally *grew* tired of playing on the swings. | The children *fussed* and *cried* after playing on the swings for an hour. |

If you find that a number of your sentences use linking verbs, try to think of a few action verbs. Often you can find a replacement for a linking verb by changing another word in the sentence into an action verb.

LINKING VERB:   In the park the flies *were* a bother to the picnickers.

ACTION VERB:   In the park the flies *bothered* the picnickers.

At other times you may have to introduce a new verb and possibly change some of the other words in the sentence. Or you may find that reversing the order of ideas in the sentence makes it possible to use an action verb.

LINKING VERB:   Many members of the audience *seemed* bored by the speaker at the podium.

NEW VERB:   Many members of the audience *yawned* as the speaker at the podium went on and on.

NEW ORDER:   The speaker at the podium *bored* many of the people in the audience.

**EXERCISE A: Using Action Verbs.** Rewrite each of the sentences on the following page by turning the word in parentheses into an action verb or by using the suggestion given in parentheses after the sentence.

EXAMPLE:   The train was late in arriving.   (arriving)

The train arrived late.

1. Mitchell's poor attendance was the ruin of his chances for a scholarship.   (ruin)
2. The space ship was in orbit for three days.   (orbit)
3. Our kite was far over our heads in just a few moments.   (soar)
4. The entire shopping center was under fifteen feet of water. (Begin the new sentence with *Fifteen feet of water* ...)
5. The distant mountains are visible on most days.   (Begin the new sentence with *We* ...)

**EXERCISE B:  More Work with Action Verbs.** Rewrite each of the following sentences by changing one of the words in the sentence into an action verb by introducing a new action verb, or by changing the order of the words in the sentence.

EXAMPLE:   The ringing telephone was a distraction for me.

The ringing telephone distracted me.

1. My best friend was the leader of the search party.
2. A mechanic was responsible for towing us to safety.
3. The weather in Hawaii seems pleasant to most visitors.
4. Requiring a special pass to get into the parking lot is the landlord's method of providing security for the tenants.
5. At noon, the sun's rays were harmful to me.

## Choosing Vivid Words

When you describe something with words, you will want your readers to form the same picture in their minds that you have in your mind. To achieve this goal, you should develop the habit of using vivid, specific words in all of your writing. If you use dull, general words, your readers may not understand what you are trying to describe.

**376**

## Choose verbs, nouns, adjectives, and adverbs that are vivid and specific.

In the following chart, you can see the difference between general and specific language.

| USING SPECIFIC WORDS INSTEAD OF GENERAL WORDS | |
|---|---|
| **Dull, General Words** | **Vivid, Specific Words** |
| To keep dry he *sat* under a *ledge.* | To keep dry he *crouched* under a *jagged outcropping of rock.* |
| The *restaurant* served *good food.* | The *steakhouse* served *crisp salads* and *tender steak sandwiches.* |
| The *diver dived* into the pool. | The *young man arched off the board* and *plunged* into the pool. |

In some sentences a general word such as *walk* may be appropriate. In many sentences, however, a more specific word will make your meaning clearer. You might use *strut, limp, hobble, stumble, trudge,* or even *tiptoe.* A dictionary or book of synonyms can help you find a word that describes the action exactly. In the following chart, note how the vivid, specific verbs help you to see the action more clearly.

| REPLACING GENERAL VERBS WITH SPECIFIC VERBS | |
|---|---|
| **Dull, General Verbs** | **Vivid, Specific Verbs** |
| The mountain goat *moved* down the steep ridge. | The mountain goat *bounded* down the steep ridge. |
| The sergeant *gave* his command to his troops. | The sergeant *shouted* his command to his troops. |

Choose nouns, adjectives, and adverbs that are as specific as possible. In the chart on the following page, the specific words on the right give the reader a clearer picture than the general words on the left.

| REPLACING OTHER GENERAL WORDS WITH SPECIFIC WORDS | |
|---|---|
| **Dull, General Words** | **Vivid, Specific Words** |
| An *unusual bird* lighted in our *tree*. | A *fierce owl with gold eyes* lighted in our *pine tree*. |
| The *music* attracted the *animals*. | The *folk songs* attracted the *nosy raccoons*. |

**EXERCISE C: Identifying Vivid Words.** Each sentence includes vivid, specific words. For each sentence list two or more words that you think are especially exact and colorful.

1. The moment passengers began to snore in their cabins, fresh winds would swoop down and jerk the ship awake. —Sid Fleischman
2. She yanked open the left top drawer, pulling out a broken comb, which she viciously jerked through the wilderness on her head, only to be defeated by a patch of bubble gum.—Katherine Paterson
3. Off somewhere a car floated by, flashing its lights in the distance.—Ray Bradbury
4. The volleying started up again until suddenly Todd hit the ball way back on Elijah's right corner.—Ellen Kester
5. The creatures were still there—so close she could see their gray faces, with their glinty eyes, twisted mouths and crooked teeth.—Ann McGovern

**EXERCISE D: Choosing Vivid, Specific Words.** Rewrite each sentence to replace the general words that are underlined with more specific and lively words.

EXAMPLE: The picture pleased many people.

The old oil painting attracted much attention from the many art lovers at the exhibition.

1. The <u>child</u> <u>sat</u> on Santa Claus's lap in Macy's.
2. Michael <u>saw</u> a <u>shape</u> creeping toward him.
3. On my way to school, a <u>car</u> blocked the <u>road</u>.
4. The <u>apartment</u> looked <u>nice</u>.
5. Pia spoke her lines in the <u>play</u> <u>well</u>.
6. The unicyclist <u>rode</u> along the <u>sidewalk</u>.
7. She told an <u>interesting</u> story about <u>people</u>.
8. Last night someone <u>took</u> <u>many</u> <u>items</u> from our garage.
9. During the storm the wind <u>blew</u> and the rain <u>fell</u>.
10. We painted the <u>building</u> a <u>fine</u> <u>color</u>.

**DEVELOPING WRITING SKILLS: Improving the Words in a Passage.** Read the following passage carefully. Notice that many of the words in each sentence are either unnecessary linking verbs or dull, general words. Rewrite the passage using action verbs and vivid, specific verbs, nouns, and modifiers.

(1) Once my friend had a pet squirrel. (2) It had fallen out of a nest in a tree and had hurt its leg. (3) Because my friend's father is a doctor, he was able to put a tiny splint on the squirrel's leg. (4) Soon the leg was better. (5) The squirrel, which my friend named Mischief, was fond of climbing the drapes. (6) One time it got into the fish bowl and almost drowned. (7) Sometimes it went to school with my friend's brother, hiding in his jacket. (8) At those times Mischief was good. (9) At other times it found things around the house and put them somewhere. (10) When Mischief was fully grown, my friend let it loose outside, but it still ran back for food.

# Avoiding Clichés and Slang 23.2

As you choose words to express your ideas, you should guard against weak word choices such as *clichés* and *slang*. This section will help you identify clichés and slang and replace these expressions with clear, understandable language.

# Avoiding Clichés

In casual conversation people often use *clichés,* but in writing clichés can sound vague and tired. Clichés such as *green with envy* and *busy as a bee* have lost their descriptive power.

**Replace clichés with clear, direct words.**

If you think you have heard an expression hundreds of times, it most likely is a cliché. When you find a cliché in your sentences, you should cross it out and think of a more exact way to express your idea.

CLICHÉ:     Linda worried that her orange tennis shoes would *stick out like a sore thumb.*

REVISED:     Linda worried that her orange tennis shoes would *make everyone in her class laugh.*

CLICHÉ:     John was *on top of the world* after winning the contest.

REVISED:     John was *unable to stop grinning* after winning the contest.


**EXERCISE A: Finding and Replacing Clichés.** Each of the following sentences contains a cliché. Rewrite each sentence, replacing the cliché with more direct words.

EXAMPLE:     Without his glasses my uncle is blind as a bat.

                 Without his glasses my uncle can barely recognize people standing just a few feet away from him.

1. The tomatoes and carrots in Miranda's garden were growing by leaps and bounds.
2. We thought that Sven's explanation was as clear as mud.
3. Rather than plan the activities for the party, we decided to play it by ear.
4. Irene said she would cut a long story short and just tell us the results.

5. The deserted puppy had never known the milk of human kindness.
6. In the twinkling of an eye, Max cleaned off the kitchen counters.
7. While discussing camp rules in the lodge, the director asked the new campers not to rock the boat.
8. After Lisa hit the scorpion with her shoe, it was dead as a doornail.
9. Hideo gave us much food for thought in his talk about Japan.
10. I was pleased as punch when Earl asked me to the dance.

# Avoiding Slang

Like clichés, *slang* is often used in casual conversations. These words, however, tend to be popular among only certain people for only a short time.

**Replace slang words and expressions with clear, direct words.**

If you find words and expressions in your sentences that only your friends would understand, these words are probably slang. The following examples show how slang can be replaced with more specific language.

SLANG:   I thought the test was *a bummer.*

REVISED:   I thought the test was *long and difficult.*

SLANG:   Mr. Harris *shot the breeze* with my father all afternoon.

REVISED:   Mr. Harris *discussed politics and education* with my father all afternoon.

**EXERCISE B: Finding and Replacing Slang.** Each of the sentences on the following page contains a slang word or expression. Rewrite each sentence, replacing the slang words with more direct words.

Having hiked five miles into the wilderness with heavy packs, we sacked out just after sunset.

Having hiked five miles into the wilderness with heavy packs, we crawled into our sleeping bags just after sunset.

1. Pamela had a wipeout on her bicycle.
2. My older brother bought the foxiest car I have ever seen.
3. Feeling lonely, I wanted to rap with someone.
4. Nanette told her younger brother to bug off while she was playing with her friends.
5. Klaus wore a cool outfit to the Halloween dance.
6. The news of her election to student government hit Faye like a ton of bricks.
7. The two sports cars burned down the road.
8. When we were having a pillow fight, our counselor told us that we should knock it off.
9. Herbert always behaves like a turkey during a crisis.
10. A group of us met Saturday afternoon to chew the fat at the beach.

**DEVELOPING WRITING SKILLS: Writing Clear Sentences.** Write five pairs of sentences. In the first sentence of each pair, use an example of a cliché or slang that has not been discussed in this section. In the second sentence, rewrite the first sentence using more direct words.

EXAMPLE: Lanie does not want to get her hopes up and is playing it cool until the winner is announced. (slang)

REWRITE: Lanie will not allow herself to get excited until she actually hears that she is the winner.

EXAMPLE: The Mitchells are as happy as two peas in a pod. (cliché)

REWRITE: The Mitchells get along very well and are quite happy.

# Skills Review and Writing Workshop

## Improving Your Use of Words

### CHECKING YOUR SKILLS

Rewrite the following paragraph, improving the choice of words.

(1) One morning in 1939, the fog over the New York airport was thick as pea soup. (2) A pilot named Douglas Corrigan took off in a broken airplane that was without a radio. (3) He was expected to fly to California; however, the plane was flown out into the fog over the water. (4) When Corrigan's plane left the fog a long time later, he found out he was over Ireland, not California. (5) For his unusual goof up, the pilot got the nickname "Wrong Way" Corrigan.

### USING COMPOSITION SKILLS

#### Writing an Adventure Story

Writers make their stories come alive by using action verbs and vivid words. They use direct, specific language rather than general terms or clichés. Imagine you are the first person to accomplish a daring feat or to explore an unknown place. Follow the steps below to write a story about your adventure.

**Prewriting:** Write one sentence stating the feat or adventure you are describing. List your actions in the order in which they occurred.

**Writing:** Begin by letting your reader know that you have taken part in a great adventure. Then describe your adventure, step by step. Use vivid words and specific details to make the events come alive for the reader.

**Revising:** First, look at your verbs. Make sure they are active and vivid. Check that nouns, adjectives, and adverbs are specific. Replace any clichés or slang with clear, direct words. After you have revised, proofread carefully.

## Chapter 24

# Improving Your Sentences

This chapter will show you how to write more interesting and varied sentences. You will learn how you can improve your sentences and you will have a chance to practice beginning your sentences in different ways.

## 24.1 Improving Short Sentences

Too many short *simple sentences* can make your writing sound choppy. You can improve short sentences in two ways. If the sentences lack details, you can add information to them. If there are too many short sentences, you can combine some of them.

### Adding Details

Adding details to short sentences can make them more vivid and interesting.

**Add details to the subject, verb, or complement of short simple sentences.**

The chart shows three ways to add details to short sentences.

| ADDING DETAILS TO SHORT SENTENCES | |
|---|---|
| **Details Added to the Subject** | |
| *A house sat on the hill.* | *An ancient* house *with six chimneys* sat on the hill. |
| **Details Added to the Verb** | |
| He walked to the front of the auditorium. | *With long strides,* he walked *proudly* to the front of the auditorium. |
| **Details Added to the Complement** | |
| The book contained a postcard. | The book contained an *old yellowed* postcard *from Paris, dated October 1920.* |

**EXERCISE A: Adding Details to Short Sentences.** Each of the following items contains a short sentence followed by three details. Rewrite each sentence, adding the three details.

EXAMPLE:   Their barn caught fire.
         a. empty   b. in the middle of the night   c. old

         In the middle of the night, their old, empty barn caught fire.

1. The couch needs to be re-covered.
   a. in the playroom   b. ragged
   c. by a professional
2. Carnations brightened the room.
   a. blue and green   b. placed on the night stand
   c. hospital
3. Dad could not start the engine.
   a. using all his patience and wisdom
   b. after it overheated   c. old truck's

**385**

4. People jogged.
   a. of all ages   b. along the sidewalk
   c. at the edge of the river
5. The sun blazed down.
   a. summer   b. on the old car
   c. stalled at the entrance to the parking lot

**EXERCISE B: Adding Your Own Details.** Rewrite each of the following short sentences by adding at least *two* details that will make each sentence more interesting.

EXAMPLE:   The muskrat scurried.

        The frightened muskrat scurried into the woods.

1. Takiko hurt her leg.
2. A deer grazed.
3. The seaplane landed.
4. Raul won the contest.
5. The traffic stopped.

## Sentence Combining

A long series of short sentences is especially likely to sound choppy. You can often improve a group of short, choppy sentences simply by combining some of the sentences.

**Combine two or more short simple sentences to make a longer simple sentence, a compound sentence, or a complex sentence.**

The chart shows several ways to combine ideas from two short sentences into a longer, more interesting sentence.

| COMBINING SHORT SIMPLE SENTENCES |
| --- |
| **Two Simple Sentences** |
| Carly and Jack sat at a roadside stand. They sold icy lemonade. |
| **One Sentence Changed to a Prepositional Phrase** |
| *At a roadside stand,* Carly and Jack sold icy lemonade. |

**386**

| **One Sentence Changed to a Participial Phrase** |
| --- |
| *Sitting at a roadside stand,* Carly and Jack sold icy lemonade. |
| **One Sentence Changed to Part of a Compound Verb** |
| Carly and Jack *sat* at a roadside stand and *sold* icy lemonade. |
| **Sentences Combined to Make a Compound Sentence** |
| Carly and Jack sat at a roadside stand, *and* they sold icy lemonade. |
| **Sentences Combined to Make a Complex Sentence** |
| *While Carly and Jack sat at a roadside stand,* they sold icy lemonade. |

**EXERCISE C: Combining Short Sentences.** Combine the short sentences using the method given in parentheses.

EXAMPLE:   The birds perched on the bobbing boat. They looked like passengers with skinny necks. (Make the first sentence a phrase.)

Perched on the bobbing boat, the birds looked like passengers with skinny necks.

1. She began her career as a laboratory technician. She worked at Huntington General Hospital. (Make the second sentence a phrase.)
2. Clint admired my poster collection. He offered to buy five posters. (Join the sentences with *and* to form a compound sentence.)
3. At the shore we bodysurfed. We played volleyball in the afternoon. (Join the sentences using a compound verb.)
4. The company changed its package design. Sales increased sharply. (Join the sentence with *when* to form a complex sentence.)
5. The hit song was played frequently. It was played on all the rock radio stations. (Make the second sentence a phrase.)

6. I continued to exercise every day. I improved my endurance. (Join the sentences using a compound verb.)
7. Lou wanted to buy a used stereo system. He needed new tires for his bicycle first. (Join the sentences with *but* to form a compound sentence.)
8. Our television's reception was poor. We added a cable adapter. (Join the sentences with *because* to form a complex sentence.)
9. In February they visited Lima. Lima is the capital of Peru. (Make the second sentence a phrase.)
10. Lynn campaigned enthusiastically and sincerely. She failed to receive a majority of the votes. (Join the sentences with *but* to form a compound sentence.)

**DEVELOPING WRITING SKILLS: Improving Short Sentences.** Read the following passage carefully and then rewrite it to make the sentences more interesting and less choppy sounding. Add details to and combine sentences as needed. You do not, however, need to change every sentence.

(1) I was fourteen years old. (2) I fell in love with Nell. (3) I spent hours with her. (4) I wanted to give her the best possible care. (5) Unfortunately, our relationship was interrupted. (6) Nell was sent away. (7) She went to a school to be trained. (8) I heard news of her. (9) I didn't see her for months. (10) I also received pictures of her. (11) They showed her looking happy and more beautiful than ever. (12) Finally, we were reunited. (13) I visited her at her school. (14) Ten months had passed. (15) Nell was still my horse.

# 24.2 Shortening Sentences That Are Too Long

Using too many long sentences can weaken your writing just as much as using too many short sentences. This section will help you improve rambling or overly complicated sentences by shortening them.

## Shortening Rambling Sentences

*Compound sentences* are sentences that contain two or more independent clauses. Although they can often be used successfully to connect ideas and add variety to your writing, you should avoid making them uncomfortably long. If you write sentences that link clause after clause with *and, but, or,* or *so,* your readers may soon grow tired.

**Separate rambling compound sentences into two or more shorter sentences.**

Notice how awkward the following rambling sentence sounds.

RAMBLING COMPOUND SENTENCE: Tony biked over to my house at dawn on Saturday, *and* then we rode our bikes to the county fairgrounds, *and* we arrived in time to watch the workers set up the booths and tents, *but* the rides were dull without people on them, *so* we rode our bikes by the stables and pens to see the prize animals.

When you find a rambling compound sentence in your writing, look for the end of each complete thought in the sentence. Then take out one or more of the coordinating conjunctions used to link these thoughts, add a period in place of each conjunction, and begin a new sentence after each period. In the following revised version of the preceding sentence, two conjunctions have been removed to make three sentences.

REVISED: Tony biked over to my house at dawn on Saturday, *and* then we rode our bikes to the county fairgrounds. We arrived in time to watch the workers set up the booths and tents. The rides were dull without people on them, *so* we rode our bikes by the stables and pens to see the prize animals.

**389**

**EXERCISE A: Shortening Rambling Compound Sentences.** Rewrite each rambling compound sentence that follows to make two or three shorter sentences.

EXAMPLE:  He rose from bed, and he stretched wearily, and he tried to shake the cobwebs from his mind, but eight weeks of steady work had exhausted him, and he tumbled back into bed and pulled up the covers.

He rose from bed, and he stretched wearily. He tried to shake the cobwebs from his mind, but eight weeks of steady work had exhausted him. He tumbled back into bed and pulled up the covers.

1. Joyce wished to enter medical school, so she joined a premedical society at college, and in addition, she worked as a volunteer in an emergency room at the university hospital, and she also worked every other Saturday in a convalescent home for elderly people.
2. A shirt begins as yarn of one or more colors, and then it is woven into a roll of fabric, and next it is sent to a factory, and there it is cut and sewn, and finally it is shipped with other manufactured shirts to a clothing store.
3. My cousin wanted to ride the giant water slide at the park or to go fishing in the river, but the rain prevented us from doing either, so instead we went to a movie, and later we had hot fudge sundaes at the ice-cream parlor on State Street.
4. I dashed down the stairs at the bus terminal, but I just missed the bus, and consequently, I had to wait an hour for the next one, and the coffee shop was closed, so I browsed in the bookstore and bought a birthday card for Art.
5. The canyon was narrow and winding, and at the bottom a stream trickled over greenish rocks, and on either side of the stream, the walls of the canyon thrust up hundreds of feet toward the racing clouds, and some parts of the cliffs had crumbled into the river, and other parts were pocked with caves carved out by the wind and storms.

## Shortening Complicated Sentences

*Complex sentences* are sentences with one independent clause joined to two or more dependent clauses. Like compound sentences, complex sentences are useful when you want to show relationships between ideas. However, overloading a complex sentence with too many dependent clauses may confuse readers.

**Separate complicated complex sentences into two or more shorter sentences.**

Notice how long and confusing the following sentence is.

COMPLICATED COMPLEX SENTENCE:   The man *who* lives in the apartment next to us has a black cat with cold yellow eyes *that* loves to sit on our patio wall, *which* is four feet high, *because* it can watch us inside our apartment *since* we have many windows and a sliding glass door.

When you find a complicated complex sentence in your writing, look for ways to simplify it. Study the subordinating words used to connect the different thoughts and decide which ones you could remove. You may also have to change some of the words at the beginning of a new sentence. In the following revised version of the sentence above, the words *that* and *because* have been removed to make three sentences.

REVISED:   The man *who* lives in the apartment next to us has a black cat with cold yellow eyes. It loves to sit on our patio wall, *which* is four feet high. From there it can watch us inside our apartment *since* we have many windows and a sliding glass door.

**EXERCISE B: Shortening Complicated Complex Sentences.** Each of the items on the following page is a complicated complex sentence. Rewrite each sentence to make two or three shorter sentences, changing words as necessary.

EXAMPLE: When I tried a Jacuzzi for the first time, I liked it very much because the hot water that swirled all around me really relaxed my aching muscles, which were tired from doing yardwork, which had involved raking leaves and digging up tree stumps.

When I tried a Jacuzzi for the first time, I liked it very much. The hot water that swirled all around me really relaxed my aching muscles, which were tired from doing yardwork. The yardwork had involved raking leaves and digging up tree stumps.

1. In the pet store, the white mice with long pink tails looked like tiny cotton puffs with pink strings attached as they huddled in the back of the cage to sleep where it was dimly lit and warm because it was out of the draft.

2. My aunt collects first editions of famous children's books, which she finds in bookstores all over the city and displays in bookcases that cover the walls in her dining room and make visitors eager to read the books.

3. Although we crossed the Mojave Desert late in the afternoon, we could hardly stand the extreme heat because we did not have air conditioning in the car, which would have allowed us to close the windows instead of suffering the fiery blasts that blew in as we drank water from our cooler and sped east.

4. The old movie that I love most is *Shane* with Alan Ladd as Shane because Shane is a farmhand with a mysterious past who tries to give up his life as a gunfighter until he becomes involved in a conflict between farmers and a cruel rancher, which is settled when Shane decides to risk his life and fight again to save the family he loves.

5. Even though more carpooling would improve traffic conditions, it alone would not cut down on the congestion that clogs the highways and creates smog because for one reason not everyone can commute with other people, who often have very different work schedules.

**392**

**DEVELOPING WRITING SKILLS: Improving Long, Awkward Sentences.** The following passage contains both rambling compound sentences and complicated complex sentences. Rewrite the passage by separating each long sentence into two or three shorter ones. Change words as necessary.

(1) The people living in the caverns below the city of Helbes differed greatly from the people living above ground, and the two groups varied in work habits and in basic attitudes toward life, and consequently, they never mixed, and in fact, they feared each other. (2) Physically the cavern people, who had very pale skin, were shorter and stouter than those of Helbes, who tended to be tall and slim and had healthy tanned skin from the bright sunshine. (3) The cavern people were serious, quiet folk who labored day and night to mine the gold in their caverns, which made them suspicious of the carefree, fun-loving people of Helbes who enjoyed easier lives on their farms and ranches, which provided for most of their needs. (4) Thus, the two groups lived near each other, but they avoided each other, and they never spoke to each other at chance encounters along the dusty paths leading to the caves, but instead they would pass by sullenly, keeping to opposite sides of the path.

# Using Different Sentence 24.3 Openers

Varying the lengths of your sentences is just one way to make your sentences more interesting for your readers. To achieve a pleasing style, you should also pay attention to the sentence openers you are using.

**Begin your sentences with different openers: subjects, adjectives and adverbs, phrases, and clauses.**

The chart on the following page shows four different ways to begin your sentences.

| DIFFERENT WAYS OF BEGINNING SENTENCES |
|---|
| **With a Subject** |
| *Someone* opened the door to allow us inside. *Yolanda* was no longer sure of the correct path through the woods. |
| **With an Adjective or Adverb** |
| *Content,* the cats curled up by the fireplace. *Softly,* she sang the baby to sleep. |
| **With a Phrase** |
| *Under the trees,* the air was cool and still. *Hearing his name,* Robby turned sharply. *To prepare for the test,* they studied every night. |
| **With a Clause** |
| *Whenever you want to see that movie,* let me know. |

Varied sentence openers make a passage more interesting and more readable, as you can see in the following chart.

| All Subject Openers | Varied Sentence Openers |
|---|---|
| *Jimmy and I* made a fine sailing team. *We* sailed the smallest boat in the regatta race. *We* were able to outmaneuver the larger boats because we used the size of our boat to our advantage. *We* proudly captured the racing title by a comfortable margin. | *Jimmy and I* made a fine sailing team. *In the regatta race* we sailed in the smallest boat. *Because we used the size of our boat to our advantage,* we were able to outmaneuver the larger boats. *Proudly,* we captured the racing title by a comfortable margin. |

**394**

**EXERCISE: Using Different Sentence Openers.** Rewrite each of the sentences by moving a word, phrase, or clause.

EXAMPLE:   They felt more secure after the first play-off game.

   After the first play-off game, they felt more secure.

1. Mr. Wu called the police just after his store was robbed.
2. The curious chimpanzee explored the house.
3. The doorbell rang at exactly midnight.
4. Their air-conditioning system failed to operate during the intense heat spell this summer.
5. Clara attended school for five more years to become a veterinarian.
6. Mother realized afterwards that she had made a mistake.
7. A clown juggled tennis balls while he walked a tightrope.
8. The sun, slipping below the horizon, hurt his eyes.
9. You should measure carefully to hang pictures well.
10. He spent his last dollar at the boardwalk on a ride.

**DEVELOPING WRITING SKILLS: Varying Sentence Openers.** The following passage contains a series of sentences that all begin with subjects. Look for different openers for *most* of the sentences. Rewrite the sentences with a variety of openers to produce a more interesting passage.

(1) The game was tied as it headed into the bottom of the ninth. (2) The pitcher, taking careful aim, delivered a curve ball, and the first batter singled. (3) The first batter then moved to second base because of a wild pitch. (4) The second batter next took a ball, and the man on base stole third. (5) The pitcher then struck out the second batter. (6) The third batter walked after only four pitches. (7) The fourth batter, with a powerful swing, hit a long fly ball. (8) The right fielder caught the ball though the sun was in his eyes. (9) The man on third base was tagged out trying to reach home. (10) The game entered the tenth as the excitement grew.

# Skills Review and Writing Workshop

## Improving Your Sentences
### CHECKING YOUR SKILLS

Rewrite the paragraph below to improve its sentences. You may combine sentences, shorten sentences, and vary sentence beginnings.

(1) A town in Alaska has a strange name. (2) It is named Chicken. (3) There are no chickens raised in the town. (4) Once, inhabiting the area near the town, were a large number of plump birds called ptarmigans. (5) People settled in the town and wanted to write their friends back home about the strange birds, but they did not want to misspell the birds' name, so the settlers called the birds chickens instead, and that is how they decided on the name for the town.

### USING COMPOSITION SKILLS
### Writing a Travel Brochure

Professional writers keep readers interested by using a variety of sentence openings and by mixing long and short sentences. Follow the steps below to write a descriptive paragraph for a travel brochure.

**Prewriting:** Think of an interesting or unusual place you have visited. Imagine you have been hired to write a travel brochure to encourage tourists to visit this place. List details about the most interesting sights you remember from your visit there.

**Writing:** Start by naming the place and telling where it is located and how to get there. Then describe the points of interest and events a visitor should be sure to see. Save the most interesting tourist attraction for last to give your description the most impact.

**Revising:** Use the chart on page 394 for different ways to begin your sentences. Check to make sure you have combined short sentences and have shortened any sentences that ramble. After you have revised, proofread carefully.

UNIT

# Composition
## Forms and Process of Writing

# Chapter 25

# Looking at Paragraphs

A *paragraph* is a group of sentences placed together to form a single unit of thought. Paragraphs are easy to recognize because the first word will generally be indented. One sentence will usually express the main idea of the whole paragraph. All of the other sentences will present information that explains the main idea.

Once you can recognize key features of paragraphs, you will find it easier to write good ones of your own.

## Recognizing Topic Sentences 25.1

The *topic sentence* tells what a paragraph is about.

**The topic sentence of a paragraph captures the main idea of the paragraph, the idea that all of the other ideas in the paragraph explain or develop.**

A topic sentence can be the first, middle, or final sentence in a paragraph. The chart on the next page shows the ways in which topic sentences work in each of these three positions.

**399**

| WHAT A TOPIC SENTENCES DOES | |
|---|---|
| **Position** | **General Use** |
| First Sentence | Introduces the main idea and prepares the reader for the information in the paragraph |
| Middle Sentence | Presents the main idea after a short introduction |
| Last Sentence | Summarizes all of the other ideas in the paragraph by presenting a main idea |

The following paragraph by a student begins with its topic sentence. This is the most common position for a topic sentence.

TOPIC SENTENCE

Supporting information

*The computer has become a major part of the lives of millions of people.* People use the computer in many ways. These ways range from business to recreation. The computer is used in the military for tracking submarines and for calculating orbits for satellites. It aids military communications and guides airplane flights. In everyday lives, the computer plays a large role: switching telephone calls, keeping track of bank deposits, and maintaining store inventories. The computer has literally changed the life style of our world.—Karla Groff

The next paragraph shows a topic sentence that comes in the middle of a paragraph, after a short introduction, which leads up to the topic sentence.

In the past many suntan lotions promised to give protection from the sun's burning rays as well as rich, deep tans. However, consumers could not always tell how much protection they could expect from one lo-

TOPIC
SENTENCE

Supporting
information

tion compared to another. *Now a number from one to fifteen, printed on the container, tells you the amount of protection you can expect from a particular lotion.* A number two lotion, for instance, provides little sunscreening. If you already have a tan, you might use a number two lotion to help you tan even more deeply. A number six or eight lotion, on the other hand, will provide moderate protection. You might use a number eight or ten lotion if you are planning to be out in a boat all day. And if you are afraid that you will burn or if your skin is very sensitive, you should choose a lotion with a high number such as twelve or fifteen.

The final paragraph shows a topic sentence at the end where it summarizes all the ideas before it.

Supporting
information

TOPIC
SENTENCE

I awoke in a small white room, furnished only with the hard cot on which I lay and a narrow table alongside the cot. When I tried the door, I found it locked. I began to pull and push at the door to see if I could force it open, but a stern cough from the other side of the door stopped me. I rattled the thick, heavy screen at the window, but it was bolted in place. Through the tiny mesh of the screen, I could glimpse a high, forbidding wall. *Escape from this prison seemed impossible.*

**EXERCISE A: Recognizing Main Ideas.** Each of the following items includes four sentences on the same topic. One sentence is the main idea; the other three sentences offer supporting information. Identify the main idea in each group.

1. a. Drivers may not be familiar with the signs or roads.
   b. Residents may have different habits, such as passing on the right.
   c. Driving in other states can challenge any driver's skill.
   d. Out-of state drivers may not know all the traffic laws.

2. a. Newspapers announce the dates and locations of sales.
   b. Newspapers inform readers of national and international events.
   c. One benefit of reading newspapers is learning about local happenings, including entertainment.
   d. Newspapers offer readers all kinds of important information.
3. a. I typed entire letters without mistakes until I got to the end.
   b. I struggled every day in typing class.
   c. I lacked the coordination to hit the keys evenly.
   d. Even though I memorized the position of the keys, I transposed letters.

**EXERCISE B: Recognizing Topic Sentences.** Write the topic sentence of each of the following paragraphs. Note that one topic sentence is at the beginning, one follows a short introduction, and one is at the end.

(1) To outlanders, California does not immediately summon images of snow-clad peaks. But Tahoe is actually a cradle of American skiing. In 1856, the legendary Snowshoe Thompson began delivering the mail on skis, crisscrossing the crest of the range from Placerville, California, to Genoa, Nevada. Ski areas began blossoming around the lake before World War II, and in 1960, television cameras showed the world the Winter Olympics from Tahoe's Squaw Valley, choreographed by one of Squaw's pioneer skiers, Walt Disney.—Adapted from Abby Rand

(2) The Parc Naturel de Guadeloupe is a French park. Though the French have a long history of nature preservation, they came late into national parks—and with their own ideas. Beginning with the establishment of the Parc National de la Vanoise in the Alps, they have made their parks a part of life, learning, and culture, as well as a museum of the outdoors. Guadeloupe, as a department of France, has benefited from this

approach. Paved roads lead to key centers, and footpaths of varying lengths lead to the slopes of the volcano and into the rain forest.—Adapted from Michael Frome

(3) Imagine yourself luxuriating in a train compartment with a hand-carved interior. The decor is Moorish with velvet draperies and onion-bulb doorways lending an *Orient Express* air of mystery. Sunken footbaths, silver and crystal dinner service, and an unparalleled wine list add to the luxury as you speed through the countryside. All of this was available, if not always affordable, during the peak of luxury railroad travel, a period that lasted from the Civil War into the 1930's.—Adapted from Kathleen Cecil

**DEVELOPING WRITING SKILLS: Writing Topic Sentences.** Write five original sentences that prepare the reader for a paragraph of information on each of the following topics.

EXAMPLE:    I saw more unusual animals in the Bronx Zoo in one day than I had seen in my whole life.

1. keeping up with the latest top-ten songs
2. unusual animals
3. visits to flea markets and bargain shops
4. favorite sport
5. how to stay healthy

# Recognizing Supporting 25.2 Information

To develop a topic sentence, a writer can use many different kinds of *supporting information:* examples, details, facts, reasons, or incidents. In some paragraphs only one of these five kinds of supporting information will be needed. In other paragraphs several different kinds of support may be needed to give the reader a full understanding of the main idea.

# Examples, Details, and Facts

The best support for many paragraphs is the specific information provided by *examples, details,* and *facts.*

**The main idea in many paragraphs can best be supported with examples, details, or facts.**

The following chart shows ways in which these three kinds of information can be used to support a main idea.

| EXAMPLES, DETAILS, AND FACTS AS SUPPORTING INFORMATION | |
|---|---|
| **Main Idea** | **Supported by Four Examples** |
| Every state has its own official flower. | Alabama's flower is the camellia. Hawaii's flower is the red hibiscus. Kansas's flower is the sunflower. Tennessee's flower is the iris. |
| **Main Idea** | **Supported by Three Sets of Details** |
| My grandmother's backyard is spacious and old-fashioned. | A weathered barn with space for five carriages takes up the rear of the yard. A patch of raspberry bushes occupies one corner. A croquet court occupies the opposite corner. |
| **Main Idea** | **Supported by Three Facts** |
| Gila monsters are dangerous lizards. | They grow up to thirty inches long. Their bite causes intense pain. The death rate is high for untreated victims. |

The number of examples, details, or facts you include in a paragraph will depend both on your topic sentence and on the information you want to give the reader. In the following paragraph, the writer has chosen three major examples and a few specific examples to explain her main idea.

TOPIC SENTENCE
Supporting information: Examples

*A person can do many things to feel healthy and physically fit.* Exercise leads to fitness. Recreational activities such as bicycling, doing calisthenics, jogging, dancing, playing tennis, and swimming are excellent ways to get the exercise one needs. A proper, well-balanced diet helps, too. The body functions best when all its nutritional needs have been met. Getting enough sleep is also important to create an all-over sense of well-being.—Anne Barrett

In some paragraphs you may want to use two or even all three of these kinds of supporting information in order to develop your main idea fully. The following paragraph includes three major examples and a number of details and facts.

TOPIC SENTENCE

Supporting information: Examples, details, and facts

*Whatever your space requirements, there are sinks made in three different types of materials—enameled cast iron, enameled steel, and stainless steel.* The most expensive is cast iron, offering the advantages of strength, durability, and choice of colors to coordinate with your appliances. Cast iron is rugged and also holds in the heat of hot water better than other materials. Enameled steel is also an excellent material, although somewhat less expensive and less durable than iron. Finally, there is stainless steel, which is long-lasting, economical, and easy to maintain, although not available, of course, in decorator colors.—Evelyn Conti and William Lass

## EXERCISE A:  Recognizing Examples, Details, and Facts.
List the supporting information used in each paragraph. State

whether the support is made up mainly of (a) different examples of the main idea, (b) descriptive details that help you visualize the main idea, or (c) specific facts that support the main idea. The topic sentences are underlined.

(1) Like any other continent, South America can be scanned but not really seen in a grand tour fashion. Just consider the realities of a single trip that would include even half of more than a dozen countries stretching from the Caribbean beaches of Panama and Colombia to the glacial parklands of southern Argentina and Chile. Or focus on the fact that Brazil is almost a continent by itself; or that the massive spine of the Andes runs some 5,000 miles tip to top along South America's Pacific coast and cradles in its highlands ruins of the most ancient civilizations, the most historic colonial towns.—Carla Hunt

(2) The phrase American architecture calls to mind a number of images which seem to have very little to do with each other. On the one hand, there is the traditional New England village with white-steepled church and clapboard-faced houses. On the other hand, there is the city with tall, gleaming towers. There is also the adobe world of the Southwest. And there are the ornate palaces of our museums, the futuristic extravaganzas of our domed stadiums, and the classical visions of our government buildings.—Adapted from Paul Goldberger

(3) When he was all afoot his scaled head, spike-crowned and triple-tongued, rose higher than the broken tower's height, and his taloned forefeet rested on the rubble of the town below. His scales were grey-black, catching the daylight like broken stone. Lean as a hound he was and huge as a hill. Ged stared in awe. There was no song or tale could prepare the mind for this sight. Almost he stared into the dragon's eyes and was caught, for one cannot look into a dragon's eyes. He glanced away from the oily green gaze that watched him, and held up before him his staff, that looked now like a splinter, like a twig.—Ursula LeGuin

**406**

# Reasons and Incidents

*Reasons* may be the best support when you need to defend your main idea. An *incident* may work best when there is a story behind your main idea.

**A main idea can also be supported with reasons and incidents.**

The following chart shows how these two kinds of supporting information can be used.

| REASONS AND INCIDENTS AS SUPPORTING INFORMATION | |
|---|---|
| **Main Idea** | **Supported by Three Reasons** |
| Roller-skating should not be allowed on sidewalks and streets. | Many roller skaters do not watch where they are going. Sidewalks and streets are rough and dangerous. Pedestrians, bicycles, and cars already fill the sidewalks and streets. |
| **Main Idea** | **Supported by One Incident** |
| Guests often cause problems for their hosts. | When we left my brother's apartment, we thought he had his key, so we locked the door. However, he never locks his door and never carries a key. He had to borrow a ladder to climb up two stories, squeeze through a small open window, dive into the room, and pick up everything he had knocked over. |

Use at least three *reasons* to support a main idea when your topic sentence expresses an opinion that calls for explanation. The following paragraph offers reasons to back up the statement that farming is not a popular occupation in Alaska.

| | |
|---|---|
| TOPIC SENTENCE | *Although many people have tried to settle in Alaska by homesteading the land, very few have been able to make their living by farming.* Alaska is not an |
| Supporting information: Reasons | agricultural state. Scattered development and undeveloped marketing facilities offer little encouragement to farmers. Except in localized areas like the Matanuscka and Tanana valleys, the soil is too thin, is poorly drained, is too steep or too cold and wet for farming. In many areas there is not much topsoil since the decomposition of humus is very slow.—Elsa Pedersen |

In other paragraphs your best support may be a brief story, or *incident,* made up of a series of events or happenings. One incident will generally be enough to develop a topic sentence.

| | |
|---|---|
| TOPIC SENTENCE | *Love and tenderness will go a long way toward bringing about a change in the neurotic dog without emotionally upsetting him.* A case in point is a young |
| Supporting information: Incident | poodle who once lived in an apartment. Like any young dog he was fond of chewing up books, with a special preference for those on the lower shelves of the bookcase. Aware of modern psychology, the master did not waste his time scolding his growing dog, but went straight to the core of the problem. He built another bookcase with shelves out of the dog's reach. As the dog grew larger, he built another; some years later, he took his few remaining volumes to the attic. His dog gave up the chewing habit completely. The master gave up reading.—Adapted from Stephen Baker |

**EXERCISE B: Recognizing Reasons and Incidents.** Read each of the following paragraphs carefully. If the paragraph includes reasons, list the reasons used to support the topic sentence. If the paragraph includes an incident, list the events in the incident. The topic sentences are underlined.

**408**

(1) Siren screaming and lights flashing, the red, white, and orange ambulance seemed to be flying as it raced through the dark streets of Darien, Connecticut, carrying the most precious of cargos—a human life. Pulling up to the hospital's emergency room entrance, the driver brought the powerful vehicle to a surprisingly gentle halt. Immediately, the back doors flew open, revealing an elderly patient and a medical team of one adult . . . and three teenagers! Actually this was just one of some 300 emergency calls handled yearly by emergency medical services Post 53 of Darien.—Adapted from Pat Rose

(2) A dog's life is becoming increasingly competitive. There are more dogs around than ever before. Everywhere the dog looks, he meets the eyes of other dogs. There are stores where dogs can be had for a price; often as many as half a dozen dogs are placed in a show window, and passers-by are apt to praise them vocally in the presence of dogs who also happen to be passing by. It comes as a shock to even the most self-confident dog that he can be replaced. —Stephen Baker

**DEVELOPING WRITING SKILLS: Selecting Supporting Information.** Make each of the following statements into a topic sentence by adding the items called for in parentheses. List at least three pieces of supporting information that could be used to develop the main idea in the topic sentence. (The events in an incident can be counted as separate pieces of information.) Be sure to list enough examples, details, facts, reasons, and incidents to develop all of the ideas fully.

1. I appreciate the invention of the __(name of an invention)__ more and more each day.
2. A __(name of a plant, animal, or thing)__ requires loving care.
3. __(Name of an actor)__ gave his best performance in __(name of a movie)__.
4. __(A place or building)__ reminded me of __(something imaginary)__.
5. Growing up can be a __(a vivid adjective)__ experience.

**409**

# 25.3 Recognizing Paragraphs with Unified Ideas

In addition to a clear main idea and plentiful supporting information, a good paragraph should have one other important feature. All of its ideas should work together to develop the main idea and to create a single *unified* paragraph.

**A paragraph will be unified if all of the supporting information works together to develop the main idea.**

A paragraph with unified ideas is easier to read and understand than one that includes unnecessary or confusing additional information. In a paragraph about the benefits of using goggles while swimming, you would not expect to find details about the benefits of using a mask and flippers while snorkeling. The following paragraph shows how awkward the addition of unrelated ideas can be. The writer changes topics in the middle of the paragraph and then returns to support the main idea at the end.

TOPIC
SENTENCE

All serious swimmers should use swimming goggles. Although goggles do make swimmers look a little like frog people, they protect swimmers' eyes from stinging, chlorinated water. Water in public swimming pools reddens eyes and may make them itchy and sore, but goggles keep the water out. Using goggles, swimmers can keep their eyes open while they are swimming. *In snorkeling also, a well-fitting mask improves the snorkelers' vision and comfort. Flippers protect the snorkelers' feet from jagged coral.* Swimmers with goggles can also avoid bumping into the sides of the pool and into other swimmers. Furthermore, goggles enable swimmers to swim in a straight line in a narrow lane so that more swimmers can use the pool at the same time.

If you reread the paragraph, leaving out the unrelated ideas (printed in italics), you will see that the unified paragraph is much easier to read. The paragraph is also clearer because all of the supporting information focuses on the main idea.

**EXERCISE: Recognizing Unrelated Ideas.** One of the pieces of supporting information for each of the topic sentences in the following items does not develop the main idea in the topic sentence. On your paper write the unrelated idea in each item.

1. Our team debated for a week about the best colors for our new uniforms.
   a. Some players voted for white pants and shirts with red numbers and letters.
   b. A few players requested red stripes on a white background.
   c. Some people wanted sneakers with extra arch supports.
   d. Other players voted for solid brown pants and white shirts with brown numbers and letters.

2. Delivering newspapers has been a rewarding experience for me.
   a. Many of my customers have become my friends.
   b. The money I earn makes me feel independent.
   c. My customers also enjoy reading magazines.
   d. Delivering papers gives me regular exercise.

3. Today's airplanes contain many types of advanced equipment that are critical to their performance in flight.
   a. The runways with bright blue lights help planes to take off and land.
   b. Well-maintained, high-performance jet engines give the power needed to gain altitude and also to reduce speed.
   c. Automatic pilot controls enable pilots to operate the huge aircraft.
   d. Advanced instrumentation monitors altitude, speed, distance from other objects, air pressure, and many other important factors.

**411**

4. In chess, pieces are allowed to move only in certain directions and only for certain distances.
   a. The king can move one space in any direction.
   b. Chess has a long history.
   c. The knight can move two spaces forward and then one space to either side, or it can move two spaces to either side and then one space forward.
   d. A rook can move any number of spaces, forward or backward.

**DEVELOPING WRITING SKILLS: Creating a Paragraph with Unified Ideas.** The following paragraph contains two ideas that stray from the main idea. Write down the unrelated information. Rewrite the paragraph by replacing the unrelated information with information that supports the main idea.

(1) Fads are constantly replacing one another, but certain fads seem to be more memorable than others. (2) College students in the 1920's took to wearing raccoon coats and playing ukuleles. (3) Their counterparts in the 1940's made flagpole sitting and goldfish swallowing their specialties. (4) Frank Sinatra was probably the most popular singer of that period. (5) Children wore Davy Crockett hats in the middle 1950's and twirled hula hoops a few years later. (6) Then in the late 1970's, disco dancing and roller-skating became national pastimes. (7) Figure skating, on the other hand, has always been practiced by a relatively small number of people.

# 25.4 Recognizing Well-Organized Paragraphs

In addition to being unified, a good paragraph should be well organized. This section will discuss common logical orders that can be used to organize paragraphs: chronological, spatial, order of importance, and comparison and contrast.

## Chronological Order

Ideas that follow a time sequence are in *chronological order.*

**Chronological order can be used to present the steps in a process or the events in an incident in the order of their occurrence.**

Chronological order is useful when you are writing about how to do or make something. You can also use it when you are explaining historical events or describing an incident.

The following paragraph explains a process—the life of a star—in chronological order. The words printed in italics help to show the order.

TOPIC
SENTENCE

Chrono-
logical
order of
ideas

From the laws of physics and observations of stars of different kinds, astronomers have worked out the sequence of events in the life of a star. *After* a star has formed, it soon settles down to a steady existence. Nuclear reactions in its innermost core convert hydrogen to helium, releasing energy at the same time. *Eventually,* all the hydrogen in the interior is consumed. Changes *then* take place in the star's internal balance. The outer layers puff out to give the star giant proportions, *while* new reactions, working on the helium, start up inside. More changes occur and the star will go through a phase of being variable. *Ultimately,* there is no source of energy left. Smaller stars shrink into white dwarfs. Massive stars blow up as supernovae. The material blasted out by a supernova becomes part of the interstellar gas, the birthplace of a new generation of stars.—Adapted from Jacqueline and Simon Mitton

**EXERCISE A: Using Chronological Order.** Each of the items on the following page contains a topic sentence followed by a list of supporting information. Arrange each list of supporting information in chronological order.

1. Meg showed the children that bowling involves a series of separate actions, smoothly executed.
   a. Finally, she released the ball, keeping her arm straight.
   b. She picked up the ball.
   c. Aiming for the middle pin, she swung her arm forward.
   d. She walked a few steps into the alley bringing her arm back.
2. The separation of the thirteen American colonies from England actually took about twenty-five years.
   a. Then the colonists and British fought a long war which ended in an American victory.
   b. Relations with England broke down and the colonies declared their independence.
   c. The American colonists objected to certain taxes levied by the British government.
   d. The newly independent country hammered out a constitution and established its own government.
   e. The colonists tried to negotiate with England to avoid an open conflict.

## Spatial Order

When details are organized according to their location, they are in *spatial order.*

**Spatial order can be used to present details according to their physical position.**

Spatial order is useful when you are describing objects, such as a building or a landscape viewed from a distance. It can also be used to describe a person or a thing.

The following paragraph describes a scene using spatial order. Note that the words in italics help to show this order.

TOPIC SENTENCE    The view from the gas station in Georgetown, Colorado, makes motorists temporarily forget their problems with their cars. *Across the highway to the left,* a granite

**414**

Spatial
order of
details

ridge soars up to the sky. *On the right,* a wide, green, fast-moving stream flashes white as it churns over and around boulders. *Beyond the stream,* houses and a few stables nestle up against the base of the mountain. *From the stream valley,* the mountain wall on the right rises thousands of feet.

**EXERCISE B: Using Spatial Order.** Each item contains a topic sentence followed by a list of supporting information. Arrange each list of supporting information in spatial order.

1. The tiny house was as unusual as the ninety-two-year-old heiress who owned it.
    a. Just in front of the house was a drawbridge spanning a pond full of snapping turtles.
    b. And this is where Miss Dudd spent her days, wrapped in a comforter and eating fresh fruit.
    c. The huge room inside was painted green and contained nothing but a huge bed.
    d. The front door opened onto an entrance way made entirely of glass.
2. The Benders tried to make their Christmas tree look exactly the same every year.
    a. The branches were laden with lights, ornaments, and tinsel.
    b. A few mismatched cardboard trees and animals always sat around the trunk.
    c. A time-honored angel perched on the very highest branch, lit by a bulb concealed in her head.
    d. The spot on which the tree stood was traditionally covered with an old spangled cloth.

## Order of Importance

A paragraph that begins with the weakest supporting ideas and builds to the strongest idea is in *order of importance.*

**415**

**Order of importance can be used to arrange examples, details, facts, or reasons from least important to most important.**

When you are defending an opinion, organizing information in order of importance enables you to lead the reader from the least convincing idea to the most convincing idea.

In the following paragraph, the pieces of support are ranked in order of importance, concluding with the most serious reason. The italics help point out the order of importance.

TOPIC
SENTENCE
Order of importance
for ideas

Overpopulation in the valley and foothills is disrupting the balance of nature. *For example,* during heavy rains, topsoil and whole hillsides are sliding into the valley because vegetation that prevented erosion has been uprooted. *Even more serious,* the new housing developments have removed fields for rabbits and reduced the coyotes' food supply. Coyotes have begun to roam neighborhoods in the hills attacking pets. *And worst of all,* continued building has strained the area's water supply. Already two natural lakes have dried up permanently, killing plants and fish and leaving several species of birds without nesting ground.

**EXERCISE C: Using Order of Importance.** Arrange, in order of importance, the list of supporting information that follows each topic sentence.

1. The committee gave several reasons to explain why it had voted against the proposed design for the civic auditorium.
   a. Some members worried that the design might look too harsh next to the old-fashioned park buildings.
   b. Worst of all, the new building would cost 50 percent more than the budget allowed.
   c. In addition, the proposed building seemed to take up too much of the city park.

**416**

    d. All the committee members objected strongly because the architect had planned for only seven hundred seats, when the city had asked for fifteen hundred.

2. Many of the Halloween costumes at our party were quite original.

    a. But my favorite was worn by the couple disguised as a walking Space Invaders game.

    b. There was also a woman who came as Boris Karloff.

    c. Several people showed up as monsters and mythological figures.

    d. One of the best costumes was worn by a man who dressed up as a parrot.

# Comparison and Contrast Order

When information is organized to show the similarities or differences in two or more things, it is in *comparison and contrast order.*

**Comparison and contrast order can be used to group information according to similarities and differences.**

Comparison and contrast order is useful whenever your main idea focuses on the way two or more things are alike or different. This order enables you to organize information in two ways: You can move back and forth between two things, comparing or contrasting point by point; or you can present all the information about first one and then the other.

The following paragraph explains the differences between two kinds of roads point by point. The words in italics draw attention to the grouping of ideas.

TOPIC     *Although* turnpikes and freeways both help people
SENTENCE   get from one place to another, the two kinds of roads have major differences. To enter turnpikes, cars pass through tollbooths and pick up mileage tickets; to get

**417**

off, drivers turn in their tickets at tollbooths and pay the correct fee. *In contrast,* to enter a freeway, cars simply merge with traffic; to leave, they simply exit using the off ramps. *Another major difference* is that turnpikes generally have fewer exits, and therefore fewer interruptions, than freeways. Freeways, *on the other hand,* have cars constantly entering, as well as a number of conveniently spaced exits. *A third difference* is that turnpikes provide gas stations and restaurants along their routes, *whereas* drivers on freeways have to exit and find fuel and food for themselves.

**EXERCISE D: Using Comparison and Contrast Order.** Each of the following items contains a topic sentence followed by a list of supporting information. Arrange each list of supporting information in comparison and contrast order.

1. My life changed a great deal after I got my paper route.
   a. I used to enjoy staying up to watch the local news.
   b. Now I am earning enough money to save up for a racing bike.
   c. Now I enjoy watching the day wake up as I start my paper route.
   d. Then I had hardly any spending money for the things I wanted to buy and could never save anything.
   e. Now I have to plan my time carefully in order to squeeze everything in.
   f. Then I had more time than I knew how to fill.
2. The television comedies *Taxi* and *Barney Miller* have similar settings and are based on similar situations.
   a. *Barney Miller* is set in an unglamorous police station in New York.
   b. *Taxi's* stories revolve around a group of strange but funny taxi drivers.
   c. *Taxi* is set in the gritty dispatch office of a small New York cab company.

    d. *Barney Miller's* stories focus on the activities of several eccentric detectives and the even more eccentric people who come to the police station.

## Other Logical Orders

Some ideas may need a special logical order.

**Some paragraphs require special logical orders of their own.**

If a paragraph does not lend itself to one of the more common logical orders, the topic sentence may help determine the order of ideas. For example, if a topic sentence mentions rubies, emeralds, and diamonds, then the paragraph should discuss these items in that order. At other times one idea may simply lead logically to the next, with all of the ideas supporting the topic sentence equally.

The supporting information in the next paragraph develops the topic sentence logically. Each sentence follows logically from the one before it.

| | |
|---|---|
| TOPIC SENTENCE | There is one important thing for skin divers to remember. Most animals in the sea eat early in the morning and again as it begins to grow dark. You |
| Logical order of ideas suited to the main idea | should stay on your own "home ground" at these times. Leave the sea to the sea creatures at dawn and at dusk—when the sea becomes a hungry jungle. Each animal, large or small, is out looking for something to eat. They are not smart enough to know that you are not just another tasty fish to add to their menu.<br>—Shaney Frey |

**EXERCISE E: Using Other Logical Orders.** Each of the following items contains a topic sentence followed by a list of supporting information. Arrange each list of supporting information logically. Then briefly explain why you chose the particular order you did for each.

1. Mr. Hodges looks as if he were born to be everyone's idea of the perfect grandfather.
   a. And he smiles often.
   b. He wears a Santa Claus suit without looking silly.
   c. His friendliness and enthusiasm are so contagious that people generally find themselves smiling back.
   d. He is a small, bubbly man with bright eyes, a thatch of white hair, and dimples when he smiles.
   e. In fact, the one time that he actually did wear a Santa Claus suit, he was so convincing in the role that his own daughter did not recognize him.
2. My mother has three completely different wardrobes in her closet: casual wear for around the house, conservative outfits for work, and vintage or antique clothes for special occasions.
   a. She works as a bank officer and must dress the part.
   b. Around the house she dresses in comfortable clothes.
   c. Another section of her closet is filled with quiet business suits and low-heeled shoes.
   d. Over the years she has also collected a few delicate Victorian dresses, flashy flapper outfits, whimsical hats, and one fur coat of uncertain but advanced age.
   e. She loves the charm of old clothing and looks for occasions to wear them.
   f. One section of the closet is filled with jeans, T-shirts, and sneakers.

**EXERCISE F: Recognizing Logical Orders.** Identify the logical order used in each of the following paragraphs as *chronological order, spatial order, order of importance, comparison and contrast order,* or *other logical order.*

(1) You can prepare hash brown potatoes from a boxed mix in a few quick steps. First stir the potato mix, salt, and three tablespoons of water together in a saucepan. Then let the ingredients stand for about five minutes. As you heat it, the mix will

soon absorb most of the water. After the ingredients begin to sizzle, turn the potatoes with a fork until they are brown and ready to serve.

(2) Dwelling on opposite sides of the street, the two dogs looked similar but could not have been more unlike each other as far as temperament was concerned. One paced up and down constantly, like a nervous general, snapping to an especially alert posture at the slightest movement. He also barked continually, as if to let the neighborhood know that he was on the job. The other dog lay flat on the sidewalk, flatter than it seemed possible for a large dog to lie, looking very much like a bearskin rug. And, of course, *he* never uttered a sound, with the exception of an occasional gentle snore.

**DEVELOPING WRITING SKILLS: Creating Organized Paragraphs.** The following item contains a topic sentence followed by disorganized supporting information. Choose the best logical order and rearrange the supporting information. Then write a paragraph based on the order you have chosen.

A line of people waiting for a movie has its own special geography.
  a. In the last part of the line, people tend to space out, resigned to their fate.
  b. People bunch up hopefully at the front of the line.
  c. At the very end, people bunch up again, afraid that some other latecomer will get ahead of them.
  d. At a point near the middle, they begin to drift apart, stepping in and out of line to see what's happening up front.

# Recognizing Smooth 25.5 Connections Within Paragraphs

Besides being well organized, the ideas in good paragraphs should also be smoothly connected. Many paragraphs include certain guiding words that help the reader follow the order of ideas. These words are called *transitions*.

**Transitions can help connect ideas clearly and smoothly while pointing out the logical order of the ideas.**

The following chart lists a number of common transitions. They are grouped according to the logical orders they are most often used with. However, you can use many of these transitions with other logical orders as well.

| COMMON TRANSITIONS | | |
|---|---|---|
| **For Chronological Order** | | |
| after | first | previously |
| afterward | formerly | soon |
| at last | last | then |
| before | later | ultimately |
| earlier | meanwhile | until |
| eventually | next | while |
| finally | now | |
| **For Spatial Order** | | |
| above | beneath | next to |
| across | beyond | on the right |
| ahead | in front of | outside |
| away | in the center | to the left |
| behind | in the distance | |
| below | near | |
| **For Order of Importance** | | |
| also | for one reason | one |
| even more serious | furthermore | perhaps the |
| finally | more | greatest reason |
| first | moreover | second |

| first of all | most important | third |
| for example | next | |

### For Comparison and Contrast Order

| although | instead | on the other hand |
| another difference | just as . . . so also | similarly |
| both | like | similar to |
| but | likewise | whereas |
| however | nevertheless | yet |
| in contrast | on the contrary | |

### For Other Logical Orders

| accordingly | for example | in fact |
| additionally | for instance | mainly |
| along with | furthermore | namely |
| and | in addition | therefore |
| as a result | in conclusion | thus |
| consequently | indeed | |

In the following paragraph, you can see how transitions (in italics) help to link the ideas smoothly and logically.

Paragraph with transitions

Only hardy nature lovers should attempt stream fishing because what makes the streams wild and beautiful makes the fishing difficult. *First of all,* fishers usually have to tramp through woods and dense thickets, humming with mosquitoes, to reach isolated streams. *Then,* to find quiet holes where fish are, they must wade across slick stones and logs, where it is easy to fall. *Moreover,* when they cast, overhanging trees and shrubbery along the stream can snag their lines. Or if the bait does plop into a deep pool, submerged logs and underwater ledges may grab the hooks. *Consequently,* fishers may spend hours wrestling with the surrounding branches and rocks. *Finally, after* all their efforts, their lines may jerk and a sparkling fish may thrash towards them—only to flip off the hook at the last minute. Only true nature lovers can feel refreshed by this kind of adventure; others would describe it as a day when nature won a battle in the age-old conflict between humans and the outdoors.

The number of transitions needed within a paragraph will vary. Some paragraphs will be clear and smooth without transitions. In other paragraphs, just one or two transitions will improve the flow of ideas. In still other paragraphs, a number of transitions may be needed to guide the reader from thought to thought.

**EXERCISE: Choosing Appropriate Transitions.** Each of the following items consists of a list of possible transitions and a paragraph with numbered blanks. Read the paragraphs carefully. Then, decide which transitions would best connect the ideas and make the paragraphs flow smoothly. Finally, rewrite the paragraphs, inserting the transitions you have chosen.

1. and    at last    beneath    but    finally    first    furthermore    however    later    then

   Ned didn't know how to tell us that he had lost our Siamese cats while he was cat-sitting for us. (1) _____, he tried to act as if nothing had happened. He couldn't keep that up for very long, (2) _____. (3) _____, he stammered and mumbled something about the cats squeezing out through an open window when he wasn't looking. (4) _____, he said that he hoped they would be back soon. The cats did come home (5) _____, and Ned was so relieved that he stayed for dinner and had three helpings of dessert.

2. accordingly    even    for example    however    in fact    mainly    meanwhile    therefore

   The Japanese people have learned how to make brilliant use of their country's limited natural resources. (1) _____, because Japan produces only a few foods in large quantities—

(2) _____ fish, rice, and a few vegetables—the Japanese have figured out ways of using these foods in many different dishes. They (3) _____ manage to make seaweed tasty and decorative in a number of different ways. Such elaborate preparation does take time, effort, and ingenuity. (4) _____, these are resources that the Japanese people possess in greatest abundance.

**DEVELOPING WRITING SKILLS: Creating Paragraphs with Smooth Connections.** Choose one of the following skeleton paragraphs and decide which order has been used to organize the supporting information. Then list *two* or *three* transitions that could be used to connect the ideas smoothly and clearly. Finally, write the paragraph, adding the transitions you have chosen.

1. Qualities necessary in a baseball pitcher
    a. stamina
    b. a sharp eye
    c. a strong arm
    d. accurate aim
    e. instinct for batter's weakness
2. Impressions of a rock concert
    a. The arena filling gradually
    b. The band's appearance in a flash of light and roar of sound
    c. The audience's frequent applause and cheering
    d. The empty stands filled with programs and other clutter
    e. The traffic jam outside with blaring horns

# Writing Workshop: Looking at Paragraphs

## ASSIGNMENT 1

**Topic**   An Object's View of the World

**Form and Purpose**   A paragraph that describes or narrates from a different point of view

**Audience**   Your classmates

**Length**   One paragraph

**Focus**   Write a description of the world from an object's point of view, without naming the object.

**Sources**   Personal observation and your imagination

**Prewriting**   Select an object that has an interesting view of life, such as a stoplight or a television tower. Then brainstorm about how the world appears through the "eyes" of your object.

**Writing**   Write a first draft using either spatial or chronological order.

**Revising**   Add transitions from the chart on pages 422–423 to connect your ideas smoothly. Check your capitalization, spelling, and punctuation. Then prepare a final draft. Read it to other classmates to see if they can guess your object.

© 1960, United Feature Syndicate, Inc.

## ASSIGNMENT 2

**Topic**   A Comparison of Two Pets

**Form and Purpose**   A paragraph that informs or explains by comparison and contrast

**Audience**   Someone who is deciding which pet to choose

**Length**   One paragraph

**Focus**   Compare and contrast two different pets, such as a dog and a cat. Concentrate on details related to behavior and temperament.

**Sources**   Personal experiences, observations

**Prewriting**   After selecting two pets, make a list of similarities and differences in their behavior.

**Writing**   Use your list to write a first draft.

**Revising**   The chart on pages 422–423 will help you add transitions that compare and contrast. Correct any capitalization, punctuation, and spelling errors. Then prepare a final draft.

# Topics for Writing: Looking at Paragraphs

Bodmer, *Buffalo and Elk on the Upper Missouri*

The painting above may suggest a writing topic to you. If so, plan and write a paragraph. If not, use one of the items below as a topic. You may have to narrow your topic to make it appropriate for a paragraph, and you may have to research your topic before writing your answer.

1. The Stanley Steamer
2. The Dodo Bird
3. Atlantis
4. American Passenger Pigeons
5. The *Titanic*
6. The Pony Express
7. Dinosaurs
8. P.T. Barnum's Fortune
9. Free Maps at the Gas Station
10. The Volkswagen Beetle

Chapter **26**

# Writing
# Paragraphs

Writing paragraphs is a three-part process. It includes a *pre-writing stage*, a basic *writing stage*, and a *revising stage*.

This chapter will suggest and explain some helpful steps that can guide you as you plan, write, and revise.

## Thinking About Your Ideas and 26.1 Your Topic Sentence

How do you begin to write a paragraph? You need something to write about—a *topic*—someone to write for—an *audience*—something specific to say about your topic—a *main idea*—and a reason for writing—a *purpose*. You must express your main idea in a topic sentence.

### PREWRITING: Discovering a Good Topic

To choose a topic, allow your mind to roam across a number of possibilities related to your personal interests, experiences, reading, and school courses. This process is called *brainstorming*.

**Brainstorm for interesting topics to write about. Then choose a topic small enough to cover in a single paragraph.**

When you brainstorm, list *all* the thoughts that come to mind without considering whether they are your best. If you make a long list of possibilities, you will have a better chance of finding the topic that you would *most* like to write about.

Once you have a list of possible topics, think about how you could turn each one into a paragraph. Some topics may be too big to be covered in a single paragraph. You should break these large, general topics down into smaller topics.

The following is a sample brainstorming list. Notice that some of the ideas have been broken down to make them more suitable for a paragraph.

---

**BRAINSTORMING FOR A PARAGRAPH TOPIC**

| | |
|---|---|
| Dangerous fish | The beach |
| Video games | —Bodysurfing |
| Odd jobs | —The appeal of the boardwalk |
| —Delivering papers | —Building sand castles |
| —Mowing lawns | Television |
| School spirit week | —Funny commercials |
| | —The value of news shows |

---

Imagine that you had made the preceding list and had particularly enjoyed the boardwalk in the summer. You might then decide to write about *The appeal of the boardwalk.*

**EXERCISE A: Breaking Down Topics That Are Too Big.**
Each topic is too general to cover thoroughly in a single paragraph. Write each topic on your paper. Then, under each, list *three* smaller topics that would make good paragraphs.

1. Rock groups     2. Professional sports     3. Dogs (or Cats)

**430**

**EXERCISE B: Thinking Up a Paragraph Topic of Your Own.** On your paper list the following five topics. Then add *five* topics of your own. If any of the ten topics seem too big for you to write about in a single paragraph, list two or three smaller, related topics under each of them. Then choose one topic that you would like to write a paragraph about.

1. Being new at school
2. Using public transportation
3. Caring for a pet
4. Raising plants
5. Losing at sports

# PREWRITING: Choosing Your Audience, Main Idea, and Purpose

As part of your planning, you should answer three basic questions. Who is the *audience* for your paragraph? What is the *main idea* you want to express about your topic? What is your *purpose* in writing—is it to explain something to your audience, is it to persuade your audience, or is it to describe something for your audience?

**Plan your paragraph by deciding on your audience, your main idea, and your purpose in writing.**

Choosing your audience means identifying the person or people to whom you wish to write. In a letter about your vacation, your audience is obviously the friend or relative to whom you address the letter. At other times your audience may be more general—the other students in your class, all the people who are interested in the topic you are writing about, or perhaps all the people who disagree with you on a topic. Whether the audience is small and obvious or large and more general, having an audience in mind can help you write a good paragraph.

The following chart contains questions that you can ask yourself to help decide what audience you will be writing for and what this audience's thoughts may be about your topic.

**431**

1. Is your audience a specific person or larger general group?
2. How much will your audience already know about your topic?
3. Is your audience likely to have a previous interest in your topic?
4. Will your audience begin by agreeing or disagreeing with you?

Thinking about your audience can help you narrow your topic into a main idea. For example, you might decide to write about the topic *The appeal of the boardwalk* for an audience that does not live near the ocean. To shape your paragraph topic into a main idea suitable for that audience, you can ask yourself a number of different kinds of questions. Ask questions about what your audience might want to learn about the topic. Ask questions that your audience itself might ask. Ask questions about why the topic interests you and why it might interest your audience. Your answers will be possible main ideas.

## ASKING QUESTIONS TO FIND A MAIN IDEA

### Paragraph Topic: The appeal of the boardwalk

| Questions | Possible Main Ideas |
|---|---|
| What do I want my audience to know about the boardwalk? | The boardwalk is the best place to spend a Saturday afternoon in the summer. |
| What is the history of the boardwalk? | From its beginning in the 1920's, the boardwalk has thrived by keeping good things from the past while changing with the times. |
| What do I especially like about the boardwalk? | The boardwalk has a unique combination of sights, sounds, and smells. |

Having chosen an audience and listed several possible main ideas, you should next consider your purpose in writing. Will you be explaining the main idea? Will you be persuading your audience to agree with the main idea? Will you be describing something in order to share an experience with your audience?

Notice in the following chart that the three ideas about the boardwalk do indeed suit three different purposes.

| IDENTIFYING PURPOSES BEHIND MAIN IDEAS | |
|---|---|
| **Possible Main Ideas** | **Purpose** |
| The boardwalk is the best place to spend a Saturday afternoon in the summer. | *To persuade:* To convince the audience that this opinion is reasonable |
| From its beginning in the 1920's, the boardwalk has thrived by keeping good things from the past while changing with the times. | *To explain:* To tell the audience about the history of the boardwalk |
| The boardwalk has a unique combination of sights, sounds, and smells. | *To describe:* To share the sights, sounds, and smells of the boardwalk with your audience |

When you have an audience in mind and several possible main ideas and purposes, you can make your final decisions. Your final choices might look like the ones in the chart.

| MAKING FINAL DECISIONS | |
|---|---|
| **Audience** | People who do not live near the ocean |
| **Main Idea** | The boardwalk has a unique combination of sights, sounds, and smells. |
| **Purpose** | To describe this observation about the boardwalk |

**EXERCISE C: Shaping a Paragraph Topic.** Using the paragraph topic you chose in Exercise B, follow these instructions.

1. Decide on your audience and briefly describe it.
2. Thinking about your audience, write down at least two questions about your paragraph topic.
3. Write short, one-sentence answers to the questions. These will be your possible main ideas.
4. Examine your possible main ideas and decide what the purpose of each main idea you have listed is (to explain, to persuade, or to describe).
5. Choose the main idea and the purpose that you want to have for your paragraph.

## PREWRITING: Deciding on Your Topic Sentence

After you have made your basic decisions about audience, main idea, and purpose, you can turn your main idea into a topic sentence.

**Use your main idea to write a clear, direct topic sentence that suits your audience and purpose.**

Although your main idea is already a complete sentence that could act as a topic sentence, it may not say exactly what you want to communicate. To find the best possible topic sentence, write several versions of your topic sentence.

| POSSIBLE TOPIC SENTENCES |
| --- |
| **Main idea: The boardwalk has a unique combination of sights, sounds, and smells.** |
| 1. The boardwalk has a unique combination of sights, sounds, and smells. |
| 2. The boardwalk has many appealing sights, sounds, and smells. |
| 3. The boardwalk offers a feast for the senses. |
| 4. The boardwalk near my home bombards the senses. |

434

Once you have several possible topic sentences, you can choose the one that you like best.

**EXERCISE D: Writing a Topic Sentence.** Use the audience, main idea, and purpose that you chose in Exercise C to write three or four possible topic sentences that are appropriate for your audience and purpose. Then choose the one you like best.

**DEVELOPING WRITING SKILLS: Planning a Paragraph.** Use all the prewriting steps in this section to prepare ideas for a paragraph. Follow these instructions.

1. Brainstorm for interesting topics to write about. List at least *five*.
2. Choose the topic that appeals to you most. If it is too big for one paragraph, break it down into smaller topics and choose one of these as your paragraph topic.
3. Choose and briefly describe your audience.
4. With your audience in mind, jot down *three* questions about your topic. Answer each question in a single sentence. Your answers will be possible main ideas.
5. Decide what purpose each main idea would best suit.
6. Choose the main idea you want to write about.
7. Write three or four possible topic sentences, and choose the one that is clearest and most suitable for your audience and purpose.

# Supporting and Writing a 26.2 Paragraph

A topic sentence provides a focus for your paragraph. To produce a paragraph, you must flesh it out with specific, well-organized supporting information. This section will take you through the prewriting and writing steps necessary to do this.

# PREWRITING: Brainstorming for Support

You should begin by concentrating on finding specific pieces of information to support your topic sentence.

**Brainstorm for examples, details, facts, reasons, and incidents that will support or develop your main idea.**

To carry out this brainstorming step, you should use whatever method works best for you. You might find that sitting quietly, thinking, and listing helps you most. You might find that talking over your ideas with another person works best. Or you might try listing a few ideas now and more ideas later.

One particularly useful method of brainstorming involves asking questions about your main idea and then answering them. To use this method, you should begin by writing your topic sentence at the top of a piece of paper. Then think of questions that your audience might ask about your main idea. Finally, answer the questions by jotting down examples, details, facts, and so on. Make your list as detailed as you can, as in the chart below and on the next page.

---

### QUESTIONING TO FIND SUPPORT FOR A TOPIC SENTENCE

**Topic Sentence: The boardwalk near my home bombards the senses.**

What sights does it offer?
—shocking pink panthers and three-foot-tall, stuffed alligators in the booths
—big-domed building with the merry-go-round
—a man carrying a shark
—vendors selling silver helium balloons and fresh flowers
—penny arcade with ringtoss and baseball-throwing games
—boardwalk has been there for years

| | |
|---|---|
| in a garbage can lid<br>—wooden horses, kangaroos, and ostriches rising and falling | —rows of chocolates in the candy shop |

What sounds strike a person's ears?

| | |
|---|---|
| —clicking, ringing, crashing of electronic games<br>—tinkling music of the merry-go-round | —whir of passing roller skaters<br>—jets passing over<br>—thump of bumper cars and shrieks of the drivers |

What other smells, sensations, and tastes does the boardwalk provide?

| | |
|---|---|
| — sugary smell of chocolates<br>—steaming hot dogs and pretzels<br>—wooden planks vibrating with people<br>—roasting chestnuts | —fishy smell from bait used at the end of the pier<br>—macaroons and chocolate chip cookies to munch on a bench<br>—moist, salty air in your hair |

Your list of supporting information should contain more information than you would want to include in one paragraph.

**EXERCISE A: Finding Supporting Information for a Topic Sentence.** Return to the topic sentence that you wrote in Exercise D of Section 26.1. Write the topic sentence at the top of your paper and then brainstorm for specific supporting information using *one* of these methods.

1. Think about your topic sentence for a while or talk about it with another person. Then list all the information that comes to mind about your main idea. Try to list at least ten specific examples, details, facts, reasons, or incidents.

2. Jot down your topic sentence and then write two or three questions that your audience might ask about your main idea. Beneath each question list all the specific information you can think of that answers the question.

## PREWRITING: Organizing Support for Your Topic Sentence

Organizing your supporting information is a two-step process. First, you should make sure that you have enough good ideas to create a paragraph. Then, you should organize your supporting information in a logical order.

**To organize your supporting information, cross out ideas that are unrelated or extra and add other pieces of supporting information so that it follows a logical order.**

Begin by examining your brainstorming list. Make sure you have a number of ideas that cover your main idea and work well together. Then cross out unrelated ideas and ideas that are not really necessary. Finally, decide if you need to add any new information. To determine what information to keep or add, ask yourself the questions in the following chart.

---

### DECIDING WHAT TO CROSS OUT OR ADD

1. Does this example, detail, or fact help a reader understand the main idea?
2. Is this piece of information related to the main idea and to the other information in the paragraph?
3. Is this piece of information really necessary?
4. Are there any pieces of information that should be added to help the audience understand the main idea?

---

Once you have chosen the ideas that will go in your paragraph, you should look for ways to arrange them. Think about your topic sentence as you examine your supporting information. Then decide which of the logical orders discussed in Section 25.4 would best organize your ideas.

When you have a logical order in mind, you should arrange your supporting information according to that order. You can simply number the pieces of supporting information on your brainstorming list. Or you can make a modified outline that lists your supporting information in logical order under your topic sentence.

The following modified outline shows a logical arrangement of the supporting information for the paragraph on the boardwalk. The details follow spatial order—the order of sight, sounds, and smells that a person walking along the boardwalk might experience.

Topic Sentence: The boardwalk near my home bombards the senses.

1. Whir of passing roller skaters by the big-domed building with the merry-go-round
2. Tinkling music of the merry-go-round
3. Wooden horses, kangaroos, and ostriches rising and falling
4. Thump of bumper cars and shrieks of the drivers
5. Vendors selling silver helium balloons, fresh flowers, and steaming hot dogs and pretzels
6. Sugary smell of chocolate from candy shop with rows of chocolates
7. Penny arcade with ringtoss and baseball-throwing games
8. Shocking pink panthers and three-foot-tall, stuffed alligators in the booths
9. Clicking, ringing, crashing of electronic games
10. Munching macaroons and chocolate chip cookies on a bench
11. Moist, salty air blowing in your hair

**EXERCISE B: Examining Your Support.** Using the brainstorming list you created in Exercise A and the questions in the chart on page 438, check each piece of supporting information in your list. Use the questions to decide which pieces of support to cross out. Then add examples, details, and facts that seem necessary to give full support to your topic sentence.

**EXERCISE C: Arranging Your Support in a Logical Order.** Read your topic sentence and the list of support that you revised. Decide what order the paragraph should follow. List your support in logical order in a modified outline.

## WRITING: Creating a First Draft

Now that you know what you want to say, you are ready to write a *first draft* of your paragraph. You can think of this as a practice version. It should contain all of your ideas in complete sentences. It does not need to be perfect because you will still have a revision stage in which to polish your ideas.

**Write a first draft, while thinking about your audience and purpose. Use your outline as a guide and add transitions as needed to connect your ideas.**

As you write your paragraph, pretend that you are talking to your audience. Focusing on your audience and purpose will help you write more clearly. Besides following your outline, you can use the ideas in the chart as a guide while writing.

| SUGGESTIONS FOR WRITING A FIRST DRAFT |
|---|
| 1. Choose words that your audience will understand. |
| 2. Add any examples, details, facts, or other information that come to mind while writing. |
| 3. Feel free to change the order of ideas to make your paragraph flow more logically. |
| 4. Use transitions to link ideas and make your writing smooth. |

The following paragraph is a complete version of the paragraph about the boardwalk. It follows the spatial order of ideas in the modified outline on page 439. Note the way in which transitions (printed in italics) help the reader follow the ideas.

TOPIC
SENTENCE

Completed
paragraph
with unified
ideas and
smooth
connections

The boardwalk near my home bombards the senses. Walking down the boardwalk, my friends and I are surrounded by sights, sounds, and smells. Roller skaters whir by us as we pass the big-domed building with the merry-go-round. Tinkling music drifts out the door, through which we can glimpse people on wooden horses, kangaroos, and ostriches that rise and fall and then disappear. *Next door* the bumper cars thump while their drivers laugh and shriek. *Along the next stretch,* vendors sell silver helium balloons, freshly cut flowers, steaming hot dogs, and huge pretzels. *Farther down* sugary smells float out of the candy shop with its rows of chocolates and saltwater taffy. The penny arcade *nearby* swarms with people tossing rings onto pegs and popping baseballs into bottles to win one of the shocking pink panthers or three-foot-tall stuffed alligators displayed on the walls of the booths. *From another gallery* we can hear the clicking, ringing, and crashing of electronic games. While we rest on one of the benches *at the end of the boardwalk,* munching fresh macaroons and chocolate chip cookies, we can feel the moist, salty air blow in our hair and see swimmers in the surf.

**EXERCISE D: Writing a First Draft.** Using the modified outline that you prepared in Exercise C, write a first draft of your paragraph, using the chart on page 440 as a guide.

**DEVELOPING WRITING SKILLS: Developing and Writing a Paragraph.** Return to the paragraph topic and topic sentence you worked with in the Developing Writing Skills in Section 26.1 for this exercise. Then follow these instructions.

1. Write the topic sentence at the top of a blank piece of paper and brainstorm for supporting information.
2. Use the questions in the chart on page 438 to help you weed out supporting information that does not fit or that is extra. Add any other ideas that seem necessary.
3. Choose the logical order that would most help your audience understand the paragraph. Then make a modified outline following the order you have chosen.
4. Finally, write a first draft of your paragraph following the ideas in the chart on page 440.

# 26.3 Revising a Paragraph

*Revising* is an important stage in the writing process. Revising means looking very carefully at the paragraph you have written and carrying out any changes needed to make your ideas as clear as possible for your audience.

This section will show you how to revise weaknesses in your paragraphs and how to proofread your writing to find and correct any mechanical errors.

## REVISING: Looking at Your Topic Sentence

When you begin to revise a paragraph, you should first check your topic sentence. If all the supporting information fits together but the topic sentence does not seem to match the paragraph, you may have one of two problems. You may have written a topic sentence that is too narrow or one that is too general. A topic sentence that is too narrow covers only part of the supporting information in the paragraph. One that is too general leads the audience to expect more information than you have included in the paragraph.

**Rewrite a topic sentence that is too narrow or too general by expanding or narrowing the main idea to cover the information in the paragraph.**

Suppose you were writing a paragraph about the many large animals in Alaska. The following topic sentence would be too narrow because it suggests that the paragraph will be about bears only.

TOO NARROW:   The wild bears of Alaska are extremely large.

The next topic sentence is too general because it suggests that the paragraph will be about both small and large animals.

TOO GENERAL:   The animals in Alaska range from tiny creatures
to giant mammals.

The final topic sentence clearly indicates to a reader that the paragraph will focus on large animals in Alaska.

CLEARLY FOCUSED:   The wild game in Alaska comes in the large
economy size.

Now see how well the clearly focused topic sentence works with its paragraph.

Paragraph with a focused topic sentence

The wild game in Alaska comes in the large economy size. Brown bears that roam the forest in southeast Alaska reach 1,600 pounds. The Kodiak bear and the brown bears of the Alaska Peninsula, stretching toward the Aleutians, rival this for size. The moose that browse on the willows and other brush of the Kenai Peninsula, the Susina Valley, and the Alaska Peninsula are among the largest game animals. — Elsa Pedersen

To revise a topic sentence, reread your paragraph and check the supporting information against the topic sentence. If the topic sentence mentions a smaller or bigger idea than that main idea, rewrite it to state the main idea exactly.

**EXERCISE A: Revising Topic Sentences.** In each of the following paragraphs, the underlined topic sentence is either too narrow or too general. Identify each problem and rewrite each topic sentence to fit the supporting information.

(1) A number of ships have been known to sink and then live again. A Swedish battleship, the *Nasa,* built in 1628, had problems with its hull and weight distribution. The ship was constructed with sixty-four guns on two of its decks. On its maiden voyage, the *Nasa* began to list dangerously after a brief storm. Shortly afterwards, it sank, killing approximately fifty persons. But more than three hundred years later, in 1956, the ship was rediscovered, refloated, and brought back to Stockholm, where today it can be visited in port.

(2) In *The Master Puppeteer* by Katherine Paterson, Jiro, the main character, leaves his home. When Jiro feels lonely and useless at home, he runs away to join the puppet theater. There, he makes friends with Kinshi. Kinshi's generosity and sense of humor help Jiro feel at home. At the theater, Jiro discovers his own daring and ambition and conquers his envy and competitiveness. He learns that he does have the talent to make puppets come alive on stage. Through his success Jiro finds a career and wins his parents' respect.

## REVISING: Looking at Your Supporting Information

When you revise a paragraph, examine your supporting information. You may be able to make your paragraph stronger by adding more information or by replacing weak information.

**Improving Paragraphs by Adding Support.** If your paragraph does not have enough supporting information to make it clear and convincing, you may have to add more information.

**Revise a paragraph that has too little support by adding more supporting information.**

**444**

The following paragraph does not cover its main idea thoroughly. It provides examples of only part of the main idea. You wonder in what ways dolphins have helped animals.

Paragraph with not enough supporting information

> Dolphins have been known to come to the aid of both people and animals. Once, dolphins carried a shipwreck victim nearly two hundred miles through choppy seas until a ship spotted her and took her aboard. Another time, dolphins came to the aid of four men who were adrift in a thick fog off the South African coast. The dolphins swam around the boat to force it to change course, thereby directing the boat away from a dangerous reef of rocks.

Another detailed example might improve this paragraph.

Paragraph developed with complete supporting information

> Dolphins have been known to come to the aid of both people and animals. Once, dolphins carried a shipwreck victim nearly two hundred miles through choppy seas until a ship spotted her and took her aboard. Another time, dolphins came to the aid of four men who were adrift in a thick fog off the South African coast. The dolphins swam around the boat to force it to change course, thereby directing the boat away from a dangerous reef of rocks. *On other occasions dolphins have aided animals. In one well-known case, a group of dolphins saved the life of a sea lion that was being attacked by killer whales. The dolphins protected the sea lion by forming a ring around it to keep the attackers away.*

**Improving Paragraphs by Replacing Weak Support.** Paragraphs supported with generalizations and weak opinions will usually be unclear and unconvincing.

Revise a paragraph with weak support by removing the weak information and adding specific supporting information.

In the following paragraph, weak support fills out the paragraph without making the meaning clear.

Paragraph with generalizations and weak opinions     The new roller coaster at Madison Park offers a spectacular ride. *The climb up the first hill was the greatest.* When the roller coaster plunged down a steep incline, it took my breath away. *Then the roller coaster performed a great trick.* By the end of the ride, I felt total exhilaration. *I felt fantastic.*

The paragraph needs specific thoughts, observations, and feelings to replace the generalizations and weak opinions.

Paragraph with specific supporting information     The new roller coaster at Madison Park offers a spectacular ride. The climb up the first hill was deliberately slow so that I could feel how high the roller coaster was climbing. When the roller coaster plunged down the first steep incline, it took my breath away and made my eyes water. And then, before I could breathe normally, it soared upward around two huge loops, turning me upside down so fast that I saw concrete and sky blurred together. By the end of the ride, I felt total exhilaration. My heart pounded like a gong, but I felt lighter than a spring breeze. I walked down the ramp wearing a big grin from ear to ear.

## EXERCISE B: Revising Paragraphs to Improve the Supporting Information.

Identify the problems in the following paragraphs as either *not enough supporting information* or *generalizations and weak opinions.* Then rewrite each paragraph.

(1) Headphones have made life much easier. Headphones are super. They have made our house quiet although we all still enjoy our stations and records. Headphones are an outstanding invention. I have quiet to do my homework, and my family has peace when I play music. They are great outdoors, too.

(2) Riding in a carpool to school has definite disadvantages. For instance, we have to leave earlier than I normally would to allow time to pick up everyone else. In addition, if I forget something, I cannot go back to my house to get it.

# REVISING: Creating Unified Ideas

When you revise, you should also make sure that your paragraph sticks to a single main idea. If the ideas in your paragraph are not unified, a reader may wonder just what topic it is that you are really writing about.

**Revise a paragraph that lacks unified ideas by removing unrelated ideas and unnecessary information.**

In the following paragraph about driving across Kansas, the writer strays from the topic twice. Notice that the information printed in italics is unrelated and even confusing.

Paragraph with unrelated information

Driving across Kansas in the summer is an unforgettable experience. The land is covered with small hills that cause the road and the cars to dip and rise. Fields of yellowish grass, with occasional clumps of trees and farms, stretch in every direction. *When travelers cross the Mississippi River, it looks wide and muddy and barely seems to move. Next, Missouri surrounds them with moist air and green scenery.* A warm wind whips over Kansas. It whistles in a lonely way when it blows through car windows and around the corners of gas stations. *Cars should always carry drinking water, a gasoline can, and a spare tire.* Thunderstorms often move in from the Texas Panhandle and Oklahoma. The storms advance into Kansas like a solid dark wall, brightened only by flashes of lightning stabbing the ground. Travelers are likely to think of Dorothy and Oz as they search the charcoal sky for tornadoes.

If you leave out the sentences in italics, you will find that the paragraph develops one main idea and is much clearer. In checking your own paragraphs for unified ideas, question the value of each piece of information and take out anything that does not contribute.

**EXERCISE C: Revising a Paragraph to Create Unified Ideas.** Write four sentences in the following paragraph that stray from the main idea. Then revise the paragraph by rewriting.

(1) Jackie Robinson had unusual athletic abilities. (2) In high school and college, he played football, basketball, baseball, and track. (3) He made money by delivering newspapers and selling refreshments at sports events. (4) He set records in the running broad jump and in basketball, and he had the highest batting average of junior college players. (5) Jackie was a well-built, six-foot-tall man, weighing 185 pounds at his best weight. (6) After playing football for UCLA, he went professional and played for the Los Angeles Bulldogs. (7) During World War II, he became a first lieutenant in the cavalry. (8) In 1945 he signed a contract to play baseball with the Montreal Royals. (9) Between baseball seasons, he played basketball with the Red Devils in Los Angeles. (10) In 1947 he signed with the Brooklyn Dodgers. (11) In 1949 he was named most valuable player in the National League. (12) That year he achieved his highest batting average—.342. (13) Jackie's older brother was also a successful athlete. (14) Jackie's lifetime batting average was .311. (15) He helped the Dodgers win the National League pennant six times and the World Series once.

# REVISING: Fixing a Weakly Organized Paragraph

When you revise a paragraph, you should also think about whether the ideas in the paragraph could be better organized. In addition, you should look for places in your paragraph where transitions could help readers follow your ideas easily.

**Revise a paragraph that has poorly organized or weakly connected ideas by arranging the ideas in a more logical order and by adding transitions.**

The following paragraph explains how to catch a wave while bodysurfing. The paragraph is difficult to understand because the steps are not in the order that a person would do them.

Paragraph with poorly organized supporting information

To bodysurf, you must position yourself correctly, find the right wave, and use careful timing. You must walk or swim out to where the medium-size waves are breaking. You should watch for a big wave and get ready to move into action. As a large wave swells toward you, you should begin to swim as fast as you can toward the beach. To do this, you must get beyond the breaking point nearest the beach. You should duck under or jump through the first row of small waves and reach a position in the water that is about waist or chest deep. If your timing is right, you will catch the crest of the wave and ride with it as it breaks around you and flows toward the beach. You should stop walking just before the next breaking point.

In the following revised version, each piece of support has been arranged according to chronological order, which makes the paragraph much easier to understand. Transitions (printed in italics) also help the reader follow the order of steps.

Paragraph with logically organized supporting information and helpful transitions

To bodysurf, you must position yourself correctly, find the right wave, and use careful timing. *First,* you must walk or swim out to where the medium-size waves are breaking. To do this, you must get beyond the breaking point nearest the beach. You should duck under or jump through the first row of small waves and reach a position in the water that is about waist or

**449**

chest deep. You should stop walking just before the next breaking point. *Then,* you should watch for a big wave and get ready to jump into action. *As* a large wave swells toward you, you should begin to swim as fast as you can toward the beach. If your timing is right, you will catch the crest of the wave and ride with it as it breaks around you and flows toward the beach.

**EXERCISE D: Revising a Paragraph to Achieve a Better Organization.** The following paragraph is poorly organized. It also needs more transitions. Rewrite the paragraph to make the information follow a more logical order. Add transitions to connect the ideas.

(1) My trip to Florida was an exciting adventure. (2) I left Florida with a golden tan and happy memories of friends, family members, and new experiences. (3) I started my vacation by flying to Orlando and going to Disney World. (4) It fascinated me with its different "worlds" and rides and gigantic water slide. (5) I drove with friends down the east coast of the state to Fort Lauderdale. (6) Just as we were to leave for the airport, I managed to practice my golf swing for a few hours at a local Florida driving range. (7) After spending a day in Fort Lauderdale visiting my friend's grandparents, we drove to Naples, Florida, where my own grandparents live. (8) They took us fishing on a rented rowboat, and I learned to snorkel.

## REVISING: Proceeding in an Orderly Fashion

So far this section has discussed *what* you should look for when you revise a paragraph. To carry out the revision itself, you can use the following two steps.

**Use at least one rereading method and a checklist to help revise the ideas in your paragraphs.**

In order to revise a paragraph, you need to recognize its

**450**

weaknesses. The suggestions in the following chart can help you "see" your writing from a fresh perspective.

## REREADING SUGGESTIONS

1. Put your paragraph aside while you do something different for at least ten minutes. Then go back and reread it.
2. Read your paragraph aloud to yourself. Listen for confusing ideas and rough places.
3. Read your paragraph to someone else. Ask the listener to spot problem areas.
4. Have someone else read your paragraph aloud to you. Listen to the places where the reader has problems and for ideas that sound weak or confusing.
5. Have someone else read your paragraph silently and comment on the ideas.

In addition to reading your paragraph in different ways, you should also use a checklist to help identify problems.

## CHECKLIST FOR REVISING A PARAGRAPH

1. Does the main idea in the paragraph cover the ideas in the entire paragraph?
2. What examples, details, facts, reasons, and incidents could you add to develop the topic sentence more fully?
3. Can you find any generalizations or weak opinions that should be replaced with specific supporting information?
4. Are there any pieces of supporting information that are unrelated to your topic sentence?
5. Would your ideas be clearer if they were arranged in another logical order?
6. Are there any transitions that could be added to help the reader follow your ideas?
7. What other changes in words or sentences would make your paragraph clearer and more lively for your audience?

The following model shows a revised first draft of a paragraph. Note that space has been left between every line of the first draft to make the revision stage easier.

> *Parakeets can be little clowns.* ~~Parakeets make entertaining pets.~~ ^They climb *For instance, they like to* on ladders in their cages, sleep *poised* ~~standing~~ on one leg, and *rock* ~~swing~~ on swings. ~~When they are comfortable, they fluff up their feathers. They are easy to care for.~~ If you let them out of their cages, they will fly around the room. *and amuse you.* They may land on your finger, *your* ~~or~~ shoulder *or even your head.* They often tweet at themselves reflected in the mirrors in their cages or tweet when they hear human voices. They seem to tweet the loudest when you are talking on the phone or when you have company. ~~Parakeets make the best pets. Their food is not expensive.~~ They *also* like shiny objects and may peck gently at rings, watches, and earrings or perform other antics. *For example, a friend's parakeet liked the Scrabble board. He would hop around the board, pecking at the tiles. Then he would hang from a macramé plant holder by one leg and chirp, "Birdie, birdie."*

The writer has revised the paragraph by crossing out three unrelated ideas and a weak opinion. The writer has also added a few small pieces of information and a final example with details. Some of the supporting information has been reorganized, and a few transitions have been added. In addition, the writer has changed the wording of the topic sentence to make it more interesting.

**452**

After you have completed these revising steps, your paragraph should look something like the one on page 452. You should treat your first draft as a scratch copy. Cross out words and ideas. Write in new words and new ideas. Circle and move ideas, and make any other changes right on your first draft.

**EXERCISE E: Using a Checklist to Revise.** Using a paragraph that you have written recently, follow one of the rereading suggestions in the chart on page 451. Then use the checklist on the same page to look for weaknesses. Revise your paragraph by crossing out words and ideas, adding new words and ideas, and circling and moving ideas right on your paper.

# REVISING: Proofreading Your Paragraph

To complete the revising stage, you should recopy your paragraph in final form and proofread it for mechanical errors.

**Use a checklist to help proofread your final paragraph.**

The following is a checklist on proofreading a paragraph.

---

**CHECKLIST FOR PROOFREADING A PARAGRAPH**

1. Does your paragraph have any sentence errors (fragments, run-ons, or problems with modifiers)?
2. Have you used verbs and pronouns correctly?
3. Have you capitalized properly?
4. Have you used periods, commas, semicolons, apostrophes, and other punctuation marks where they are needed?
5. Have you checked the spelling of any words that do not look right or that you often misspell?

---

You may be able to correct most errors you catch right on your final copy. If you find major errors or a number of errors, you should recopy the paragraph and proofread it again.

**EXERCISE F: Proofreading a Paragraph.** Make a final copy of the paragraph you revised in Exercise E. Then read your final version slowly and carefully, using the checklist on page 453 to help proofread for mistakes. Finally, make your corrections neatly on your final copy or, if there are too many mistakes, recopy the paragraph and proofread it again.

**DEVELOPING WRITING SKILLS: Practicing Your Revising Skills.** Use a paragraph that you have recently written or write one now using the planning and writing steps you have learned in this chapter. Then follow these directions.

1. Exchange paragraphs with a partner.
2. Pretending that your partner's paragraph is your own, follow the second rereading suggestion in the chart on page 451.
3. Then use the checklist on page 451 to find weaknesses in the paragraph.
4. Write directly on your partner's first draft. Revise the paragraph by crossing out words and ideas, adding new words, and moving ideas as necessary.
5. Then exchange paragraphs again, and recopy your own paragraph in final form following the revisions your partner has made if you think they are good. In addition, make any other improvements that you think are necessary.
6. Then proofread your paragraph and make any corrections that are needed.

# Writing Workshop: Writing Paragraphs

## ASSIGNMENT 1

**Topic**   Settling the West: One Major Problem

**Form and Purpose**   A paragraph that informs an audience about a historical event

**Audience**   Readers of a history textbook

**Focus**   Concentrate on one major problem that settlers encountered when they moved westward. Explain the importance of the problem and how it was solved.

**Sources**   History texts, biographies of settlers

**Prewriting**   Narrow the topic to a specific problem. Formulate a main idea and write notes that support that idea.

**Writing**   Using your notes, write a first draft with a topic sentence and support.

**Revising**   Use the checklists on page 451 to revise your first draft. Prepare a final draft.

"WHEN HE'S FINISHED, LET'S ASK HIM TO GIVE US THAT LECTURE ON SPORTSMANSHIP AGAIN."

## ASSIGNMENT 2

**Topic**   What Is Sportsmanship?

**Form and Purpose**   A paragraph that persuades a reader of your interpretation of sportsmanship

**Audience**   A group of junior high school coaches

**Length**   One paragraph

**Focus**   State your main idea about the definition of sportsmanship. Then give facts, details, and/or examples to support your main idea.

**Sources**   Personal experiences in and observations of sports events

**Prewriting**   Decide on your main idea. Brainstorm for specific facts, details, and examples that support your main idea. Outline your ideas and information in a logical order.

**Writing**   Follow your outline as you write a first draft.

**Revising**   Revise your paragraph using the checklists on page 451. Prepare a final copy.

# Topics for Writing: Writing Paragraphs

The moon shot above may suggest a writing topic to you. If so, plan and write a paragraph. If not, choose one of the following general topics. Make sure that you narrow your topic so that it can be easily covered in one paragraph. If necessary, research your final topic.

1. The First Moon Landing
2. A Theory About the Formation of the Moon
3. A Lunar Eclipse
4. The Moon as a Symbol in Literature or Myths
5. The Full Moon: Does It Really Affect Animals and People?
6. Moon Craters
7. The Dark Side of the Moon
8. Comparison of the Moon and Sun
9. An Explanation of Lunar Phases
10. Exploring the Moon: What Did We Learn?

# 27

# Kinds of Writing

When you write, your purpose may be to *explain*, to *persuade*, or to *describe*. Each purpose creates a different kind of relationship between you and your audience. This chapter will give you a chance to practice all three kinds of writing, using the paragraph as a model.

## 27.1  Writing to Explain

The purpose of much writing is to *explain*. You may write a report for a science that explains an experiment. You may complete an application or write a test answer or a letter in order to explain or inform.

### The Features of Paragraphs That Explain

When you write to explain something, your paragraphs should have certain basic features.

**A paragraph that explains should have a factual main idea developed with specific, factual support expressed in clear, direct language.**

The topic sentence in a paragraph that explains should be factual. It should indicate that you want to share information with a reader. It should also tell a reader what information the paragraph will develop.

Notice the difference between the two topic sentences. Only the first one would suit a paragraph meant to explain.

FACTUAL TOPIC SENTENCE:   You can follow three methods to improve your memory.

OPINIONATED TOPIC SENTENCE:   One method for improving a person's memory works better than all the others.

In addition to having a factual topic sentence, a paragraph that explains should have supporting information that is factual and well organized. The support should *not* consist of opinions; rather, examples, details, facts, and incidents should be used.

Another important feature of paragraphs that explain is clear, direct language. Your words should suit your purpose and your audience. Think about what your audience already knows about your topic. Use words that your audience will understand, and define any difficult or specialized terms. For instance, in a paragraph about rock climbing written for beginners, you might want to define the term *chimney* as "a deep, narrow crack in the face of a cliff." You should also use specific language rather than vague, general language. Try to give a reader an exact idea of your topic.

In the paragraph on the following page, notice the factual idea stated in the topic sentence. Notice also that the supporting information is plentiful, specific, and factual. It is arranged in a logical order that is easy to understand. Finally, notice that the language is clear and direct.

**459**

TOPIC
SENTENCE
(Factual
statement)

Specific,
factual
support in
logical
order

The life of the Hawaiians was not all hard work. They had actually many hours of leisure and a great variety of sports, games, and entertainment. Everyone enjoyed the healthful and invigorating sports of swimming and of surf-riding on carved boards, at which the Hawaiians became amazingly skillful. Coasting down steep hill courses on narrow sleds was a daring sport practiced by the chiefs; children in similar fashion slid down hills on *ti* leaves and coconut fronds, a game still common among the youth of the islands. Boxing, wrestling, and foot-racing were popular sports. The Hawaiians had a form of bowling, several kinds of dart and throwing games, guessing games, and one called *konane* that was something like checkers. Many of these sports and games furnished entertainment for spectators, as did military exercises, sham battles, and hula exhibitions. The hula had a threefold value: It was a religious exercise, a system of physical training, and a form of entertainment.—Ralph S. Kuykendall and A. Grove Day

**EXERCISE A: Examining a Paragraph That Explains.** Answer the questions on the following paragraph.

What happens if you come upon a Portuguese man-of-war or a stinging jellyfish? If you are wearing a wet suit, it will protect you from stings. If not, you will get stung. And it hurts. First, rub all the tentacles off your skin with sand or a towel. Douse the area with diluted ammonia or alcohol or gasoline. Then use a soothing lotion to relieve the stinging. If you run into a big one and feel sick, go to a doctor right away.—Shaney Frey

1. What is the main idea of the paragraph?
2. For whom do you think the paragraph was written?
3. What supporting information is used?
4. How is the supporting information organized?
5. Is the language clear and direct? Why or why not?

# Pointers for Writing Paragraphs That Explain

When you write a paragraph that explains, you should think about the basic features of an explanatory paragraph, while keeping your audience in mind.

**As you write a paragraph that explains, focus on your purpose and your audience.**

The suggestions in the following chart will help you focus on your specific purpose.

| SUGGESTIONS FOR WRITING PARAGRAPHS THAT EXPLAIN |
| --- |
| 1. Choose a topic that you know well enough to explain to someone else. |
| 2. Focus your main idea in a factual topic sentence that clearly indicates what the paragraph will explain. |
| 3. Gather specific examples, details, facts, and incidents that will help your audience understand your main idea. |
| 4. Organize this information clearly. Particularly, make sure that the steps in any instructions you give are clear and logical. |
| 5. Use words that are specific, exact, and understandable to the audience. Define any difficult terms. |

**EXERCISE B: Planning and Writing a Paragraph That Explains.** Choose *one* of the topics that follow or make up one of your own. Think about a paragraph that you could write about this topic. Then follow the planning, writing, and revising steps that you have learned, as well as the pointers in this section, to write a paragraph that explains.

Ways to save water
How to raise a cat
An important local event

What causes lightning
Exhibits in a museum

**DEVELOPING WRITING SKILLS: Writing Paragraphs That Explain.** Think of a topic that you know well to use as a basis for a paragraph that explains. Then follow these instructions.

1. Choose *two* different audiences.
2. Follow the basic planning and writing steps to write *two* different paragraphs on the same topic for your two different audiences.
3. Exchange first drafts of both your paragraphs with a partner. Read your partner's paragraphs and try to identify the two audiences. Then use the checklist on page 451 to suggest improvements.
4. Consider your partner's comments and revise your own paragraphs.
5. Make final copies of your paragraphs and proofread them using the checklist on page 453.

# 27.2 Writing to Persuade

In many writing situations, you must do more than simply explain; you must use special skills to *persuade.* In your social studies class, for example, you may need to write a paragraph giving your views on a political issue. In your school paper, you may want to present reasons for a change in after-school activities. This section will help you to write convincing persuasive paragraphs.

## The Features of Paragraphs That Persuade

Persuasive paragraphs should always have certain special features.

**A paragraph that persuades should have an opinion for its main idea. The main idea should be supported with specific evidence arranged logically and presented reasonably.**

The topic sentence of a persuasive paragraph should be a statement with which some people might disagree—an opinion. It should also be a statement that you can back up with specific supporting information. You should state your opinion firmly, but at the same time, you should not make fun of those who disagree with you.

Notice that both of the topic sentences in the following chart express opinions in a reasonable but definite way.

| TOPIC SENTENCES FOR PARAGRAPHS THAT PERSUADE |
| --- |
| The national and state governments should make every effort to protect our parks from commercial development. |
| People in our community should vote now to make motorcycle riding illegal on the hills outside of town. |

The supporting information in a persuasive paragraph should defend the opinion in the topic sentence. The support will generally include reasons in favor of the opinion. Examples, incidents, and facts can also be used to convince readers to accept the opinion. Above all a persuasive paragraph should have enough support to make the opinion seem reasonable.

Your support should be organized in a way that will help convince your audience that your opinion is right. One especially effective way to present your support is to arrange it in order of importance, building from your least important to your most important reason or piece of evidence. By organizing your paragraph in this way, you can leave the reader thinking about your strongest point.

Like the language in your topic sentence, the language throughout the paragraph should be firm but reasonable. When you are discussing a topic about which you feel strongly, it is easy to become overly emotional. Name-calling seldom convinces someone to agree with you. Instead, take care to make all of the paragraph as reasonable as possible.

**463**

In the following paragraph, the supporting information, arranged in order of importance, backs up the opinion in the topic sentence.

TOPIC SENTENCE (Opinion)

Specific evidence in order of importance

Many of today's campers are missing the true joys of camping. For many people camping has come to mean nothing more than moving all the comforts of home out into a wilder setting. Throughout the summer most campgrounds are densely packed with recreational vehicles. These homes on wheels bring the lights, sounds, and crowds of civilization with them. Many of these campers spend more time carrying on their typical home activities—watching television and listening to the radio—than they do appreciating the unique chances to exercise and get fresh air that the campgrounds offer. More important than the activities are the basic attitudes. Many people seem to have forgotten the point of camping: to enjoy the mountains, the forests, the wild animals, and the quiet—the things not made by human hands.

**EXERCISE A: Examining the Features of a Paragraph That Persuades.** Read the following paragraph carefully. Then answer the questions that follow it.

Let's declare war on noise pollution at Jackson School. How many times have we gotten headaches from lockers banging in the halls or from students pounding on the piano in the music room or blasting radios on the lawn at lunch? We all can learn to close our lockers quietly, and those students who use the music room or who play radios can change their habits. All of us can remember not to yell across the courtyard during lunch, and especially when classes are in session. We can also practice walking instead of running down the corridors. Finally, and perhaps most important, students who do not have classes can try to remember not to stand around talking by the doors to rooms in which classes are being held. Instead, we can all spend more time in the cafeteria, on the far lawn, or in the library. With a little effort on everyone's part, we can make Jackson a more peaceful, relaxing place to learn.

1. What is the main idea of the paragraph?
2. For what kind of audience was this paragraph written?
3. What supporting information is used?
4. How is the supporting information organized?
5. Is the language reasonable and specific? Why or why not?

## Pointers for Writing Paragraphs That Persuade

When you plan and write persuasive paragraphs, you should follow the usual planning and writing steps. But you should also concentrate on the special features of persuasive writing.

**As you write a paragraph that persuades, focus on your purpose and try to convince your audience.**

The suggestions below can be used along with the steps of the writing process to write persuasive paragraphs.

### SUGGESTIONS FOR WRITING PARAGRAPHS THAT PERSUADE

1. Choose a topic about which you have strong feelings or definite ideas. Make sure that you can support your opinion.
2. Focus your opinion in a topic sentence that indicates what opinion you will be defending in the paragraph.
3. Gather specific support that will help convince your audience to consider and accept your opinion.
4. Organize your evidence logically in an order that will seem most convincing to your audience.
5. Use words that are reasonable and specific.

**EXERCISE B: Planning and Writing a Paragraph That Persuades.** Choose one of the following topics or make up one of your own. Think about an opinion you have on that topic. Then follow the planning, writing, and revising steps that you have learned, as well as the pointers given in this section, to write a paragraph that persuades.

Table manners                    Violence in movies

A famous performer            Smoke alarms

School dances

**DEVELOPING WRITING SKILLS: Writing Paragraphs That Persuade.** Think of a topic that interests you and about which you have strong feelings. Then follow these instructions.

1. Choose *two* different audiences (for example, people who agree with you and people who do not).
2. Follow the basic planning and writing steps to write *two* different paragraphs on the same topic for your two different audiences.
3. Exchange first drafts of your paragraphs with a partner. Read your partner's paragraphs and try to identify the two audiences. Then use the checklist on page 451 to suggest improvements.
4. Consider your partner's comments and revise your paragraphs.
5. Make final copies of your paragraphs and proofread them using the checklist on page 453.

# 27.3  Writing to Describe

Descriptive writing is needed in many different situations: in letters to friends, in stories, and even in reports. To write good descriptive paragraphs, you must use your powers of observation to make a scene or an experience come alive for your audience. This section will help you write descriptive paragraphs that are both vivid and effective.

# The Features of Paragraphs That Describe

Paragraphs that *describe* should have a number of special features.

**A paragraph that describes should present a dominant impression of a person, place, or thing as its main idea. This dominant impression should be supported with vivid details presented in language that is especially colorful.**

The focus of a descriptive paragraph should be a *dominant impression* of the person, place, or thing that is being described: the overall feeling you have about your topic. Your dominant impression of a garden might be that the garden has a perfect order and harmony. Your dominant impression of an elderly man on a bus might be that he is an old-fashioned gentleman.

Because the dominant impression is the main idea of the paragraph, you will often want to present it in a topic sentence at the beginning of the paragraph. However, you may also end your paragraph with your dominant impression, or you may build up to it and lead away from it by putting it in the middle of the paragraph. In some descriptive paragraphs, the dominant impression is implied throughout but not directly stated anywhere. For now, however, you should present your dominant impression in a topic sentence.

The topic sentences in the following chart both state dominant impressions.

| TOPIC SENTENCES FOR PARAGRAPHS THAT DESCRIBE |
| --- |
| The moored sailboat bounced lightly on the waves, eager to race the wind. |
| The airport surrounded us with fumes and noise. |

The supporting information in a descriptive paragraph should develop the dominant impression with vivid details.

Your detailed observations of shape, color, size, and texture can help the reader picture the topic. To present a person, for example, you should try to capture the person's appearance, movements, and facial expressions. You might mention the way a person walks, blinks, or grins, concentrating on those details that make this person unlike every other person.

The arrangement of details should suit the dominant impression and help the audience see or experience the topic. If you are describing a scene, spatial order will often be the most useful order because it allows you to present each detail in relation to another. If you are describing the minute-by-minute changes in a scene such as a sunrise, you may want to use chronological order. At other times you may want to arrange your details in a special logical order that suits your particular topic.

In writing a descriptive paragraph, you should use words that will help the reader picture the scene—strong verbs, precise nouns, and vivid modifiers. Instead of saying that a basketball player made a *good* shot, you may want to say that he *launched* himself from the floor and *tapped* the ball through the hoop.

You may also want to include *sensory impressions*—that is, combinations of words that make sights, sounds, smells, tastes, and sensations real for your audience.

SENSORY IMPRESSIONS:   The gritty crunch of sand in a sandwich

The smooth, slippery feeling of mud between your toes

The sickly sweet smell from a ketchup factory.

The sudden, piercing bark of a tiny dog

You can also use imaginative comparisons. Comparing one thing with another can help your audience see what you are describing by emphasizing whatever the two things have in

**468**

common. When such a comparison includes the word *like* or *as,* it is called a *simile.*

SIMILES:   The man looked *as* tense *as* a cat ready to pounce.

The grill on the car was *like* a grinning pumpkin.

*Metaphors* are another kind of imaginative comparison. They compare two different things directly, by stating that one thing *is* another thing.

METAPHORS:   The mountain ridge was a sleeping giant.

The siren was a tortured monster shrieking in pain.

The following descriptive paragraph presents a dominant impression in its topic sentence and then develops it with carefully chosen details. Notice that the details of the scene are arranged in spatial order, moving from near to far. Notice also that the language is especially colorful.

TOPIC
SENTENCE
(Dominant
impression)

Vivid,
specific
details in
spatial
order

We opened our shades and windows on a whipped-cream world. Cool, frosty air filled our noses and lungs as we gazed at the sparkling whiteness under the china blue sky. Right outside the windows, the bushes hung limply under white blobs like drippings from a giant's spoon. Our railing and front steps stood oddly taller, raised by the five inches of white fluff. Across the courtyard white frosting capped each branch, so that the limbs of the trees were mostly white trimmed with grayish brown. Around the trees even the most wiry branches of the smallest bushes had delicate creamy lacing. The sidewalk on the edge of the courtyard stretched out like a narrow white rug, dirtied by only a few footprints. The mailboxes beyond the sidewalk sported white top hats. Glistening white snow coated the telephone wires and formed little mounds on the knobs on the telephone poles.

**EXERCISE A: Examining the Features of a Paragraph That Describes.** Read the following paragraph carefully. Then answer the questions that follow it.

Close to, the fire on the mountain was very much more alarming than it had seemed from a distance. They could smell it now, and hear it; smell the smoke more bitter than a farm bonfire; hear the soft, dreadful sound of flames consuming the bracken, like paper crumpled in the hand, and the sudden crackling roar as a bush or a patch of gorse went up. And they could see the flames, leaping high, bright red and yellow at the edges of the fire but ferocious and near invisible at its heart.
—Susan Cooper

1. What is the dominant impression presented in the paragraph?
2. What are *three* vivid details used to develop the dominant impression?
3. How is the supporting information organized?
4. To what senses do the sensory impressions in the paragraph appeal?
5. What examples of imaginative comparisons does the paragraph contain?

## Pointers for Writing Paragraphs That Describe

When you plan and write descriptive paragraphs, you should use the planning and writing steps. Also, pay particular attention to the special features of paragraphs that describe.

**As you write a paragraph that describes, focus on painting a verbal picture or recreating an experience for your audience with specific details and vivid words.**

The suggestions in the chart can be used along with the basic steps of the writing process to write descriptive paragraphs.

**470**

## WRITING PARAGRAPHS THAT DESCRIBE

1. Choose a topic that stands out in your mind.
2. Zero in on one dominant impression of your topic. State this dominant impression in a topic sentence.
3. Gather specific, vivid details to support the impression.
4. Organize your details in an easily followed order.
5. Use strong verbs, precise nouns, vivid modifiers, sensory impressions, and a few similes and metaphors, if you can, to make your topic sharp and clear.

**EXERCISE B: Planning and Writing a Paragraph That Describes.** Choose one of the topics that follow or make up one of your own. Then follow the planning, writing, and revising steps you have learned, as well as the pointers in this section, to write a descriptive paragraph.

| | |
|---|---|
| A plane taking off | A lake |
| A frightening building | A stranger you |
| Your favorite movie star | would like to meet |

**DEVELOPING WRITING SKILLS: Writing Paragraphs That Describe.** Think of *two* different topics. Decide on a dominant impression of each. Then follow these instructions.

1. Use the basic planning and writing steps to write *two* different descriptive paragraphs on the two different topics.
2. Exchange first drafts of your paragraphs with a partner. Read your partner's paragraphs and identify the dominant impression in each. Then suggest improvements using the checklist on page 451.
3. Consider your partner's comments and revise your paragraphs.
4. Make final copies of your paragraphs and proofread them using the checklist on page 453.

# Writing Workshop: Kinds of Writing

## ASSIGNMENT 1

**Topic**   An Invention that the World Really Needs!

**Form and Purpose**   A paragraph that explains to readers the functions and importance of a future invention

**Audience**   Readers of a magazine called *Futurerama*

**Length**   One paragraph

**Focus**   Tell what your invention is and why it is needed. Then explain how it works. Conclude with a statement about how it will affect the world.

**Sources**   Books, your imagination

**Prewriting**   Brainstorm alone or in a small group to come up with ideas about future inventions. Make notes about the features, use, and importance of one invention.

**Writing**   Follow the checklist of suggestions on page 461 as you write a first draft.

**Revising**   Correct any errors in capitalization, spelling, and punctuation. Then prepare a final copy.

## ASSIGNMENT 2

**Topic**   One Sure Way to Improve School Spirit!

**Form and Purpose**   A paragraph that persuades readers of your viewpoint

**Audience**   The school principal

**Length**   One paragraph

**Focus**   State your opinion in a topic sentence. Then support that opinion with facts, details, examples, and/or reasons.

**Sources**   Personal observations, interviews with other students, parents, teachers, or administrators

**Prewriting**   Write a topic sentence that clearly expresses your opinion. Brainstorm for support.

**Writing**   Using your notes, write a first draft.

**Revising**   Check to be sure that all of the supporting sentences actually support your opinion. Correct any errors in spelling, punctuation, and capitalization. Then prepare a final copy.

**473**

# Topics for Writing: Kinds of Writing

The Pentagon, Washington, D.C.

The photo above may suggest a writing topic to you. If so, plan and write an explanatory, descriptive, or persuasive paragraph about that topic. Other possible topics are listed below. You may have to narrow the topic you choose to cover it adequately in a single paragraph.

1. What the Term "Bureaucracy" Means to Me
2. The Size of the Federal Government
3. An Interesting Career in the Federal Government
4. An Impressive Building or Monument in Our Nation's Capitol
5. The Tax Dollar: How It Is Divided
6. Persuading Your Senator to Take a Stand
7. The Construction of the Nation's Capitol
8. The High Price of Maintaining the Federal Government
9. The Growth of the Federal Deficit
10. How Important a Role Does the Federal Government Play in Your Life?

# 28

# Writing Essays

An *essay* is a group of paragraphs written to communicate one main point. This chapter will explain the parts of an essay in more detail and give you a chance to plan, write, and revise your own essays.

## Looking at Essays 28.1

In some ways an essay is like a paragraph, only on a larger scale. A paragraph has a main idea expressed in a topic sentence; an essay has a *main point* presented in a *thesis statement.* A paragraph is made up of information that supports the main idea; an essay has a number of *body paragraphs* that present information to support the main point. Because an essay is larger, however, it contains a few special parts of its own: a *title,* an *introduction,* and a *conclusion.*

### The Parts of an Essay

Each of the essay parts has special functions.

**An essay has a number of basic parts: a title, an introduction with a thesis statement, two or more body paragraphs, and a conclusion.**

**475**

The following chart explains how each of these parts helps to present and develop an essay's main point.

| THE PARTS OF AN ESSAY | |
|---|---|
| **Part** | **How It Works** |
| Title | The title comes at the beginning of the essay.<br>—It catches the reader's interest.<br>—It reveals something about the essay's topic. |
| Introduction | The introduction is the first paragraph of the essay.<br>—It makes the reader want to read the essay.<br>—It presents the topic and any necessary background information.<br>—It leads into and includes the thesis statement. |
| Thesis Statement | The thesis statement is usually one sentence at the end of the introduction.<br>—It presents a focused statement of the main point that the writer wants to develop in the essay.<br>—It suits the audience and purpose. |
| Body Paragraphs | The body paragraphs are two or more paragraphs that form the middle of the essay.<br>—They present specific supporting information to develop the main point.<br>—Each one will generally focus on one aspect—or *subtopic*—of the main point.<br>—They are organized in a logical order. |

| Conclusion | The conclusion is usually the final paragraph.<br>—It reminds the reader of the thesis statement.<br>—It ends the essay smoothly with a final example, an incident, a striking quotation, or a clever statement (called a *clincher*). |

**EXERCISE A: Recognizing the Parts of an Essay.** Identify each of the following by writing *title, introduction, thesis statement, body paragraph,* or *conclusion.*

1. It offers supporting information.
2. It reminds the reader of the main point.
3. It leads into the main point.
4. It tells the main point.
5. It is the first thing to catch the reader's attention.

# How the Parts of an Essay Work Together

The main point presented in the thesis statement holds all the parts of the essay together. The title and introduction introduce the topic and the thesis statement, which contains the main point. The body paragraphs explain and back up the main point. The conclusion summarizes the development of the main point.

**The title, introduction, thesis statement, body, and conclusion all work together to present and support the essay's main point.**

The following essay about doodles shows how all of the parts work together. The essay explains a theory about doodling to a general audience. It has three body paragraphs that develop three aspects or subtopics of the thesis statement.

**477**

| | |
|---|---|
| Title | Doodles Talk |
| Introduction | No two people doodle exactly alike, according to people who study handwriting. These graphologists (as they are called) believe that doodles are expressions of a person's inner self and that doodles hint at unconscious thoughts and feelings. Graphologists |
| Thesis statement | propose the theory that doodling reveals clues about mental abilities, social attitudes, and personality. |
| First body paragraph (Develops subtopic on mental abilities) | Graphologists say that different patterns of doodling can indicate general mental ability. For example, a person who draws intricate geometric patterns probably has a well-organized mind. A person who scribbles in no definite pattern, however, may not think clearly or with much concentration. Such people may become frustrated by minor problems. |
| Second body paragraph (Develops subtopic on social attitudes) | Other patterns of doodling can indicate a person's social attitudes. People who draw smiling faces tend to enjoy the company of others and like to meet new people. People who draw frowning or twisted faces, on the other hand, might dislike people or be critical of them. Someone who draws wide, airy circles is likely to be open and even naive about people—a person who trusts others and sees their brighter sides. |
| Third body paragraph (Develops subtopic on personality) | Graphologists also point out that doodling can offer clues about personality. Competitive people generally draw doodles that resemble games such as tic-tac-toe or targets or arrows. Sensitive, artistic people tend to doodle in graceful arching or waving lines. Tender, protective people may draw flowers or plants, and people who draw little hearts may be sentimental. |
| Conclusion with reminder of thesis statement | While doodling is by no means a totally accurate method of judging people, a person's doodles may indicate something about his or her thinking, attitudes toward others, and character. Even though doodling |

**478**

may seem to be an idle habit, graphologists feel that doodles may really be a form of self-expression. In a sense, when a person doodles, he or she may be drawing a self-portrait. — Adapted from Dorothy Sara

**EXERCISE B: Understanding the Parts of an Essay.** Read the essay on doodles again. Then answer the questions.

1. How does the title catch the reader's interest? What other title might have been used?
2. What information does the introduction contain?
3. How does the thesis statement prepare the reader for the order of the body paragraphs?
4. Which sentence in the conclusion reminds the reader of the thesis statement?
5. What other information does the conclusion contain?

**DEVELOPING WRITING SKILLS: Planning the Parts of an Essay.** Choose one of the following two thesis statements and then follow the instructions given below.

    a. A friend's most valuable quality is a sense of humor.
    b. Movies that have sequels entertain viewers and give them something to look forward to.

1. Think of a title for the essay.
2. Write a short introduction that ends with your thesis statement.
3. List at least five major pieces of supporting information that could go in the body paragraphs.
4. Write a conclusion that refers to the thesis statement and ends the essay in a memorable way.

# Planning an Essay 28.2

Once you understand the parts that an essay must include, you are ready to plan an essay of your own. As you will see, planning an effective essay involves many of the same prewriting steps that planning an effective paragraph does.

# PREWRITING: Discovering a Good Topic

To find a topic for your essay, you should brainstorm for ideas. Brainstorming means letting your mind work freely.

**Brainstorm for interesting topics. Narrow down any topics that are too large or too general to cover well.**

You can carry out this step by sitting quietly with a paper and pencil, jotting down as fast as you can all the ideas that occur to you. Or talk to friends or relatives, flip through magazines, or browse in a library, and then write down your ideas.

In the following chart is a list of possible essay topics similar to the list you should make. Note that large or general topics are broken down into smaller, more specific topics.

| BRAINSTORMING FOR AN ESSAY TOPIC | |
| --- | --- |
| Scuba diving | Putting on a neighborhood |
| Dress codes | play |
| —Dress codes at private | Radio stations |
| schools | —Features of a good rock |
| —Dress codes at public | station |
| schools | —A good local news |
| —A dress code at River | station |
| Valley School | Public transportation |
| Unusual pets | —The need for more |
| —Raising bees | public transportation |
| —Building an ant farm | —A few success stories in |
| —The habits of gerbils | public transportation |

When you have a list that includes some good possibilities, choose a topic that interests you greatly, that you already know something about, or that you want to explore.

**EXERCISE A: Thinking Up Essay Topics.** Brainstorm for essay topics by listing as many ideas as you can. Think about television shows you have seen recently, books you have read lately, news events, activities at your school, or something new you have learned about your hobby. Jot down at least five possible topics. If a topic is too large, break it down into smaller topis. Then choose a topic that you want to write about.

# PREWRITING: Choosing Your Audience, Main Point, and Purpose

After you have chosen your topic, your next prewriting step involves making three important decisions. First, you should choose your audience—the people to whom you are "speaking" in your essay. Second, you should decide what particular point you want to focus on. And third, you should decide your purpose in writing: to explain or to persuade.

**Focus your essay topic by deciding on your audience, main point, and purpose. Then write a thesis statement that shows the results of these decisions.**

You should begin by deciding who your audience is. Is your audience a specific person or group, or would you rather write for a larger, more general audience? How old is your audience? How much does your audience know about your topic? Is your audience likely to agree or disagree with you?

Once you have an audience in mind, you can decide on a main point. One method of finding a main point is to ask yourself questions about your topic. Think particularly about what you and your audience might want to know about your topic. For example, if you had chosen to write about the topic *A dress code at River Valley School,* you might decide that your audience would be other students at the school. With this audience in mind, you could ask yourself questions like those in the chart on the following page to zero in on a main point.

**481**

| ZEROING IN ON A MAIN POINT | |
|---|---|
| **Essay Topic: A dress code at River Valley School** | |
| **Questions** | **Possible Main Points** |
| Why is the topic of a dress code at River Valley School important right now? | The administration is considering returning to a formal dress code to make the school more formal and orderly. |
| What are my feelings about having a dress code at River Valley School? | A formal dress code would harm the pleasant, relaxed atmosphere we now have at the school. |
| What view would I like to see taken by the other students at River Valley School? | River Valley School should not return to a formal dress code. |

Your answers to these questions will be a list of possible main points. When you look at these possible main points, you will probably find that they suit different purposes. In the preceding chart, the first main point informs readers about the dress code; the second and third main points persuade readers to accept the writer's opinions. If you were to decide that the third main point was the point you wanted to cover in your essay, your purpose would be to persuade the other students in the school to agree with you. You would now have chosen your audience, your main point, and your purpose.

The next step is to turn your main point into a thesis statement. You should express your main point as clearly as you can in a complete sentence. Think about your audience and purpose as you try different ways to state your main point. The chart on the following page shows three possible thesis statements for an essay on the dress code.

**482**

| **POSSIBLE THESIS STATEMENTS** |
| :--- |
| **Main Point: River Valley School should not return to a formal dress code.** |
| 1. River Valley School should not return to a formal dress code. |
| 2. River Valley School does not need a formal dress code. |
| 3. River Valley School should not return to a formal dress code because it would create problems for everyone and it would take away many of our responsibilities and privileges. |

When you have several versions of your thesis statement, decide which one you like best. Having a thesis statement in mind will help you focus your ideas for the rest of your essay.

**EXERCISE B: Making an Essay Topic into a Thesis Statement.** Using the essay topic you chose in Exercise A, follow these instructions.

1. Decide who your audience is, and then write a sentence describing your audience.
2. Write down *three* questions that you or your audience might ask about your topic. Then write one-sentence answers to your questions that could be used as main points for your essay.
3. Decide which purpose each main point would serve, and think about which purpose you would like to have.
4. Choose your main point. Then write two or three slightly different thesis statements expressing your main point.
5. Choose the thesis statement you want to use.

## PREWRITING: Finding Support for Your Thesis Statement

Once you have a thesis statement, you are ready to brainstorm for specific information that will explain or support your thesis statement. Thinking about your audience and purpose

**483**

will help you find the best supporting information. For instance, if your purpose is to explain, you should think of all the examples and facts that your audience needs to understand your main point. If your purpose is to persuade, you should think of examples, facts, and reasons that will make your audience agree with your main point.

**Think about your audience and purpose as you brainstorm for examples, details, facts, reasons, and incidents to support and develop your thesis statement.**

Begin by writing your thesis statement at the top of a blank piece of paper. Then think about your audience and purpose, and list all your ideas about your thesis statement. At this stage do not try to sort out information that may not belong. Instead, try to list *more* specific information than you will need in your essay. If you think your mind is straying too far from your main point, however, read your thesis statement over again.

The following is a brainstorming list for the essay about a dress code at River Valley School.

---

**BRAINSTORMING FOR SUPPORTING INFORMATION**

| Thesis Statement: | River Valley School should not return to a formal dress code because it would create problems for everyone and would take away many of our responsibilities and privileges. |
|---|---|

—formal dress code to begin next semester
—would lose responsibility to make our own decisions
—need to discover our own identities
—need time to find out what styles are good for us
—express individuality with clothing
—explore different attitudes toward society
—boys to wear dark slacks and solid-colored shirts (no jeans, T-shirts, or pullover shirts allowed)

—girls to wear pleated pastel skirts or dark slacks and solid-colored blouses (no jeans, dresses, or shorts allowed)

—more work for administrators to make sure students follow code

—more record keeping for teachers in addition to the usual absences and locker and book checks

—more detention for deans to supervise

—return to River Valley School's formal dress code of ten years ago

—need to buy those special kinds and colors of slacks, shirts, skirts, and blouses

—already bought special gym clothes

—need to see how others respond to our own choices of clothes

—"uniforms" would make school serious, formal, no longer casual and fun

—need to think of an alternative to a formal dress code or a compromise

—administration wants formal school atmosphere

—dullness of having to wear only certain styles

—"uniforms" not useful outside school

—already have rules about footwear and short shorts

**EXERCISE C: Brainstorming for Supporting Information.** Write your thesis statement from Exercise B at the top of a blank piece of paper. Then list as many examples, details, facts, reasons, and incidents related to your thesis statement as you can.

## PREWRITING: Organizing Your Supporting Information

As a final step in the prewriting stage, you should organize your ideas.

**Choose your best pieces of supporting information and group them logically by making an outline for the body of your essay.**

**485**

The steps in the following chart will help you decide which pieces of information you should include in your essay and in what order you should present them. You can do your crossing out and organizing right on your list.

---

**SUGGESTIONS FOR SORTING AND ORGANIZING SUPPORTING INFORMATION**

1. Read over each piece of information on your brainstorming list. Cross out any ideas that are not closely related to your main point.
2. If some ideas are important but do not belong in the body of your essay, put them aside for the introduction or conclusion.
3. If you think of new ideas that develop your main point, add them.
4. Examine your thesis statement and your list of support to find logical groupings for your support. These groupings will be your subtopics. You can plan to use one body paragraph for each subtopic you choose.
5. Decide on a logical order (chronological order, spatial order, order of importance, comparison and contrast order, or some other logical order) for your subtopics.
6. To see your essay more clearly, prepare a modified outline for the body of your paragraph.

---

For the essay on the dress code, the supporting information could be grouped under two subtopics taken directly from the thesis statement. The first body paragraph might cover the problems created for everyone. The second body paragraph might cover the way a dress code would take away student responsibilities and privileges. These two subtopics fall into a natural order of importance since the second subtopic is likely to be more convincing to an audience made up of other students. The following modified outline shows how you might arrange the supporting information in the body of this essay.

**486**

Thesis Statement: River Valley School should not return to a formal dress code because it would create problems for everyone and would take away many of our responsibilities and privileges.

Subtopic 1: Would Create Problems for Everyone
1. Need to buy special kinds and colors of slacks, shirts, skirts, and blouses
   —already have school clothes this year
   —"uniforms" not useful outside school
   —already bought special clothes for gym
2. More work for faculty and administrators to enforce code
   —more record keeping for teachers in addition to the usual absences and locker and book checks
   —more detention for deans to supervise

Subtopic 2: Would Take Away Many of Our Responsibilities and Privileges
1. Would take away our responsibility to make our own decisions
2. School years are a time to discover our identities
   —express individuality with clothing
   —find out what styles are good for us
   —see how others respond to our choices
   —explore attitudes toward society
3. Choosing clothes is part of maturing

**EXERCISE D: Sorting and Arranging Supporting Information.** Use the brainstorming list that you prepared in Exercise C and the suggestions in the chart on page 486 to sort out and organize your supporting information. Show your decisions by writing a modified outline of the body of your essay.

**DEVELOPING WRITING SKILLS: Preparing an Essay.** Follow the prewriting steps in this section and the instructions on the following page to plan another essay.

1. Brainstorm for a topic, or choose one from the list of topics you made in Exercise A.
2. Choose an audience and purpose that differ from those you chose for your first essay. Zero in on a main point and express your main point as a thesis statement.
3. Brainstorm for supporting information.
4. Weed out unrelated ideas. Add new ideas, and group your support logically by subtopics of your main point.
5. Prepare a modified outline for the body of your essay.

# 28.3 Writing and Revising an Essay

The planning you have done so far should give you confidence as you approach the writing of your essay. Having gathered and organized the support for your main point, you now need to put the parts of the essay together.

## WRITING: Creating a First Draft with an Introduction, Conclusion, and Title

Because your essay needs an introduction, you should think of ideas for your introduction before you begin to write the first draft. Jotting down ideas for your conclusion and title can also help.

**Think of ideas for your introduction, your conclusion, and your title. Then write your first draft.**

You can plan your introduction by thinking of the best way to introduce your topic and make it interesting to your audience. Try to think of a "hook" to grab the audience's attention. What examples, quotations, questions, statements, or incidents would appeal to the audience and lead into your thesis statement? Check your brainstorming list for good ideas that you are not using in the body paragraphs. Your introduction should also give any background information that the audience needs to know to understand the essay. In addition, your introduction should make your purpose clear, and it should end with your thesis statement.

Just as your introduction should "hook" readers, your conclusion should leave readers with a strong impression of your essay. As you jot down ideas for your conclusion, try to think of a way to tie together all of the essay's ideas. Somewhere in the conclusion, you should refer to the thesis statement without repeating it exactly. Look also for a few examples, unusual facts, or a striking statement that you can use at the end to make the audience remember your essay. Finally, jot down two or three possible titles that would make the audience want to read the essay.

Once you have ideas for all parts of your essay, you can write your first draft. Use your notes about the introduction and conclusion and your modified outline as a guide. You can also use the suggestions in the following chart.

## POINTERS FOR WRITING A FIRST DRAFT OF AN ESSAY

1. Use words that your audience will understand and language that suits your purpose. If you are explaining, be direct and exact. If you are persuading, be firm but reasonable.
2. If new and related information occurs to you, add it.
3. Make sure that each of your body paragraphs has a topic sentence.
4. Connect the parts of your essay by using transitions where they are needed.

**EXERCISE A: Writing a First Draft.** Return to the essay you organized in Exercise D of Section 28.2. First jot down ideas for your introduction, conclusion, and title. Then write your essay in complete sentences using your modified outline and the pointers presented in the preceding chart.

# REVISING: Polishing and Proofreading Your Essay

After you have written a complete first draft of your essay, you should revise it.

**Reread your essay several times and then use a checklist to revise it. Complete the revising stage by making a final copy and proofreading it carefully.**

To revise your essay, you should begin by trying to see it from a fresh perspective, just as a reader would. Rereading your essay silently and aloud can help you find areas that are awkward or unclear. You should also use a checklist to evaluate the essay point by point. Follow the suggestions in the checklist to revise your essay.

| CHECKLIST FOR REVISING AN ESSAY |
| --- |
| **Title** |
| 1. Does the title suggest the essay's topic and purpose? |
| 2. Is there another more interesting title for the essay? |
| **Introduction and Thesis Statement** |
| 1. Do opening remarks catch the reader's attention? |
| 3. Have you included necessary background information? |
| 3. Does the thesis statement fit the essay? |
| 4. Is there any way the thesis statement could express your main point more clearly? |
| **Body** |
| 1. Are the body paragraphs arranged in the best order? |
| 2. Does each body paragraph have a clear topic sentence? |
| 3. Should you take out any pieces of support? |
| 4. Have you included enough support? |

| **Conclusion** |
| --- |
| 1. Does the conclusion refer to the thesis statement and tie the essay together? |
| 2. Is there any way you could improve the conclusion? |

Changes can be made right on your first draft. If you change the order of ideas, circle the ideas and draw arrows to the places where they belong. When you are satisfied with your improvements, make a final copy.

The last step in the revising stage is proofreading. Read your essay carefully, looking for mistakes overlooked earlier or added in recopying. Use the proofreading checklist for paragraphs on page 453 to proofread each of your paragraphs.

Notice in the final copy of the dress code essay the new ideas that have been added and the transitions (printed in italics) that help make the ideas flow.

Title                       Addressing the Dress Code

Introduction       Schools have changed in many ways over the years. *For example,* in many schools, dress codes have relaxed or disappeared. Most students at River Valley School value the freedom to choose what to wear to school. *But* did you know that River Valley School had a formal dress code ten years ago? Are you aware that the administration wants to return to that dress code next semester? The code would require boys to wear dark slacks (no jeans) and solid-colored shirts (no T-shirts or pullover shirts). Girls would wear pleated pastel skirts or dark slacks (no jeans) and solid-colored blouses. The student council opposes this change in school policy. River Valley School should

Thesis
statement      not return to a formal dress code because it would create problems for everyone and would take away many of our responsibilities and privileges.

**491**

Establishing a formal dress code at our school this year would create problems for us and for the faculty and administration. *First,* we would have to buy the slacks, shirts, skirts, and blouses to meet the code's requirements. *But* we already have school clothes for this year, and most of these outfits can be worn outside school as well. The "uniforms" for the code, *on the other hand,* would not be very useful outside school. *Furthermore,* we have already had to purchase special clothes for gym. The dress code would *also* create more work for the faculty and administrators. They would have to be prepared to enforce the code by punishing those students who are "out of uniform." In addition to the record keeping that teachers already do—recording absences and checking lockers and books—teachers would have to keep track of those students who wore jeans or T-shirts on a particular day. *And* the deans would have to supervise detention for violators of the dress code.

Second
body
paragraph
(Develops
second
subtopic)

*Even more important,* a formal dress code would take away many of our responsibilities and privileges. We would lose one major opportunity to make our own decisions. Our school years are a time for us to discover our identities. Choosing our own clothes gives us a chance to express our individuality. Experimenting with different outfits gives us a chance to decide what styles are appropriate for us and to see how others react to our choices. Within reasonable limits school should be a testing ground, a place for us to take responsibility for how we appear.

For these reasons a formal dress code would disrupt River Valley School rather than make it more orderly, and it would take an important responsibility away from us. If you agree with these arguments, you should speak to your parents about the dress code.

**492**

Then, either with them or on your own, you might write a polite letter to the school board. You can *also* send suggestions for alternatives to the student council. Show that you are responsible and that you are concerned about the school by acting now.

**EXERCISE B: Using Checklists to Polish and Proofread an Essay.** Reread the first draft of the essay you wrote in Exercise A. Then use the checklist for revising an essay to identify and improve any weaknesses in your essay. Rewrite your essay in final form. Then proofread it, using the checklist for proofreading a paragraph on page 453.

**DEVELOPING WRITING SKILLS: Practicing Drafting and Revising.** Use the essay that you planned in the Developing Writing Skills at the end of Section 28.2, and complete the following steps.

1. Jot down ideas for the introduction, conclusion, and title.
2. Draft your essay using these ideas and your modified outline.
3. Read your essay aloud to someone in your class.
4. Use the person's comments and the checklist for revising to improve your essay. Then make a final copy and proofread it.

# Writing Workshop: Writing Essays

## ASSIGNMENT 1

**Topic**  Recycling: Unpiling the Trash Pile

**Form and Purpose**  An essay that explains a problem and persuades a reader of a solution to the problem

**Audience**  Citizens voting on the construction of a recycling center

**Length**  Four to six paragraphs

**Focus**  In your introduction, discuss the importance of proper trash disposal and develop a thesis statement about recycling. In the body, concentrate on explaining the benefits of various recycling methods. Conclude with a reminder of your thesis statement.

**Sources**  Books, magazine and encyclopedia articles, local recycling centers

**Prewriting**  Research your topic. Formulate a main idea and brainstorm for support. Use the checklist on page 486 to organize your support.

**Writing**  Use your outline to write a first draft.

**Revising**  The checklist on pages 490–491 will help you to make changes in your draft. Then prepare a final copy.

*"They spend years teaching us how to talk —and now they say children should be seen and not heard."*

## ASSIGNMENT 2

**Topic**   Probing a Puzzling Inconsistency in Life

**Form and Purpose**   An essay that explains or persuades

**Audience**   Readers of a humorous feature column in a newspaper

**Length**   Four to six paragraphs

**Focus**   Adopt an informal style and humorous tone. Develop a thesis statement about the puzzling inconsistency in your first paragraph. Then support your thesis statement with examples, facts, and details.

**Sources**   Personal experiences and observations

**Prewriting**   Brainstorm for a specific topic. Develop a list of supporting facts, details, and examples. Organize your notes into a modified outline.

**Writing**   Use your outline to write a first draft.

**Revising**   Use the checklist on pages 490–491 to revise your paper. Then prepare a final copy.

# Topics for Writing: Writing Essays

Christopher Columbus

If the above painting suggests a writing topic to you, plan and write an essay about the topic. Other possible topics are listed below. If you choose one, you may have to research and narrow it to a more specific topic.

1. Magellan's Great Voyage
2. The Vikings
3. The First Settlement in Your Town or City
4. Cortés and Montezuma
5. Stanley and Livingstone
6. The Polynesians: Masterful Sailors
7. The Importance of James Cook's Voyages
8. Ancient Maps: What Do They Reveal?
9. The Human Urge to Explore: Why?
10. Exploration: Where to Next?

# Chapter **29**

# Writing Reports

Throughout your school years, you will probably be asked to write a number of *reports* on material you have read and studied. These reports usually contain research information taken from several sources. When you write reports, you can use many of the skills you learned in writing paragraphs and essays. However, reports also have special features of their own.

## Looking at Reports 29.1

In some ways, a *report* is like an essay. It has a title, an introduction with a thesis statement, a body, and a conclusion. It develops one main point with supporting information. However, it differs from an essay because it is based on information gathered from research.

### Sources of Information

A report should be based on information found in books, magazine articles, encyclopedias, and other reference sources. The report should bring together facts, examples, and other pieces of information you have found through your reading. In the report you must give credit for information from other sources by including *footnotes* and a *bibliography*.

**497**

**Footnotes.** To give readers the source of specific information used in your report, you will need to write footnotes. A footnote gets its name from the fact that it is often placed at the bottom, or foot, of the page where the information appears.

**A report should include footnotes that credit sources of specific information.**

Writing a footnote is fairly simple. First, you should place a small number—a 1, 2, 3, and so on—right after and slightly above the information that you have included in your report. Then you should identify the source at the bottom of that page or in a numbered list at the end of the paper as shown below.

| WRITING FOOTNOTES FOR DIFFERENT SOURCES | |
| --- | --- |
| **Kind of Source** | **Footnote** |
| Book with one author | [1]Moira Johnston, The Last Nine Minutes, p. 51. |
| Book with two authors | [2]Ralph S. Kuykendall and A. Grove Day, Hawaii: A History, p. 158. |
| Magazine or newspaper article (author given) | [3]Carol Collins, "Safety First," Hockey World, January 1980, p. 56. |
| Magazine article (no author given) | [4]"Toys for Tots," Time, December 14, 1981, p. 68. |
| Encyclopedia article (author given) | [5]The World Book Encyclopedia, 1981 ed., "Flag," by Whitney Smith. |
| Encyclopedia article (no author given) | [6]The World Book Encyclopedia, 1981 ed., "Skiing." |

There are three specific cases in which a footnote must be used. You must use one whenever you quote someone's exact

**498**

words. The words themselves must be placed in quotation marks. You must also use a footnote whenever you take ideas from another source and rewrite them in your own words. Finally, you must use a footnote whenever you include a fact that is not well-known.

**Bibliography.** Besides footnotes a report should include a bibliography.

**A report should include a bibliography at the end that lists all the sources used in preparing the report.**

A bibliography is really nothing more than an organized list of sources at the end of a report, usually on a separate page. A bibliography entry differs only slightly from a footnote. In a bibliography entry for a book, for example, you should write the author's last name first. You should also reverse the indentation and list the sources alphabetically by the first letter of each entry. The following chart can guide you in writing your own bibliographies.

| WRITING BIBLIOGRAPHY ENTRIES | |
|---|---|
| **Kind of Source** | **Bibliography Entry** |
| Book with one author | Johnston, Moira. The Last Nine Minutes. New York: Avon Books, 1976. |
| Book with two authors | Kuykendall, Ralph S. and Day, A. Grove. Hawaii: A History. Englewood Cliffs, N.J.: Prentice-Hall, Inc., 1961. |
| Magazine or newspaper article (author given) | Collins, Carol. "Safety First." Hockey World, January 1980, p. 56. |
| Magazine article (no author given) | "Toys for Tots." Time, December 14, 1981, p. 68. |

| Encyclopedia article (author given) | The World Book Encyclopedia, 1981 ed., "Flag," by Whitney Smith. |
| Encyclopedia article (no author given) | The World Book Encyclopedia, 1981 ed., "Skiing." |

**EXERCISE A: Practicing Citation of Sources.** In the library, find two or more books about an interesting place, a famous person, or some event of importance. Find a newspaper or magazine article about the same topic, using *The Readers' Guide to Periodical Literature.* Write a footnote for each source. Then make a bibliography of all your sources.

## The Basic Structure of a Report

A report is similar to an essay in structure, but it also shows the research that has gone into planning and writing it.

**A report is a paper on a single topic, based on information gathered through research. It has a title, an introduction with a thesis statement, body paragraphs, footnotes, a conclusion, and a bibliography.**

Your report should be a unified paper that combines your own ideas on a topic with supporting information taken from other sources. The main point should always be your own idea.

As in an essay, all of the various parts of the report should work together. The title, introduction, thesis statement, body paragraphs, and conclusion should serve the purposes outlined in the chart on pages 476–477. Footnotes and the bibliography should show the reader the research you have done in preparing the report. The following report shows how all of these parts work together. Note the way in which the footnotes are abbreviated when a source is used a second time.

Title

The Fearsome Beastie of Loch Ness

Introduction

According to ancient legends and many modern-day witnesses, a large, mysterious creature lives in the deep, dark waters of Loch Ness, Scotland's largest lake. Over the centuries many people claim to have seen this Loch Ness monster. In 525 A.D. St. Colomba, an Irish missionary, was bothered by a "fearsome beastie" while he was swimming one day.[1] In the twentieth century, over three thousand people have reported sightings.[2] But since no one has a photograph or any evidence of what they have seen, most zoologists do not believe that the creature really exists. The

Thesis
statement

debate between the believers and the skeptics continues, with the believers—convinced by personal sightings or by the numerous reports of eyewitnesses—struggling to supply the proof that skeptics demand.

First
subtopic:
skeptics'
point of
view

Those who doubt the existence of the Loch Ness monster point out that most of the sightings of the creature are brief and occur during the summertime on the misty waters of the lake. These skeptics claim that the differences between the temperatures of the cool water surface and the warmer air above it produce distortions, or "mirages." Because of these mirages, people mistake a glimpse of an ordinary object for the legendary beast.[3]

Second
subtopic:
witnesses'
descriptions

But there have been a number of accounts of sightings, both in water and on land, which are difficult to explain. One witness said that he saw a huge, snail-like creature crossing a road. It had a long neck "a little thicker than an elephant's trunk." He added that just part of the creature had covered the entire width of the road.[4] Other witnesses have estimated the length of the animal they saw at twenty to thirty feet. Most of the accounts describe a creature with a small head and a long, slender neck. The bulky body has

**501**

several fins at the sides and at least one large hump on the back.[5]

**Third subtopic: attempts to provide proof**

In recent years several attempts have been made to track the Loch Ness monster systematically and photograph it clearly. In 1972 Dr. Robert Rines, president of the Boston Academy of Applied Science, used a sonar-activated underwater camera. He produced a photograph of what seems to be a diamond-shaped fin, much like the flipper described in many sightings.[6] In the summer of 1979, Dr. Rines had hoped to increase his chances of photographing the creature. His idea was to attach sonar and camera equipment to a pair of trained dolphins that would swim about in the lake. But one of the dolphins died before the experiment began and Dr. Rines was forced to drop the project.[7]

**Conclusion**

And so the debate goes on. No conclusive evidence has been found to prove that the Loch Ness monster really exists. Yet no argument has explained away the large number of similar descriptions of sightings. Both skeptics and believers are still free to argue as they like—as free, some would say, as the elusive Loch Ness monster roaming in its dark, secret home.

---

[1]William S. Ellis, "Loch Ness: The Lake and the Legend," *National Geographic,* June 1977, p. 763.

[2]Ellis, p. 763.

[3]Marcia F. Bartusiak, "Will the Real Nessie Please Stand Up?" *Science News,* August 18, 1979, p. 566.

[4]F.W. Holiday, *The Great Orm of Loch Ness,* p. 31.

[5]Holiday, pp. 26–36.

[6]Robert H. Rines and Howard S. Curtis, "The Big One Got Away—Again," *Technology Review,* June/July 1979, p. 15.

[7]"Loch Ness Mission Delayed After Training Dolphin Dies," *The New York Times,* June 28, 1979, p. A16.

BIBLIOGRAPHY

Bartusiak, Marcia F. "Will the Real Nessie Please Stand Up?" Science News, August 18, 1979, pp. 565–566.

Ellis, William S. "Loch Ness: The Lake and the Legend." National Geographic, June 1977, pp. 758–779.

Holiday, F.W. The Great Orm of Loch Ness. New York: W.W. Norton & Company, Inc., 1969.

"Loch Ness Mission Delayed After Training Dolphin Dies," The New York Times, June 28, 1979, p. A16.

Rines, Robert H. and Curtis, Howard S. "The Big One Got Away —Again." Technology Review, June/July 1979, pp. 14–16.

Whyte, Constance. More Than a Legend. London: Hamish Hamilton, 1957.

**EXERCISE B: Examining a Report.** Read the report again. Then answer the following questions.

1. How many footnotes does the report contain?
2. How many entries does the bibliography contain?
3. In what order are the entries listed in the bibliography?
4. What different kinds of sources are used?
5. What are two other sources on this topic that can be found in your school or local public library? List these as bibliography entries.

**DEVELOPING WRITING SKILLS: Looking at Reports.** Find an article on the topic you chose for Exercise A. Be sure that the article has footnotes and a bibliography. Write an analysis that includes the following information.

1. The number of footnotes the writer used
2. The number of sources
3. The kinds of sources (newspaper, book, magazine article)
4. The thesis statement
5. The subtopics you find
6. How the conclusion summarizes the information in the thesis statement

**503**

# 29.2 Writing a Report

Several practical prewriting steps will help you as you prepare your report.

## PREWRITING: Planning Your Report

If you take time to plan a report carefully, you will find that the actual writing will be easy. The four prewriting steps which follow give you a good, workable plan for your report.

**Finding a Good Topic.** A good topic for a report is one that interests you. Your topic must also fit your assignment and be one that you can research.

**For a report, choose a topic that you want to read and write about and one for which you can find at least three good sources of information.**

Make a list of at least five topics you would like to know more about. They may be subjects you read about, heard about on the radio, or saw on television. Look up these possible topics in encyclopedias, the library card catalog, and *The Readers' Guide to Periodical Literature.* These general sources can help you in many ways. They can give you an overview, help you find ways to narrow down a topic so that it can be covered in a report, and help you see how much information is available.

**Making Bibliography Cards.** *Bibliography cards* can help you keep track of the sources.

**Make a bibliography card for every book, magazine, or other source that you plan to use.**

Before you start reading and taking notes on your sources, prepare note cards that list all of the sources you might use. To prepare your cards, go to the card catalog, *The Readers' Guide,* or other sources of information that you have found. The following chart gives guidelines for preparing your cards.

## GUIDELINES FOR PREPARING BIBLIOGRAPHY CARDS

1. Use one note card for each source.
2. On each card write all of the information that you will need for a bibliography entry.
3. For a book in the library, note the call number.

**Taking Notes on Your Sources.** After you have listed your sources begin taking notes.

**Begin your research by making up questions about your topic and by writing a rough thesis statement. As you read and take notes, look for information that answers your questions and that relates to your thesis statement.**

## SUGGESTIONS FOR TAKING NOTES FOR A REPORT

1. Take notes on cards. Use a new card for each new subject or source.
2. In the upper left-hand corner, write the author and title of the source.
3. In the upper right-hand corner, write a heading that tells the subject of the information on that card.
4. Write each quotation, idea, or fact on your cards exactly. Copy quotations word-for-word and put them in quotation marks. Put a page number next to each piece of information.
5. Keep the note cards from each source together.

Begin with a source, such as an encyclopedia, that will give you an overview of your topic. First skim your sources and then reread them carefully while taking notes. Focus on information that answers your questions and that relates to your thesis statement.

The cards on the following page show the basic format.

**505**

Subject heading ────────────────────────────

Authors, article, magazine, and date

> Jerry Adler and Joe Contreras,      Saturn's Moon
> "A Voyager's Close-up of Saturn,"    Hyperion
> Newsweek, September 7, 1981

Exact quotation with page number

> "Passing by at a range of less than 300,000 miles, Voyager 2 showed [the moon Hyperion] to have the shape of a squat cylinder, 220 miles across and 130 miles thick, a shape variously likened to a tuna-fish can, a hockey puck, and a hamburger." (p 58)

Subject heading ────────────────────────────

Authors and title

> Jacqueline and Simon Mitton,    Surface of Mars
> The Prentice-Hall Concise
> Book of Astronomy

Facts written in note-taker's own words with page numbers

> – red dust in air makes Mars look red (p 48)
> – sometimes winds blow at hundreds of kilometers per hour and move dust around, changing the colors of the surface (p 48)
> – many craters caused by meteorites crashing into the planet (p 49)
> – old lava flows (p 49)

**Organizing the Report.** When you finish taking notes, you can move on to the final prewriting step.

**Organize your Ideas in a modified outline.**

## STEPS FOR ORGANIZING A REPORT

1. Decide what aspects of your main point to develop in the body of your report. These will be your subtopics.
2. Group your note cards according to your subtopics.
3. Decide on a logical order for presenting the subtopics.
4. Write a modified outline of the subtopics and the supporting information under each one.

**EXERCISE A: Choosing a Topic and Preparing Bibliography Cards.** Write down *five* topics. Go to the library, and check to see whether you can find *three* sources for one of them. Prepare bibliography cards for the sources.

**EXERCISE B: Taking Notes on Your Sources.** Write three or four questions about your topic and a rough thesis statement. Read your sources, looking for answers to the questions, and making notes. Make a card for each bit of information, even if two or more come from the same source.

**EXERCISE C: Organizing Your Report.** Using your rough thesis statement and note cards, follow the chart on this page to organize your report. Arrange your subtopics so that your report is as clear and logical as you can make it.

## WRITING AND REVISING: Creating a First Draft and Polishing

You are now ready to write the first draft of your report. This section will guide you through the steps for writing and revising your report.

**Your Paper.** Before you write your report, you may find it useful to jot down some ideas for your introduction, conclusion, and title. Then you can write the first draft using these ideas, your outline of the body paragraphs, and your note cards.

**Write a first draft of your report, including footnotes and bibliography. Revise your report by making improvements, writing a final copy, and proofreading.**

As you write your report, think about presenting your information clearly and accurately. Begin with an introductory paragraph that has a clear thesis statement. The body should de-

**507**

velop your thesis statement with effective information, and a conclusion should end the report. Connect your ideas with transitions. When you use a source, write a footnote. Finally, prepare a bibliography and add a title.

Allow time to revise. Check the content and organization of your paper as you would for an essay. Check footnotes and bibliography as well. The following checklist can help you correct any weaknesses.

---

### CHECKLIST FOR REVISING A REPORT

1. Does the thesis statement present the main point clearly?
2. Does any information *not* develop the statement? Is there other information you could add?
3. Have you written footnotes for all quotations, borrowed ideas, and little-known facts?
4. Do your footnotes follow the correct form?
5. Are your sources listed correctly in the bibliography? Are the entries listed alphabetically?

---

**EXERCISE D: Writing and Revising Your Report.** Using your outline and note cards from Exercises A, B, and C, write a first draft. Use every other line on your paper to leave space for revising. Write a bibliography. Then revise your draft, following the checklist above.

**DEVELOPING WRITING SKILLS: Writing a Report.** Exchange the reports written for Exercise D with another student. Write an evaluation of your partner's report noting the following elements: thesis statement, main idea, subtopics, footnotes, bibliography, and the strong and weak points of the report. What logical order did the writer use in arranging subtopics? Is there enough information for each topic? What, if anything, should the writer change? Try to judge your partner's report fairly and thoroughly.

# Writing Workshop: Writing Reports

## ASSIGNMENT 1

**Topic**   Radio as an Entertainment Medium

**Form and Purpose**   A report that informs readers

**Audience**   Readers of a Sunday news magazine

**Length**   Four to six paragraphs

**Focus**   Narrow the general topic to one aspect of radio. Develop a thesis statement in your introduction. Support your thesis statement in the body paragraphs with direct quotations and information from other sources. Conclude with a restatement of your thesis.

**Sources**   Books, magazines, interviews with grandparents

**Prewriting**   Narrow the topic and research it. Take notes on bibliography cards. Organize your notes into a modified outline.

**Writing**   Use your outline and notes to write a first draft. Credit all direct quotations and other source ideas by including footnotes. Prepare a bibliography.

**Revising**   Use the checklist on page 508 to revise your paper. Then prepare a final copy.

Sound devices used for an early radio show

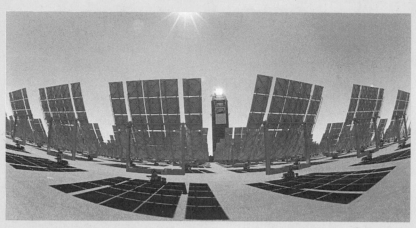

Solar power

## ASSIGNMENT 2

**Topic** Future Energy Sources

**Form and Purpose** A report that informs readers of the topic and persuades them of your viewpoint

**Audience** People concerned about our limited energy resources

**Length** Four to six paragraphs

**Focus** In your introduction, develop a thesis statement about the potential of one future energy source. Then support your thesis statement with documented information from other sources. Conclude with a reminder of your thesis.

**Sources** Books, magazines, newspapers, encyclopedias, science museum exhibits

**Prewriting** Research the topic and take notes on bibliography cards. Organize your notes into a modified outline, and write a thesis statement.

**Writing** Use your outline and notes to write a first draft. Include footnotes and a bibliography.

**Revising** Use the checklist on page 508 to revise your draft. Then prepare a final draft.

**510**

# Topics for Writing: Writing Reports

If the photo above suggests a topic to you, then research, plan, and write a report about it. If not, use one of the topics below.

1. The Big Business of Fishing Tackle
2. A Fish-Stocking Program in Your State
3. The Effect of Acid Rain on Freshwater Fish Populations
4. Life Cycle of the Salmon
5. A Career in Fish Management
6. The Growth of Freshwater Tournament Fishing
7. A Fish Hatchery in Your State
8. Fish as a Food Source
9. A Profile of One Species of Fish (brown trout, pike, catfish)
10. Altering the Environment: A Report of Its Effects on Fish Populations

# Chapter *30*

# Writing Book Reports

Book reports have some of the features of other reports, but they also have characteristics of their own. This chapter will explain the kinds of information you should include in a book report. It will guide you in planning, writing, and revising the book reports you will be asked to do for many classes.

## 30.1 Looking at Book Reports

You have probably read many book reports. If so, you have seen that a book report can be almost any length and can be arranged in many different ways. However, all good book reports have certain things in common. A good book report will identify the book and give a short summary of the contents. It will discuss certain interesting features of the book, and it will give some idea of whether or not the book is worth reading.

### The Format of a Book Report

To cover all of these details in your own book reports, you can use a three-part format.

**A book report can be arranged in three parts. An introductory paragraph can be used to identify the title and author of the book and give a short summary. Body paragraphs can be used to discuss one or more features of the book. A concluding paragraph can be used to make a recommendation.**

The following chart gives more information about these three parts.

| ONE USEFUL FORMAT FOR A BOOK REPORT | |
|---|---|
| **Part** | **What It Does** |
| Introduction | The introduction covers basic information in one short paragraph at the beginning of the report.<br>—It gives the title and author of the book.<br>—It tells what kind of book it is (for example, a mystery, a biography, or an adventure novel).<br>—It presents a short summary of what the book is about. |
| Body Paragraphs | The body paragraphs cover interesting features of the book.<br>—Each paragraph presents a main idea about one of the features of the book (for example, a character, an incident, or the setting in which the story takes place).<br>—The main idea in each paragraph is supported with specific examples, details, and facts taken from the book. |

| Conclusion | The conclusion offers an opinion about the book in one short paragraph. |
|---|---|
| | —It tells other readers whether or not the book is worth reading. |
| | —It backs up this opinion with a few general or specific comments. |

The second part of your report is the most important part. In it you should focus on one or more features of the book, usually devoting one body paragraph to each feature you choose to discuss. You could tell your reader whether the author makes the characters seem real, and if so, how. You could comment on the author's description of the setting and whether the location affects one or more characters. Without telling every event in the story, you could give the reader an idea of the plot, especially how it causes the characters to act or to change.

The following chart lists some of the features found in books and offers suggestions for writing about each of them.

## FEATURES TO WRITE ABOUT IN A BOOK REPORT

| Feature | What to Write About |
|---|---|
| **Characters:** Characters are the people in a story. The reader gets to know characters through their actions, their speech, their thoughts, other characters' reactions to them, and descriptions of them. | 1. Your favorite or least favorite character<br>2. How a main character changes through the incidents in the story<br>3. Why a character is believable or unbelievable |
| **Setting:** The setting of a story is the time it takes place (the year, the season, the time of day) and the | 1. How the setting plays an important part in what happens to the characters in the story |

location where it takes place (one particular house, one country, another planet).

2. Why you would (or would not) like to live at the particular time and place of the story
3. How well the setting is described

**Plot:** The plot is the order of incidents in a story. It is based on a *conflict*, or problem, that a character or several characters must face and solve. Usually the incidents in a story lead up to one main incident, or *climax*, when the conflict is settled.

1. Why a particular incident is the most interesting, exciting, amusing or memorable in the book
2. A problem that a main character has and how he or she overcomes it
3. How the author creates suspense in an incident
4. How quickly or how slowly the story moves

**Theme:** A theme is a central idea or general truth about life: the meaning behind the story. A theme is usually shown through the characters' actions, the plot, and the setting, rather than stated directly.

1. Something a character learns about himself or herself or about life through the story
2. How the book changed your mind about some-thing or made you see something in a new way
3. Why you agree or disagree with the author's observation of life presented in the story

**EXERCISE A: Looking at Book Reports.** Answer the following questions about the features of a book report.

1. What are the three parts of a book report format?
2. What should be included in the introductory paragraph?

3. What is the most important part of a book report? What can the writer tell the reader in the most important part?
4. What element should be part of the concluding paragraph?
5. What are four major features of a book on which a book report might focus?

## Examining a Sample Book Report

The following book report is on the award-winning novel *A Wrinkle in Time* by Madeleine L'Engle. Notice that it has all the parts of a book report mentioned in the chart on pages 514–515. Notice also that in its body paragraphs it covers two different features of the book.

Report on <u>A Wrinkle in Time</u>

Introduction     <u>A Wrinkle in Time</u> is a fantasy written by Madeleine L'Engle and published in 1962. In this story two teenagers, Calvin O'Keefe and Meg Murry, and Meg's brilliant five-year-old brother, Charles, travel across the universe to find Meg and Charles's father. Their father, a physicist, disappeared while doing top-secret experiments on space travel for the government. On their journey Calvin, Meg, and Charles meet friendly creatures on other planets, but in the end they must fight by themselves against the evil IT on the planet Camazotz.

First feature     Right from the beginning, the novel catches the reader's interest with a mysterious incident. Restless because of a storm, Meg, Charles, and their mother gather in the kitchen in the middle of the night and talk about the tramp who has been stealing things in the neighborhood. This talk and their dog's growling creates the suspense. Then a noise in the laboratory turns out to be a small old lady dressed in odd clothes of many colors. She says that the wind blew her off course. This comment is strange, but her X-ray vision and her knowledge about Mr. Murry's secret experiments are even more eerie. Charles calls this peculiar woman Mrs. Whatsit and reveals that he has met her at a deserted house in the woods. This incident makes the reader want to know who and what Mrs. Whatsit really is and what she knows about Mr. Murry's disappearance.

**Second feature**
Besides having suspenseful incidents that make the reader read faster and faster, the novel focuses on a character who struggles with important problems and wins. In the course of the story, Meg learns to accept herself and to act responsibly. At the beginning of the novel, Meg hates herself. She hates her looks—her braces and plain hair. She is not doing well at school and does not get along with her teachers, the principal, or other students. However, when Meg meets Calvin and starts to look for her father, she realizes that she is likable and useful. Discovering that Calvin likes her personality and her eyes helps her like herself. In addition, Meg discovers that her nerve and impatience are useful in the search for her father. She is the one who insists they go on, and it is she who charges ahead into the cell where he is imprisoned. Through these dangers Meg also learns that she cannot expect others to solve all her problems. Instead, she must use her intelligence and courage. For example, she must return alone to Camazotz to save Charles from the evil IT that has captured his mind. By taking responsibility and risking her life for others, Meg comes to understand that she is a valuable human being.

**Conclusion**
A Wrinkle in Time is well worth reading. It whisks the reader from one planet to another, from danger to greater danger with Meg and the other characters, who are people the reader cares about. The book offers the reader new worlds, some beautiful and some terrifying, but all unforgettable.

**EXERCISE B: Examining a Sample Book Report.** Read the report on *A Wrinkle in Time* again carefully. Then answer the following questions about it.

1. What information is given in the introduction?
2. What is the first feature of the book the report focuses on?
3. What are *three* examples or details from the book that are used to develop this feature?
4. What is the second feature that the report focuses on?
5. How is this feature developed?
6. What is the writer's opinion of the book?

**DEVELOPING WRITING SKILLS: Writing About Book Reports.** Find two short book reports. (You may also use book reviews.) Answer the questions in Exercise B as they relate to first one of the reports, and then the other. Then write two or three paragraphs comparing the two reports. Comment on the introductions, the body paragraphs, and the concluding paragraphs. Finally, write a few lines telling which report you prefer and why.

# 30.2 Writing a Book Report

You are now ready to begin planning, writing, and revising a book report of your own.

## PREWRITING: Planning Your Book Report

Preparing your book report involves many of the same prewriting and writing steps that you used for writing paragraphs and essays.

**To prepare your book report, decide what features of the book you want to discuss. Find and list information from the book that is related to these features. Then follow the writing and revising steps for paragraphs and essays.**

Your first prewriting step is to decide what you want to say about the book. From the chart on pages 514–515, choose one or more features to focus on. Once you have chosen the features for your focus, you can begin to list the information you will use.

The next step is to write down the information you will present in the introduction. Give the title, author, kind of book, and a short summary. Then decide what main idea you want to use in presenting each of the features in your body paragraphs. To support your ideas, make a brainstorming list by skimming the book and listing examples, facts, incidents, and quotations that explain or back up your ideas. The final step is to decide on your recommendation.

**EXERCISE A: Planning a Book Report.** Choose a book that you have read recently to write about in a book report. Then, using the chart on pages 514–515, choose at least *two* features of your book that you will focus on and write them on your paper.

**EXERCISE B: Gathering Information for a Book Report.** On a blank piece of paper, jot down information for your introduction. Then decide on a main idea for each of the features you have chosen to write about and look back through the book to find as many examples, details, facts, reasons, and incidents as you can that relate to your main ideas. List this information on your paper. Finally, jot down ideas for your conclusion.

## WRITING and REVISING: Creating a First Draft and Polishing Your Paper

The next step is writing a first draft. The following chart will guide you as you write.

## SUGGESTIONS FOR WRITING A BOOK REPORT

1. Make your introductory paragraph brief but helpful.
2. Write a clear topic sentence for each of your body paragraphs.
3. Link your ideas with transitions.
4. Use either the present tense for your verbs ("The book *is* ..." or "The character *learns* ...") or the past tense ("The book *was* ..." or "The character *learned* ...").

Once you have drafted your report, reread it carefully several times and use a checklist to revise it. The following checklist will remind you of the various parts of a book report.

## CHECKLIST FOR REVISING A BOOK REPORT

1. Have you mentioned the title, the author, and the kind of book in your introduction?
2. Have you given enough but not too much information about the contents of the book in your introduction?
3. Should you include more information from the book to support your main ideas about the features of the book?
4. Is any of the information you have taken from the book unnecessary?
5. Does your conclusion make a recommendation?
6. Have you linked your ideas with transitions?

As a final step in revising your book report, you should re-copy it and proofread it carefully.

**EXERCISE C: Writing a Book Report.** Following the suggestions in the first chart above, write a first draft of your report.

**DEVELOPING WRITING SKILLS: Revising a Book Report.** Using the checklist above, revise your report. Proofread it carefully.

**520**

# Writing Workshop: Writing Book Reports

## ASSIGNMENT

**Topic**   A Science-fiction Novel

**Form and Purpose**   A book report that informs and expresses an opinion

**Audience**   Readers of a magazine entitled "Popular Science Fiction"

**Length**   Four to five paragraphs

**Focus**   Provide a short summary of the book in your introduction. Then discuss two or more features of the book. Conclude by expressing your opinion about the book and making a recommendation.

**Sources**   Science-fiction novels

**Prewriting**   Choose a science-fiction novel to read, or choose one you have already read. Decide what features of the book you want to discuss. Take notes about each of these features. Then prepare an outline.

**Writing**   Use your outline to write a first draft.

**Revising**   Review your paper to see if you have included enough details to support your thesis statement adequately.

# 31

# Personal Writing

Personal writing tells about the writer's own life. A *journal* is one kind of personal writing. Sometimes, when something interesting happens to you, you may feel that you want to remember it always. Writing about events in a journal is a good way to collect memorable moments of your life and what you felt or thought about them.

In this chapter you will learn about journals and how to write one of your own.

## 31.1 Understanding the Purpose of Journals

In one way, all journals are alike. The overall purpose of any journal is to record events and the writer's thoughts and feelings about them.

**A journal is a record of a writer's experiences, observations, and personal feelings.**

There are several good reasons for writing about daily activities, friends or family, and the exciting or unusual things that occur in your life. Writing about them helps you to recall the events later. Once you write an account of an experience in a journal, you can reread it and enjoy it as often as you like.

Another reason for writing about people, places, and events, is that you come to understand them more clearly. But perhaps the most important reason for keeping a journal is that by writing and rereading it regularly, you come to know yourself better. People who begin keeping journals when they are young can read them years later and see how they have changed over the years. This helps them to understand the way they think, behave, and relate to other people.

Although every journal records the details of someone's life, all journals do not have the same style, form, or length. In fact, no two journals are identical. There are as many styles as there are journal writers. This variety is what makes journals truly personal writing. Writers using this form have given us some of our most enjoyable reading and shared their thoughts and feelings most fully.

The section that follows will help you see how journal writers plan their journals and select material for individual entries. It will guide you through the different kinds of journals, and show you how the individual purpose of any journal tells the writer how often to write in it. It will also show you how journal writers decide what to write in their journals. Finally, it will show you the way writers use description, action, and personal thoughts and feelings to make their journals interesting and enjoyable to read.

## A Place for Ideas

In writing paragraphs and reports, you may have used information and opinions collected from books, newspapers, magazine articles, and other people. A journal is a place to express your own personal opinions.

Journals vary with the people who keep them. It will help you to decide what kind of journal you want to write if you understand something about the kinds of journals, and the kinds of entries they contain.

**Kinds of Journals.** Some famous writers have published journals in which they wrote every day and seemed intent on noting every detail, even tiny, common ones. Others, equally well-known, wrote only twice a week or once a month. Some of these latter journal writers also concentrated on small details. Others were content to write down their general thoughts and feelings about their experiences.

Some journal writers expect other people to read their work; others write only for their own enjoyment or to collect material for other kinds of writing. Many people start journals for the first time because they are planning a special vacation or a move to a new town or city. They sense that the experience will be important in their lives, so they decide to make a permanent record of it.

The chart below describes some kinds of journals. Notice that the frequency of writing depends on the writer's intentions in keeping a journal.

| Purpose of Journal | Probable Writing Time |
| --- | --- |
| To summarize everyday experiences | Daily |
| To express personal feelings and insights | Daily or several times a week |
| To keep track of important events | Several times a week |
| To record special experiences | As each occasion arises |

**Kinds of Entries.** Each section in a journal is called an *entry*. Journal entries vary, just as whole journals do. Some writers prefer chatty, long entries that are like letters to friends or relatives. Others write accounts that link events and quote people, so that they seem like short stories. Still other journal entries are short comments that simply record feelings or sudden

**524**

thoughts that interest the writers and move them to make entries in their journals. Usually the purpose of the journal accounts for the kind of entries used.

No matter how long or short, or what style a writer uses, journal entries usually describe people, places, and activities, and give the writer's reactions or impressions. Often, dates and locations are noted at the beginning of an entry. These personal ideas make journals enjoyable for others to read. Readers get the feeling that they are being let in on another person's private experiences. Also, journal entries often seem to be more frank and honest than other kinds of writing. They can be especially pleasant for the writer to reread after a long time. They allow the writer to renew past experiences and to see them in a new and different way.

The journal entry below recounts part of the first day of a writer's driving tour of the United States. Notice the use of chronological order, the colorful details, and the mention of the writer's feelings.

| | |
|---|---|
| Descriptive details | The early darkness came on. My headlamps cut only a forty-foot trail through the rain, and the dashboard lights cast a spectral glowing . . . I bent over the wheel to steer along the divider stripes . . . Then onto I-64, a new interstate that cuts across southern Illinois and Indiana without going through a single town. If a world lay out there, it was far from me. On and on. Behind, only a red wash of taillights. |
| Action | At Grayville, Illinois, on the Wabash River, I pulled up for the night on North Street and parked in front of the old picture show. The marquee said TRAVELOGUE TODAY, or it would have if the *O*'s had been there. I should have gone to a café and struck up a conversation; instead |
| Personal feelings | I stumbled to the bunk in the back of my rig, undressed, zipped into the sleeping bag, and watched things go dark. I fought desolation and wrestled memories of the Indian wars.—William Least Heat Moon |

**525**

**EXERCISE: Understanding a Journal.** Reread the journal excerpt on the previous page and answer the following questions.

1. What event does the entry describe?
2. Why do you think the author chose to write about this experience?
3. What time span does the entry seem to cover?
4. Pick out the descriptive details that make you see the scene.
5. What thoughts and feelings has the writer included?

**DEVELOPING WRITING SKILLS: Understanding Journals.** Ask your librarian to help you find a published journal. Describe the journal, telling what kind it is, and what purpose you think the author had in writing it. Pick an entry you liked and answer the questions in the exercise above.

# 31.2 Keeping a Journal

Now that you understand the purpose and kinds of journals and the entries that they contain, you are ready to start a journal that will record actual events of your life.

## Planning a Journal

Because journals are an informal, personal type of writing, there are almost no hard and fast rules for writing them. However, there are some steps that will help you to plan your journal entries.

**Use your journal to record events, observations, and ideas from your own experience.**

You will find journal keeping easier and more enjoyable if you plan ahead. You can begin by writing down the purpose of your journal, then listing the things you want to cover in your first entry. If your purpose is to keep an account of your first term in a new school, list the classes, students, teachers, and new activities you encounter. If you prefer to write a journal of your daily life, you will need to keep notes of the things you do each day and the people with whom you do them. You will have to form the habit of jotting down descriptive details as soon as possible after you notice them, before they fade from your memory. It is helpful to do your writing at nearly the same time every day.

The following chart will help you to plan your journal to suit your own purpose.

---

### PLANNING YOUR JOURNAL

1. Decide on the purpose of your journal: to record daily or special events, set down ideas and feelings, and so on.
2. Decide how often you will write entries. Consider your purpose and your own habits: How much time do you want to commit to keeping a journal?
3. Take notes about things that happen to you. Jot down as many answers as you can to the questions: Who? What? When? Where? and Why?
4. Brainstorm for descriptive details about the people, places, and things that you will write about, and add them to your notes.

---

The following chart will help a writer who is planning to record a summer at a music camp. Notice how the four questions focus the entry material.

---

### PREPARING TO WRITE A JOURNAL ENTRY

| | |
|---|---|
| When? | During the summer vacation |
| Who? | A classmate and me |
| Where? | In the northern part of Michigan |
| What? | Cello lessons, new instructors, playing in an ensemble, recreational activities |

---

**EXERCISE A: Planning a Journal.** Decide what kind of journal you want to keep. Write your purpose. Below it, write the number of times you will write in a week. Then make notes for your first entry.

## Putting Your Ideas Into Writing

The planning you have done will make the writing step easy and pleasant. As you write, think of all the interesting details that will help the reader to see, hear, and feel the experience you are relating. Describe the people, the places, the spirit of the event, and any other telling details you can recall. Words that appeal to sight, hearing, and feeling will help readers to share the experience.

Organize the information chronologically, so the reader can follow the progress of your account. Be sure to write your own impressions and feelings about the things you mention.

The journal entry below comes from the journal of a student at a summer music program. Notice that the writer arranges events in the order in which they happened. Transitions like *soon* and *after that* help readers to follow the sequence of events. See if you can pick out the descriptive details that make the entry interesting and the personal observations that tell you something about the writer.

Time and place

*Music-by-the Lake, July 10*

Steve and I got to the little Michigan town in the late afternoon. When we got off the train, clutching our cellos, the camp van was waiting for us at the old-fashioned red wooden station. Meg, the van's driver, told us that she had been coming to the camp for eight years—since Steve and I were in fourth grade!

It was hot in the sunlight. The train had been air-conditioned, and the rattly van was not. But as soon

**528**

as we started up, the breeze cooled us and made us comfortable again. We chugged down the one street of the town past two churches, a post office, a general store, and a gas station that also sold fishing bait and snowmobiles. Then we passed a few scattered houses, and that was all.

Descriptive details

Soon, Meg was driving us through deep and dark evergreen forests, along a road that was paved at first, then turned to gravel, and finally to dirt. Just when I began to wonder if we were lost, the van broke out of the forest, and the bright blue lake lay ahead.

Chronological order

We checked in at the office, got our cabin keys, and walked to Number 6 cabin, right above the dock. After we unpacked our duffel bags and put away our cellos, the dinner bell rang, and we followed the other campers to the long, low dining hall made of logs. As we filed into the sweet-smelling building, and I caught a glimpse of sparkling water in the lake nearby, I felt as if the whole thing were a dream.

Personal observation

**EXERCISE B: Writing a Journal Entry.** Use the notes you wrote for Exercise A and write a first entry. You may want to give your reasons for starting your journal, your feelings about journal keeping, or a description of something unusual that happened to you recently. Use colorful descriptions, helpful transitions, and conclusions that share your feelings with a reader.

**DEVELOPING WRITING SKILLS: Keeping a Journal.** Think of some recent happening in your life about which you feel strongly. The feeling you had about the occurrence might have been excitement, happiness, fright, sadness, or any other emotion. Write a journal entry relating the incident and expressing your feelings.

# Writing Workshop: Personal Writing

## ASSIGNMENT 1

**Topic**  People-Watching

**Form and Purpose**  Journal entries describing a variety of people

**Audience**  Yourself; possible resource for characters when you write short stories

**Length**  One entry every day over a three-week period

**Focus**  Write daily journal entries describing people you have observed. Include details that clearly convey your dominant impression of each person.

**Sources**  Personal observations

**Prewriting**  Observe as wide a variety of people as possible and write descriptive notes about each one that interests you.

**Writing**  Use your notes when you write each journal entry.

**Revising**  Make sure that you have clearly conveyed your dominant impression of each person.

## ASSIGNMENT 2

**Topic**   Recording Your Deepest Thoughts

**Form and Purpose**   Journal entries recording your thoughts and feelings

**Audience**   Yourself

**Length**   One entry each day over a two-week period

**Focus**   Write daily journal entries recording thoughts and feelings that you feel you cannot share with others.

**Sources**   Personal thoughts and feelings

**Prewriting**   During the day, record your thoughts and feelings by taking notes.

**Writing**   At the end of each day, use your notes to write a journal entry.

**Revising**   Review your journal entries to make sure that you have described your thoughts and feelings accurately.

# Topics for Writing: Personal Writing

If the photo above suggests a writing topic to you, keep a journal for several weeks that explores that topic. Other related topics that may also be explored in your journal are listed below.

1. Am I Many Other People Than Just "Me"?
2. Are We Really "The *ME* Generation"?
3. What Makes Me Angry?
4. What Makes Me Sad?
5. When Am I Happiest?
6. Do I Really Identify with and Understand Other People's Problems?
7. What Would I Like to Change About Myself?
8. Am I a Giver or a Taker?
9. What Do I Like Best About Myself?
10. Where Would I Like To Be in Ten Years? Why?

# Chapter 32

# Writing
# Short Stories

Stories are fun to read, and they can also be fun to write. This chapter will give you suggestions to follow in creating stories of your own.

## Planning a Story 32.1

A story should have a number of parts woven together. It should have a *main character* and a small cast of other characters. It should have a *conflict,* or problem, that the main character faces. This problem should be shown and solved in an incident or a series of incidents, which form the *plot* of the story. A story also needs a storyteller, or *narrator.*

### PREWRITING: Thinking Up Characters and a Conflict

The *characters* in a story should be believable people who act, think, and have things happen to them. In order to make the *plot* interesting, the characters should have *conflicts* that they must solve.

**533**

**Think up a main character who seems real to you. Decide what conflict, or problem, this character will face in your story. Then imagine a few other characters you will need in order to show this conflict.**

To launch your story, think up a main character who really interests you. You may get your ideas from observing people you actually know, from your reading, from family stories, or from experiences you have had or might have had.

Make your main character come alive by listing details about the person as in the following chart.

| SKETCHING YOUR MAIN CHARACTER | |
| --- | --- |
| **Details to Include** | **Examples** |
| 1. Give your character a name and an age. | Kerry Fliegel, thirteen years old |
| 2. Describe the character by giving a few striking physical characteristics that tell something about the person. | —long, straight brown hair<br>—slim, muscular legs<br>—wears shorts, leotards, or jeans and bright print blouses |
| 3. Imagine important details about the character's family and past. | —only child with two working parents<br>—has just moved to a new apartment |
| 4. Describe the character's interests and personality (including both good and bad qualities). | —loves gymnastics and biking<br>—can play the piano<br>—quiet but friendly<br>—usually kind to people<br>—has developed poor study habits and gotten poor grades for two years |

5. Describe the character's behavior: facial expressions, gestures, the way he or she acts toward other people, and what other people think of the character.

—often frowns slightly when thinking
—winds her hair around her fingers
—enjoys spending time alone or with a few friends
—usually talks politely

The details on your list will make your character seem more real even if your story does not include all of them.

As you think about your main character, you should think about the problem, or conflict, your character will face in the story. Begin by giving your character a goal. What does he or she want? Decide who or what could prevent your character from achieving the goal. The problem your character faces in achieving the goal will be the conflict. Finally, you should state the conflict in a few short sentences, mentioning in the final sentence a choice your main character must make.

The following chart shows a conflict that includes a goal, a problem, and a choice.

| DEVELOPING A CONFLICT FOR A STORY | |
|---|---|
| **Main Character** | **Statement of the Conflict** |
| Kerry | Kerry must raise her grades to *B*'s in all her classes in order to visit her best friend during Christmas vacation. But the next door neighbor always seems to find a way to interrupt Kerry's studying time. Kerry must choose between finding a way to make the woman stop or letting the woman continue to bother her. |

Thinking about your conflict will help you think of other characters for your story. Include characters who work against your main character and those who help your main character. The conflict in the chart on page 535 mentions a character whose habits work *against* the main character. If you were creating this story, you might also want to add more helpful characters. After you have chosen the additional characters you need, make brief character sketches of them just as you did of your main character.

**EXERCISE A: Examining Characters in Stories.** Choose *two* characters from a story that you have read and list a number of details about each of them—appearance, personality, interests, behavior, and so on.

**EXERCISE B: Creating a Main Character.** Think of a character for a story of your own. At the top of your paper, write the name and age of your character. Then brainstorm for details about the character. Use the chart on pages 534–535.

**EXERCISE C: Choosing a Conflict.** Look again at the rough sketch you made of your main character in Exercise B. Then follow these instructions.

1. Choose a goal for your main character.
2. Decide what is preventing your main character from reaching the goal.
3. Now state the conflict in a few sentences. Include the goal, the problem, and the choice that the character must make.

**EXERCISE D: Choosing Your Other Characters.** Using the main character and the conflict from Exercises B and C, decide on your other characters. Use the chart on pages 534–535 to make a character sketch of each of your other characters.

# PREWRITING: Deciding Who Will Tell the Story

Your ideas about your characters and conflict are the basis for a story. Now you need a storyteller—a *narrator.*

**Choose a first-person or third-person narrator for your story.**

First-person and third-person narrators are explained below.

| CHOOSING A NARRATOR FOR A STORY | |
| --- | --- |
| **Narrator** | **How It Works** |
| First-Person Narrator | The main character or another character in the story tells the story, using the words "I" and "me." This narrator can tell the reader his or her own unspoken thoughts and feelings but cannot see into the minds of any other characters. |
| Third-Person Narrator | Someone outside the story tells the story, using the names of the characters and the words "he" and "she." This narrator can see into the mind of at least one character and report unspoken thoughts and feelings. This narrator can also report the thoughts of all the characters. |

Choice of narrator will determine how much detail you can include about your characters' actions, thoughts, and feelings. In the story about Kerry, either narrator could be used.

First-person narrator (Kerry)    I was trying to study on our deck. I had only been reading ten minutes when I heard a sliding door open. "Mrs. Maddox is watering her fuchsias," I thought. I began to worry, thinking that she would probably start talking to me.

| Third-person narrator | Kerry was trying to study on her deck. She had only been reading ten minutes when she heard a sliding door open. "Mrs. Maddox is watering her fuchsias," she thought. Kerry began to worry, thinking that Mrs. Maddox would probably start talking to her. |

Stick with your choice of narrator throughout your story.

**EXERCISE E: Choosing a Narrator.** Think about the characters and conflict you created in Exercises B, C, and D. Decide who will tell your story. Do you want your main character to tell his or her own story? Do you want a third-person narrator to tell the story from outside the story but through your main character's eyes? Write a short passage of your story using two different narrators. Decide which one you will use.

## PREWRITING: Plotting Your Story

You are now ready to *plot,* or map out, your story. Your story should build up to a *climax,* the point at which the main character must make a decision and take action.

**Plot your story by deciding on the time the story will cover, the number of incidents it will have, the opening incident, the other incidents, and the climax.**

In plotting your story, you should first decide how much time it will cover. Does your main character need a few hours or a few days to struggle with and end the conflict? Or should your story take place over two or three weeks or even a year? A short time span is usually easier to handle than a long one.

Next, you should decide how many incidents your story will include. An incident is a scene or an important event. Each incident should show the main character trying to reach the goal. A story can have one incident that ends with the climax or a number of incidents leading to the climax.

**538**

If you plan more than one incident, your next step is to think about your opening incident. The opening incident of your story should make both the main character's goal and the conflict clear. It should also grab the reader's interest by showing your main character doing something or speaking.

After planning the first incident, think how the other incidents will show the conflict growing, and the main character dealing with the need to make a choice.

Finally, you must decide what the climax will be. What will happen? What decision will your main character make? What action will your main character take? The decision and action should fit the character and should end the conflict.

List all of the incidents, including the climax. If you wish, you can briefly describe each one.

| DEVELOPING A PLOT OUTLINE FOR A STORY | |
|---|---|
| **Time Covered** | Three weeks in October |
| **Opening Incident** | Mrs. Maddox interrupts Kerry while she is studying. Kerry pretends the phone is ringing. Conflict: Kerry must study to get good grades, but Mrs. Maddox is always bothering her. |
| **Second Incident** | Two weeks later Mrs. Maddox starts playing the piano and singing in the afternoons. Kerry cannot study. |
| **Third Incident** | Kerry and her friend Dennis plan to show Mrs. Maddox how terrible her singing is. |
| **Climax** | Mrs. Maddox has an upsetting talk on the phone with her son, and Kerry discovers how lonely Mrs. Maddox is. She decides not to carry out her plan but instead to figure out some other way to study. |

As you think more about your story and as you write it, you may change or add incidents. Having a plot outline will help you focus on the conflict and on the action in your story.

**EXERCISE F: Making a Plot Outline.** Use the story you have been planning in this section to make a plot outline. Follow these instructions.

1. On your paper write how much time your story will cover.
2. Decide how many incidents you will have.
3. Briefly describe the opening incident.
4. Briefly list and describe each of your other incidents.
5. Then describe what happens at the climax.

**DEVELOPING WRITING SKILLS: Rewriting a Story.** Reread the story read for Exercise A. Follow these directions:

1. Write three or four sentences telling about the main character, the conflict, and the type of narrator.
2. Rewrite a paragraph from the story using a type of narrator different from the one used in the story.

# 32.2  Developing Your Story

In addition to characters, a conflict, a storyteller, and a plot, your story should have a *setting*—a specific time and location. You may also want to add *dialogue,* or conversation between your characters, to make your characters and what happens to them seem more real. After you have considered these last two parts of a story, you will be ready to write and revise your story.

## PREWRITING: Choosing Details of the Setting

Before you write your story, imagine the details of your *setting,* even if you include only a few of these details in your story.

**Imagine the time and place of the actions in your story. List details that will help you and the reader see the setting.**

If you have a clear picture in your mind of your setting, your story will seem more lifelike to the reader. If possible, list details that appeal to the five senses—sights, sounds, and so on—as you describe your setting.

---

**LISTING DETAILS FOR THE SETTING OF A STORY**

| | |
|---|---|
| **Setting** | 1980's, October |
| | An apartment building in Concord, California |
| **Details** | —modern concrete three-story apartment buildings with decks |
| | —view of the small oval pool and of the purple mass of Mount Diablo |
| | —thin-walled apartments |
| | —small wooden fences about chest-high, dividing the decks of the apartments |
| | —purple and red fuchsias hanging in pots on Mrs. Maddox's deck |
| | —sunshine beating on the decks and flashing on the pool |
| | —faint ringing of phones from open windows |

---

**EXERCISE A: Finding Details for Your Setting.** Return to the story that you planned in Section 32.1. Write the specific time and place of your story. Then brainstorm for details that will help you and your reader see the setting.

## PREWRITING: Considering Dialogue

When you develop your story, you should also decide whether or not you want to add *dialogue*—that is, to have your characters speak to each other.

**541**

**Plan if and where you will use dialogue in your story.**

You may want to include dialogue at most or all of the important points in your story. Use the following suggestions.

| USING DIALOGUE IN A STORY |
|---|
| 1. Decide if and where you want your characters to speak and mark these places on your outline. |
| 2. Always set the scene briefly and make it clear who is speaking. |
| 3. Make what the characters say and how they say it (the words, the length of the sentences, the expressions) fit their personalities. |
| 4. Enclose all words spoken by characters in quotation marks and begin a new paragraph with each new speaker. (See Section 20.7 about using quotation marks.) |

The following passage of dialogue could be part of the first incident in the story about Kerry.

Dialogue between two characters
"Great day, huh, Kerry?" Mrs. Maddox said, looking at me from her side of the deck.

"Oh, hi, Mrs. Maddox. It *is* warm for October," I replied, barely raising my head from the book.

"Almost makes me want to jump in the pool," she said, leaning over the divider.

**EXERCISE B: Deciding Where to Use Dialogue.** Think about the story you worked with in Exercise A, and reread your plot outline for it. Then decide at what points in the story you could have your characters speak. Write "dialogue" on your plot outline in those places.

**EXERCISE C: Practicing with Dialogue.** Write the dialogue for one part of your story, following the suggestions in the chart above.

## WRITING: Creating a First Draft

You are now ready to write a first draft of your story using your ideas about your characters, your plot outline, and your notes about the setting.

**As you put the pieces of your story together in complete sentences and complete paragraphs, concentrate on the action in the story and try to make the story flow smoothly.**

As you write, follow your plot outline and think about ways to connect the incidents in your story. The transitions between incidents can be just a few words such as "next week" or "twenty minutes later." Or they can be sentences or short paragraphs that tell something about what has happened between the incidents. Whatever transitions you use, they should be as short and direct as possible and should help the reader follow the passage of time in your story.

Your goal in writing a first draft should simply be a complete version of your story. You should not worry a great deal about fine points at this time. The revision stage will give you a chance to polish your work.

When you have finished writing your story, you should think of a title for it. The title should hint at the conflict in your story and should make the reader want to read the story.

**EXERCISE D: Writing a First Draft.** Using the story you worked with in Exercise C, write a first draft. Connect the incidents in your story with a few words, sentences, or short paragraphs to indicate that time is going by. Give your story a title.

## REVISING: Polishing Your Story

Revising is a time to sharpen and polish your story.

**Try to look at your story from a reader's point of view. Then revise your story using a checklist.**

You should set your story aside for at least a few hours after you finish writing it. When you return to it, pretend that you are reading it for the first time. Read it aloud. If you can, have someone else read and comment on it. Then use the following checklist to examine the different features of your story.

---

### CHECKLIST FOR REVISING A STORY

1. Does your title fit the story?
2. Is the beginning of your story likely to catch the reader's interest?
3. Will the reader be able to imagine your characters and the setting clearly?
4. Do your characters' actions and thoughts show their personalities?
5. Does your dialogue fit your characters' personalities?
6. Does your story move smoothly from one action and time to the next?
7. Is the ending of the story clear and believable?
8. Have you used one narrator consistently throughout?

---

The checklist should help you smooth out rough spots in the story. When you think you have polished your story so that it will catch and hold the reader's interest from the beginning to the end, rewrite it in final form and proofread it.

The following is the final version of the story about Kerry.

| | |
|---|---|
| Title | Solo |
| Opening incident | I was reading and tanning on the deck of our new apartment overlooking the little oval swimming pool and the purple mass of Mount Diablo. My parents had grounded me for my low grades so I was studying at home every day. They had told me that I could visit my best friend in Colorado during Christmas vacation if I got *B*'s in all my classes. Eager to go to Colorado, I was plowing through the last fifty pages of *The Martian* |

*Chronicles* for my book report due the next day when I heard a sliding door open, followed by a steady dripping sound. "Mrs. Maddox is watering her fuchsias," I thought. "And she probably wants to talk to me. Maybe if I look very busy she will leave me alone." But I was wrong.

Dialogue "Great day, huh, Kerry?" Mrs. Maddox said, looking at me from her side of the deck.

"Oh, hi, Mrs. Maddox. It *is* warm for October," I replied, barely raising my head from the book.

"Almost makes me want to jump in the pool," she said, leaning over the divider so that I could see her curlers under the green scarf around her round, soft face.

I felt like saying, "I wish you would jump in the pool," but I didn't.

"You know I won the bingo championship last Friday," she continued. "I've been playing three years now, but this is the first time I've ever won five games in one night. The first card I didn't have a chance, but after the second one, I had all the right numbers."

"Really?" I answered. It was becoming very obvious that any chance of reading on the deck was all over. Why did she always manage to catch me out here and talk on and on about bingo, the lines at the grocery store, or the rude teller at the bank? I had three hours of homework to do that night so I pretended I heard the phone ringing.

"Excuse me. I think that's our phone. It might be Mom," I said, snatching up my book and racing inside.

Transition The next week Mrs. Maddox met me three times at the mailboxes. Each day, sticky from gymnastics and from riding my bike, I squirmed while she babbled on for over twenty minutes. I tried to look as tired as I felt as I shifted my books and heavy binder from arm to arm. Finally, I pushed by her and headed for the eleva-

**545**

tor, and she followed, talking all the time about the new shopping center in Pleasant Hill and her son, Robbie, who lives in Indianapolis.

Second incident

By the following week I really regretted our move to that apartment. I was trying to study for the exams coming up at the end of the quarter when I heard this plunking on a piano, her piano, right against our living room wall. Soon a flat, raspy voice started to sing "White Christmas." She stumbled through it once, played "Alley Cat," and then tried to croon "Moon River."

I jumped up from the kitchen table and ran to my room. "How was I ever going to study with Mrs. Maddox practicing up for the holidays in October?" I thought.

Transition

She played the piano and croaked every day that week. By Thursday, I was so tense that I went over to my

Third incident

friend Dennis's house after school even though I had promised my parents that I would go right home after gymnastics every day.

Dialogue

"Look," Dennis said. "If she's that bad, why don't you send her an anonymous note. You could say,

> 'Roses are red
> Tires are black.
> You think you can sing
> But you only quack.' "

"Sure," I said. "She wouldn't get it. She wouldn't figure out that I can hear her lousy singing. You know what we could do, though?" I had just had a delightful idea.

"What? Tell me." Dennis danced around.

"I am going to get the music for 'White Christmas' and practice it on our piano," I said. "Do you think you could sing it in a screechy voice, kind of slow and raspy?"

"Yeah. What's the plan?"

"Well, if I can hear her so well, she should be able to hear us too. She always sings her solos at about 4:30. You come to our apartment next Thursday, and as soon

**546**

as we hear her start that song, we'll play the same thing. We can mimic her and drown her out. Then maybe she'll realize how terrible she sounds and how much she bugs me."

"Tremendous. I like it," Dennis said.

**Transition**

I could hardly wait for Thursday. Monday, Tuesday, and Wednesday afternoons, Mrs. Maddox chirped and screeched again. Her concerts lasted longer and longer. She had added "Jingle Bells," "Sleigh Ride," and "Deck the Halls" to her repertoire. I shut myself in the bathroom each afternoon and turned on the fan so that I could do my reading and studying for our Constitution test.

**Incident leading to climax**

At 4:10 on Thursday, Dennis buzzed our apartment, and I let him in. He was grinning, cracking jokes, and threatening to yodel as he walked in our front door.

**Dialogue**

"Are you ready for this?" he said, taking a bow near the piano and getting ready to perform.

"The music is open to the page. Now we just have to wait for Mrs. Melody Maddox," I said.

We chatted softly about the upcoming school assembly. Then we heard Mrs. Maddox talking on the phone. Her voice got louder. We put our ears to the wall. Dennis tried the glass trick. Mrs. Maddox's voice sounded angry, then desperate.

"Robbie, you've got to come to California for Christmas vacation. I'll fly to Indianapolis, then. Are you telling me that you don't want to see me? Robbie, I miss you. Please."

Then all we could hear was sobbing, hysterical crying, and silence. About ten minutes later we heard a few weak chords on the piano. She started to choke out "White Christmas," stopped, and started again.

**Climax with dialogue**

"Now!" Dennis said as he hopped over to the piano. "Hit it!"

I was still sitting by the wall. "Hey, Den. Forget it."

**547**

"What do you mean? Are you chickening out? Hurry up."

But I couldn't get this picture out of my mind: Mrs. Maddox in her worn purple housecoat and her fuzzy yellow slippers sitting in a dark apartment alone on Christmas Day singing "White Christmas" and "Jingle Bells." I felt really sad.

"The plan's off," I said as Mrs. Maddox moaned a few more bars of the song.

"Well, it's your study time and your sanity," Dennis shrugged his shoulders. "Guess I'll go home." He picked up his books and headed for the door.

"Yeah. Thanks anyway," I mumbled. I closed the door and watched him step into the elevator. "There's always the library," I thought. "And if that doesn't work, I can use one of our big pillows to make the bathroom floor more comfortable."

**EXERCISE E: Polishing Your Story.** Reread silently and aloud the first draft of the story that you wrote in Exercise D. Then use the checklist for revising a story on page 544 to find weak spots in the story and to make improvements in it. When you are satisfied with it, complete your revising by rewriting your story in final form and proofreading it.

**DEVELOPING WRITING SKILLS: Rewriting a Story.** Using the story you wrote for Exercises D and E, follow these directions.

1. Think about how your story would change if it were told from a different point of view. For example, if you used first person, rewrite the story in third person.
2. Find a passage in the story that could be told in a different way. For example, choose a passage telling us about the plot or characters and write it as a dialogue between two characters.

# Writing Workshop: Writing Short Stories

## ASSIGNMENT 1

**Topic**   You Are There Stories

**Form and Purpose**   A story that entertains readers

**Audience**   Producer of a television series called *Halls of History*

**Length**   Two to four pages

**Focus**   Develop a historical account of an event into a short story. Use a historical figure who was involved in this event as the narrator of your story.

**Sources**   History texts, biographies, your imagination

**Prewriting**   Develop a sketch of the main character by using ideas such as those on pages 534–535. Then create a plot outline.

**Writing**   As you write a first draft, follow your plot outline. Include dialogue to make your characters more believable.

**Revising**   Use the checklist on page 544 to revise your story. Then prepare a final copy.

Washington at Valley Forge

© 1974 United Feature Syndicate

## ASSIGNMENT 2

**Topic**   A Story Based on a Moral or a Saying

**Form and Purpose**   A story that entertains and teaches a moral lesson

**Audience**   Readers of the book *Old Morals in Modern Fables*

**Length**   Two to four pages

**Focus**   Like a fable, your story should have a moral. Unlike a fable, your story should have a modern setting and characters who are people, not animals. At the end of the story, write the moral that you used.

**Sources**   Fables, reference books of quotations and sayings

**Prewriting**   Use the checklists on pages 534–535 and 539 to develop character sketches and a plot outline.

**Writing**   Use your sketches and outline to help you write a first draft. Include dialogue and descriptive details.

**Revising**   Use the checklist on page 544 to revise your story. Then prepare a final copy.

# Topics for Writing: Writing Short Stories

Edward Hopper, *House by the Railroad*, The Museum of Modern Art, New York

If the painting above suggests a setting for a short story to you, develop it into a short story with characters and a plot. Other possible story settings are listed below; choose one, if you prefer.

1. The Subway Tunnels Beneath a City
2. A Runaway Train Traveling Through the Canadian Wilderness
3. An Island on a Large Lake
4. An Abandoned Factory
5. Space Station Orbiting the Earth
6. An Ocean Oil Rig and Platform
7. Inside a Missile Silo
8. Mountains Surrounded by Deserts
9. Deep in the Heart of a Jungle
10. A Transatlantic Airplane Flight

# Chapter 33

# Writing Letters

From time to time you may need to write letters to friends and relatives or to write letters concerning business matters. This chapter will show you the forms that should be used for *friendly letters, social notes,* and *business letters*.

## 33.1 Looking at Friendly Letters, Social Notes, and Business Letters

The letters you write should all follow certain special forms. The form for friendly letters and social notes is different from the form for business letters.

### The Form for Friendly Letters and Social Notes

A *friendly letter* is written to communicate with a friend, acquaintance, or family member. A *social note* is used to offer an invitation, to accept or decline an invitation, or to express congratulations or sympathy.

All of your friendly letters and social notes should follow the same basic form.

**The Parts of the Letter or Note.** Any friendly letter or social note should have five basic parts.

**A friendly letter or social note should include a heading, a salutation, a body, a closing, and a signature.**

The *heading* of your letter or note should contain your address as well as the date on which you write the letter. On the first line, you should write your street address. On the second line, you should write your city or town, the state, and the ZIP code. And on the third line, you should write the date.

HEADING:   44 Homer Drive
               Bronx, New York   10465
               January 17, 1982

The *salutation* is the part that greets your reader. The words you use will depend upon how well you know your reader. Note that all salutations for friendly letters and social notes end with a comma.

| FORMAL SALUTATIONS: | Dear Dr. Broden, | Dear Mrs. Martland, |
|---|---|---|
| | Dear Aunt Milly, | Dear Ms. Mullen, |
| LESS FORMAL SALUTATIONS: | Hi, | Hello, Suzie, |
| | Greetings, | Howdy, |

The *body* of the letter or note should contain your message—all of the things you want to say in the letter. In a letter to a friend, you might write several paragraphs sharing news and ideas. In a letter inviting someone to a party, you might need to write only three or four sentences.

The *closing* should signal the end of the letter or note. It can be one word or it can be a short phrase. Note in the following examples that all closings begin with a capital and end with a comma.

| CLOSINGS: | Sincerely yours, | Bye for now, |
|---|---|---|
| | Cordially, | Love, |

Your *signature* ends the letter or note. You should sign the name that the reader uses to address you.

A sixth part, an *R.S.V.P.*, may be added at the bottom of a letter of invitation. This abbreviation tells your reader that you want a response.

**A Style for the Letter or Note.** Style refers to the way the parts of a letter are positioned on the page.

### Use a consistent style for all friendly letters and social notes.

When you write a friendly letter or social note, you should place the different parts of the letter in certain expected positions. The heading belongs in the upper right-hand corner. The salutation goes several lines beneath it along the left margin. The body, the central part of the letter, follows beneath the salutation. The closing belongs in the lower right-hand section of the letter, about two or three lines beneath the body. And your signature follows beneath the closing. If you need to add an *R.S.V.P.*, place it in the lower left-hand corner.

The following example shows the arrangement of the five parts.

**A Style for Friendly
Letters and Social Notes**

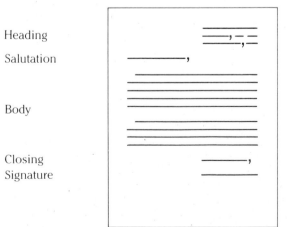

Heading

Salutation

Body

Closing
Signature

**An Envelope for the Letter or Note.** Once you have written your letter, you must prepare an envelope.

**Prepare an envelope that has the correct mailing address of the letter's receiver, and include your full return address.**

As you prepare the envelope, use the guidelines in the following chart.

---

### PREPARING AN ENVELOPE FOR A FRIENDLY LETTER OR A SOCIAL NOTE

1. Use an envelope that matches the paper or stationery of the letter.
2. Place the mailing address in the center of the envelope; give the person's name on the first line, the street address on the second line, and the city or town, state, and ZIP code on the third line.
3. Place your complete return address in the upper left-hand corner.
4. Avoid any abbreviations that might be unclear.
5. Be sure to include ZIP codes in both addresses.

---

Your envelope should resemble the one in the following example.

Return address

Mailing address

**Mailing the Letter or Note.** To mail your letter, you should carry out a simple but important step.

**Fold your letter properly and place it into your envelope.**

If you are writing on small-size stationery, you will usually be able to fold the paper in half and slip it into the envelope. In some cases, you may find that your stationery is cut to fit into an envelope without folding. In other cases, however, you may need to fold your letter more than once. The method shown in the following diagram can be used with most large pieces of stationery.

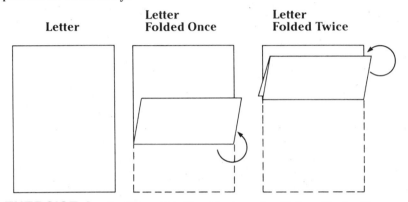

Letter | Letter Folded Once | Letter Folded Twice

**EXERCISE A: Setting Up the Parts of a Friendly Letter or Social Note.** Use one piece of paper to make a skeleton letter that shows the arrangement of the parts of a friendly letter or social note. Use your own address and today's date for the heading. Choose someone to write to and write his or her name in the salutation. Draw lines for the body and add a proper closing and signature.

**EXERCISE B: Preparing an Envelope for a Friendly Letter or Social Note.** Use the chart on page 555 to prepare an envelope for the skeleton letter in Exercise A. Then fold the letter and place it into its envelope.

## The Form for Business Letters

You may need to write *business letters* for a variety of purposes: to order merchandise, to answer an advertisement, to state a complaint, and so forth. All business letters should include certain special parts and all of them should follow a special style. As you will see, the parts and the style discussed in the following paragraphs are similar to those in friendly letters and social notes.

**The Parts of a Business Letter.** A business letter should have six basic parts.

**A business letter should include a heading, an inside address, a salutation, a body, a closing, and a signature.**

The *heading* of a business letter is exactly like the heading of a friendly letter. It should contain your street address, town or city, state, and ZIP code, as well as the date on which you write the letter.

The *inside address* is the address of the person or business to whom you are writing. It begins with the name of the person or business, followed by the other details needed in a full address.

INSIDE       Mrs. Doris Jones, President
ADDRESS:   Data Base Electronics, Inc.
               21000 Veneto Boulevard
               Encino, California   90106

The *salutation* of a business letter should be a formal greeting. It should also be followed by a colon, not a comma, as in the following examples.

SALUTATIONS:   Dear Sir or Madam:   Gentlemen:
               Dear Mrs. Jones:     Dear Dr. Scott:

The *body* of a business letter should contain your message. It can be a few sentences or a few paragraphs, but it should always be clear and direct.

The *closing* of a business letter should be just as formal as the salutation. Like the closing in a friendly letter, it should begin with a capital and end with a comma, as in the examples shown on the next page.

CLOSINGS:    Sincerely yours,     Very truly yours,
               Cordially,          Sincerely,

The *signature* in a business letter should also be formal. You should sign your full name without, however, adding any title.

**A Style for a Business Letter.** Style is even more important in business letters than in personal ones.

**Use a consistent style for all business letters.**

A business letter can be set up almost the same as a friendly letter and social note. The only difference is in the addition of the inside address, which is placed on the left just above the salutation.

The arrangement of the parts is shown below.

**A Style for Business Letters**

| | |
|---|---|
| Heading | |
| Inside address | |
| Salutation | |
| Body | |
| Closing | |
| Signature | |

**An Envelope for a Business Letter.** Most business letters are written on white, business-size stationery. The envelope for a business letter should also be white and business-size.

**Prepare an envelope that has the correct mailing address of the letter's receiver, and include your full return address.**

As you prepare the envelope, use the guidelines in the chart on page 555. Your completed envelope should resemble the envelope for a friendly letter shown on page 555.

**Mailing a Business Letter.** Almost all business letters will need to be folded twice. Follow the diagram on page 556.

**Fold your business letter properly and place it into its envelope.**

**EXERCISE C: Setting Up the Parts of a Business Letter.** Use a sheet of business-size paper to make a skeleton letter that shows the arrangement of the parts of a business letter. Use your own address and today's date for the heading; use the information given after these instructions to write an inside address. Choose an appropriate salutation and draw lines for the body. Then add a closing and signature.

Mrs. Judith Baldwin, President of Nature Book Club, Inc., Box 400, Baltimore, Maryland, ZIP code 20552.

**EXERCISE D: Preparing an Envelope for a Business Letter.** Obtain a business-size envelope to go with the letter that you set up in Exercise C. Prepare the envelope, fold the letter properly, and place the letter into the envelope.

**DEVELOPING WRITING SKILLS: Writing Letters.** Choose two of the ideas below and write a friendly letter and a business letter. Include all the necessary parts for each one using your own name and address for the heading.

1. Write an invitation to neighbors inviting them to a cookout.
2. Write to a friend who has moved away, bringing him or her up to date on your life and the lives of mutual friends.
3. Write a business letter ordering merchandise from an advertisement.
4. Write a business letter to complain about a product.
5. Write to a friend to express sympathy over the loss of a pet.

# 33.2 Writing Different Kinds of Letters

Whenever you write letters of any kind, it helps to keep both your reader and your purpose in mind as you write the letters. This section will offer a number of suggestions that you can use to write letters, social notes, and business letters to many different people for a number of different purposes.

## Writing Friendly Letters

A friendly letter is a personal letter. It can be informal, and it can be enjoyable to write because it gives you a chance to express your thoughts and feelings. Your audience is probably someone you know quite well. Your purpose may be to inform, to persuade, to describe, to entertain, or some combination of all of these different purposes for writing.

**A friendly letter shares personal news with friends and family, continues the communication of earlier letters, or simply maintains relationships between people.**

When you write a friendly letter, you should "talk" to your reader. Ask questions about that person's activities and thoughts. Answer any questions that the person has asked you in a letter you have already received. Make your letter a pleasure to read by including specific details and interesting or amusing incidents that will appeal to your reader.

A friendly letter can be casual, but it should include all the necessary parts of a friendly letter, from heading to signature. You should also try to write clear sentences in readable writing. Check your grammar, punctuation, and spelling by reading your letter aloud and by proofreading it before you send it. This will help you make sure that your reader will be able to understand what you have written.

On the following page is a sample of a friendly letter.

102 Riverside Drive
Phoenix, Arizona 85036
April 23, 1986

Dear Tina,

It was great to see you during spring vacation. What a surprise! I still can't believe that you took that long bus ride just to see me. After hiking and riding in the mountains with you again, I realized just how much I miss you. How was your trip home?

I'm glad you visited last week and not this week. Yesterday, winds ripped through the valley and blew down power lines. The gusts spread a brush fire into a blaze that burned ten homes and many acres of land right near where we went hiking. Do you remember Danny? His family had to leave their home and spend the night in a local high school with the Red Cross. Danny's house survived, but the fires really scared me.

Are you nervous about the big speech tournament? I know you will do well. Let's make plans for the summer soon. I'll let you know how my ballet recital goes. Say hello to your parents and your sister for me. Write soon.

Love,
Emily

**EXERCISE A: Writing a Friendly Letter.** Write a friendly letter that includes two of the following kinds of information.

An event at your school   News about a friend
An amusing incident       A movie or book

# Writing Social Notes

Social notes are short letters usually written for one definite purpose. They should be to the point, briefly stating the exact purpose of the note and giving the reader specific information.

**561**

**Writing Invitations and Letters of Acceptance and Regret.** Perhaps the most common social notes you will use are *invitations*.

**A letter of invitation invites someone to a special event; a note of acceptance or regret answers an invitation.**

Whenever you write a letter of invitation, you should include the five parts of a social note as well as certain special details. Your reader will need to know the date and time of the event, the location and nature of the event, and possibly what he or she should bring or wear. When sending an invitation, always try to put yourself in the reader's place. Think about what he or she needs to know.

As in the following sample, you can include a request to *R.S.V.P.* if you need a reply from your reader to help plan the event.

> 4 Regatta Road
> Lyons, Tennessee 37352
> August 27, 1986
>
> Dear Hill,
>
> I am planning a surprise birthday party for Bill Mackenzie at my house on September 8. All guests should arrive by 4:00 p.m. that afternoon, so that we can surprise Bill, who will arrive at 4:30 p.m.
>
> Dress is casual. Please bring joke presents, Frisbees, and other forms of entertainment. I hope you are free that day.
>
> Yours truly,
> Henrietta Rice
>
> R.S.V.P.

If you receive a letter of invitation, you should answer it promptly, especially if it has an *R.S.V.P.* To accept an invitation, you should state that you will attend. Then you should repeat the date, time, and place so that there will be no confusion later on. If, instead, you must decline the invitation, be sure to give a reason. Whether you accept or decline, you should always express your appreciation for having been invited.

**Writing Letters of Thanks and Other Social Notes.** The greatest use of social notes is for sending and receiving invitations. They are also appropriate at other times.

**Social notes can be used to express thanks or congratulations or to offer comfort.**

If you receive a present, you may want to write a thank-you note telling how much you enjoy the gift or at least say thanks to the giver for thinking of you. You may also want to use a letter to thank a host or hostess for entertaining you for an evening or a weekend. You might want to offer congratulations to a person who has won a prize. If someone close to you is ill or has been injured, you might write a note of sympathy.

**EXERCISE B: Writing a Social Note.** Choose one of the following ideas to write a social note. Include all five parts of a social note, and make sure that the purpose of your note is clear. Then prepare an envelope and place the note into it.

1. A friend has moved away to a nearby town. You would like to have him or her visit your family for a weekend next month. Write a letter of invitation that gives information about the visit.
2. A former coach or teacher has invited you to a barbecue and reunion of students. Accept or decline the invitation. Make up the details.
3. One of your relatives has sent you a birthday present. Write a letter of thanks.

# Writing Business Letters

Business letters are a useful and often necessary way to carry on business with other people. If you focus on your audience and the purpose you want to achieve in writing the letter, you will usually find it relatively easy to write good business letters.

In writing a business letter, you should constantly think about your audience. You should try to make a good impression by following correct form, by being polite, and by being neat and accurate. You should also try to be direct so that you do not waste the reader's time. Include all the necessary information as quickly and as simply as possible.

In addition to thinking about your audience, think about the results you want to achieve with your letter. State what you want clearly and politely, and give the reader enough facts so that he or she can understand what you want.

Because business letters must be brief yet easily understandable, you should plan to revise and proofread your business letters carefully. You should also pay special attention to the kind of business letter you are writing.

**Writing Order Letters.** Perhaps the most common kind of business letter is the *order letter*.

**An order letter states a specific request for merchandise and includes all necessary ordering information.**

An order letter should have all six parts of a business letter as well as certain other important information. Early in the letter, you should mention the specific item or items you want to buy. If the items are from a catalog and have order numbers, include these. Also include any sizes, prices, or amounts to help your reader fill your order. If you include money, state the amount and enclose a check or money order for the total amount. Do not send cash. The following is an example of an order letter.

```
                            1320 Oak Drive
                            Westbury, New York  11592
                            February 20, 1986

        Order Department
        Phillips Ski Equipment, Inc.
        4400 Central Highway
        Denver, Colorado  80217

        Dear Sir or Madam:

            From your 1986 winter catalog, I would like

        to order the following items:

                Amount    Item                    Price

                   1      Ski bindings          $ 90.00
                          No. 123

                   1      Set of ski poles      $ 23.99
                          No. 432
                                                -------
                TOTAL                           $113.99

            I have enclosed a check for the total amount

        ($113.99), and I understand that this amount in-

        cludes all handling charges. Thank you for fill-

        ing this order.

                            Sincerely,

                            Ben Brubaker
```

**Writing Other Business Letters.**  In addition to placing an order, business letters can be used for a number of other purposes.

**Business letters can be used to request information, file a complaint, or express an opinion.**

In writing reports or planning parties or trips, you may sometimes find it necessary to write a letter to a business or agency,

**565**

asking for specific information. Occasionally, you may also need to write a letter to correct a problem. For example, if you buy something that does not work, you may have to write to the company informing them of the problem and asking them to correct it. Or you may want to complain about poor service, suggesting some way to improve it. Sometimes you may want to express your opinion to a newspaper or a television station.

Letters requesting information should be clear, direct, and polite. Letters making complaints or offering opinions need a few additional items. They should be well supported with facts and they should be persuasive. Try to convince your reader to agree with you and to take action.

**EXERCISE C: Writing Business Letters.** Select any one of the following ideas for a business letter. Include all six parts of a business letter, and use your own address for the heading. Invent a person to whom you are writing and invent an address for the person, business, or organization. Finally, when you have written, revised, recopied, and proofread your letter, prepare an envelope for it.

1. Obtain a mail order catalog for clothing or sporting goods. Write an order letter that includes all necessary ordering information for two items that you want.
2. Write to a local travel agent. Ask for information about the sights to visit in some other city.
3. Write to a national magazine expressing your opinion of a story or article that you recently read in that magazine. Address the letter to the editor.

**DEVELOPING WRITING SKILLS: Writing a Friendly Letter, Social Note, or Business Letter.** Identify a purpose that you have for writing a friendly letter, social note, or business letter. Use the guidelines in this chapter to plan and write the letter. After drafting your letter, revise it, rewrite it, and proofread it. Then prepare an envelope for it.

**566**

# Writing Workshop: Writing Letters

## ASSIGNMENT 1

**Topic**   Letters for an Advice Column

**Form and Purpose**   Two friendly letters that request, inform, and offer advice

**Audience**   Yourself

**Length**   One to two paragraphs

**Focus**   In a friendly letter, state a problem that you have, give some background information, and request some advice. In a second letter, provide advice that may or may not solve the problem.

**Sources**   Letters in advice columns in newspapers, yourself

**Prewriting**   Plan your letter by stating the exact nature of the problem and making notes that give background information.

**Writing**   Use your notes to write a first draft.

**Revising**   Check the position of all letter parts. Proofread your letter, and prepare a final copy.

## ASSIGNMENT 2

**Topic**   Traveling to the Stars

**Form and Purpose**   A business letter that requests information

**Audience**   A travel agency

**Length**   Two to three paragraphs

**Focus**   In your letter to a travel agent, explain exactly where you would like to travel to in our galaxy, what you expect to see, and how much you can spend. Request information about such flights, sights, and rates.

**Sources**   Travel ads, astronomy books, and your imagination

**Prewriting**   Brainstorm and make notes about the contents of your letter.

**Writing**   Use your notes to write a first draft.

**Revising**   Check the position of all letter parts. Proofread your letter, and prepare a final copy. Then prepare an envelope for your letter.

# Topics for Writing: Writing Letters

© 1974 United Feature Syndicate

The cartoon may suggest an idea for a business or friendly letter. First, decide on your audience and purpose. Then plan and write your letter. If you prefer, choose one of the related topics.

1. Telling What a Great Time You Had When Not Doing Your Chores or Homework
2. Telling a Relative that You Can't Come for a Holiday
3. Advising Someone How Not to Clean Their Room
4. Explaining What You Were Doing When You Were Not Paying Attention in Class
5. Telling a Business Why You Will Not Buy Their Product(s)
6. Explaining to a Coach Why You Do Not Need to Practice So Much
7. Advising a Friend About Why He or She Should Not Act or Behave a Certain Way
8. Persuading Someone That a Movie You Saw Was Not Very Good
9. Advising Someone Not to Make the Same Mistake You Once Made
10. Requesting that a Certain School Regulation Not Be Enforced (or Changed)

# Chapter 34

# Taking Essay Exams

When taking examinations, you are often asked to write essay answers to questions. Some essay exam questions may seem at first to be difficult or challenging. However, if you apply what you know about writing good paragraphs, answering these questions will become easier.

## 34.1 Preparing Answers to Essay Exams

An important step toward success with essay exams is to learn to manage your time well.

**Schedule time for planning, writing, and checking all the answers on the exam and stick to your schedule.**

At the beginning of a test, read all test directions first, skimming each question. You may see that you have more to say about one question than about another, and will need to allot more time to it. If you can estimate which questions will take the most time, you can then budget your time for the entire test. Plan to use about half the time in planning and the other half for the actual writing and proofreading of your answers.

# Understanding the Question

It is important that you make sure you understand what a question asks of you.

**Read each question on the exam to be sure you know what information it asks for.**

You may need to read a question twice to be certain about its meaning. When you read the question, watch for key words that tell you what the question asks for and that guide you in preparing your answer.

The following chart gives some typical key words from exam questions. Then it explains the kind of answer you should give when you see each of these words.

| Key Word | What You Should Do |
| --- | --- |
| Compare | Point out similarities |
| Contrast | Point out differences. |
| Define | Tell what something is; use examples. |
| Describe | Give features, details, organization. |
| Explain | Give information that makes something clear. |

**EXERCISE A: Understanding Essay Exam Questions.** Underline the key words in the questions below and explain how you would answer each question.

EXAMPLE:   Describe the Monarch butterfly.
　　　　　Give the features of the Monarch.

1. Define an equilateral triangle.
2. Compare the climates of North and South America.
3. Contrast the Appalachian and Rocky Mountains.
4. What is the cause of erosion?
5. How do the three branches of the federal government work together?

# Outlining Your Answer

Once you understand what the question is asking, you can begin to plan your answer. Think. Try to recall all the facts, ideas, and other information that you will need for your answer. Jot down this material as it comes to mind, without regard for what you will use and what you will discard.

**Plan your answer by collecting all the information you know about the subject and arranging it in modified outline form.**

State your main idea. Then list the major details you will use in your answer. (Modified outlines are discussed in detail in Chapter 37.)

# Writing Your Answer

Begin with a topic sentence if your answer is to be one paragraph long. If you plan to write an essay-length answer, begin by writing a thesis statement. Follow your modified outline to write your answer. End with a conclusion that summarizes your main point and refers back to your topic sentence or thesis statement.

Below is a one-paragraph answer to the question "Name the major gases in the atmosphere and tell why each one is important."

TOPIC
SENTENCE
Supporting
information

The atmosphere is made up of five major gases that are necessary to the well-being of all living things. Nitrogen, which is necessary for cell growth and repair, makes up 78 percent of the atmosphere. It cannot be used directly, but must be taken from the soil by plants and from food by animals. Oxygen is necessary for breathing, or respiration, and makes up about 21 percent. Other gases are found in smaller quantities. Carbon dioxide is the gas plants require to make their food. Water vapor is important to weather and prevents the atmosphere from becoming too hot. Argon is the gas used in light bulbs and has other industrial uses. There are also trace gases, which occur in very small amounts. Each of these gases has an important role to play in the life of plants and animals.

**EXERCISE B: Outlining Your Answer.** Using a question from Exercise A, make a modified outline for a paragraph-length answer.

**EXERCISE C: Writing Your Answer.** Write an essay answer one paragraph long using the outline you created above.

## Checking Your Answer

Check each answer before handing in your examination.

**Proofread your paper, checking for accuracy.**

| CHECKING YOUR ANSWER |
| --- |
| 1. Did you answer the question directly and clearly? |
| 2. Did you write a clear topic sentence or thesis statement? |
| 3. Did you offer enough supporting information? |
| 4. Did you use correct grammar, spelling, and mechanics? |

**EXERCISE D: Checking Your Answer.** Check the paragraph you wrote for Exercise C. If the questions above show you ways to improve your answer, change it.

**DEVELOPING WRITING SKILLS: Preparing Answers to Essay Exams.** Gather essay questions from some of your other classes. Using the guidelines you learned in this chapter, write an essay-length answer to one of them.

**573**

# Writing Workshop: Taking Essay Exams

## ASSIGNMENT

**Topic**   Comparing and Contrasting Musical Elements

**Form and Purpose**   An essay-exam answer that informs by comparing and contrasting two subjects

**Audience**   A music teacher or instructor

**Length**   One to three paragraphs

**Focus**   First, narrow the topic and write an essay-exam question. In your essay answer, explain the similarities of and the differences between the two subjects or elements you selected.

**Sources**   Personal observations and experiences

**Prewriting**   After narrowing your topic and formulating an exam question, make a chart that lists similarities and differences related to the two subjects.

**Writing**   Use your chart to write a first draft of your answer.

**Revising**   Add transitions that help connect or contrast related ideas. Then proofread your answer.

# *Vocabulary and Spelling*

# Chapter 35

# Building Your Vocabulary

Every day you come into contact with new words. A good vocabulary can add to your understanding of books and conversation. It will help you to develop your own ideas effectively and to share them with others.

Reading is your most common source of new vocabulary words. If you enjoy reading, you may already have a good foundation of words to build upon. This chapter will present a number of helpful methods for learning and remembering new words. As you read, decide which method or methods work best for you.

## 35.1 Adding Words to Your Vocabulary

The easiest and most effective way to build your vocabulary is to make vocabulary improvement a special part of your reading program. When you start reading a new book or a new chapter in a textbook, get in the habit of looking up in a dictionary any new words that you meet. Record the meanings of these words in a special vocabulary notebook. Whenever the author repeats a word whose meaning you have already looked up and recorded, refer back to your list for the meaning. After meeting the word a few times, you will find that you have learned it by heart. By the end of the book, you will find that you have added quite a few new words to your vocabulary.

## Recording Vocabulary Words in a Notebook

The method described above for learning new words works best if you begin with a special vocabulary notebook.

**To expand your vocabulary, keep a dictionary and a vocabulary notebook handy when you read.**

The following illustration shows one way in which you can list the words in your notebook.

Chapter 5: The Early Nation

| Words | Definitions | Examples |
|---|---|---|
| anticipate (an tis′ ə pāt′) | look forward to; expect | Did the British anticipate an early end to the war? |
| repeal (ri pēl′) | withdraw officially or formally; revoke | Congress decided to repeal the law. |
| embargo (im bär′ gō) | a government order prohibiting the entry or departure of commercial ships to its ports | What is the purpose of imposing an embargo? |

In setting up a vocabulary notebook, you may find it useful to make separate divisions for vocabulary words from each of your subjects. Each time you begin a new chapter in one of your textbooks, use the title of the chapter as a heading and record beneath it any new words that you meet in that chapter. Each entry should include the word and its pronunciation, a dictionary definition, and a sentence that uses the word, as shown in the illustration on page 577.

You can also set up a separate section of your notebook for words from the books that you read for pleasure. Your entries in this section should be similar to those from your texbooks. Instead of chapter titles, the headings will be the titles of the books in which you met the words.

**EXERCISE A: Setting Up a Vocabulary Notebook.** Select one of the subjects you are studying this year. As you complete your current reading assignment, jot down any unfamiliar words. When you are finished, look up the meaning of each word in a dictionary and enter the information under the chapter heading in your vocabulary notebook.

| EXAMPLE: | Words | Definitions | Examples |
|---|---|---|---|
| | pagoda | Eastern temple | The pagoda |
| | (pə gō′ da) | | looked like |
| | | | a house with |
| | | | many roofs. |

**EXERCISE B: Starting a Section in Your Vocabulary Notebook for Recreational Reading.** Choose one of the books that you are currently reading on a subject that particularly interests you. If you do not have such a book, go to the library and select one. Read a chapter of the book and write down any words that are new to you. Then look up the words in a dictionary, and record them under the title of the book in the part of your vocabulary notebook set aside for recreational reading.

EXAMPLE:    <u>Words</u>          <u>Definitions</u>        <u>Examples</u>

metropolis         a large city       They lived in
(mə träp′′l is)                       the center of
                                      the metropolis.

## Studying and Remembering Vocabulary Words

There are a variety of ways in which you can study the new words you meet in your reading. You may want to vary your technique if you find that one method is more appropriate for certain words than another method.

**Select at least two review methods to help you learn new vocabulary words.**

Try each of the following techniques to see which ones are most convenient and effective for you.

**Using Your Vocabulary Notebook to Review New Words.** Before you begin a new chapter in a textbook or in a book that you are reading for recreation, open your notebook to the entries you have made for the previous chapters of the book. Skim over the words on your list to refresh your memory. You can use this quick review method: Cover the definition and example sentence for each word and try to remember the meaning of the word. If you have trouble, look at the example sentence. Finally, uncover the definition and read it.

If writing out a new word helps you to remember it, you may want to write a sentence giving the word and its definition.

EXAMPLE:    The word *anticipate* means "to look forward to" or
            "to expect."

**Using Flash Cards to Study Vocabulary Words.** Vocabulary flash cards are a particularly convenient method of studying new words. Not only are they easy to carry with you, but with them you can study by yourself, with a member of your family, or with a friend. Use a set of index cards for your words. On the front of the card, write the vocabulary word. On the back of the card, write the definition. In the upper lefthand corner, write the subject area or book from which the word was taken. Usually this information will be all that you will need. However, if you have trouble pronouncing a word, you may also want to include its phonetic spelling. In addition, if the meaning of the word is hard for you to remember, you can include a short example sentence.

**Front**            **Back**

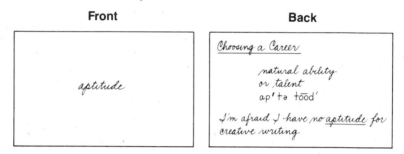

**Using a Tape Recorder to Review Word Meanings.** If you have access to a tape recorder, you may want to try the following method of reviewing vocabulary words and their meanings. Some people learn more easily when they can hear the words and their meanings over and over.

## STUDYING WITH A TAPE RECORDER

1. Read a vocabulary word into the tape recorder.
2. Leave about ten seconds of blank space on the tape and then give the definition.
3. Leave another ten seconds of blank space on the tape and give a sentence using the word.
4. Continue this procedure with the remainder of the words.
5. Then replay the tape, filling in the first blank space with a definition and the second blank space with a sentence using the word.
6. Rerun the tape until you are able to give all of the definitions and sentences quickly and easily.

**580**

After you have learned the words, you can listen to your tape once or twice a week as reinforcement.

**EXERCISE C: Reviewing with Your Vocabulary Notebook.** Setting a time limit for yourself, study a group of words from your vocabulary notebook according to the method described on page 579 in this section. Write down the words and then close your notebook. Write the definition and a sentence for each word.

| EXAMPLE: | Words | Definitions | Sentences |
|---|---|---|---|
| | porter | a person who carries luggage | The porter took my bags. |

**EXERCISE D: Making Flash Cards or Tapes.** Make a set of flash cards or a tape using the procedures described in this section. Use five of the following words, concentrating on those whose meanings you do not know. Then learn these new words using the cards or tape.

1. chaos
2. doubloon
3. elude
4. squid
5. annihilate
6. theory
7. depreciate
8. impeach
9. nonchalant
10. unequaled

**DEVELOPING WRITING SKILLS: Evaluating Your Vocabulary Progress.** After using the methods described in this section for at least two weeks, make a chart similar to the one on page 582 to show your vocabulary progress. List the vocabulary words that you have learned and the source of each word (for example, science, social studies, or the title of a book). Then check the method or methods you used to learn the word. When you have completed your chart, use each of the vocabulary words you have listed in the chart in a sentence of your own.

**581**

| Vocabulary Progress Chart | | | | |
|---|---|---|---|---|
| Word | Source | Method | | |
| | | Notebook | Flash Cards | Tape |
| osmosis | science | ✓ | ✓ | |
| | | | | |
| | | | | |
| | | | | |
| | | | | |
| | | | | |

# 35.2 Learning Words by Using Context

Sometimes when you come across an unfamiliar word in your reading, you may not have to turn immediately to a dictionary. The author may have already given you enough clues to the word's meaning for you to figure it out by yourself.

**Use context clues to help figure out the meanings of new words.**

The *context* of a word is created by the group of words that surround it. The following approach may help you use the context of a word to find clues to its meaning.

## USING CONTEXT CLUES

1. Read the sentence carefully, concentrating on the unknown word.

   **Sentence:** Jane was never a lazy girl, so I was not surprised to learn that she was a *diligent* art student.

2. Look for clues in the surrounding words.

   **Clues:** "never lazy," "not surprised"

3. Use these clues to guess the meaning of the new word.
   **Guess:** hard-working
4. Reread the sentence, substituting your meaning for the new word to see if it makes sense.
   **Substitution:** Jane was never a lazy girl, so I was not surprised to learn that she was a *hard-working* art student.
5. Then look up the new word in a dictionary to see how accurate your definition is.
6. Add the new word and its dictionary definition to the appropriate section of your vocabulary notebook.

Now you are ready to put your skills into practice. The rest of this section is devoted to using context clues in different kinds of reading situations.

# Using Context Clues in Social Studies

The following paragraphs are typical of the kind of material you might find in a social studies textbook. Read each paragraph carefully, looking for context clues to the meaning of each underlined word. Then write down what you think each word means.

EXAMPLE:  With the Louisiana Purchase of 1803 and the explorations led by Lewis and Clark and their guide Sacajawea, there was increased interest in extending the American frontier as far westward as possible. In the first few <u>decades</u> of the nineteenth century, this newly acquired land was made <u>accessible</u> to new settlers.

   The early <u>pathfinders</u>, or explorers, of the West were the hardy people who were engaged in fur trapping and trading. One of these people who left a <u>chronicle</u> of his adventures was Jim Beckwourth. Like those of many other trappers of that time, Beckwourth's <u>endeavors</u> were made in the interest of one of the private fur trading companies that were

**583**

being established at the time. He started out with General William Ashley's Rocky Mountain Fur Company but later joined the American Fur Company, founded by John Jacob Astor.

Beckwourth would set out on an <u>enterprise</u> of one or two years' <u>duration</u> with a group of other experienced trappers. The size of the group varied from about thirty to more than a hundred people. By traveling with a group of trappers, Beckwourth found it easier to <u>cope</u> with the terrible hardships of an expedition into uncharted territory. Although the life of a fur trapper was never lacking in adventure, too often it was also accompanied by hunger and danger.

We, the <u>descendants</u> of these explorers, are indebted to them. Many of the trails that they made for themselves and their horses were the <u>forerunners</u> of the railroad lines and highways that we use today.

**EXERCISE A: Defining Words.** Use your guesses from the preceding passage to answer the following. Choose the definition that most closely matches the meaning of each word as it was used in the selection. Then check your answers in a dictionary. Record in your vocabulary notebook any words that you missed.

EXAMPLE: extend    (a) cancel; (b) stretch out; (c) contract; (d) squeeze

                     b

1. accessible    (a) hard to find; (b) easy to reach; (c) sharp; (d) far away
2. chronicle    (a) a record; (b) constant; (c) illness; (d) ship
3. cope    (a) give to; (b) deal with; (c) hide; (d) steal
4. decade    (a) ten-year period; (b) one-hundred-year period; (c) twenty-year period; (d) twenty-five-year period

5. descendant      (a) a forefather; (b) admirer; (c) offspring; (d) friend

6. duration      (a) strength; (b) hard; (c) longer lasting; (d) length of time

7. endeavor      (a) problem; (b) earnest attempt; (c) debt; (d) conclusion

8. enterprise      (a) opening; (b) closing; (c) reward; (d) undertaking

9. forerunner      (a) something that comes before; (b) first; (c) athlete; (d) something that follows

10. pathfinder      (a) detective; (b) adventure; (c) explorer; (d) trail

# Using Context Clues in Science

In the following paragraphs, you will find material similar to that found in science textbooks. Some of the words in such books may have specialized meanings used only in scientific contexts. However, even with these words, you will often find context clues that can help you understand the material.

As you read each paragraph, look for context clues to the meaning of each underlined word.

EXAMPLE:      Although some animals stay in the same region all year long, there are many kinds of animals who have more than one home. These animals travel, or migrate, from one home to another seasonally in their quest for an adequate food supply and a safe place to raise their young. The migratory habits of animals have fascinated scientists for years.

     The Arctic tern breeds in the Arctic regions of the far North and then travels southward to the Antarctic area when it is summer there. Mallards, unlike domestic ducks, commence their journey northward in early January. In early September, Monarch butterflies gather in large flocks and fly southward to Florida and California. Some of these flocks are made up of millions of butterflies. Upon arriving at their destination, these butterflies <u>consistently</u> seek out the same trees to hang from in a kind of hibernation during the winter.

A number of different kinds of bats migrate northward in the spring and travel south again in the fall. They hang upside down in the same caves year after year for their winter sleep. Normally, bats travel at night and navigate by sending out high-pitched squeaks, <u>inaudible</u> to the human ear. By listening for the echoes that come back, they are able to "see" objects even in total darkness. However, scientists are not sure if bats use this method to set their course on the longer migratory journeys they make each spring and fall.

**EXERCISE B: Defining Words.** Use your guesses to answer the following multiple choice questions. For each word choose the definition that most closely matches the meaning of the word as it was used in the selection. Then check your answers in a dictionary. Record in your vocabulary notebook any words that you missed.

EXAMPLE:  navigate      (a) lead the way; (b) steer a course; (c) swim; (d) float

b

1. adequate       (a) enough;  (b) extra;  (c) not enough; (d) delicious
2. Antarctic      (a) near the North Pole; (b) cold; (c) icy; (d) near the South Pole
3. breed          (a) make wide;  (b) live;  (c) produce young; (d) make narrow
4. commence       (a) plan;  (b) attend;  (c) travel;  (d) begin
5. consistently   (a) differently;  (b) thoughtfully;  (c) sometimes; (d) always in the same way

6. inaudible      (a) not able to be heard; (b) difficult; (c) not fit to be eaten; (d) unfriendly

7. mallard      (a) hammer; (b) domestic duck; (c) wild duck; (d) song

8. migratory      (a) moving from one region to another; (b) farmer; (c) staying in one place; (d) powerful

9. quest      (a) escape; (b) search; (c) ask; (d) odd

10. tern      (a) revolve; (b) rear end of a ship; (c) sea bird; (d) strict

# Using Context Clues in Literature

The following paragraphs are typical of the kind of material you might find in a literature textbook. Read carefully, looking for context clues to the meanings of the underlined words.

EXAMPLE:      Jack London was born in San Francisco in 1876. When Jack was young, the London family moved to Oakland. Jack was very close to his stepfather. <u>Despite</u> the fact that Mr. London tried to earn a <u>livelihood</u>, the family was usually poor. As a boy Jack <u>delivered</u> newspapers to contribute to the family income. After graduating from grammar school, he worked in a factory for a while. But he felt he was <u>destined</u> for a life on the sea.

     He bought a small boat, added a sail, and made many <u>jaunts</u> on San Francisco Bay. When he was seventeen, Jack got a job as a seaman on a sealing schooner headed for Alaska. Although he was <u>relatively</u> young, Jack was strong and proved himself equal to the tasks that he was given. At the journey's end, Jack received his <u>compensation</u> and gave most of it to his family.

     Soon after, Jack London <u>attained</u> his first bit of literary <u>recognition</u>. He entered a story that he had written about his adventures on the voyage in a contest backed by a San Francisco newspaper. London was the <u>recipient</u> of the first prize, and his story was published in the newspaper.

At the age of nineteen, Jack decided to go back to school. He finished high school in two years and went on to college. After he had completed a year of college, adventure once again beckoned him. Jack joined the Klondike gold rush and journeyed to Alaska. There he found plenty of adventure, but little gold. However, when Jack returned home, he used his experiences in Alaska to gain <u>prominence</u> as a writer.

**EXERCISE C: Defining Words.** Answer the following multiple choice questions. For each word choose the definition that most closely matches the meaning of the word as it was used in the selection. Then check your answers in a dictionary. Record in your vocabulary notebook any words that you missed.

EXAMPLE: schooner    (a) luxury train;   (b) car;   (c) plane; (d) ship with sails

           d

1. attain           (a) hold back; (b) fail to reach; (c) achieve; (d) take care of

2. compensation    (a) essay; (b) a change from gas to liquid; (c) friend; (d) pay

3. despite          (a) for spite; (b) without any hope; (c) without pity; (d) in spite of

4. destined        (a) blamed; (b) stretched; (c) intended; (d) famous

5. jaunt           (a) short trip; (b) visit; (c) long journey; (d) cheap restaurant

6. livelihood       (a) means of support; (b) full of life; (c) activity; (d) nice neighborhood

| 7. prominence | (a) fame; (b) a long walk; (c) insurance; (d) agreement |
| 8. recipient | (a) giver; (b) receiver; (c) replacement; (d) list of ingredients |
| 9. recognition | (a) unfavorable notice; (b) payment; (c) favorable notice; (d) determination |
| 10. relatively | (a) somewhat; (b) like a big family; (c) hardly; (d) extremely |

**DEVELOPING WRITING SKILLS: Using Vocabulary Words to Write a Friendly Letter.** Write a letter to an imaginary friend, using at least ten of the underlined words from the passages you have read. Exchange letters with a partner and write an answer to the other person's letter. Show your understanding of the vocabulary words used in the letter.

# Learning Words by Using 35.3 Word Parts

The more you know about the structure of words, the faster you can enlarge your vocabulary. Three different word parts—*prefixes, roots,* and *suffixes*—are used to construct words. The word *invisible* offers an example of a word made up of all three parts. If you know the meanings of the individual parts, you can figure out the meaning of the word.

PREFIX: *in-* means "not"

ROOT: *-vis-* means "to see"

SUFFIX: *-ible* means "capable of being"

WORD: *invisible* means "not capable of being seen"

A prefix, such as *in-*, is one or more syllables added to the beginning of a root to form a new word. A root, such as *-vis-*, is the main part—the base—of the word. A suffix, such as *-ible,* is one or more syllables added to the end of a root to form a new word.

**Use the meanings of prefixes, roots, and suffixes to help determine the meanings of unfamiliar words.**

The only word part that can ever stand alone is the root. The word *move,* for example, consists of a root alone. Some words, such as *remove,* have a prefix and a root. Other words, such as *movable,* have a root and a suffix. Still others, such as *removable,* contain all three parts—a prefix, a root, and a suffix.

## Using Prefixes

A simple way to build your vocabulary is to learn a few *prefixes.* Then you can add them to words or roots that you already know to form new words. Using this method, you can add a surprising number of new words to your vocabulary.

The following chart contains some of the many prefixes that can be added to roots.

| FIVE COMMON PREFIXES | | |
|---|---|---|
| **Prefix** | **Meaning** | **Example** |
| ex- | from, out | ex- + -change   to change from one thing to another |
| mis- | wrong | mis- + -place   to put in the wrong place |
| re- | back, again | re- + -call   to call back |
| trans- | over, across | trans- + -port   to carry over a distance |
| un- | not | un- + -seen   not seen |

**EXERCISE A: Using Prefixes to Make New Words.** Using the chart above, join a prefix to each of the words or roots on the following page. Each new word that you write on your paper should match the definition in the second column.

EXAMPLE: _____ + -consider   to think about again

      reconsider

1. _____ + -calculate       to count or judge incorrectly
2. _____ + -defined         not explained
3. _____ + -pel             to drive out by force
4. _____ + -deem          to buy back, to recover
5. _____ + -foreseen       not expected
6. _____ + -late            to change from one language to another
7. _____ + -quote         to use another's words incorrectly
8. _____ + -tain           to hold back, to keep
9. _____ + -pand         to spread out or stretch out
10. _____ + -form         to alter the form or appearance of

**EXERCISE B: Making More Words with Prefixes.** Divide your paper into two columns. In the first column, make ten words by adding each of the prefixes from the chart to two words or roots that you know. In the second column, write a short definition of each word, using your knowledge of the meanings of these prefixes. When you have finished, check each of your definitions in a dictionary. If you have made up a real word but given a wrong definition, write the word in your vocabulary notebook along with its correct definition.

EXAMPLE:    <u>Words</u>      <u>Definitions</u>

       unpleasant     not nice

## Using Roots

The *root* of a word is the most important part because it contains the basic meaning of the word. The chart on the following page lists five common roots. Notice that each of the roots listed has more than one spelling. An additional spelling for each is shown in parentheses.

| FIVE COMMON ROOTS | | |
|---|---|---|
| **Root** | **Meaning** | **Example** |
| -mit- (-mis-) | to send | trans-+-mit to send from one place to another |
| -mov- (-mot-) | to move | mot-+-ion movement |
| -ven- (-vent-) | to come | con-+-vene to come together, to meet |
| -vert- (-vers-) | to turn | re-+-vers-+-al turning around |
| -vid- (-vis-) | to see | vis-+-ion ability to see |

**EXERCISE C: Using Roots to Determine the Meaning of Words.** Match each word in the first column with its correct meaning in the second column.

EXAMPLE:   remote

       far away

1. convention
2. revise
3. dismiss
4. intervene
5. missionary
6. motive
7. reverse
8. promote
9. visual
10. introvert

a. to correct by looking at again
b. a reason for taking action
c. a coming together of a group
d. to send away
e. to move forward
f. able to be seen
g. a person sent out to teach others
h. a person who turns his or her thoughts inward
i. to come between
j. to turn back

**EXERCISE D: Using Roots in Sentences.** Think of (or look up) two words for each root in the chart above. Check your definitions in a dictionary. Then use each new word in a sentence.

**592**

EXAMPLE:  mission

The spy carried out the mission very carefully.

## Using Suffixes

A *suffix* is one or more syllables added at the end of a root to form a new word. When a suffix is added to a root, the part of speech of the new word that is formed is usually different from that of the root. For example, the suffix *-less* changes the noun *sleeve* to the adjective *sleeveless*.

The following chart contains four suffixes, their meanings, and examples of words formed with them. It also shows the parts of speech formed by the suffixes. Two of the suffixes have more than one spelling. The additional spellings are shown in parentheses.

By studying the chart carefully, you can master these suffixes and build new words by adding them to words or roots that you already know.

| FOUR COMMON SUFFIXES | | | |
|---|---|---|---|
| **Suffix** | **Meaning** | **Example** | **Part of Speech** |
| -able (-ible) | capable of being | vis- + -ible | adjective |
| -ly | in a certain way | swift- + -ly | adverb or |
| | | heaven- + -ly | adjective |
| -ment | the result of being | command- + -ment | noun |
| -tion (-ion, -sion) | the act or state of being | predic- + -tion | noun |

**EXERCISE E: Using Suffixes to Make New Words.** Complete each of the sentences on the following page with a word made by adding a suffix from the chart above to the underlined word. You may have to drop the final letter or letters in the underlined word before adding the suffix. In some cases you may have to add a letter. Consult a dictionary if you need to.

EXAMPLE: A person who <u>retires</u> from a job is in a state of
_____.

retirement

1. A person who wants to be <u>employed</u> is seeking _____.
2. The act of <u>preserving</u> a forest is called _____.
3. A teacher who <u>assigns</u> a composition is giving an _____.
4. If you <u>judge</u> another person's actions, you are making a
_____.
5. A person capable of being <u>believed</u> is _____.
6. A police officer who acts in a <u>courageous</u> way acts
_____.
7. The act of <u>exploring</u> a country is known as _____.
8. A woman who delivers a speech in a <u>confident</u> way speaks
_____.
9. A dog that <u>confronts</u> an enemy has a _____.
10. A bottle capable of being <u>reused</u> is _____.

**EXERCISE F: Making More Words with Suffixes.** Divide your paper into three columns. In the first column, write two new words for each suffix in the chart on page 593. In the second column, write a short definition of each word using your knowledge of the meanings of the suffixes. In the third column, write the part of speech of each word you have made. When you have finished, check your answers in a dictionary.

EXAMPLE:   <u>Words</u>       <u>Definitions</u>       <u>Parts of Speech</u>
          readable     able to be read       adjective

**DEVELOPING WRITING SKILLS: Forming Words from Word Parts.** Choose a total of ten word parts from the three charts in this section. Combine them with words or word parts you already know to make ten complete words. Then use each word in a sentence of your own.

EXAMPLE:    mis- + -take

mistake

People often mistake her for her twin sister.

# Exploring the Origins of Words 35.4

You probably know the meaning of most of the following words: *diesel, nicotine, boycott, sideburns, sandwich, macadam,* and *watt*. However, you may not know that all of these words have something in common. They are all "people" words—each has its origin in the name of a person. You can find information about the origin and history of a word—its *etymology*—in most good dictionaries. If you wish to learn more about a word's origin, the best place to look is in the 420 section of the library. Here you will find some fascinating books about the origin and history of words.

Knowing the history of a word often helps in remembering its meaning. In this section you will learn something about the origins of the preceding "people" words and of a number of other interesting words.

## Borrowed Words

Many words in the English language have interesting and sometimes surprising origins. Thousands of them have been borrowed from the languages of other countries. These are called *loanwords*. You probably use many of these loanwords constantly without ever realizing that they come from other languages.

**Loanwords are words in the English language that have been borrowed from other languages.**

Some examples of foreign words that have become part of the English language are *mosquito* (Spanish), *prairie* (French), *kindergarten* (German), and *piano* (Italian).

**595**

Besides loanwords taken from the languages of other countries, there are a number of words that have been borrowed from the languages of the Native Americans. Many are place names in the United States.

EXAMPLES:  Kentucky     Iroquoian, meaning "level land, plain"

Mississippi  Algonquian, meaning "big river"

Missouri     Algonquian, meaning "people of the big canoes"

Arkansas     Siouan, meaning "downstream people"

## EXERCISE A: Discovering the Origins of Loanwards.
Using a dictionary that provides etymologies, match the words in the first column with their languages of origin in the second column. If necessary, use the guide to abbreviations at the front or back of the dictionary.

EXAMPLE:  raccoon

Native American

| | |
|---|---|
| 1. pretzel | a. Eskimo |
| 2. skunk | b. French |
| 3. algebra | c. Spanish |
| 4. karate | d. Norwegian |
| 5. ski | e. Native American |
| 6. kayak | f. German |
| 7. tomato | g. Arabic |
| 8. spaghetti | h. Japanese |
| 9. ketchup | i. Italian |
| 10. restaurant | j. Chinese |

# New Meanings for Old Words

Another way that speakers of English have expanded their language is by adding new meanings to existing words.

**The English language grows by giving new meanings to existing words.**

Sometimes a word simply acquires another meaning, and the original meaning fades away. The word *nice,* for example, originally meant "strange, lazy, or foolish."

Words also acquire new meanings by working together. *Airline, airmail, airplane,* and *airport* are all examples of existing words that have been paired to create new words for new ideas.

**EXERCISE B: Finding Old Words with New Uses.** List and define five words whose current meanings have been added to the English language over the last few hundred years. Begin by looking up such words as *space, sun,* and *moon* in the dictionary.

EXAMPLE:   spaceman

a crew member on a spaceship

# Invented Words

Besides borrowing words and giving new meanings to old words, the English language continually grows in another way. Words are invented to describe new products and ideas. These are called *coined words*.

**The English language grows by the addition of coined words.**

There are a number of methods of coining words. One method, mentioned at the beginning of this section, is to name a discovery or an invention after a person.

**"People" Words.** The words mentioned in the first paragraph of this section are just a few of the many words in the English language that have as their origin the names of people. The *diesel* engine, for example, is named for its designer, a German engineer named Diesel.

**Brand Names.** Manufacturers have been responsible for introducing many words. Among them are *Xerox, Band-Aid,* and *Levi's. Levi's* is both a brand name and a "people" word since Levi Strauss was the first manufacturer of jeans.

**Acronyms.** An *acronym* is a word coined from the first letter or first few letters of each of the words in a series of words. Acronyms have occasionally been used to describe new scientific processes. It is certainly more convenient, for example, to speak of a *laser* than to speak of *l*ight *a*mplification by *s*timulated *e*mission of *r*adiation. Acronyms are used even more often for political or military organizations, such as NATO (*N*orth *A*tlantic *T*reaty *O*rganization).

**EXERCISE C: Finding the Origin of Invented Words.** In a dictionary with etymologies or a book from the 420 section of the library, look up the words. Write each definition and origin.

EXAMPLE:  cardigan

       a sweater, named after the Earl of Cardigan

| | | | |
|---|---|---|---|
| 1. sonar | 4. VISTA | 7. Popsicle | 9. silhouette |
| 2. OPEC | 5. Kleenex | 8. sandwich | 10. gardenia |
| 3. Pyrex | 6. boycott | | |

**DEVELOPING WRITING SKILLS: Working with Etymologies.** Look up five of the following words in a dictionary that provides etymologies or a book from the 420 section of the library. Then write a short account of the etymology of each.

EXAMPLE:  gung-ho

       Chinese for "work together"

| | | |
|---|---|---|
| 1. coin | 5. caterpillar | 9. democracy |
| 2. camera | 6. Fahrenheit | 10. acrobat |
| 3. magazine | 7. raccoon | |
| 4. volcano | 8. Chicago | |

# Skills Review and Writing Workshop

## Building Your Vocabulary

### CHECKING YOUR SKILLS

Use context clues to write a definition for each underlined term in the following paragraph.

(1) Tennis is a game of *strategy*; it is played with your head as well as your arms and legs. (2) Physical skills such as running and hitting are *essential*. (3) Mental skills, however, are even more *crucial*. (4) A successful tennis player uses both physical and mental skills with *consistency*. (5) Without consistency, you never get a chance to improve your strokes or *hone* your mental skills. (6) Instead, tennis becomes a *random* activity of casual strokes, brilliant shots, and silly flubs. (7) To develop consistency, you have to practice your strokes until they become *routine*. (8) You have to develop the ability to *volley* patiently with your opponent until you can hit the ball so that it cannot be returned. (9) You have to develop perfectly placed *lobs* that will send your opponent scurrying away from the net. (10) Then you can begin to *acquire* the art of placement, putting yourself as well as the ball in the right place at the right time.

### USING VOCABULARY SKILLS IN WRITING
### Writing a Sports Story

To write well, the writer must have a large vocabulary and must also know any special words or terms connected with the subject. Follow the steps below to write a sports story.

**Prewriting:** Make a list of words that are special to your favorite sport. Briefly outline the sequence of the action.

**Writing:** Following the outline, write your story chronologically, using your vocabulary list of special words. Conclude by telling why you think the team or individual won.

**Revising:** Change any words that could be more accurate or descriptive. After you have revised, proofread carefully.

# 36

# Improving Your Spelling

Good spelling is an important skill that you can easily learn. Good spelling means that your writing will be free of the kinds of spelling errors that may distract your readers from what you are saying.

The first section of this chapter will help you to identify and learn words that have been hard for you to spell. The second section will deal with certain kinds of spelling problems.

## 36.1 Solving Your Spelling Problems

A successful spelling program should begin with the words you use every day. This section will help you find out which words you commonly misspell and show you how you can learn to spell them correctly.

### Using a Dictionary

When you are doing your homework or writing a report, it is always a good idea to have a dictionary on hand.

**Acquire the "dictionary habit" as a first step in improving your spelling.**

A dictionary is a book about words. It can tell you how to pronounce a word, how to spell it, and what it means. If you use a dictionary to look up any words whose spelling you are unsure of, you will accomplish two things. First, you will soon be able to identify those words that you use frequently but may be misspelling. Second, your written work will be free of many of the spelling errors that you may have made in the past.

**EXERCISE A: Correcting Misspelled Words.** Gather together the papers that your teachers have returned to you in the past month. Use a dictionary to look up the correct spelling of any words you misspelled. Write the words correctly in your notebook. You can refer to these words later when you are making up your personal spelling list.

EXAMPLE: library

## Starting Your Personal Spelling List

Whenever you need to look up the spelling of a word in a dictionary, you should consider adding the word to a personal spelling list. This is especially true if the word is one that you use often rather than a specialized word that is used in only one subject at school. More specialized words should be checked in a dictionary, but you may not want to add them to your personal spelling list.

For a spelling improvement program to be successful, it should fit a person's own needs. Your personal spelling list should be different from those of your classmates. Your list should reflect not only your personal spelling problems but also your personal interests. You must decide which of the words that you most frequently use give you problems. These are the words that you should begin with.

**Select the words you want to include in your personal spelling list, enter them in your notebook, and study them regularly.**

Every time you have to look up the spelling of a common word for a homework assignment or a report, add the word to your personal spelling list. You will also want to review your corrected spelling tests, reports, or compositions for any spelling errors you have made. These incorrectly spelled words should also be added to your personal spelling list. If you do this on a regular basis, your spelling list will always be up-to-date.

Use a special section of your notebook to list your spelling words. Each entry should include the word, its pronunciation, and a simple definition. Look up this information in your dictionary. Leave room in each entry for a short sentence or a memory aid in case you decide that you need one.

The following illustration shows how you might set up your own list.

| | Word | Pronunciation | Definition | Sentence / Memory Aid |
|---|---|---|---|---|
| | audience | ô'dē əns | a group assembled to see and hear a play or concert | Debbie saw her mother and father in the audience. |
| | decision | di sizh'ən | the act of deciding something | Jack had a difficult decision to make. |
| | license | līs'əns | formal or legal permission to do something specified | Does your sister have a driver's license? |

**EXERCISE B: Working with Spelling Words.** Read each of the following sentences and look carefully at the underlined word. If the word is spelled correctly, write *correct* on your pa per. If the word is misspelled, write the correct spelling of the word. When you are finished, check each underlined word in the dictionary. Add any words that you misspelled to your personal spelling list.

EXAMPLE:   On the <u>eigth</u> try, they succeeded.

   eighth

1. The general store in the old village had a <u>barrel</u> of apples for sale.
2. Do you know which city is the <u>capitol</u> of the state of Illinois?
3. Sally goes to an <u>exercize</u> class three times every week.
4. I wonder <u>weather</u> it will rain tomorrow.
5. Will you drop this <u>envelope</u> in the mailbox on the corner?
6. I need a pair of <u>scissers</u> to open this package.
7. The soccer team worked hard to <u>acheive</u> its goal of a winning season.
8. The person in the picture did not look <u>familiar</u> to any of us.
9. Is it <u>necessary</u> to make reservations for dinner ahead of time?
10. Jane didn't want to <u>dissappoint</u> her brother by missing his swim meet.

# Learning Your Spelling Words

After choosing the words for your personal spelling list, you should begin to study these words regularly.

**Review your spelling words several times a week using the following method.**

With a little practice, you will find that you can follow the steps on the following page very easily.

**603**

## A METHOD FOR STUDYING YOUR SPELLING WORDS

1. *Look* at each word. Notice any unusual features about the spelling of the word. For example, in the word *argument,* the *e* in *argue* is dropped before the ending is added. Concentrate on the part of the word that gives you the most trouble. Then cover the word and try to picture it in your mind.
2. *Say* the word aloud. Then sound the word out slowly, syllable by syllable.
3. *Spell* the word by writing it on a sheet of paper. Say each syllable aloud as you are writing it down.
4. *Compare* the word that you wrote on the paper with the word in your notebook. If you spelled the word correctly, put a small check in front of the word in your notebook. If you misspelled the word, circle the letter or letters on your paper that are incorrect. Then start over again with the first step.

Do not attempt to master your complete list of spelling words in one week. Divide the words into groups of five or ten words and study each group for a week. Be sure to study all of the words in the group at each practice session, including those which you may have spelled correctly in previous sessions. Spelling a word correctly once or twice does not necessarily mean you know that word by heart.

You can study the words almost anywhere. One good time might be just before the start of each of your classes. If the occasion arises, you can also try to use the words in the writing you do in class.

Usually after a few practice sessions you will begin to make progress. If, however, you find that there are some words that are still giving you trouble, you may want to do some additional drills with these words.

To reinforce the correct spelling of these words in your mind, you may want to write them down five or ten times or use them in sentences. You can also ask a friend or classmate to pronounce each problem word and then listen as you spell the word aloud.

Once a week have a friend or someone in your family read your spelling words aloud to you. Write the words down, and then compare the words on your paper with the ones in your notebook. Any misspelled words should be included in the group of spelling words that you study the following week. In your writing assignments for the next few weeks, you should also try to use the words you spelled correctly. This will help to reinforce the correct spelling.

**EXERCISE C: Choosing the Correct Spelling.** Read each of the following sentences, looking carefully at the pair of words in parentheses. Select the word that is spelled correctly and write it on a sheet of paper. When you are finished, check each word in a dictionary. Enter in your personal spelling list any words that you misspelled. Review these words using the four-step method described on page 604.

EXAMPLE:  We will decide what to do with the elephant (tommorrow, tomorrow).

tomorrow

1. David (accidently, accidentally) stepped out of bounds.
2. We took our grandparents out to dinner on their (anniversary, anniversery).
3. Kim ordered chocolate ice cream for (desert, dessert).
4. Have you visited the (Capital, Capitol) building in Washington, D.C.?
5. Greg spent the afternoon doing research in the (library, libary).
6. Do you (beleive, believe) the story that Jason told us?
7. Patsy danced to the (rythm, rhythm) of the music.
8. Will you call up Cindy to see (whether, weather) she can come?
9. A historic (cemetary, cemetery) stood at the top of the hill.

10. Don't (mispell, misspell) any names on the program.
11. Marilyn stayed after school to (rehearse, reherse) for the class play.
12. My next-door (neighbor, neighber) has a collie.
13. Jerry left his (mathematics, mathmatics) book in the gym.
14. Are you (familar, familiar) with the works of Robert Louis Stevenson?
15. A flash of (lightning, lightening) lit up the countryside.
16. One of the pirates wore a blue (hankerchief, handkerchief) on his head.
17. Tracy likes to (exercize, exercise) before running around the track.
18. Are you on the decorating (committee, comittee) for the spring dance?
19. Beth is in the (labratory, laboratory) finishing an experiment.
20. Reggie circled his birthday on the (calendar, calender).

## Using Memory Aids

One effective way to learn the spelling of some particularly difficult words is to make up a sentence that helps you remember the troublesome letter or letters in the word. This kind of sentence is called a *memory aid*.

**Use memory aids to help remember the spelling of words that are difficult for you.**

In one kind of memory aid, you can associate the troublesome letter or letters in a problem word with the same letters in a word that you know.

EXAMPLES:  It is w*ise* to exerc*ise*.

The capt*ain* steered the boat in the *rain*.

In another kind of memory aid, you can find a shorter word within the difficult word.

EXAMPLES:   Will you *hand* me a *hand*kerchief?

Kings and queens *reign* in some fo*reign* lands.

My *neigh*bor has a horse that *neighs*.

*Cloth*es are made from *cloth*.

**EXERCISE D: Making Memory Aids.** Make up a memory aid for each of the following spelling words.

EXAMPLE:   mathematics

Please give <u>them</u> your ma<u>them</u>atics book.

| | | |
|---|---|---|
| 1. believe | 5. curious | 9. misspell |
| 2. calendar | 6. familiar | 10. secretary |
| 3. cemetery | 7. knowledge | |
| 4. committee | 8. laboratory | |

**EXERCISE E: Writing Your Own Memory Aids.** Select five words from your personal spelling list, each of which contains a shorter word. In your notebook write a memory aid for each

EXAMPLE:   There is a lot of <u>air</u> on a pr<u>air</u>ie.

## Studying Spelling Demons

Another way to improve your spelling is to study a list of words that are frequently misspelled. Words that are difficult to spell are called *spelling demons*.

**From a list of spelling demons, select words that you find hard to spell and enter them in your notebook.**

The list of spelling demons on the following page contains fifty words that students your age often misspell. Divide the words into five groups of ten each. Then use the four-step method you have learned to study the words. If you have trouble spelling any of the words correctly, add them to your personal spelling list.

## FIFTY COMMON SPELLING DEMONS

| | | | |
|---|---|---|---|
| accidentally | curious | knowledge | rhythm |
| achieve | deceive | laboratory | scissors |
| anniversary | desert | library | secretary |
| barrel | dessert | lightning | similar |
| behavior | disappear | mathematics | sincerely |
| believe | disappoint | misspell | spaghetti |
| calendar | eighth | necessary | straight |
| capital | emergency | neighbor | substitute |
| capitol | envelope | opinion | succeed |
| captain | exercise | prairie | tomorrow |
| cemetery | familiar | probably | whether |
| clothes | foreign | rehearse | |
| committee | handkerchief | restaurant | |

**EXERCISE F: Adding the Missing Letters.** Each of the following spelling demons has one or more missing letters. Write the complete words on your paper. Then check your spelling of the words against the way the words are spelled in the chart of common spelling demons. Add to your personal spelling list any words that you misspelled.

EXAMPLE:     str __ __ ght

straight

1. accident __ __ __ y
2. annivers __ ry
3. barr __ l
4. behav __ __ r
5. cur __ ous
6. di __ appear
7. exer __ __ __ e
8. famil __ __ r
9. handkerch __ __ f
10. knowle __ __ e
11. light __ ing
12. n __ __ ghbor
13. opin __ __ n
14. pra __ __ ie
15. prob __ bly
16. secr __ tary
17. simil __ r
18. sin __ erely
19. su __ __ eed
20. wh __ ther

**608**

**DEVELOPING WRITING SKILLS: Using Spelling Words in a Newspaper Article.** Pretend you are a reporter for your school newspaper. Write an article for the paper using at least five words from the chart of common spelling demons on page 608 and five words from your own personal spelling list. You may write a news article, a feature story, or a sports article. Underline the spelling words you have used in the article. Check your work for any spelling errors. Correct these as well as any other errors you may have made.

# Using Basic Spelling Rules  36.2

The spelling of some words in the English language must be memorized because the words do not follow any specific rule. However, many other words are spelled according to one of several basic rules. You will work with these rules in this section. Learning each rule will enable you to spell correctly the whole group of words to which the rule applies.

## Forming Plurals

Many people occasionally find it hard to change a word from its singular form to its plural form. Fortunately, most nouns form their plurals according to the basic rule that follows. These nouns have *regular plurals*. The nouns that do not follow this rule have *irregular plurals*.

**Regular Plurals.** Most nouns in the English language have *regular plural* forms.

**Nouns that are regular form their plurals by adding either -s or -es.**

To form most regular plurals, simply add -s. The chart on the following page shows you how to form other regular plurals. Notice that in some words the spelling of the singular word is changed slightly before the plural ending is added.

## FORMING REGULAR PLURALS

| Word Ending | Rule | Examples |
|---|---|---|
| -s, -ss, -x, -z, -sh, -ch | Add -es. | gas, gases<br>dress, dresses<br>ax, axes<br>buzz, buzzes<br>splash, splashes<br>lunch, lunches |
| -o preceded by a consonant | Add -es. | potato, potatoes<br>EXCEPTIONS:<br>piano, pianos<br>(and other<br>musical terms) |
| -o preceded by a vowel | Add -s. | rodeo, rodeos |
| -y preceded by a consonant | Change y to i and add -es. | pony, ponies<br>daisy, daisies |
| -y preceded by a vowel | Add -s. | boy, boys<br>donkey, donkeys |
| -ff | Add -s. | cliff, cliffs<br>cuff, cuffs |
| -fe | Change f to v and add -es. | life, lives<br>wife, wives |
| -f | Add -s.<br>OR<br>Change f to v and add -es. | chief, chiefs<br><br>elf, elves<br>wolf, wolves |

**Irregular Plurals.** Some nouns are *irregular* and do not follow the preceding rules. The plurals of irregular nouns are listed in the dictionary after the pronunciation of the word.

**Use the dictionary to look up the correct spelling of words with irregular plurals.**

The following chart lists a number of irregular plurals.

| FORMING IRREGULAR PLURALS | |
|---|---|
| **Rule** | **Examples** |
| Add -*en.* | ox, oxen |
| Add -*ren.* | child, children |
| Change vowels. | goose, geese<br>woman, women |
| Change vowels and one other letter. | mouse, mice |
| Use singular form as plural. | sheep, sheep<br>deer, deer |
| Use plural form only. | clothes<br>scissors |

**Plurals of Compound Nouns.** Compound nouns, composed of two or more words, may be one word *(baseball)*, a hyphenated word *(mother-in-law)*, or separate words *(cable car)*.

**Most compound nouns written as single words form their plurals regularly.**

EXAMPLES:  flashlight     flashlights

toothbrush     toothbrushes

If, however, one part of the compound noun is irregular, the plural of the compound will be irregular.

EXAMPLE:  snowman     snowmen

Some compound nouns use the following rule.

**Most compound nouns written with hyphens or as separate words form the plural by making the modified word plural.**

**611**

EXAMPLES:   son-in-law     sons-in-law

gold mine     gold mines

**EXERCISE A: Writing Plurals.** On your paper write the plural form for each of the following words. Use your dictionary to check the spelling of any words you do not know. Then add to your personal spelling list the plural words you looked up.

EXAMPLE:   monkey

monkeys

1. class
2. valley
3. circus
4. shelf
5. story
6. sister-in-law
7. moose

8. diary
9. railroad
10. zoo
11. pajamas
12. loaf
13. catfish
14. tax

15. sheriff
16. ostrich
17. supply
18. radish
19. tomato
20. foot

## Adding Prefixes

A prefix is one or more syllables added at the beginning of a word.

**When a prefix is added to a root word, the spelling of the root word stays the same.**

The spelling stays the same even when the last letter of the prefix is the same as the first letter of the root word.

EXAMPLES:   re- + -fill = refill

un- + -noticed = unnoticed

dis- + -solve = dissolve

**EXERCISE B: Working with Prefixes.** Make new words by combining the prefixes and root words on the following page.

EXAMPLE:   re- + -read

reread

1. dis-+-appear
2. un-+-necessary
3. mis-+-behave
4. re-+-entry
5. mis-+-take
6. dis-+-satisfied
7. un-+-able
8. re-+-decorate
9. in-+-experienced
10. dis-+-service
11. in-+-accurate
12. re-+-elect
13. dis-+ appoint
14. de-+-press
15. mis-+-match
16. circum-+-navigate
17. re-+-build
18. im-+-movable
19. co-+-operate
20. un-+-expected

## Adding Suffixes

A suffix is one or more syllables added at the end of a word.

**When a suffix is added to a root word, the spelling of the root word often changes.**

There are a number of different kinds of spelling changes that can take place when a suffix is added to a word. The following chart tells you what the changes are and when to make them.

| SPELLING CHANGES WHEN ADDING SUFFIXES | | |
|---|---|---|
| **Word Ending** | **Rule** | **Examples** |
| -*y* preceded by a consonant | Change *y* to *i*. | beauty, beautiful  EXCEPTIONS: Most suffixes beginning with *i:* try, trying baby, babyish |
| -*y* preceded by a vowel | Make no change. | joy, joyous EXCEPTIONS: day, daily gay, gaily |

| -e | Drop the final *e* if suffix begins with a vowel. | love, lovable<br>use, usable<br>EXCEPTIONS:<br>change, changeable<br>peace, peaceable<br>agree, agreeable |
|---|---|---|
| -e | Make no change if suffix begins with a consonant. | hope, hopeful<br>late, lately<br>EXCEPTIONS:<br>true, truly<br>argue, argument |
| One-syllable word ending in a single consonant preceded by a single vowel | Double the final consonant if suffix begins with a vowel. | drop, dropped<br>grin, grinned<br>EXCEPTIONS:<br>Words ending in *x* or *w:*<br>mix, mixing<br>blow, blowing |
| Word ending in a single consonant preceded by a single vowel and having the accent on the final syllable | Double the final consonant if suffix begins with a vowel. | permit, permitted<br>EXCEPTIONS:<br>Words in which the accent shifts when the suffix is added: refer′, ref′erence |

**EXERCISE C: Working with Suffixes.** Make new words by combining the following words and suffixes. Check the spelling of the new words in the dictionary.

EXAMPLE:   care- + -ful

careful

**614**

1. run-+-er
2. encourage-+-ment
3. bare-+-ly
4. value-+-able
5. complete-+-ly
6. stop-+-ed
7. hungry-+-ly
8. change-+-able
9. enjoy-+-ment
10. dry-+-ing

11. sleepy-+-ly
12. comfort-+-able
13. care + less
14. myster-+-ous
15. grow-+-ing
16. commit-+-ed
17. prefer-+-ence
18. nerve-+-ous
19. easy-+-ly
20. bow-+-ing

## Using *ie* or *ei*

Many people do not know when to use *ie* and when to use *ei* in words containing a combination of those letters. If you need practice in this area, the following rules should help you.

**When a word has a long e sound, use *ie*.**

**When a word has a long a sound, use *ei*.**

**When a word has a long e sound preceded by the letter c, use *ei*.**

Some of the words covered by these rules are listed below.

| COMMON *ie* AND *ei* WORDS | | |
|---|---|---|
| **Long e Sound Use *ie*** | **Long a Sound Use *ei*** | **Long e Sound Preceded by c Use *ei*** |
| achieve | eight | ceiling |
| believe | freight | deceive |
| field | neighbor | perceive |
| grief | reign | receive |
| piece | vein | |
| thief | weigh | |

Some of the exceptions to the preceding rules are listed on the next chart.

| SOME EXCEPTIONS TO THE RULES | | |
|---|---|---|
| either | neither | seize |

**EXERCISE D: Spelling *ie* and *ei* Words.** On your paper write the incomplete word from each of the following sentences, filling in either *ie* or *ei* in the blanks. When you are finished, check each word in your dictionary. Add to your personal spelling list any words you misspelled.

EXAMPLE:   She wanted n __ __ ther the reward nor the publicity.

   neither

1. Samantha went to the doctor to get her ears p __ __ rced.
2. At the campground we cooked w __ __ ners over a fire.
3. R __ __ ndeer live in the colder regions of the world.
4. Did you rec __ __ ve a birthday package from your great-grandmother yet?
5. The soldiers lay s __ __ ge to the fort.
6. Several foreign ships were lined up at the p __ __ r.
7. The bride wore a shoulder length v __ __ l.
8. The nurse measured Bill's height and w __ __ ght.
9. The cashier stapled the rec __ __ pt to the bag.
10. In this state you have to be __ __ ghteen to drive.

## Using -*cede*, -*ceed*, and -*sede*

Words ending in -*cede*, -*ceed*, and -*sede* are often confused by spellers. Since there are very few words that end this way, it is easiest simply to learn them by heart.

**Memorize the words that end in -*cede*, -*ceed*, and -*sede*.**

The following chart gives those words that you are most likely to meet.

| Words Ending in *-cede* | | Words Ending in *-ceed* | Words Ending in *-sede* |
|---|---|---|---|
| concede | recede | exceed | supersede |
| intercede | secede | proceed | |
| precede | | succeed | |

**EXERCISE E: Working with Words That End in** *-cede,* *-ceed,* **and** *-sede.* Make up five sentences, each using one of the words listed in the chart. Look up the definitions of any unfamiliar words. You may want to add a few of the more common words in the chart to your personal spelling list.

EXAMPLE:    concede

The candidate conceded the election at midnight.

**DEVELOPING WRITING SKILLS: Using Spelling Rules in Writing a Humorous Story.** Write a humorous story using words that follow the spelling rules you have learned in this section. Use at least three words that illustrate the rules for plurals, three words that illustrate rules for prefixes and suffixes, and three words that illustrate rules for *ie* and *ei* words. Your story should also include one word with a *-cede, -ceed,* or *-sede* ending. Underline the words that represent spelling rules, and then choose an appropriate title for your work. Check the spelling in your story when you are finished.

# Skills Review and Writing Workshop

## Improving Your Spelling

### CHECKING YOUR SKILLS

Rewrite the following paragraph, correcting all errors in spelling.

(1) The musical porgram consists of two parts: three traditional peices and then, after intermission, a new work. (2) The orchestra will begin with a traditional Irish melody, "The Children's Gooses." (3) After that begining, the orchestra will procede to Hungary for a whirl of Hungarian dances. (4) Next there will be a duet for two pianoes with orchestral acompanyment. (5) Their will be a shirt intermission of ten minutes. (6) Thier will be no smokeing in the hall. (7) Mr. Jones, our principle, will begin part two by introducing the composor, Miss Smyte. (8) She will describe her work, "Aniversary Rythm." (9) Then she will derect the schoul orchestra in playing her own work. (10) Refreshmints will be served after the consert.

### USING VOCABULARY AND SPELLING SKILLS IN WRITING

#### Writing a Program Guide

Correct spelling is particularly important in a guide such as a musical program guide. Follow the steps below to write a musical program guide that is correctly spelled.

**Prewriting:** Imagine that you are directing a concert. List the names of the players in the order they will appear, and their selections.

**Writing:** Begin by telling how the entire musical event is organized. Then identify each musician or group and the selection that will be played. Briefly describe each selection.

**Revising:** Check your spelling of the musicians' names and their selections. Make any other changes in your program that will improve it. After you have revised, proofread carefully.

# *Study and Research Skills*

# Basic Study Skills

Study skills are tools that will help you to understand, remember, and use what you need to learn. If you work at the exercises in this chapter to make them habits, you will be able to study well without having to think about it all the time. Once you develop good study habits, you will have more time to spend on leisure activities.

## 37.1 Establishing Good Study Habits

This section you will help you develop good study habits by showing you how to choose a useful study setting, how to schedule your study time, and how to keep an assignment book.

### Choosing a Study Setting

Even though you can probably get some studying done at school, you should set up a study area at home. Make a habit of studying in the same place every day. Keep everything you need in your study area, so you will not have to interrupt your studies to hunt for pencils, paper, and so on.

**Establish a study area that works well for you.**

The following chart contains a list of features that a good study area should have.

| FEATURES OF A GOOD STUDY AREA |
| --- |
| 1. The same every day |
| 2. Off-limits to other people |
| 3. Free from constant interruption |
| 4. Attractive so that you enjoy being there |
| 5. Equipped with a comfortable chair that is good to work in and a table or desk at a good height for working |
| 6. Well-lit with a special lamp for your desk area if the existing room light is not enough |
| 8. Equipped with all the supplies needed for studying |
| 9. Well-organized and neat |
| 10. A study schedule posted |

The following list includes supplies that you will need in your study area.

| SUPPLIES A STUDY AREA SHOULD HAVE | | |
| --- | --- | --- |
| eraser | paper clips | stapler and staples |
| ruler | scissors | pencil sharpener |
| folders | glue | markers/colored pencils |
| index cards | dictionary | paper/notebooks |
| tape | pens/pencils | wastepaper basket |

You may also want a compass, a protractor, a slide rule, a calculator, a typewriter, art supplies, and a thesaurus or other reference books.

**EXERCISE A: Rating Your Study Area.** List the features and supplies that your study area has. Compare your list with the lists you have just studied. Then write a paragraph describing how you could improve your study area.

**621**

# Scheduling Study Time

You will have enough time to complete all of your homework assignments and still have time for other activities if you plan your time carefully.

### Schedule regular periods for studying.

To plan a study schedule, write after-school hours divided into half-hour segments down the left-hand side of a piece of paper. Next to the times, write the activities you are going to do at that time. First, write in regularly scheduled after-school activities such as sports practice, family chores, and dinner. Schedule at least two hours for homework. Break these into two blocks and write it on your chart. Allow at least half an hour before bedtime for pleasure reading. Then fill in the remaining time with leisure activities.

Write out two copies of this schedule: one to keep in your school notebook and one to post in your study area.

| SAMPLE STUDY SCHEDULE | |
|---|---|
| 3:30–4:00 | Softball Practice |
| 4:00–4:30 | Softball Practice |
| 4:30–5:00 | Homework |
| 5:00–5:30 | Homework |
| 5:30–6:00 | Chores |
| 6:00–6:30 | Dinner |
| 6:30–7:00 | Homework |
| 7:00–7:30 | Homework |
| 7:30–8:00 | Television |
| 8:00–8:30 | Television |
| 8:30–9:00 | Pleasure Reading |

Be sure to schedule study time at nearly the same hour every day. You may have to revise your study schedule a few times until it works well for you. Once you have created a study schedule that works for you, stick to it. It is important to follow your plan until it becomes a habit.

**EXERCISE B: Preparing a Study Schedule.** Plan your own study schedule. If you have different after-school activities on different days of the week, you may have to write more than one schedule. Follow your plan for one week and then evaluate it. Did it help you complete your work on time? Did you allow the correct amount of time for each activity? Did you follow it every day? Revise your schedule based on your evaluation and follow the revised version.

## Keeping Track of Assignments

It is important to keep track of the papers, reading assignments, and tests due in each class. Do this by keeping an assignment book or a special assignment section in your notebook. Write down each assignment as you get it. This will help you plan what to work on in your scheduled study time. Keeping an assignment book will help you to complete each assignment on time and to be prepared for any in-class discussions or tests.

### Use an assignment book to record homework assignments and due dates.

Set up your assignment book by making five columns on each page. Use the first column for the date you received the assignment, the second for the subject, the third for the assignment itself, as well as any directions the teacher gave about how to do it. In the fourth write the date the assignment is due. The fifth column is for a checkmark that says you have completed the assignment. Look at the sample assignment book page that appears at the top of page 624.

| Date | Subject | Assignment | Due | Completed |
|------|---------|-----------|-----|-----------|
| 10/15 | History | Read Ch. 6, pp. 55–75 | 10/18 | |
| 10/16 | English | Answer questions on pp. 76 & 77 —in note form | 10/17 | √ |

**EXERCISE C: Setting Up an Assignment Book.** Set up an assignment section in your notebook or in a separate assignment book by following the directions you have just read. Use it for a week. Then, if you find it necessary, revise it. You may want to make changes like leaving more room for writing down assignments, using a red marker to indicate tests, and so on.

**DEVELOPING WRITING SKILLS: Good Study Habits.** Write a paragraph about your efforts to create a useful study area, schedule study time, and keep an assignment book. Discuss whether you studied more efficiently, completed all your assignments on time, and if you could improve your study habits still more.

# 37.2 Developing Your Note-Taking Skills

Taking good notes is an important and useful study skill. Taking notes in a class helps you remember what you heard, and taking notes while reading helps you remember what you read. Later, you can use your notes to study for a test or just to review the information you have learned.

In this section you will learn how to organize your notebook and keep your notes in order. You will also learn two methods that you can use for taking notes: the modified outline and the formal outline.

## Keeping an Organized Notebook

A neat, well-organized, and complete notebook can be your most helpful study tool. Your notebook can remind you what went on in class on any particular day. You can also use it to keep track of notes you take while reading or studying at home.

**Keep a neat, well-organized, and complete notebook.**

---

### TEN STEPS TO A WELL-ORGANIZED NOTEBOOK

1. Use a three-ring looseleaf binder, so you can remove, replace, and rearrange your notes as necessary.
2. Keep a good supply of looseleaf paper in your binder, so you always have enough to take notes.
3. Use dividers to separate each subject in your notebook.
4. Keep all notes on the same subject in the section you have marked for that subject.
5. Label all notes by subject and write the date they were taken.
6. Rewrite any notes that are messy or hard to read, and throw away the messy copy when you are finished.
7. Use gummed reinforcements on any torn pages, so they do not fall out of your notebook.
8. Keep any tests or homework assignments in their subject section. They may be useful for future studying.
9. Include a special section to keep track of homework assignments, or keep a separate assignment book.
10. Place a copy of your class and study schedules on the inside front cover of your notebook for easy reference.

---

Since taking notes is part of the process of learning and remembering, it is always best to take your own notes. However, to keep your notebook complete and up-to-date, be sure to get notes from a classmate if you must miss a class. You can also ask your teacher how you can make up what you missed.

**625**

**EXERCISE A: Evaluating Your Notebook.** Compare your notebook to the items on the chart on page 625. Give yourself one point if you rarely follow the suggestion; two points if you sometimes follow it; three points if you follow a suggestion often or always. A score of twenty-five or more points means you have a notebook that really works for you. Use your score to guide you to the areas that need improvement.

## Making Modified Outlines

A modified outline is a method of taking notes quickly and easily. It can help you to recall the main points and major details from your class or your reading. It can also be used to organize ideas for a short essay or writing assignment.

**Use a modified outline to take notes while listening or reading.**

Read the following passage and look at the modified outline that follows it. Notice how the main points are underlined and the major details are numbered.

PASSAGE:   The cartoon character Bugs Bunny was created by Bob Clampett, a Warner Brothers artist. Clampett was watching a 1934 movie called *It Happened One Night* and saw actor Clark Gable munching on a carrot in one scene. Clampett began drawing. Soon he came up with a rabbit that looked a lot like Clark Gable, munching on a carrot.

Bugs Bunny made his first movie appearance in a 1938 Porky Pig cartoon called *Porky's Hare Hunt*. But he looked very different at that time from the Bugs Bunny we know today. He was very short, had black and white fur, and squinty eyes. His name wasn't even Bugs—it was Happy! And his favorite expression was different, too. In those days he would poke his head up from the ground and say "What's cooking?" Today, of course, he says "Eh, what's up, Doc?"

Bugs changed because audiences were not happy with Happy. So several Warner Brothers artists, including Tex Avery, Chuck Jones, and Ben "Bugs" Hardaway all tried different ways of drawing the rabbit. In the end they came up with Bugs Bunny as we know him today. This totally new Bugs made his first movie appearance in the 1940 movie *A Wild Hare*.

MODIFIED OUTLINE:

Bugs Bunny created by Bob Clampett
1. Warner Brothers artist
2. Saw *It Happened One Night* (1934 movie)
3. Based drawing of rabbit on actor Clark Gable munching on carrot
4. First movie: Porky Pig cartoon called *Porky's Hare Hunt* (1938)

Different from what he is today
1. Looks short, black and white fur, squinty eyes
2. Other differences—named "Happy," favorite expression "What's cooking?"

Why and how Bugs changed
1. Audiences did not like Happy
2. Other Warner Brothers artists worked on him: Tex Avery, Chuck Jones, Ben "Bugs" Hardaway
3. New Bugs's first movie: *A Wild Hare* (1940)

**EXERCISE B: Making a Modified Outline.** Arrange the following words into three groups, using a modified outline. Decide which three words are the main points and underline them. Then, under the headings, list the words that are related details.

| | | |
|---|---|---|
| 1. ball | 6. sneakers | 11. skates |
| 2. horse | 7. tennis | 12. net |
| 3. puck | 8. beam | 13. stick |
| 4. rings | 9. hockey | 14. gymnastics |
| 5. helmet | 10. bar | 15. racket |

# Making Formal Outlines

A *formal outline* is used for organizing ideas and information for a written report or for taking detailed notes from textbooks. Formal outlines follow strict rules of organization.

**Use a formal outline to arrange ideas when preparing major written and oral assignments.**

Roman numerals (I, II, III) are used to label main ideas in a formal outline. Main ideas begin at the left. Major details that support a main point are indented under it and labeled with a capital letter (A, B, C). Minor details that relate to a major detail are further indented and labeled with numbers (1, 2, 3). Subdetails are indented still further and labeled with small letters (a, b, c).

To make a formal outline, follow the five rules shown in the chart below.

---

### RULES FOR MAKING FORMAL OUTLINES

1. Every level of importance must have at least two items. An outline must have a I. and a II.; an A. must have a B.; a 1. must have a 2.; and so on.
2. Main ideas begin at the left. Every new level of information must be indented.
3. All roman numerals should be lined up vertically, all capital letters should line up, and so on.
4. The first word in each item should be capitalized.
5. A period should be placed after each number or letter.

---

Look at the formal outline on the following page on the passage about Bugs Bunny. Then compare it with the modified outline on page 627. Notice that this formal outline is similar to the modified outline on the same passage. However, the formal outline breaks the information down into more detail and arranges it according to its level of importance.

FORMAL OUTLINE:

BUGS BUNNY

I. Created by Bob Clampett
   A. Warner Bros. artist
      1. Saw *It Happened One Night* (1934 movie)
      2. Based drawing of rabbit on actor Clark Gable munching on carrot
      3. First movie: Porky Pig cartoon called *Porky's Hare Hunt* (1938)
   B. Different from what he is today
      1. Looked different
         a. Very short
         b. Black and white fur
         c. Squinty eyes
      2. Other differences
         a. Named Happy
         b. Favorite expression was "What's cooking?"
II. Why and how Bugs changed
   A. Audiences did not like Happy
   B. Other Warner Brothers artists worked on him
      1. Tex Avery
      2. Chuck Jones
      3. Ben "Bugs" Hardaway
   C. New Bugs's first movie *A Wild Hare* (1940)

**EXERCISE C: Making a Formal Outline.** Write a formal outline of the contents of this chapter. Use the section titles that are numbered 37.1 and 37.2 as your main ideas and label them I and II. Then look for major details for each main point and indent them under each heading, labeling them with capital letters. Continue looking for minor details and subdetails, indenting and labeling them according to the rules you learned.

**DEVELOPING WRITING SKILLS: Writing About Your Notebook.** Write a paragraph on "How I Use My Notebook."

# Skills Review and Writing Workshop

## Basic Study Skills

### CHECKING YOUR SKILLS

Take notes on the following paragraph, using either a modified outline or a formal outline (in either sentence or topic form).

### AMPHIBIANS

Amphibians include such animals as frogs, toads, and salamanders. Amphibians are animals that can live both in water and on land. They live part of their life in the water because water is necessary for their reproduction and the development of their fertilized eggs.

In the beginning of their lives, amphibians live in the water and are called tadpoles. Tadpoles breathe with gills, have a two-chambered heart, and two legs. After undergoing a series of changes, or metamorphosis, the tadpole becomes an adult amphibian.

Adult amphibians live on land. They breathe with lungs, have a three-chambered heart, and four legs. They return to the water to lay their eggs, and the cycle begins all over again.

### USING STUDY SKILLS IN WRITING
### Writing an Essay

**Prewriting:** Get the modified outline you wrote in Exercise B on page 627 of this chapter. Use this outline as the basis for a short essay.

**Writing:** Expand on the details you noted down in your outline. Do some research on the three items, if you wish, or write about any personal experience you may have with them.

**Revising:** Read what you have written. Does it hold together well? Do you want to add anything, or take anything out? After you have revised, proofread your work, checking for any spelling, grammar, and punctuation errors.

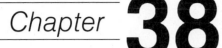

# Critical-Thinking Skills

When you think critically, you analyze and evaluate information. You can get this information from reading and listening. This chapter will help you develop skills for thinking clearly about material you read or listen to.

## Forms of Reasoning  38.1

There are two critical-thinking skills you will study in this chapter. First, you will learn how to decide whether or not the information you are examining is *reliable*. Second, you will learn how to decide if the author's thinking is *valid,* or sound.

### Using Fact and Opinion

The first step in thinking critically is to determine if the information you are examining is *reliable*. Is the material based on proven facts, or is it merely an unsupported opinion?

**Analyze your material to determine whether or not it is based on reliable information.**

In order to analyze material in this way, you must be able to tell statements of *fact* from statements of *opinion*.

**Fact.** You can *verify* a statement of fact, or prove it to be true. Facts can be verified by personal observation or experimentation; by consulting authoritative sources such as a dictionary, encyclopedia, or other reference book; or by speaking to a human authority on the subject.

FACT:    The sun is a ball-shaped object made up of hot gases.

The statement of fact above can be verified by research in an encyclopedia or earth science textbook.

**Opinion.** You cannot verify a statement of opinion, but you can *validate* it. Opinions can express a person's feelings, judgments, or predictions about a given situation.

PERSONAL FEELING:    Lying in the sun is boring.

JUDGMENT:    Solar energy is more promising than fossil energy since we will soon use up all of the fossil fuels.

PREDICTION:    The sun will continue to release energy for another five billion years, according to NASA.

The first statement is a personal feeling without any related facts given to support it, so it is an *invalid opinion*. The second statement is a judgment, supported by related facts, so it is a *valid opinion*. The third statement is a prediction and cannot be proved or disproved until the event takes place. However, it is a valid opinion since NASA bases its prediction on facts.

---

**QUESTIONS TO ASK TO TELL FACTS FROM OPINIONS**

1. Can the statement of fact be checked to *verify*, or prove, that it is true? How? (dictionary, reference book, human authority, personal observation, or experimentation)
2. If the statement cannot be verified as fact, it is opinion. Are there supporting facts to make the opinion *valid*?

**632**

**EXERCISE A: Analyzing Fact and Opinion Statements.**
First, identify each of the following statements as *fact* or *opinion*. Then analyze whether each fact statement is *true* or *false* and give your sources for verification. Then analyze whether each opinion statement is *valid* or *invalid*.

1. In 1976, two Viking spacecraft landed on Venus.
2. Randall Jarrell wrote *The Great Brain*.
3. Juliet has been training hard. She will win the marathon.
4. E. B. White wrote *Charlotte's Web*.
5. *The New York Times* reported that the Senate passed the tax bill.
6. Hawaii is the fiftieth state to join the United States.
7. Fried eggs taste awful.
8. My cousin Sarah makes fried eggs by cooking them in castor oil. They taste awful.
9. Ken is a talented writer who has been published in three different literary magazines.
10. *Ghostbusters* is the greatest movie ever made.

# Using Inference and Generalization

It is important to be able to think reasonably about the information you are examining. When you think logically, you observe details of the material you have been given and draw valid conclusions from it.

### Think logically to draw valid conclusions.

Two forms of reasoning that can be used to draw valid conclusions are *inference* and *generalization*. They can also be misused to draw invalid conclusions.

**Inference.** Sometimes the main idea of what you read or hear is stated directly. More often, the author or speaker *implies,* or hints at this main idea. When you think critically, you examine details and make *inferences* about the main idea from them. Any conclusions you draw must be based on the details of the information you have been given.

**633**

A *valid inference* is a reasonable conclusion based on the information you are examining. An *invalid inference* is an interpretation or statement that does not follow from the information you are working with.

INFORMATION GIVEN:    Joanne works hard at her job in a fast-food restaurant every day after school.

VALID INFERENCE:    Joanne probably earns a fair amount of money per week.

INVALID INFERENCE:    Joanne will own a restaurant someday.

The first statement is a *valid inference* because one can draw the conclusion that Joanne earns money from the information given–that she works hard at a job. The second statement is an *invalid inference* because it is not based on the facts given. Just because Joanne works hard in a fast-food restaurant does not show that she has either the desire or the ability to own a restaurant someday.

The following chart lists questions you can ask yourself to help you draw valid inferences from the material you are examining.

| QUESTIONS TO ASK TO DRAW VALID INFERENCES |
| --- |
| 1. What details give clues to the main idea of the material? |
| 2. What main ideas do you conclude from these details? |
| 3. Do your conclusions follow reasonably from the inferences you have made? |
| 4. Are there other conclusions you could draw from the same details? What are they? |

**Generalization.** You make a *generalization* by examining a number of facts or cases and drawing a conclusion from all the information you have. A *valid generalization* is a conclusion based on a large number of examples. It takes into account any exceptions or qualifying factors. A *hasty generaliza-*

**634**

*tion* is one based on too few examples or one that ignores exceptions and qualifying factors.

| | |
|---|---|
| VALID GENERALIZATION: | Except for three girls who run faster than any-one else (they are on the track team and train all the time), all the boys in my seventh-grade class can run faster than the girls. Therefore, in seventh grade, most boys can run faster than most girls. |
| HASTY GENERALIZATION: | Craig can run faster than Diane. Therefore, boys can run faster than girls. |

The second statement is a *hasty generalization* because it is based on only one example.

The chart lists questions you can ask yourself to help you make valid generalizations from the information given.

---

**QUESTIONS TO ASK TO MAKE VALID GENERALIZATIONS**

1. What facts or cases are presented to make the generalization?
2. Will the generalization you make hold true for all or most cases? Are there any exceptions to the statement?
3. Are enough cases given to make a valid generalization?

---

**EXERCISE B: Analyzing Forms of Reasoning.** Identify whether *inference* or *generalization* is used in each of the following statements. Explain whether each conclusion is *valid* or *invalid*.

1. All *G*-rated movies are babyish and boring.
2. Jean attends the School of American Ballet, so she must be a good dancer.
3. Carl got 62 in a math test, so he knows nothing about math.
4. Children may mistake medicine for candy. Therefore all medicine bottles should have child-proof caps.
5. I got sick eating strawberries. Nobody should eat them.

**635**

**DEVELOPING WRITING SKILLS: Analyzing Writing.** Read the following passage. First, analyze all statements of *fact* and *opinion* in it, and explain whether they can be verified or validated. Then, make *inferences* and *generalizations* to draw your own conclusions about the material. Write a paragraph about the conclusions you have drawn and the methods you used.

American youth has gotten fatter than it was in the '60s, according to HHS [Health and Human Services] tests. Young people spend an average of 13 hours a week in sports or other exercise. They spend three to four times that watching TV and playing video games. Schoolchildren's scores are now declining for strength, power, speed, agility, and cardiovascular fitness. The Amateur Athletic Union reports that 36% of youngsters meet its standards for push-ups, high jumps, long jumps, endurance runs, and sprints. Just a few years ago, the number was 42%.

# 38.2 Language and Thinking

People think by using language. We express thoughts to ourselves and explain them to one another in words. We also use words to express our feelings to one another. Critical thinking includes analyzing how words are used to express thoughts and feelings. This helps us evaluate a writer's or speaker's purpose.

## Uses of Language

Language can be used to communicate information honestly. It can also be used to distort information and attempt to make you think about it in a certain way.

**Learn to identify different uses of language.**

**Word Meanings.** Words can be used in a *denotative* manner, in which they present facts or describe a situation objectively, in a neutral tone. Words can also be used in a *connotative* manner, in which they imply a particular point of view, and convey a positive or negative tone. The connotations of words can cause an emotional response to the material.

DENOTATION:   The movie contains many chase and fight scenes.

CONNOTATION:   The movie is a drawn-out car chase, interrupted only by staged fistfights.

The first statement uses words in a denotative manner, describing the movie in a neutral tone. The second statement implies that the movie is unpleasant and boring.

**Jargon.** Jargon is the use of words with specialized meanings in a particular trade or profession. Jargon is meant to have very precise meaning. However, it is often used to obscure ideas that anyone could understand if they were stated directly.

JARGON:   Aspire to your proficiency-achievement level.

DIRECT:   Work to the best of your ability.

**EXERCISE: Analyzing Uses of Language.** Analyze each pair of sentences below for use of *denotation/connotation* and *jargon/direct language*.

1. Rita refused to discuss the problems.
   Rita declined to discuss the situation.
2. Security personnel apprehended the perpetrator.
   The guards caught the burglar.
3. He raced across the piazza and drew her into his arms.
   He walked across the square and put his arms around her.
4. They finalized a strategy to minimize system down-time.
   They figured a way to avoid machine breakdowns.
5. The man was dressed in a blue suit.
   The gentleman was outfitted in a midnight-blue tuxedo.

**DEVELOPING WRITING SKILLS: Using Critical Thinking in Writing.** Rewrite the passage from Developing Writing Skills on page 636 so that it communicates honestly and simply.

**637**

# Skills Review and Writing Workshop

## Critical-Thinking Skills

### CHECKING YOUR SKILLS

Read the following selection, and list facts, opinions, denotations, connotations, and jargon. Use inference and generalization to draw conclusions about the material presented. Write a sentence or two describing its main idea.

As schools reopen this month, the number of computers in U.S. classrooms has reached some 1 million (up from 630,000 last year). . . .

But the educational benefits claimed for computer programming have been difficult to prove. One study of sixth-grade Logo programmers found that 69% had memorized the commands that tell the computer to draw a 90° angle on the screen, but only 19% knew how to draw the same angle on paper.

### USING CRITICAL-THINKING SKILLS IN WRITING

### Writing a Parody of a Speech

Follow the steps below to write a parody of a pompous, overblown speech.

**Prewriting:** For a humorous tone, pick a topic such as "how to feed your cat," and use lots of big words. For a more serious tone, pick an important topic, and use jargon and connotations of words to confuse your audience.

**Writing:** Use a thesaurus to find little-used words and phrases to make your speech sound pompous. Make use of the connotative effects of words and jargon. State opinions, judgments, and predictions without facts to back them up—or use made-up "facts." Make hasty generalizations and inferences about your subject matter.

**Revising:** Look over your speech. Does it open with an attention-getting line? Does it set the humorous tone for what is to follow? Does it use enough exaggeration and parody to help your audience see that they could be misled by speakers? After you have revised, proofread carefully.

**638**

# Chapter 39

# Reading and Test-Taking Skills

You have probably been using textbooks as long as you have been in school. This chapter will help you learn how to read and use a textbook more effectively. These reading skills are an important part of preparing for and taking tests in school, and this chapter will also help you improve your test-taking ability.

## Reading Textbooks

To get the most out of reading textbooks requires special reading skills. First, you should examine the special features that your textbooks have.

### Examining Your Textbooks

Most textbooks have special sections and features to help you use them more effectively. Familiarize yourself with these so you know what they are when you need them.

**639**

**Identify and make use of the special sections at the front and back of your textbooks.**

Most textbooks have some or all of the following special sections: table of contents, preface or introduction, index, glossary, appendix, and bibliography.

Once you know which of these reading aids your textbook offers, you will want to use them to help you in your studying. Following are descriptions of the special sections found in most textbooks that tell where they are located and that give some suggestions on how to use them.

**Table of Contents.** The table of contents is located at the front of the textbook. It lists the sections and chapters of the book in order and the pages on which each section begins. It can be used to help you locate general information or a particular section.

Read through the table of contents when you first receive a textbook to get an overview of what it covers. You can also use the table of contents to test yourself at the end of a chapter by looking at the listings and seeing how much detail you can remember about each section.

**Preface or Introduction.** This section is also located at the front of the book. The preface or introduction states the author's reason for writing the book. It often has ideas about how to use the textbook's special features.

Read the preface or introduction when you first get your textbook to help you get the most out of it.

**Index.** The index is found at the back of the book. It lists all the subjects covered in the book in alphabetical order and tells on which pages they can be found.

You can use the index to find all of the references to a particular topic in the entire textbook, or to help you find one particular entry on that topic.

**Glossary.** The glossary, which is located at the back of the book, lists and defines a number of words or special terms that are used in the textbook.

Read the glossary first to help you understand the terms as they come up in your reading. Also, if you run across a term you do not understand or do not remember while you are reading, you can turn quickly to the glossary and look it up.

**Appendix.** Located at the back of the book, an appendix contains supplementary material such as documents, charts, graphs, maps, and essays. They add information related to material in the book.

You can use an appendix to save time. You will not have to look for outside reference books and materials that contain that particular information about the subject.

**Bibliography.** A bibliography may be located at the back of the book. Sometimes, however, a bibliography may appear at the end of each chapter or unit of a book. A bibliography is a list of books, pamphlets, magazines, and other publications. Sometimes, the bibliography is a list of materials that the author used to write the textbook. In your textbooks the bibliographies will usually be a list of materials that the author recommends for further reading on the subject.

Sometimes, you may have questions on the material you are studying that are not answered in your textbook. At other times you may simply want more information on the subject, or you may want to write an in-depth report on it. Then, you can use the bibliography to find additional material to read and study.

Other features of your textbook can also help you in your studying. *Chapter titles, headings,* and *subheadings* are usually printed in large, bold, heavy, or colored type. Headings divide each chapter into smaller, easier-to-read sections. You can skim through the chapter, reading only headings and subheadings to locate, preview, or review the material. Also, as you read, you can turn each heading into a question and then read the following material to answer the question. This helps you remember what you read.

*Questions* and *exercises* can help you test your knowledge and skills. They are generally located at the end of each chapter or section. Glance at them before reading the chapter itself to see what you are expected to master by the end of it. When you finish reading, use the questions and exercises to see how much you remember and how well you can use your new skills.

*Pictures* and *captions* are used to illustrate or add information to the text in which they are found. They are located throughout the book. Pictures and captions can help you transfer what you have read into a visual image, making the knowledge easier to remember.

Flip through a chapter looking only at pictures and captions to see how much you remember of what you have read. Ask yourself questions such as "What is this picture here for? What does it illustrate or explain?"

An outline of what the aim or content of each chapter is appears in the *chapter introductions*. It will be located at the beginning of each chapter. Read the chapter introduction carefully to help guide and focus your reading.

At the end of each chapter, you may find a *chapter summary*. It is a brief review of the main ideas and major details of the entire chapter.

Use the chapter summary to solidify and check your knowledge. If something mentioned in the summary is vague or unclear to you, go back and reread the section on that topic in detail.

When you use a textbook to study, be sure to take advantage of the special sections and features it offers. They can save you time in both finding and learning information.

**EXERCISE A: Examining and Using the Special Features of a Textbook.** Examine one of your textbooks. Notice especially the special sections and other features it contains. Then answer the following questions about the book.

1. How many units and chapters does the book have?
2. Are chapters divided into smaller sections in the table of contents?

3. Where is the glossary found in the textbook? What two types of information can you learn from it?
4. How are the listings in the index arranged?
5. Does the textbook contain an appendix? If so, what kind of information does it include?
6. Where is the bibliography located and what is the purpose of the materials listed there?
7. What do chapter titles, headings, and subheadings look like? How do they differ in appearance from one another?
8. Does each chapter contain an introduction and a summary?
9. What kind of pictures does the textbook contain? Do the pictures have captions? Do the pictures and captions simply illustrate material in the book or do they add new information?
10. Where are questions and exercises located in the textbook? In what two ways can they be used to help you study the information presented in the book?

## Using Textbooks to Study

After you have examined the special sections and features of your textbooks, you can use their organization to help you study better.

**Use the organization of your textbooks to help you study them effectively.**

The following chart contains suggestions that you can use when you use your textbooks to study.

| SUGGESTIONS FOR STUDYING TEXTBOOKS |
| --- |
| 1. *Think* about the assignment or about why you are reading the textbook. Remember reasons such as class discussions or upcoming tests for which you will need the information in your textbook. You will remember more if you are aware of what and why you want to learn. |

2. *Preview* the material you want to cover. Skim through the chapter and decide what you will read at one sitting. Take note of chapter headings and subheadings, words printed in boldface or in color, pictures and captions, and so on. These will give you clues as to what is important in the chapter.

3. *Read* through the material with close attention. Set yourself a time limit (minimum one-half hour; maximum one hour). Say "I will read for 45 minutes, and during that time I will not think about anything else." This will help you focus your attention on the immediate goal of completing the reading.

4. Make *questions* out of what you are reading. When you reach a chapter heading or subheading, turn it into a question. Then read the paragraph beneath it to find the answer to the question.

5. Take *notes* on what you are reading. As you think about your assignment and ask yourself questions, take notes on the main ideas and major details of what you are reading. The action of note-taking itself helps you remember what you have read. You can also review the notes later to refresh your memory before writing a paper or taking a test.

6. *Recite* aloud important sections of the textbook or the notes you have taken. Hearing the information in this way will help to fix it in your mind.

7. *Review* your notes at the end of your reading period. Check what you have learned. You may wish to skim through the material once more to make sure you have not skipped anything important. This immediate review will help you when you use the notes again at a later date. If you wait too long to review your notes, they may seem unfamiliar to you and be less useful than they could be.

**EXERCISE B: Using a Texbook to Study.** Follow the suggestions in the chart on pages 643 and 644 to study a textbook chapter that has been assigned to you. Then list three ways in which the suggestions helped you to study the chapter.

# Reading Critically

When you read, the first step is to understand and remember the main ideas and major details of the material you are reading. The second step is to read critically so you can analyze and evaluate the material. When you read critically you ask yourself questions to help you analyze and evaluate what you read.

**Read critically in order to question, analyze, and evaluate what you read.**

When you read critically, you use critical-thinking skills to think clearly and reasonably about what you are reading. A full discussion of critical thinking is found in Chapter 38.

The chart below briefly describes the main skills you need to be able to read critically.

| CRITICAL-READING SKILLS |
| --- |
| 1. Understanding the difference between statements of *fact* and statements of *opinion* |
| 2. Making *inferences* from the material presented to come to a conclusion about the main idea in the writing |
| 3. Recognizing the author's *attitude* toward the subject and noticing how it gives clues to the author's purpose |
| 4. Recognizing any *persuasive techniques* used and what effects they have |

**Fact and Opinion.** When you read critically, the first thing you should do is separate factual statements from opinion statements. You can always *verify* a statement of fact or prove it to be true. You can do this by consulting a written or a human authority, by direct personal observation, or by experimentation.

The chart on the following page gives examples of statements given as fact and the sources to verify them.

| Fact Statements | Sources to Verify |
|---|---|
| The sun rises in the east and sets in the west. (True) | Science textbook, encyclopedia, direct personal observation |
| Beverly Cleary is the author of *Ribsy*. (True) | Library, biographical reference book |
| There are fifty-one states in the United States. (False) | Research, encyclopedia, social studies textbook, almanac, atlas |

You cannot prove a statement of opinion to be true. However, you can *validate* it, or find material that supports it. Supporting material includes related facts or an authoritative source. The chart below gives examples of valid and invalid opinion and sources you can use to validate an opinion.

| Opinion Statements | Sources to Validate |
|---|---|
| Research scientists believe that saccharin can cause cancer based on experiments done on laboratory animals. (Valid opinion) | This opinion is validated by authoritative sources. |
| Saccharin causes cancer. (Invalid opinion) | This opinion is not validated by facts or authority. |

**Inference.** Sometimes an author states the main idea of the material in direct language. Many times, however, the author hints at main ideas rather than stating them directly. To discover the main idea of a piece of writing, you must observe clues and draw logical conclusions from the material that is presented. This is called making *inferences*. An inference you draw is *valid* if it is supported by the details in the material you are examining. Below are examples of valid and invalid inferences drawn from the same information.

INFORMATION GIVEN:    Lawrence won first place at the swim meet for the butterfly stroke.

VALID INFERENCE:    Lawrence won first place at the swim meet for the butterfly stroke, so he is a very good swimmer and probably trains very hard.

INVALID INFERENCE:    Lawrence won first place at the swim meet for the butterfly stroke, so he will win first place for the backstroke and diving, too.

To infer that John's backstroke or diving abilities are good enough to win first place does not follow from the information given. The information given implies only that he is a good swimmer who trains hard and won first place in the butterfly stroke.

**Denotation and Connotation.** An author reveals his or her attitude toward the subject in writing by the choice of words. The author's choice of words affects your response to the material. Words can be used in a *denotative* manner. This means they can be used to communicate information as objectively as possible, in a neutral tone. Below is an example of the denotative use of language.

DENOTATION:    The production of nuclear energy also produces a large amount of radioactive waste. Safe means of disposing of this material has yet to be developed.

Words can also be used in a *connotative* manner. This means that they are used to create a particular tone or atmosphere and to communicate a particular point of view. An example of the *connotative* use of language is on the following page. Notice how the emotionally charged words reveal the author's attitude toward the subject.

CONNOTATION:   The mindless production of nuclear energy also creates massive quantities of dangerous radioactive waste. At this time, there is no safe way of disposing of this deadly material.

Words such as "mindless," "massive," "dangerous," and "deadly" can create emotions of anger or fear in the reader. The author may hope these emotions will lead the reader to take a negative attitude toward the subject being described and possibly to take action against it.

**Persuasive Techniques.** Authors can use the connotations of words to make you think or feel a certain way about a subject. Politicians and advertisers often use words in this way to convince you that their policies are right or to get you to buy their product. Since a skilled writer can bend the truth to fit his or her purpose, it is important to be able to read critically and recognize any persuasive techniques the writer may be using. Otherwise you may take what is written as true, without thinking for yourself and drawing your own conclusions.

*Jargon* is language that seems to be technical or scientific. An author can use jargon to appear to be an expert in the field. Although specialized terms are meant to have very precise meanings, jargon is often used in a vague and confusing way by authors who wish to deceive the reader, rather than inform the reader about something. Following is an example of jargon and a translation of it in direct language.

JARGON:   Any student who exhibits a tendency toward tardiness must interface with guidance personnel.

DIRECT LANGUAGE:   Any student who is late must go to the guidance office.

**EXERCISE C: Applying Critical-Reading Skills.** Look in a newspaper or a magazine and find an article that interests you. Then answer the questions on the following page, using that article as your source.

**648**

1. Find one statement of fact and one statement of opinion. Note if these statements are verified or validated in the article.
2. What inferences or conclusions did you draw about the main idea or ideas in the article?
3. What was the author's attitude toward the subject matter? Describe any connotative use of language in the article and note the effect it had on you as a reader.
4. Did the author use any persuasive techniques, such as jargon? If so, quote them and rewrite in direct language.
5. What do you think the author's purpose is in writing this article? Use the answers to the four questions above to help you come to your conclusion.

**DEVELOPING WRITING SKILLS: Evaluating Your Reading Skills.** After a week of practice, write a paragraph about your reading skills. Include your answers to the following questions.

1. Have you been using the special sections and features of your textbooks?
2. Which suggestions for studying textbooks have you found most useful?
3. What have you read recently which required you to use critical-reading skills?
4. What were some of the critical-reading questions that you asked to help you analyze and evaluate what you read?
5. What do you need to concentrate on in the future in order to improve your reading skills?

# Taking Tests 39.2

The ability to take tests well affects your performance in every class. Students often feel nervous about taking tests. This section will help you learn how to prepare for and take tests.

If you practice the suggestions and exercises in this section, you will gain confidence and lose some of the nervousness you may feel when you are about to take a test. You may even start seeing tests as a way to check your progress.

## Preparing for Tests

Preparing properly to take a test is the most important part of test-taking. Be sure to set aside plenty of time to study for a test for several days beforehand. Effective test preparation requires time, organization, and concentration.

**Schedule time for several days before a test in order to prepare for it.**

Schedule time for test preparation on your study schedule. This ensures that you will have enough time to review and memorize all the material you need to know for the test.

The following chart shows ways to prepare for a test.

| PREPARING FOR TESTS |
| --- |

1. Find out about the nature of the test and what sorts of questions will be on it. This will help you direct your studying. It will also take away some of the nervousness about not knowing what kind of test it will be.
2. Review any class or reading notes that relate to what you are going to be tested on. This aspect of test preparation actually begins much earlier. You should review your notes three times altogether: once on the day you take them, once a few days later, and once the night before the test.
3. Check your knowledge. Make up questions on the material you will be tested on, and write out the answers. Any weak spots will show you where you need to do additional studying. Work with a friend on this. Make up questions for each other. If one of you knows more on the subject, that one can help the other learn what he or she does not know.

4. Memorize material by going over it repeatedly for several days before the test. This helps to fix it in your mind. Have someone quiz you on the material to make sure that you know it and to test yourself before the actual test.

Do not try to do all your studying at the last minute. Your studying will not be effective at all. It leaves you feeling tired and tense. This can hurt your test performance a lot, since being relaxed and well rested is the best state to be in to take a test. It also has no long-term value as you will probably forget everything within a few days.

Test preparation should be the final stage of your studying. If you practice all your other study skills and make an effort to be active in class, preparing for tests will be much easier. You will be building on work you have already done, rather than trying to memorize information you never really learned.

**EXERCISE A: Preparing for a Test.** Use the suggestions in the chart on pages 650 and 651 to study for your next test. After you have taken the test, list several ways that the suggestions helped your performance.

## Taking Objective Tests

Many of the tests that you take in school will be objective tests. When you take an objective test, you will usually choose the correct answer from several possibilities that are given, you will answer either True or False, or you will fill in a blank with a short answer.

There are three steps in taking an objective test. The first is to look over the test to get an overview of its content and format. The second step is to answer the questions, beginning with the easiest ones. The last step is to proofread your work to make sure you have not made any careless mistakes. Budget the time during your test period so you can do each of these steps thoroughly.

**Budget your time among looking over the test, answering the questions, and proofreading your work.**

Looking over the test and proofreading shouldn't take more than 15 percent to 25 percent of your time. You want to allow the largest amount of your time for answering the questions.

You will be less nervous and more confident if you arrive at the test on time. If possible, arrive a few minutes early so that you can be even more relaxed.

Be sure to bring a watch, pens, pencils, erasers, and paper, as well as any books or other materials you may have been told to bring. Sit down, arrange your things, and wait for the test to be handed out.

Once you receive the test and are told to begin, start looking over the test immediately. The following chart lists steps you may follow when looking over a test.

---

### STEPS FOR LOOKING OVER A TEST

1. First, write your name on every sheet of paper you will have to hand in.
2. Next, look over the entire test to see what types of questions it has and how they are arranged.
3. Find out whether you lose points for incorrect answers. If you do, do not guess at answers.
4. Decide how much time you plan to spend answering the questions in each section of the test. Make a small checkmark next to the most difficult questions and those that are worth the most points. Allow the most time for these questions.

---

After you have looked over the entire test and decided how you are going to work on it, you should begin to answer the questions.

Several hints for answering questions on an objective test appear in the chart on the following page.

**652**

## ANSWERING QUESTIONS ON A TEST

1. If you are allowed to use separate scratch paper, use it freely for jotting down notes or information, making outlines, calculations, and so on.
2. Answer all the easy questions first. This leaves most of your time for tackling the difficult questions.
3. Get to work on the difficult questions. Concentrate on one question at a time. If you have difficulty remembering certain information, try to relax your mind and see if the information comes up by itself. If not, answer the question to the best of your ability and move on. If the material comes to you later, go back and add it on.
4. If you do not know the answer to a question at all, move on to the next question. Make a checkmark next to the question so you can return to it if you finish the other questions.
5. Be sure to follow the directions carefully and completely.

Once you have answered all the questions, take a few minutes to go over your work and proofread it. This allows you to catch any careless mistakes you may have made out of nervousness or rushing. It also permits you to double-check that you have answered all the questions and followed all the directions completely.

Below are steps to follow when you proofread your test answers.

## PROOFREADING TEST ANSWERS

1. Make sure your name is written on each sheet of paper you have to hand in.
2. Make sure you have followed the test directions accurately and completely and that you have answered all the questions.
3. Read all the test questions and your answers. Correct any punctuation or spelling errors you may find. You can also add to, elaborate, or clarify any of your answers at this time.

**EXERCISE B: Evaluating Your Test-Taking Skills.** Give short answers to the following questions about a test you have taken recently.

1. Did you give yourself enough time to study beforehand?
2. How could you have improved your test score by better use of your study time?
3. Did you come on time or early?
4. Did you bring all the materials you needed with you?
5. Did you look the test over carefully?
6. Did you make marks next to the hard questions so that you could come back to them later?
7. Did you answer all the easy questions first?
8. Did you allow enough time for difficult questions or for questions that were worth more points?
9. Did you proofread carefully, catching all mistakes, and making sure you answered all the questions?
10. Did you miss any questions or give wrong answers you could have corrected if you had proofread it more thoroughly?

**DEVELOPING WRITING SKILLS: Writing About How to Improve Your Test-Taking Skills.** Write a brief paragraph about how you can strengthen your test-taking skills. Use your answers to the questions above to help you guide your evaluation of previous test performance and how it could be improved.

# Skills Review and Writing Workshop

## Reading and Test-Taking Skills
### CHECKING YOUR SKILLS

Use one of your textbooks to practice the following skills. Look up a chapter title. Look up the definition to a specialized term. Find pages on which there are references to a specific topic. Review what you have learned from a special chapter. (How many ways can you do this?) Practice some of your other skills in using the special features of your textbooks.

### STUDY SKILLS IN WRITING
### Review and Compare Two Textbooks

**Prewriting:** Look at two textbooks from two different classes (for example, one from science and one from social studies). What special features does each of the two textbooks have? Does one have more special features than the other? Is one easier to read or use? Why? Does one of the textbooks have a clearer table of contents, a better introduction, more appendixes, a bigger glossary? Make a list containing two columns to compare the features, both good and bad, of each of the two textbooks.

**Writing:** Describe the two textbooks in terms of the questions you asked yourself in the prewriting exercise. Then evaluate them, describing which one you liked better and why.

**Revising:** Make sure the paper is organized in a logical fashion. Begin with a paragraph describing the two books, and then go on to give your opinion on them. Do not mix up the description and the review when you are writing. Correct any spelling, grammar or punctuation errors. Make sure the final copy is neat and readable. After you have revised, proofread carefully.

# 40

# Library and Dictionary Skills

Whether you want to know the date of the first President's birth or of the first space-shuttle flight, your best source of information will generally be the library. Both your school and public libraries hold a vast amount of knowledge. There you can find an answer to almost any question. You just have to know how to look for the answers.

The first two sections of this chapter will show you how to use the library's resources. The third section covers the features of the dictionary.

## 40.1 Using the Library

Because the library is a place for many people, it helps when everyone shows the same consideration for others. Try not to talk loudly. Most people need quiet in order to concentrate. Return materials on time and in the same condition that you found them. Treat all library equipment, such as copying machines and microfilm readers, with care. If you do not know how to use a certain machine, ask the librarian. He or she can also help you with any question you may have about the use of the library. But before asking the librarian for help, learn how to use the card catalog yourself.

## The Card Catalog

Inside the library you will find a file cabinet that contains many cards. Just like the index of a book, the *card catalog* tells you where to find certain information.

**Use the card catalog to find materials in the library.**

The drawers of a card catalog contain cards arranged in alphabetical order. These cards identify all of the materials in the library. The label on the front of each drawer shows a part of the alphabet. If you read the drawers in columns from top to bottom beginning at the left and moving slowly to the right, you will see the entire alphabet.

The cards inside each drawer match the alphabet label. For instance, the drawer Di-E contains all of the cards that begin with letters of the alphabet from Di to E. Some of the cards are *guide cards*. Their tabs list major subjects that fall within that section of the alphabet.

**Kinds of Catalog Cards.** Each catalog card lists information about one book. The top line of the card identifies it as an *author card*, a *title card*, or a *subject card*.

**Use the three types of catalog cards—author, title, or subject—to find books.**

Suppose you want to find a book and you know only that it was written by June Callwood. You would then look for the book's author card. In checking the card catalog under C, the first letter of the author's last name, you would find a card such as the one at the top of the next page.

Perhaps you know only that the title of the book is *Portrait of Canada*. Then you would look for a title card, under P such as the middle card on page 658.

When researching a report, you often may have neither an author's name nor a title. However, you will know the subject of your report, so you can look for books by checking subject cards. If you look up the subject *Canada,* you would find a card such as the last one on this page.

AUTHOR CARD:

```
971      Callwood, June ————————————— Author of book
C        Portrait of Canada.
         Doubleday 1981.

         378p.
```

TITLE CARD:

```
971      Portrait of Canada ———————————— Title of book
C        Callwood, June

         Portrait of Canada.
         Doubleday 1981.

         378p.
```

SUBJECT CARD:

```
971      CANADA ———————————————————— Subject of book
C
         Callwood, June
         Portrait of Canada.
         Doubleday 1981.

         378p.
```

Sometimes nothing may be listed in the catalog under the first subject heading that you check. However, a *cross-reference card,* called a *see* card, will often refer you to a subject that the library does list. If you look for a book under *French-Canadian folksongs,* you might find a *see* card telling you that the library lists the subject as *Folksongs, French-Canadian.*

CROSS-REFERENCE CARD:

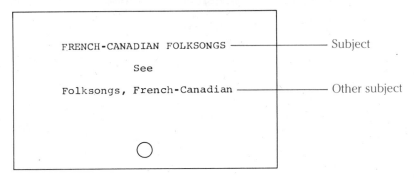

Another cross-reference card, a *see also* card, can be used to find additional, related subjects. You will often be able to find exactly what you want to know about a general subject by checking the more specific subjects listed on such card. The following card suggests specific subjects related to the general entry *Accidents.*

CROSS-REFERENCE CARD:

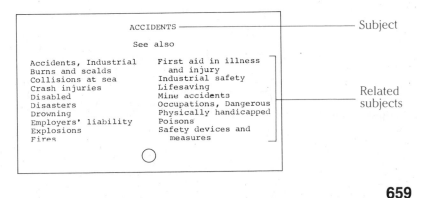

The card catalog may file all of the different kinds of cards together. In some libraries, however, the subject cards are placed in a separate file. Notice that each author, title, and subject card gives the same information. Only the top lines are different.

**Information on Catalog Cards.**   After you find the card for the book you want, take time to study the card. The catalog card shows more than the author, title, and subject of the book.

**Use a catalog card to learn about a book before you look for it on the shelves.**

Notice all the information that the following author card shows. The copyright date tells you when the book was published. You can then decide if its information is current enough for you. The card also tells you the book's length. You may find that the book is either too brief or too detailed for your use. In addition, the card describes certain other useful features of the book. If the book has illustrations, you may understand its ideas better. If it has a bibliography, you will have a list of other materials related to your subject. If it has an index, you may find it easier to locate specific facts. The card may also list, at the bottom, one or more subject headings under which you may look for additional books. When you decide to look at the book itself, the *location symbol* in the upper left corner will show you where to find it.

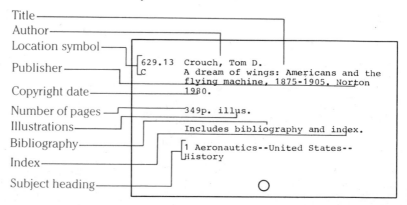

**Arrangement of Catalog Cards.** Cards are arranged alphabetically by word in the card catalog.

**Use word-by-word alphabetizing to find cards in the card catalog.**

There are two kinds of alphabetical order. In *word-by-word alphabetizing*, the first word in a group of words is considered separately. In this system *home run* comes before *homeroom* because the word *home* comes before the word *homeroom*. In the other system, *letter-by-letter alphabetizing,* all of the letters in a listing are considered as a single block. If the listing has more than one word, the space between them is ignored. In this system *homeroom* comes before *home run.*

| TWO WAYS OF ALPHABETIZING | |
| --- | --- |
| **Library's Method: Word-by-Word** | **Other Method: Letter-by-Letter** |
| home economics | homecoming |
| home run | home economics |
| homecoming | homemade |
| homemade | homeroom |
| homeroom | home run |

The following chart shows some other rules that libraries use when alphabetizing catalog cards.

| OTHER ALPHABETIZING RULES |
| --- |
| 1. The words *a, an,* or *the* at the beginning of a listing are ignored. For example, *The Moon* would be filed under *M.* |
| 2. All abbreviations are filed as if they were spelled out. For example, *Mt. St. Helens* would be filed as *Mount Saint Helens.* |
| 3. *Mc* is filed as if it were spelled *Mac.* For example, *McCall* would be filed as *MacCall.* |

**661**

**EXERCISE A: Using the Card Catalog.** Use a catalog card in your library to provide the following information. If the card does not have the kind of information listed, write *none*.

1. Location symbol
2. Author
3. Title
4. Copyright date
5. Publisher
6. Number of pages
7. Illustrations
8. Bibliography
9. Subject headings
10. Kind of card

**EXERCISE B: Alphabetizing in Card Catalog Order.** Arrange the following items in card catalog order.

1. Newman
2. news
3. New Deal
4. Newton
5. New Guinea

## Finding the Book You Want

How does the catalog card lead you to the book on a shelf? The location symbol is the key. Look at the upper left corner of the card. This corner will tell you whether the book is fiction or nonfiction. Works of *fiction* are "made up" stories that come from an author's imagination. *Nonfiction* books contain facts or opinions about real events. Most libraries keep fiction and nonfiction in separate areas. If you know the location symbol, you will know which section to check.

**Finding Fiction.** If the upper left corner of the catalog card shows an F or Fic, the book is *fiction*. Often the first letter or letters of the author's last name will also be written, beneath the F. The author's name is the key to the order on the shelves.

**Find fiction arranged on the shelves alphabetically by the last name of the author and then by the title.**

Several books by the same author are alphabetized by the first words of the titles. The words *a, an,* and *the* are ignored.

**Finding Nonfiction.** If the catalog card shows a number and one or more letters in the upper left corner, the book is *nonfiction.* This number and letter combination is known as a *call number.* The number is a special classification. The letters represent the author's last name. The call number also appears on the spine of the book.

**Find nonfiction arranged on the shelves from left to right in call-number order.**

Most public and school libraries use *Dewey Decimal numbers* to classify nonfiction books. This system is named for an American librarian, Melvil Dewey, who suggested that books could be classified into ten main groups. The following chart shows these groups.

| DEWEY DECIMAL SYSTEM | |
|---|---|
| **Numbers** | **Groups** |
| 000–099 | General works (such as encyclopedias) |
| 100–199 | Philosophy |
| 200–299 | Religion |
| 300–399 | Social sciences (such as education) |
| 400–499 | Language (such as dictionaries) |
| 500–599 | Pure sciences (such as chemistry and mathematics) |
| 600 699 | Technology, or applied sciences (such as business, engineering, and medicine) |
| 700–799 | The arts (such as music and painting) |
| 800–899 | Literature (such as criticism and poetry) |
| 900–999 | General geography and history |

Each of these main groups can be divided again and again into more specific categories. The example on the following page shows how the general classification 900 can be broken down to represent a very specific subject.

EXAMPLE: 900     General history and geography

970     General history of North America

973     United States history

973.7     The administration of Abraham Lincoln

Books are grouped on the shelves by their Dewey Decimal numbers. Ones with the same number are arranged alphabetically by the last names of the authors. The books generally show both numbers and letters as the full call numbers.

**Finding Books in Special Collections.** Most libraries separate fiction, nonfiction, and other special sections.

**Learn the symbols your library uses for its own special collections.**

Most libraries have a section for *reference books.* The letter *R* in front of the call number indicates these books. (Section 40.2 has more about reference books.)

Books that are of interest to teenagers may be placed in a *young-adult section.* The letters *YA* in front of the call number show that a library has this section.

Most libraries also have a collection of biographies and autobiographies. A *biography* is a factual account of a person's life. If that person wrote his or her own story, it is called an *autobiography.* These books have the letter *B* or the number *92,* followed by all or part of the last name of the book's subject. Unlike fiction, biographies are arranged alphabetically by the last name of the book's subject, not the book's author.

**EXERCISE C: Finding Fiction.** Arrange the following books in the order you would find them on the shelves.

1. *The Witch of Blackbird Pond* by Elizabeth Speare
2. *Cave Beyond Time* by Malcolm Bosse
3. *I Am the Cheese* by Robert Cormier
4. *Summer of the Swans* by Betsy Byers
5. *The Adventures of Tom Sawyer* by Mark Twain

**EXERCISE D: Finding Nonfiction.** Arrange the following call numbers as they would appear on the shelves.

| 1. 973.7 | 3. 301.42 | 5. 613.5 | 7. 301.3 | 9. 746 |
|----------|-----------|----------|----------|--------|
| G | B | A | Z | R |
| 2. 301.415 | 4. 613.2 | 6. 342.73 | 8. 423 | 10. 422 |
| A | B | G | F | W |

**EXERCISE E: Finding Biographies.** Arrange the following biographies in the order you would find them on the shelves.

1. *Up From Slavery,* autobiography of Booker T. Washington
2. *James Monroe* by Edwin P. Hoyt
3. *The Electrical Genius of Liberty Hall,* a book about Charles Steinmetz by Olga Maynard
4. *Somebody's Angel Child,* a book about Bessie Smith by Carman Moore
5. *Loretta Lynn* by Robert K. Krishef

**DEVELOPING WRITING SKILLS: Using Your Library Skills.** Pick a topic. In your school or public library, find three books about your topic in the card catalog. Go to the shelves to find the books. Then, list and describe each of the books chosen. Finally, write a paragraph explaining how you chose them and how well they cover your topic.

# Finding Reference Books 40.2 in the Library

When you need information quickly, the first place to look will generally be the reference section of your library. There you will find such books as dictionaries, encyclopedias, and almanacs. The spines of these books will have an *R* in front of the call number. Reference books are seldom allowed to be taken out of the library.

Reference books are set up so you can find information in them quickly. For instance, a book of names might be set up in alphabetical order. A book on history might be set up by dates.

Most reference sections contain general books that cover a wide range of knowledge and special books that focus on only one topic. You can also find various magazines that supply assorted, up-to-date information of general and special interest.

## General Reference Books

General reference books cover a wide variety of subjects. They can supply you with a small bit of information or give a large amount of background detail. The following pages discuss the information that can be found in general encyclopedias, almanacs, and atlases. (See Section 40.3 for a discussion of the information in general dictionaries.)

**Encyclopedias.** If you have been asked to write a report on a subject you know nothing about, you may find it useful to begin with an *encyclopedia.* It will give you an overview of the subject. It may also highlight facts with charts, maps, or photographs. In addition, you may find references to related articles or books at the end of the article.

**Use encyclopedias for basic facts, background information, and bibliographies.**

How do you use an encyclopedia? Most encyclopedias consist of several *volumes.* The spine of each book is marked with letters covering a part of the alphabet. Each volume contains articles on subjects that begin with those parts of the alphabet. For example, an encyclopedia marked Be-Co could contain articles on Belgium, Biology, Canoes, and the Continental Divide. At the top of each page, *guide words* show the subjects covered on that page.

An encyclopedia usually has an *index.* This is an alphabetical list of all the major subjects in a book or set. If you cannot find a complete article on your subject, turn to the index to find information on related topics.

Look at the following example from the index of the *Encyclopedia Americana.* The major entry, National Park (U.S.), tells you that there are articles in volume 19, page 766, and volume 21, page 334. Articles on more specific subjects are listed below. At the end of the entry, there is a *see also* reference to other topics.

INDEX ENTRY:

Page number ——————— **NATIONAL PARK** (U.S.) **19—** ——— Volume number
766; 21–334
Alaska 1–470
California 5–209
Conservation 7–634
list 19–774
Public Land 22–753
Roosevelt, T. 23–778
wilderness areas 7–632
Map 19–773
*See also* ——————— *See also* individual parks
reference             and monuments, such as
Independence   National
Historical Park
**National Park Museum** (U.S.)
19–639
**National Park Service** (U.S.)
19 768
**National parkways** (U.S.) **19–**
775

Encyclopedias may also have yearbooks. Each year, the major events and developments of that year are written up and published in an encyclopedia yearbook.

Your library probably has more than one general encyclopedia. The following chart lists some of the most popular.

| POPULAR ENCYCLOPEDIAS | |
| --- | --- |
| *Collier's Encyclopedia* | *Encyclopedia Americana* |
| *Compton's Pictured* | *Random House* |
| *Encyclopedia* | *Encyclopedia* |
| *The Encyclopaedia* | *The World Book* |
| *Britannica* | *Encyclopedia* |

**Almanacs.** When you want to find specific facts quickly, you can check an *almanac.* This yearly publication can be your source of facts and statistics in many areas. These include business, entertainment, government, population, sports, and current as well as historical events.

### Use almanacs to find specific facts about a variety of information.

Like encyclopedias, almanacs cover a wide range of knowledge. However, unlike encyclopedias, they provide little background information. Most facts are presented in tables, charts, or lists. These lists are usually categorized by general topics. If you wanted to know which is the tallest tree in the United States, you would first check the index under *Trees*, which would give you a page reference.

INDEX ENTRY:

| | | |
|---|---|---|
| Subject —— | **Trees—** | |
| | Giant (U.S.) . . . . . . . . . . . . | 163-164 —— Page numbers |
| | Oldest (Cal.) . . . . . . . . . . . . . . | 609 |
| | State (official) . . . . . . . . . . . . | 607-632 |
| | **Tribes, Amer. Indian** . . . . . . . . . . | 441 |
| | **Trieste** (Italy) . . . . . . . . . . . . . | 511 |
| | **Trinidad and Tobago** . . . . . . . . . . | 544 |
| | Aid, U.S. . . . . . . . . . . . . | 565 |
| | Ambassadors . . . . . . . . . . | 563 |
| | Petroleum . . . . . . . . . . . . | 131 |
| | Trade . . . . . . . . . . . . | 140, 544 |

When you turn to page 164, you would see a list of trees in the United States, with the date the tree was measured, its height, and the state in which it can be found.

TEXT ENTRY:

| | | |
|---|---|---|
| | Plum, American (1972) . . . | 35 | Oakland Co., Mich. |
| | Poison Sumac (1972) . . . . | 20 | Robin's Island, N.Y. |
| | Pondcypress (1972) . . . . . | 135 | nr. Newton, Ga. |
| | Poplar, Balsam (1982) . . . | 98 | South Egremont, Mass. |
| | Possumhaw (1981) . . . . . | 42 | Congaree Swamp, S.C. |
| Tallest tree —— | Redbay (1972) . . . . . . . | 58 | Randolph City, Ga. |
| in the U.S. | Redwood, Coast (1972) . . . | 362 | Humboldt Redwoods State Park, Cal. |
| | Royalpalm, Florida (1973) . | 80 | Homestead, Fla. |
| | Sassafras (1972) . . . . . . | 100 | Owensboro, Ky. |
| | Seagrape (1972) . . . . . . . | 57 | Miami, Fla. |
| | Sequoia, Giant (1975) . . . . | 275 | Sequoia Natl. Pk., Cal. |

The two best-known almanacs are *The World Almanac and Book of Facts* and the *Information Please Almanac.*

**Atlases.**   Books of maps, called *atlases,* give information about geography. Maps show the earth's division into continents and countries, as well as the locations of cities, towns, mountains, and oceans. Through the use of symbols and color, atlas maps may also show climate, kinds of crops and industry, and population.

### Use atlases to find information about countries, parts of countries, and bodies of water.

The index of an atlas will direct you to the page showing the map you want. For example, if you wanted to find a map of the island Crete, you would look up the island in the index.

INDEX ENTRY:

```
                    Creswell, Oreg...........D3  201
                    Crete, Ill..................B6  178
                    Crete, Nebr  ...........D9  191
                    Crete, N. Dak.............C8  198
Subject ──────────  Crete, isl., Grc...........E5  69 ────────── Page number
                    Crete, sea, Grc...........D5  69
                    Cretone, It................g9  67
                    Creuse, riv., Fr...........D4  58
                    Creutzwald, Fr...........C7  58
```

Using the information in the index, you would find the map of Crete on page 69.

The following chart lists some well-known atlases.

## GENERAL ATLASES

*Goode's World Atlas*
*Hammond's World Atlas*
*Prentice Hall Illustrated Atlas of the World*
*The National Geographic Atlas*

**EXERCISE A: Using Encyclopedias and Almanacs.** Find the following information, using encyclopedias and almanacs. On your paper write each piece of information and the title of the book you used to find it.

1. The world's longest railway tunnel
2. The birth date and birthplace of Woody Allen
3. The country that won the World Cup for soccer in 1970
4. The population of Alabama in 1980
5. The two largest cities in Kentucky
6. Five major historical events of the nineteenth century
7. Five independent countries
8. A description of Alaska's state flag
9. The state motto of Idaho
10. The population of the United States in 1980

**EXERCISE B: Using Atlases.** Use atlases to find the following information. On your paper write each piece of information and the book you used to find it.

1. The three largest cities in New York State
2. The countries that border on the Sea of Japan
3. Two counties in North Dakota that border on South Dakota
4. The countries that border on Venezuela
5. The states that border on Arizona

## Special Reference Books

Some reference books cover one subject in great detail. These special reference materials may be dictionaries, encyclopedias, or biographical reference books.

**Special Dictionaries.** Dictionaries contain alphabetical listings of words and names. *Special dictionaries* give detailed information only about one specific subject.

**Use special dictionaries to find definitions and other information about one subject.**

Some special dictionaries cover specific aspects of the English language such as slang, rhyming words, or *synonyms*—words that have similar meanings. Others cover a specific subject area such as music, history, or art.

A dictionary of synonyms can be useful when you write. If you want to use a certain word but have already used it several times or if you find that the word you have in mind is not the exact word you want, check a dictionary of synonyms.

Dictionaries of synonyms include *Roget's International Thesaurus* and *Webster's New Dictionary of Synonyms.* Some show words listed in alphbetical order. Others are arranged by categories according to an alphabetical index. In this second type of dictionary, if you wanted to find a synonym for *genuine*, you would first look up that word in the index. Under the word you would find various meanings of the word, each with a category number and a paragraph number. The following example shows the list of meanings given for the word *genuine* in one index.

INDEX ENTRY:

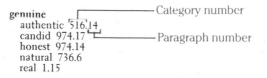

After studying the meanings listed under *genuine* in the index, you would choose the one that best fits the meaning you have in mind. If you want a word that means "authentic," you would look for category 516, paragraph 14, in the main part of the book. The guide numbers at the top of the pages will help you find the right entry.

GUIDE NUMBER:     516.12–517.1

Once you find the entry, you can choose a word. The partial text entry on the following page shows only a few of the many words you could pick.

TEXT ENTRY:     .14 genuine, authentic, veridical, **real, natu-**
**ral, realistic, naturalistic,** true to reality,
**true to nature, lifelike,** true to life, veri-
similar; **literal,** following the letter, true
to the letter; verbatim, verbal, **word-for-**
**word;** true to the spirit; **legitimate,** right-
ful, lawful; **bona fide,** card-carrying [in-
formal], **good,** sure-enough [slang]...

The following chart lists other useful special dictionaries
that cover particular fields or topics.

| SPECIAL DICTIONARIES |
|---|
| *Abbreviations Dictionary* <br> *The Dictionary of American History* <br> *The Dictionary of American Slang* <br> *James' Mathematical Dictionary* <br> *Science Dictionary in Basic English* |

**Special Encyclopedias.** *Special encyclopedias* are organized and used in much the same way as general encyclopedias. However, each special encyclopedia covers only one
field and has much more detailed information than a general
encyclopedia would have on its particular subject.

**Use special encyclopedias to find detailed in-
formation about a subject.**

The chart below gives examples of special encyclopedias.

| SPECIAL ENCYCLOPEDIAS |
|---|
| *The Encyclopedia of Pop, Rock, and Soul* <br> *Encyclopedia of World Art* <br> *Funk & Wagnall's Wildlife Encyclopedia* <br> *Peoples of the Earth* <br> *The Reader's Encyclopedia* |

**Biographical Reference Books** Have you ever needed to
find basic information about a famous person? Besides reading

**672**

a complete book about that person, if one is available you can also check *biographical reference books.*

### Use biographical reference books to find information about people.

One of the best general sources of information about people in the news today is *Current Biography.* Each volume covers one year, dating back to 1940. Within each volume are biographies of well-known people in all fields—athletes, politicians, actors, scientists, writers, and others. Each article runs about one to two pages long, is illustrated, and ends with a bibliography of sources where more information about the person can be found.

Articles in *Current Biography* are arranged alphabetically according to the last name of the person. The indexes at the back of most recent volumes cover articles published over a series of years. The 1980 edition contains a ten-year index with references to articles dating back to 1971. There is also a cumulated index volume that covers the thirty-year period from 1940 to 1970.

Suppose you wanted to find information on baseball player Dave Winfield. First, you might check in the index of the 1984 volume of *Current Biography* to see if his name is listed there.

In the 1984 volume, you would then look under the *W*'s for the article on Dave Winfield.

INDEX ENTRY:

```
                    Wilson, Kenneth G(eddes) Sep
                       83
                    Wilson, Peter (Cecil) obit Aug
                      ·84
                    Winchell, Constance M(abel)
                       obit Sep 84
        Subject ———Winfield, Dave Jan 84}————— Volume year
                    Winger, Debra Jul 84
                    Wise, James DeCamp obit Apr
                       84
                    Wood, John Apr 83
                    Wood, Natalie obit Jan 82
                    Woods, Donald Feb 82
```

TEXT ENTRY:   **Winfield, Dave**

*Oct. 3, 1951– Baseball player. Address: b. New York Yankees, River Ave. and E. 161st St., Bronx, N.Y. 10451*

When David M. Winfield left the University of Minnesota in 1973, he was a multi-threat natural athlete of such potential that professional teams in three sports drafted him. He opted for baseball—specifically the San Diego Padres of the National League. After "eight years of mediocracy" (his agent's phrase) as an outfielder in San Diego, Winfield jumped leagues to sign with "a winner," the New York Yankees, who gave him not only the most lucrative contract in the history of sports but also a star-class showcase for his prowess. With his size (six feet six, 220 pounds) and speed, Winfield the outfielder foils home runs with leaping catches that only a man of his height and body control could make. It is at the plate, however, that he is most feared. Always a powerful batter, he used to describe himself as "a wrist hitter, a line-drive hitter." Ironically, since arriving in Yankee Stadium (the structure of which is not conducive to ho-

The following chart lists other biographical reference books and describes their contents.

| BIOGRAPHICAL REFERENCE BOOKS | |
| --- | --- |
| **Example** | **Description** |
| *Contemporary Authors* | Articles give coverage about writers throughout the world |
| *McGraw-Hill Encyclopedia of World Biography* | Short illustrated articles give information about well-known subjects who are no longer living. |
| *Who's Who* | Different subject volumes give short descriptions of various people. |

**674**

**EXERCISE C:  Using Special Reference Books.** Use special reference books to find the following information. Write each piece of information and the book you used to find it.

1. The definition of *de-orbit*
2. The titles of two books by Jane Austen
3. The meaning of the campaign slogan "Tippecanoe and Tyler too"
4. The definition of *mish-mash*
5. A synonym for *wealthy*
6. A synonym for *poor*
7. The year Aldous Huxley was born
8. The reason why Diana Nyad is well-known
9. The reason why Jomo Kenyatta was famous
10. The definition of *mud puppy*

# Periodicals

Printed materials that are published at regular intervals, or periods, are called *periodicals*. They may be issued daily, weekly, monthly, every two months, or every three months. The periodicals you will probably use most often are magazines.

**Use periodicals to find accurate, up-to-date information.**

Periodicals provide the most recent information about a wide variety of subjects. A book provides more detailed information. But new discoveries or events can change the accuracy of an older book. In this case a current periodical may be best.

How do you find the periodical—generally, the magazine—that has the information you need? Just as you use the card catalog to find books in a library, you can use a special index to find magazine articles. The most useful index is *The Readers' Guide to Periodical Literature.* Published since 1900, it indexes over 180 general magazines. In paperback form *The Readers' Guide* is published twice a month. The cover of each biweekly issue shows the dates it covers. At the end of the year, information from all of the different issues is gathered together and bound in a hardcover, yearly volume.

*The Readers' Guide* indexes magazine articles by author and subject. Main entries are listed in alphabetical order. If you know either the author or the subject of a magazine article, you can find the name of the magazine that has that article.

If you were writing a report on apples, you would turn to the main heading—*Fruit.* There you would find a number of articles along with other more specific subheadings. Each entry would tell you the title of an article and generally the name of its author. It would also give you the name of the magazine and the information you need to find the magazine and article. In most cases this information would consist of the volume of the magazine, the page number or numbers on which the article is found, and the date of the magazine. If the article is illustrated, the abbreviation *il* would be included. To interpret the entries, you may sometimes need to turn to the front of the volume, where there is an alphabetical list of the abbreviations used.

ENTRY FROM THE READERS' GUIDE:

```
Fruit                                                  ——— Main subject
    See also ┐                                             heading
  Cooking—Fruit ├───────────────────────────────────— Cross-reference
    See also names of fruit                          ——— Author of article
Fruit for all seasons. E. W. Stiles. il Nat Hist 93:42-53
    Ag '84                                           └—— Title of article
Fruit selection. N. Nevins. il South Living 19:144 Ag
    '84
Sweet summer sensations. il Glamour 82:188-91 Jl '84 ——— Magazine title
Winter temptations. il Glamour 82:302-5+ N '84
              Diseases and pests ——————————————————— Subheading
    See also
  Codling moths
  Fruit flies
              Drying
Stretch summer flavor with dried produce. M. Chason.  ——— Volume; page numbers;
    il, South Living 19:188+ Je '84                       and date
              Preservation
Keeping fruit fresh [polyethylene film wrap] Consum ┐
    Res Mag 67:2 F '84                              └— Illustrated
              Ripening
Ripe promises. E. W. Stiles. Nat Hist 93:51 Ag '84
              Varieties
Have you grown new fruit varieties? Sunset 172:256
    Je '84
```

**676**

Once you have found the article you need, you then need to find the magazine. A library may keep its magazines in different forms and in several places. Recent magazines may be kept on open shelves, allowing you to pick up the ones you want to read. Older magazines may be stored elsewhere and perhaps bound into annual volumes. Some libraries keep all magazines in a separate area and require you to fill out a request form to get even the most recent copies. When you want a magazine that is not available on the shelves, use a request form to write down the information that you found in *The Readers' Guide*. The following request form shows a request for the magazine that contains the first article in the entry on page 676.

---

**PERIODICAL REQUEST FORM**

Name of Periodical:  *Natural History*

Date: *August 1984*

Check if circulating copy preferred
(if available) . . . . . ✔ . . . . .

Microfilm . . . . . . . . . .

Your Name: *Mary Robbins*

---

**REPORT**

No circulating copy available  . . . . . . . . . . .

Issue(s) missing or in use  . . . . . . . . . . .

Do not have  . . . . . . . . . . . .

Check at desk for locations at other libraries.

---

In some libraries, magazines are photographed and stored on microfilm (rolls) or microfiche (sheets). To read one of these magazines, you must view the film through a *reader*. Ask your librarian for help when using these microfilm or microfiche viewers.

**EXERCISE D: Interpreting *The Readers' Guide*.** Look at the following excerpt from *The Readers' Guide*. Choose one magazine entry and write it in your paper, using complete words for all abbreviations. Then explain how you would find that article in your library.

**Computerphones**
The computerization of the telephone. K. McKean. il
*Pers Comput* 8:102-4+ Jl '84
The debut of the computer-phone [Rolm's Cedar]
*Newsweek* 104:83 N 12 '84
Is the 'computer-phone' market ready to explode? il *Bus Week* p101-2 Ag 13 '84
Now let your computer reach out. A. Seelig. il *Comput Electron* 22:56-9+ Ap '84

**EXERCISE E: Using *The Readers' Guide*.** Use a recent *Readers' Guide* to find two articles about a topic that interests you. Write out all information about the articles.

**DEVELOPING WRITING SKILLS: Using Research Tools.** Choose the best reference book to find each of the following pieces of information. On your paper list each piece of information and the book you used to find it.

1. Two synonyms for *hesitate*
2. The governor of Texas in 1952
3. The number of births in Alabama in 1978
4. The countries bordering on Lake Victoria
5. The name by which Hector Hugh Munro is better known
6. The profession and birth date of Sherrill Cleland
7. Two countries where the official language is German
8. The world's largest dam
9. Two synonyms for *generous*
10. The Oscar-winning best film of 1975

**678**

# Using the Dictionary 40.3

You probably use a dictionary more often than any other reference book. A dictionary is the first place you should look for quick answers to questions about the spelling and meaning of words. Of course, it takes time to look up words in the dictionary. However, with practice, you should be able to find what you are looking for quickly and easily. Developing the habit of using a dictionary regularly can be a valuable study skill, one that can help you improve your school work.

This section will show you how you can use the dictionary more efficiently. It will also show you how you can make better use of the great variety of information that can be found in a general dictionary. As a result you will soon see how you can use the dictionary both to increase your knowledge of words and to earn better grades.

## Using a Dictionary to Check Spelling

You may ask, "How can I look up a word if I can't spell it to begin with?" Checking the spelling of a word in a dictionary *can* be difficult because the English language often has many different spellings for the same sound.

**Become familiar with the different spelling patterns of the sounds in English words.**

The best way to begin looking up the spelling of a word is to listen to the sound of the word. Make a guess about what letters make those sounds and look up that spelling. It is likely that you will find the word you are looking for after just a few tries. The more spellings you know for each sound, the better your chances of finding the word quickly.

Some dictionaries provide a chart or list that shows the different spellings a sound may have in English.

Part of such a chart is shown on page 680. It is from *Webster's New World Dictionary*, Student Edition.

**679**

| WORD FINDER CHART | | |
|---|---|---|
| If the sound is like the . . . | try also the spelling . . . | as in the words . . . |
| a in fat | ai, au | plaid, draught |
| a in lane | ai, ao, au, ay, ea, ei, eigh, et, ey | rain, goal, gauge, ray, break, rein, weigh, sachet, they |
| a in care | ai, ay, e, ea, ei | air, prayer, there, wear, their |
| a in father | au, e, ea | gaunt, sergeant, hearth |

Suppose, for example, that you had written "The brane is protected by the skull." When you got back your paper, you found that your teacher had marked the word *brane* wrong. If you were to look up this spelling in the dictionary, you would not find any word spelled in this way listed there. To guess which letter or letters are incorrect, you would then have to think about the different sounds in the word. You might guess that the problem involved the *a*-sound. You could then look at the Word Finder Chart or you could rely on your knowledge of other ways to spell an *a* sound in the English language. According to the Word Finder Chart, the letters *ai* can have a long *a* sound. Try using the letters *ai* to spell the word *brain*. If you look up this spelling in the dictionary, you will see that it is correct.

**EXERCISE A: Correcting Spelling with a Dictionary.** The following words are misspelled. The incorrectly spelled sounds are underlined. Using a dictionary, write the correct spelling of each word.

1. ratlesnake
2. conshous
3. flavering
4. ocasion
5. esteam
6. recieve
7. slugish
8. tyme
9. embarass
10. rejister

# Finding Words Quickly

When you come across an unfamiliar word in a sentence, a quick check with the dictionary can often help you better understand what you are reading.

**Learn to use alphabetical order quickly to find words in the dictionary.**

Flipping aimlessly through the pages of a dictionary to find a word's meaning can be frustrating. Three simple steps will help you find any word quickly.

| STEPS FOR FINDING WORDS QUICKLY |
| --- |
| 1. Use the Four-Section Approach. |
| 2. Next use the guide words. |
| 3. Then follow strict, letter-by-letter alphabetical order. |

**The Four-Section Approach.**  Most dictionaries can be divided into four roughly equal quarters.

FOUR SECTIONS:  ABCD
              EFGHIJKL
              MNOPQR
              STUVWXYZ

If you know the quarter of the dictionary in which a word will be found, you can open the book to that general area right away. For example, the word *lynx* will be near the middle of the book, *cravat* near the beginning, and *tarragon* toward the end. With practice you will often be able to open the dictionary right to the first letter of the word you want.

**Guide Words.**  Once you have narrowed your search down to the first letter of a word, begin using the *guide words*. These are the two words printed in large type at the top of each page in a dictionary. The one on the left tells you the first word on that page. The one on the right tells you the last word. If, for example, the guide words at the top of a page are *flashy* and *fleet,* you know the word *flaunt* is on that page.

**Letter-by-Letter Alphabetical Order.** All the items in a dictionary are listed in *strict alphabetical order*—that is, letter by letter right to the end of the item. Thus, a word beginning with *a* comes before a word beginning with *b,* a word beginning with *ac* comes before one beginning with *ad,* and so on. This order holds true even if an item is made up of more than one word.

EXAMPLES:  fizzy *before* flab

flab *before* flipper

flipper *before* flip side

**EXERCISE B:  Putting Words in Alphabetical Order.** Alphabetize in the order you would find the words in a dictionary.

| | | |
|---|---|---|
| 1. hate | 5. hautboy | 9. hatchet |
| 2. hasty pudding | 6. Hastings | 10. haunt |
| 3. hand | 7. haughty | |
| 4. haste | 8. hat tree | |

**EXERCISE C:  Finding Words Quickly.** Using the three steps for finding words quickly, look up the following items in a dictionary. On your paper write the guide words on the page on which each item is found.

| | | |
|---|---|---|
| 1. smock | 3. ostracize | 5. yellowtail |
| 2. recumbent | 4. bola | |

## Using Main Entries

The words you look up in a dictionary combined with all the information given about them are called *main entries.* The words themselves, in heavy type, are called *entry words.* The following chart shows some of the kinds of entry words found in dictionaries.

| | KINDS OF ENTRY WORDS | | |
|---|---|---|---|
| Single Word | **hope·ful·ly** (-ē) *adv.* **1.** in a hopeful manner **2.** it is to be hoped (that) [*hopefully* we will win]: regarded by some as a loose usage | | |
| Compound Word | **lesser panda** a reddish, raccoonlike mammal of the Himalayan region | | |
| Abbreviation | **prec.** preceding | | |
| Prefix | **pre-** [< Fr. *pré-* or L. *prae-* < L. *prae*, before: for IE. base see FAR] *a prefix meaning:* **1.** before in time, place, or rank [*pre-war*] **2.** leading up to, in preparation for [*preschool*] | | |
| Suffix | **-less** (lis, ləs) [OE. *-leas* < *leas*, free] *a suffix meaning:* **1.** without, lacking [*valueless*] **2.** that does not [*tireless*] **3.** that cannot be [*dauntless*] | | |
| Person (Family Name Usually First) | **Hop·kins** (häp′kinz) **1. Gerard Man·ley** (man′lē), 1844–89; Eng. poet & Jesuit priest **2. Mark,** 1802–87; U.S. educator | | |
| Place | **Hoover Dam** [after Pres. HOOVER] dam on the Colorado River, between Ariz. & Nev.: formerly **Boulder Dam** | | |

As you can see in the chart, the information following an entry word varies depending upon the kind of word it is.

**Learn to recognize and use the different kinds of information contained in a main entry.**

**Spelling.** Most words have only one correct spelling, which is shown in the entry word. Some words, however, can be spelled in more than one way. The most common spelling is called the *preferred spelling.* Less common spellings are called *variant spellings.* If the form of a word you are looking up is a variant spelling, the entry will refer you to another main entry that will give the preferred spelling.

**Ma·hom·et** (mə häm′it) *same as* MOHAMMED —**Ma·hom′-et·an** *adj., n.*

**Mo·ham·med** (mō ham′id) 570?–632 A.D.; Arabian prophet: founder of the Moslem religion

If two entry words are given, the spelling of the word listed first is preferred.

EXAMPLE:  **kash·rut, kash·ruth** (käsh ro͞ot′, käsh′ro͝ot) *n.* the dietary regulations of Judaism: see KOSHER

**Syllabification.**   Centered dots, spaces, or slashes in an entry word show how that word may be divided into *syllables.* In the example, the dots indicate the syllables.

See Section 21.9 for rules about breaking words into syllables when you write.

**Pronunciation.**   The dictionary tells you how to pronounce a word by respelling it in a *phonetic alphabet.* This alphabet is made up of special symbols. Each symbol is assigned a certain sound. Phonetic alphabets vary from one dictionary to another. To become familiar with the one in your dictionary, look at the *pronunciation key* at the front or back of the book. Most dictionaries for students also print short pronunciation keys at the bottom of every other page.

The dictionary also shows you which syllables are stressed. The syllable that gets more emphasis than any other has a *primary stress.* This is usually shown by a heavy mark after the syllable (′). Words of more than one syllable may also have a *secondary stress.* This is shown by a shorter, lighter mark (′).

When two or more pronunciations of a word are given, the pronunciation shown first is the one most frequently used. Additional pronunciations are usually shown in abbreviated form.

MORE THAN ONE PRONUNCIATION:

**main·land** (mān′land′, -lənd) *n.* the main land mass of a continent, as apart from nearby islands, etc. —**main′land′er** *n.*

**684**

**Part-of-Speech Labels.** *Part-of-speech labels* tell you whether a word is generally used as a noun, a verb, or one of the other six parts of speech. This information is given in abbreviated form, usually right after the pronunciation. When a word can be used as more than one part of speech, the word's meanings are grouped under each part-of-speech label.

After the appropriate part-of-speech label, the dictionary may also show the plural forms of nouns, the principal parts of verbs, or the various forms of adjectives or adverbs.

EXAMPLE:

Noun —

Plural forms of noun

**bus** (bus) *n.,* *pl.* **bus′es, bus′ses** [< (OMNI)BUS]  **1.** a large motor coach for carrying many passengers, usually along a regular route; omnibus  **2.** [Slang] an automobile  **3.** *Elec.* a conductor used as a common connection for three or more circuits: in the form of a bar, also called **bus′bar′** —*vt.* **bused** or **bussed, bus′ing** or **bus′sing** to transport by bus —*vi.* **1.** to go by bus ☆**2.** to do the work of a busboy

Principal parts of verb

Transitive verb —

Intransitive verb

**Definitions.**  A word's meaning is called its *definition.* Some words have just one meaning; others have more. When a word has more than one definition, the dictionary will give each of the definitions a number and group them according to their parts of speech. Related definitions may be divided further by letters.

EXAMPLE:

**burst** (burst) *vi.* **burst, burst′ing** [< OE. *berstan* & ON. *bresta,* both < IE. base *bhres-,* burst, break]  **1.** to come apart suddenly and violently, as from pressure within; fly into pieces; explode *[the balloon burst]*  **2.** to give sudden expression to some feeling; break (*into* tears, laughter, etc.)  **3.** to go, come, start, etc. suddenly and with force *[he burst into the room]*  **4.** *a)* to be as full or crowded as possible *[a room bursting with visitors]* *b)* to be filled (*with* anger, pride, etc.) —*vt.* to cause to burst —*n.* **1.** a bursting; explosion  **2.** the result of a bursting; break  **3.** a sudden, violent display of feeling *[a burst of anger]*  **4.** a sudden action; spurt *[a burst of speed]*  **5.** a single series of shots from an automatic firearm —**burst′er** *n.*

Numbered definitions

Definition with two lettered parts

Examples of word in use

As you can see, many definitions are followed by a helpful phrase or sentence showing the word in use.

**Etymologies.** The origin and history of a word is called its *etymology*. The etymology often appears in brackets after the pronunciation of part-of-speech label. In some dictionaries the etymology may appear at the end of the main entry. In the examples on page 685, the etymology shows that *bus* is a shortened form of the word *omnibus*. The etymology of *burst* shows that it came from Old English and Old Norse words, which both came from an Indo-European word. The abbreviations used in etymologies are usually explained in the front of a dictionary. (See Section 35.4 for more about etymologies.)

**Derived Words.** Words formed by adding a common suffix, such as *-er, -ly,* or *-ness,* to an entry word are called *derived* speech. Most dictionaries list derived words at the end of a main entry. In the definition of *burst* on page 685, the noun *burster* is a derived word.

**Usage and Field Labels.** In the dictionary *usage labels* indicate nonstandard usages such as *Archaic* (old-fashioned), *Obsolete, Slang,* and so forth. Notice the slang label for the second definition of *bus* in the example on page 685.

A *field label* indicates an occupation, activity, or area of knowledge in which people use the word in a special way. Notice the field label for *Electricity* for the third definition of *bus* on page 685.

**Synonyms.** Words that have similar but not identical meanings are called *synonyms*. After some main entries, you may find a block of words beginning with the label *SYN*. Here synonyms are given and the differences in meaning among synonyms may be explained. *Antonyms,* words opposite in meaning, are sometimes found here, too, preceded by *ANT*.

**law·yer** (lô′yər) *n.* a person whose profession is advising others in matters of law or representing them in lawsuits
**SYN.**—**lawyer** is the general term for a person trained in the law, who advises or represents others in legal matters; **counselor** and **attorney** are now general synonyms for **lawyer,** but in earlier use **counselor** referred to a lawyer who conducts cases in court, as does the British **barrister,** and **attorney** referred to one who prepares briefs, draws up contracts and wills, etc., as does the British **solicitor; counsel,** often equivalent to **counselor,** is frequently used for a group of lawyers working together to advise a client or conduct a case in court

———— Synonyms

**EXERCISE D:  Understanding the Parts of Main Entries.**
Read the following main entries and then answer the questions
that follow.

> **hon·ied** (hun′ēd) *adj. same as* HONEYED
> ☆**honk** (hôŋk, häŋk) *n.* [echoic]  **1.** the call of a wild goose
> **2.** any similar sound, as of an automobile horn —*vi., vt.* to make
> or cause to make such a sound —**honk′er** *n.*
> **Hon·o·lu·lu** (hän′ə loo′loo, hō′nə-) [Haw., lit., sheltered bay]
> capital of Hawaii: seaport on Oahu: pop. 325,000 (met. area
> 631,000)

1. In which quarter of the dictionary would these entries be
   found?
2. Is *honied* a preferred or a variant spelling?
3. Which two syllables in *Honolulu* are stressed? Which of
   these syllables receives the greater stress?
4. As how many parts of speech can *honk* be used?
5. Write the derived word found in the excerpt. Include its
   part-of-speech label.

**DEVELOPING WRITING SKILLS:  Using a Dictionary to
Answer Questions.** Use a dictionary to answer the following
questions. Write your answers in complete sentences.

1. Who was Minerva?
2. Which is the preferred spelling—*theatre* or *theater?*
3. Who killed the Minotaur?
4. What is *chicory?*
5. What is the Milky Way?

# Skills Review and Writing Workshop

## Library and Reference Skills

### CHECKING YOUR SKILLS

Take notes on this selection from a magazine.

Theodore Roosevelt, President of the United States from 1901 to 1909, was a hunter and naturalist. Once he and some friends were hunting bears in Mississippi. Their time was running short, and no bears had been seen. A guide found an old, half-blind bear and tied it to a tree for the President to shoot. Roosevelt, to whom honor was the greatest virtue, refused to shoot the bear. His companions told the story to newspaper reporters. A political cartoonist drew the incident, but he used a bear cub in the cartoon. Later Roosevelt was asked for permission to name a toy stuffed bear after him. The President agreed. Thus, the teddy bear reminds us today of the country's twenty-sixth President.

### USING STUDY SKILLS IN WRITING

#### Writing a Report

You will find books and periodicals in the library that contain information you need to write a research report. You might use one aspect of the paragraph above about President Theodore Roosevelt and teddy bears to write a report.

**Prewriting:** Decide what aspect you want to write about. Use general reference books and more specialized reference books such as a biography or *The Reader's Guide*. Take notes and make an outline for your report.

**Writing:** Begin your report by introducing your topic and why you are writing about it. Then, clearly present your information. Conclude your report by making a statement that summarizes the main ideas.

**Revising:** Carefully read over your report to make sure that it contains all the information from your outline. After you have revised, proofread carefully.

# Speaking and Listening

# Chapter **41**

# Speaking and Listening Skills

You listen and speak every day. They are both part of one process. When you speak, someone else listens. If you speak well, you can express your ideas clearly. If you listen well, you can remember more of what you hear.

## 41.1 Informal Speaking Skills

Informal speaking skills include talking with friends or family, discussing in class, giving directions, and making introductions. This section will help you improve these skills.

### Speaking in Class Discussions

You can improve both your speaking and listening skills by taking part in class discussions. If you plan what you want to say before you say it and practice taking part in class often, you will increase your skills and confidence as well.

**Develop confidence about participating in class through preparation and practice.**

690

You can develop your informal speaking skills by answering when the teacher asks the class a question. You can comment on another student's remarks or ask questions about the topic being discussed. You can also volunteer to share an example from your own experience or your reading that will illustrate what is being discussed.

The more well prepared you are for a class, the more you will be able to contribute to it and the more you will get out of it. The chart below offers some suggestions on how to prepare yourself for taking part in class discussions.

---

**SUGGESTIONS ON HOW TO TAKE PART IN CLASS DISCUSSIONS**

---

1. Set a goal for yourself about taking part in class. For example, you might decide to speak at least once during each class.
2. Do whatever homework and reading are required so that you are well prepared. Extra reading on the subject you are studying can help you say something of special interest to the class.
3. If possible, plan what you might say before the discussion begins.
4. Do not wait for the teacher to call on you. Raise your hand and volunteer to contribute your thought.
5. Listen to the discussion carefully so that what you say will be to the point.
6. Observe other students who make good contributions to the class, and learn from their example.
7. Ask questions about what you do not understand, or what you want to know more about.

---

Practice these suggestions to develop your speaking skills and build self-confidence about speaking in front of others. This will help you to contribute more freely and regularly to class discussions in the future.

**EXERCISE A: Improving Class Participation Skills.** For each of your classes, keep a record of your contributions for two weeks. Try to increase the number and the quality of your comments.

## Giving Directions

You may be asked directions about how to get somewhere or how to do something. If you can give clear and accurate directions, people will be able to follow them easily.

**When giving directions, be as clear and accurate in your langauge as possible.**

As you can see below, it is much easier to follow the second set of directions than to follow the first set.

VAGUE DIRECTIONS: Walk down the street for several blocks. Then turn left and keep going until you see the library.

CLEAR DIRECTIONS: Walk straight ahead for three blocks. When you reach the corner of Elm and Park streets, turn left. Walk one block, and the library will be on the corner to your right.

The following chart gives some suggestions for giving clear and accurate directions.

| SUGGESTIONS FOR GIVING DIRECTIONS |
|---|
| 1. Think through the directions carefully before you speak. |
| 2. Speak slowly so that your listeners can follow your directions without difficulty. |
| 3. Choose your words carefully, being as specific as you can. |
| 4. Use short sentences, so your listener can remember each one. Give only one step of the directions in each sentence. |
| 5. Remember to give the most important details, but do not confuse your listener with unnecessary information. |

**EXERCISE B: Giving Clear Directions.** Rewrite the following directions so that they are clear and accurate. Then give the directions to a classmate and ask the person to evaluate your directions for clarity and accuracy.

To get from here to the grocery store, walk on Main Street for a while, keeping to the right-hand side of the street. You will pass a 5&10, a bowling alley, a movie theater, a restaurant, and a few private houses. When you reach the corner of Fifth and Main, right in front of a donut house, take a right and walk east on Fifth Street for a minute, again on the right side of the street, and you'll see the grocery store—it has a big glass front, so you can see inside. They sell the best ice cream ever.

# Making Introductions

Let us say you want to introduce one friend to another or to your parents, a new student to the teacher or to the whole class. How do you make a good introduction? The most important thing is to remember the person's full name and to pronounce it correctly. You should also mention something of interest about the person you are introducing.

**Introduce people by their full names and tell something of interest about them.**

Notice the difference between these two introductions:

INTRODUCTIONS:    Mom, this is Penny. I know her from school.

Mom, I'd like to introduce my friend Penny Marshall. She lives right down the street. We're in the same math class. Penny, I'd like you to meet my mother, Mrs. Thurgood.

Which of the introductions do you think is better?

If you are introducing a new student at school, try to find out other information about that person to share with your teacher or your class, such as what school he or she used to attend, favorite hobbies or sports, if he or she has any brothers or sisters, any past accomplishments, and so on. This helps make the person you are introducing feel comfortable with a new group of people right away.

**EXERCISE C: Writing an Introduction.** Write an introduction in which you present a famous person to your class. Use interesting details about the person you are introducing. Present your introduction to the class, but leave out the person's name. See if your classmates can guess who the person is from the rest of your introduction.

**DEVELOPING WRITING SKILLS: Writing About Informal Speaking Skills.** Write a brief paragraph about why you think informal speaking skills are important. Think of speaking with friends or family, participating in class discussions, and giving directions. Are there other times you speak in informal situations? Do you think what you learned in this section will help you there, too?

# 41.2 Formal Speaking Skills

You use formal speaking skills when you speak to an audience. These skills can help you give a class presentation or a speech. Being able to give a speech is one of the most useful and widely admired abilities you can develop. What makes this hard to do is nervousness about speaking before a group. Two things can help: having experience and being well prepared.

## Recognizing Different Kinds of Speeches

There are three main kinds of speeches: *explanatory* speeches, *persuasive* speeches, and *entertaining* speeches. The kind of speech you decide to give will depend on two things. The first is your purpose in giving the speech. The second is the age and background of your audience.

**Choose the kind of speech you will give by considering both the purpose of the speech and your audience.**

An *explanatory* speech explains an idea, an object, or an event. Possible topics for an explanatory speech might include stamp collecting, how to grow herbs, and why the sky is blue.

A *persuasive* speech is used to get your audience to agree with your point of view or to take some action. You might give a persuasive speech about why the band needs new uniforms.

An *entertaining* speech is given to amuse the audience. A good speaker also makes use of entertaining material to enliven an explanatory or persuasive speech. This relaxes the audience so that they are better able to listen to the informative or convincing material.

**EXERCISE A: Identifying Kinds of Speeches.** Identify the speech topics below as *explanatory, persuasive,* or *entertaining*.

1. The history of the piano
2. Why we should watch less TV
3. Eagles
4. Ten great excuses for not doing your homework
5. The need for more teachers and smaller classes
6. Famous baseball players
7. My visit to Planet X
8. The importance of health and fitness
9. How you can help protect the environment
10. How to ask someone to dance

## Planning Your Speech

Preparation is the most important part of giving a speech. When you are asked to give a speech, begin by thinking carefully about the purpose of your speech and the audience you will be speaking to. This will help you choose the kind of speech you will give, the topic of the speech, and the way in which you will present your material. Select a topic you enjoy or know a lot about. The more interested you are in your subject and the more you know about it, the better your speech will be.

**Choose a subject that you know or like in order to interest your audience.**

Choose your topic and gather all the information on it that you need. Then, organize it in outline form. The outline below is for a speech about George Willig, the "human fly" who climbed the World Trade Center in New York City. As you study the outline, notice that it contains only main ideas and supporting details.

SAMPLE OUTLINE:   G. Willig's Climb
1. May 26, 1977—scaled 1,350 feet up World Trade Center
2. Took three and a half hours

First Results of Climb
1. Charged with breaking the law
2. City sued him for $250,000

Later—Mayor's News Conference
1. Charges dropped
2. Fined only $1.10
3. Willig saluted as hero

Next write the main ideas and major details for your speech topic on note cards. Note cards can be read quickly and easily as you deliver your speech. As you finish reading from each card, turn it over and go on to the next card. Note cards will help you cover everything you want to, while speaking in a natural, conversational manner. The chart below gives suggestions for preparing note cards for a speech.

---

### PREPARING NOTE CARDS FOR A SPEECH

1. Use only a few 3″ × 5″ index cards.
2. Print all information neatly on the cards.
3. Write out quotations or facts that you want to remember exactly.
4. Write out beginning and ending statements if you think they will be useful.
5. Rely mainly on key words and phrases or clear abbreviations to jog your memory.
6. Use a clear outline form and indent all of the details under the ideas they support.
7. Use underlining and capital letters to make important information stand out.
8. Number your cards to help keep them in order.

---

**EXERCISE B: Planning Your Speech.** Prepare a short demonstration speech on one of the topics below or choose one of your own. Remember to select a topic that interests you and one about which you have information. Think about who your audience will be. Gather any information you will need and organize it in outline form. Then write note cards to use during your speech, following the suggestions in the chart above.

How to make origami birds
Tying knots
How to tell a joke
Magic tricks
Throwing a football

How to care for tropical fish
How to prepare tasty and
    nutritious after-school
    snacks
Braiding hair
How to train a dog
Taking care of a
    mischievous younger brother

## Delivering Your Speech

How do you overcome nervousness, so you can relax and speak naturally to your audience? By doing one thing: practicing.

Practice giving your speech as you plan to give it in class. Use the note cards you have prepared and deliver your speech several times alone in front of a mirror and then to your parents or a friend. The more practice you get, the more confidence you will have when you deliver your speech in class.

**Practice your speech to gain confidence.**

---

### SIX THINGS TO REMEMBER WHEN DELIVERING A SPEECH

1. Do not read to your audience. Refer to your note cards and speak in a natural, relaxed manner.
2. Pronounce your words clearly, and do not speak too hurriedly or too slowly.
3. Be aware of nonverbal language, such as your movements, posture, facial expressions, and gestures, while you practice and deliver your speech.
4. Stay within the time limit you were given for your speech.
5. Be prepared to answer questions from your audience.

---

If you work on these suggestions while practicing your speech, when the time comes to actually deliver your speech, they will have become habits. Then you won't have to think about them constantly. They will come naturally, allowing you to focus on the content of your speech, rather than on the manner of your presentation.

**EXERCISE C: Practicing and Delivering a Speech.** Take the note cards you wrote for a speech in Exercise B. Practice giving the speech several times, following all the suggestions given. Then deliver your speech in class.

**DEVELOPING WRITING SKILLS: Writing About Formal Speaking Skills.** Write a paragraph that includes the main points and major details of this section. What are the difficulties of giving a speech? What are some suggestions on how to overcome these difficulties? What is important to remember when planning a speech? What is important to remember when delivering a speech?

# Listening Skills 41.3

Listening is something we do every day. But there are so many sounds to hear that we must be selective in what we actually listen to. Imagine if you tried to listen to everything—the birds, the traffic, conversations around you, the song running through your head, the sounds of chairs scraping on the floor, or pencils scratching on paper. You would certainly have difficulty trying to listen to the discussion going on in class as well.

Thus, it is important to distinguish between *hearing* (what happens automatically when sounds reach your ear) and *listening* (actively paying attention to and attempting to understand and retain what you hear).

Being a good listener is important for your development not only as a student but also as a human being who cares about what others have to say.

## Preparing Yourself to Listen

In order to listen well, you must give the speaker your complete attention. Nearly 75 percent of your time in school is spent listening. You listen to teachers, friends, announcements, movies, records, tape recordings, instructions, and so on. To do all that listening well you must be prepared to listen.

**Prepare yourself to listen by giving the speaker your complete attention.**

**699**

Listening effectively requires concentration and attention. The ability to concentrate and pay attention is like a muscle: It has to be built up, by practice. It is easy to say "pay attention!" But how do you do it? The chart below gives seven suggestions that will help you learn to build the muscle of attention, by repeating them over and over. Practice them daily in your classroom and whenever someone is speaking to you.

## SUGGESTIONS FOR PREPARING TO LISTEN

1. Start with a positive attitude. Say to yourself, "I am going to concentrate on what is said and pay attention." Avoid daydreaming by actively trying to listen, understand, and remember what is being said.
2. Do not look around at your friends in class, out the window, at books on your desk or anything else that would distract you from the speaker. Focus your eyes and ears on the speaker.
3. Concentrate on *what* the speaker is saying and try not to be distracted by his or her looks or manner of speaking.
4. Block out any distractions such as noises inside or outside the classroom, or any concerns or thoughts you had earlier in the day. Do not try to think of questions or answers to what the speaker is saying now—put all your energy into listening and taking in what is being said.
5. Put away anything that may detract from your paying attention to the speaker, such as books, magazines, homework schedules, and so on.
6. Keep a pencil and paper handy in case you want to take notes, but avoid doodling or writing things unrelated to the discussion.
7. Try to find out in advance what main topic will be discussed. That way you have some idea of what to focus on while you are listening. However, do not ignore the speaker because you think you already know what he or she is going to say. You may be surprised by what you hear if you really pay attention.

Your physical condition also affects your ability to pay attention. Therefore, you should get enough rest, eat properly, and get enough exercise. Otherwise, you will be distracted by your body saying "I'm tired! I'm hungry! I want to run around!" when you should be listening and you will not be able to concentrate on listening well in class.

**EXERCISE A: Developing Your Listening Skills.** Read through the seven suggestions on page 700 and try to practice them in one particular class. At the end of the class, grade yourself on how well you listened by answering the following questions.

1. Did I begin with a positive attitude, reminding myself to listen and pay attention?
2. Did I avoid daydreaming?
3. Did I focus my eyes and ears on the speaker?
4. Did I concentrate on *what* the speaker was saying?
5. Did I block out distractions such as noises inside or outside the classroom?
6. Did I stop thinking about personal concerns and thoughts unrelated to the class?
7. Did I put away distracting items such as books, magazines, and so on?
8. Did I take notes?
9. Did I avoid doodling?
10. Did I find out the topic of discussion in advance and use that knowledge to direct my listening?

## Selecting Information to Remember

In order to listen well, you must learn what to listen to. Can you identify main ideas and major details while listening to a speaker? Identifying the speaker's main ideas and major details will help you know what information you want to remember after the speaker is done.

**701**

**Identify and remember the main points and major details while you are listening to the speaker.**

Below are seven questions that will help you identify main points and major details. Read through them, and ask yourself these questions when you are listening in class.

---

### IDENTIFYING MAIN IDEAS AND MAJOR DETAILS

1. What is the opening sentence about? This is often the topic sentence that tells you the general topic.
2. What is the last sentence about? This is often a restatement of the main topic.
3. What important points are being made about the topic?
4. What needs to be remembered about each point?
5. What clues is the speaker giving about something's importance? For example, does he or she begin by saying "Remember . . .," "Most of all . . .," "Importantly . . .," or "To sum up . . ."?
6. Does the speaker repeat an idea or phrase a number of times or emphasize its importance by his or her tone of voice or by using gestures?
7. What is written on the blackboard? What do the visual aids, or supporting materials (if any) tell me about the main idea and major details of what I am listening to?

---

If you practice asking yourself these questions while you are listening carefully, you will eventually become an active and effective listener. You will find that you can get much more out of a class or out of any other listening situation by developing your listening skills.

**EXERCISE B: Practicing Listening Skills.** Work with another student on this exercise. One of you should read the first announcement below aloud, while the other listens for the main idea and major details, writing them down after the reading is completed. Then switch roles and repeat the process with the second passage.

1. There will be a special performance of *You're A Good Man, Charlie Brown* on Friday night, October 21, in the Hayes auditorium. Student-price tickets will be available tomorrow only from 8:30 to 1:30 in Room 242, at $4.00. There will be no student tickets available at the time of the performance.

2. The Explorer's Club will be having its first meeting on Wednesday, April 6, at 3:30 p.m. The registration fee is $3.00, and you need a permission slip from your parents. Come to the school gym, and bring any suggestions or ideas for outings.

**DEVELOPING WRITING SKILLS: Writing About Listening Skills.** Continue to practice the seven suggestions for preparing yourself to listen, and at the end of one week, answer the following questions again. Do you see any improvement? Has your attention-paying muscle begun to get stronger? What areas still need work? Write a paragraph describing any improvements in your ability to listen effectively. Then write a paragraph explaining ways in which you can further improve your listening skills.

# Skills Review and Writing Workshop

## Speaking and Listening Skills
### CHECKING YOUR SKILLS

Working with another student, give oral directions on how to get from one place to another in your school or in the town or city where you live. Do not tell where you are leading your partner. See if the other person can follow the directions in his or her head and figure out where they lead to. Then switch roles, and try it again.

### USING SPEAKING AND LISTENING SKILLS IN WRITING

#### Writing a Speech

Watch a TV news program. Pay close attention, using the suggestions on preparing yourself to listen on page 700 and the questions to help you identify main points and major details while listening on page 702. Take notes while watching and listening to the program. Then, write a speech on what you have seen and heard, following the suggestions below.

**Prewriting:** Look over your notes and try to reconstruct the show. What were the show's main points? What were the major details? What is the purpose and audience for the speech you are preparing?

**Writing:** Organize your material in outline and note-card form, following the suggestions for planning a speech on pages 696 and 697. Then, write out the speech as you would deliver it in class.

**Rewriting:** Look over what you have written. Does it read well? Does it sound natural? Are your main point and major details clear and easy to understand? Proofread your speech carefully, correcting any spelling, grammar, and punctuation errors.

**704**

# Preparing Papers

This short section on preparing papers will give you a style to use in setting up your papers. It will also suggest questions you can ask if you are having problems with grammar, usage, mechanics, or spelling. Finally, it will give you a few useful symbols that you can use when you revise and proofread.

## Setting Up Your Papers

Neatness counts. It may sometimes be a part of your grade, and it will almost always have a favorable effect on your reader. If you use the suggestions in the following charts, your reader will be able to concentrate on your ideas, not on the physical appearance of your paper.

**Setting Up a Handwritten Paper.** Use the following guidelines for a handwritten paper.

### HANDWRITTEN PAPERS

1. Use white, lined, notebook-sized paper. Do not, however, use pages ripped from a spiral binder.
2. Use either blue or black ink.
3. Leave a margin of space on the right side.
4. Indent each paragraph.

**Setting Up a Typed Paper.** Use these guidelines for a typed paper.

### TYPED PAPERS

1. Use white, unlined, notebook-sized paper.
2. Use a clear black ribbon.
3. Leave a margin of space on all sides.
4. Double-space all lines and indent each paragraph.

**Identifying Your Papers.** Your teacher may have a form for you to follow in identifying your papers. If not, use one of the two forms below. The example on the left shows a full title page for long papers. The example on the right works best for short papers.

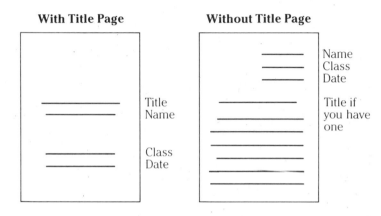

| With Title Page | Without Title Page |
|---|---|

The second page and all additional pages should carry your name and the page number in the upper right-hand corner.

## Checking for Errors

In revising papers look for errors in grammar, usage, mechanics, and spelling. The following charts will help.

**Errors in Grammar.** Common errors in grammar are fragments, run-ons, and errors in modifiers.

| Problems | Questions to Ask | Text Sections |
|---|---|---|
| Fragments | Does each sentence have all of the necessary sentence parts? | 12.1 |
| Run-ons | Are any of your sentences really two sentences? | 12.2 |
| Misplaced Modifiers | Are all modifiers as close as possible to the words modified? | 12.3 |

**Errors in Usage.** Agreement causes problems in usage.

| Problems | Questions to Ask | Text Sections |
|---|---|---|
| Subject-Verb Agreement | Do subjects and verbs agree in number? | 16.1 and 16.2 |
| Pronoun-Antecedent Agreement | Do all the pronouns agree in person and number with their antecedents? | 16.3 |
| Special Problems with Verbs, Modifiers, and Other Words | Have you chosen the wrong verb from certain troublesome pairs? Have you chosen the wrong adjective or adverb? Have you used the wrong word? | 14.4 for Verbs 17.4 for Modifiers 18.2 for Words in General |

**Errors in Mechanics.** Capitals and a few widely used punctuation marks cause the most problems in mechanics.

| Problems | Questions to Ask | Text Sections |
|---|---|---|
| Capitals | Are all proper nouns and adjectives capitalized correctly? | 19.2 for Nouns 19.3 for Adjectives |
| End Marks | Does every sentence have the correct mark at the end? | 21.1 |
| Commas | Do you have a good reason for every comma used? | 21.2–21.4 |
| Apostrophes | Are apostrophes used incorrectly in personal pronouns such as *its*? | 21.10 |

**Errors in Spelling.** Misspellings are common errors.

| Problem | Question to Ask | Text Sections |
|---|---|---|
| Misspelled Words | Have you used a dictionary to check every word you are not sure of? | 36.1 and 36.2 |

## Using Correction Symbols

Correction symbols are special marks that make it easier to show where changes are needed in a paper. The following chart shows some of the most common.

| Symbol and Meaning | Corrected Example | Final Version |
|---|---|---|
| —— take out | Randy admired the ~~the~~ lake. | Randy admired the lake. |
| ∧ add | It was a *deep* blue color. | It was a deep blue color. |
| ¶ paragraph | ¶ Along the lake four hikers were walking. | Along the lake four hikers were walking. |
| *frag* fragment | Very hungry and tired. *frag* | They looked very hungry and tired. |
| *RO* run-on | The group had left camp at dawn, *RO* they had hiked for hours. *mod* | The group had left camp at dawn, and they had hiked for hours. |
| *mod* misplaced modifier | Distant, Randy pointed to the campsite. | Randy pointed to the distant campsite. |
| *sp* spelling | They headed down the trale. *sp* | They headed down the trail. |

# Index

Bold numbers show pages on which basic definitions and rules can be found.

**710**

verbs, 97–**98**, 124
*see also* Compound nouns
Concluding expression, with direct
    quotation, **333**–334
Conjugation, **200**–202, **205**–207
Conjunction, **77**–80
    capitalization in titles, 286
    coordinating, **77**–78, 174
    correlative, **79**–80
    diagraming, 123
    identifying, 85
    subordinating, 152
Connotation, 647–648
Context, word recognition from, **582**–589
    in literature, 587–589
    in science, 585–587
    in social studies, 583–585
Contractions, **355**–356
Coordinating conjunction, **77**–78, **174**
Correction symbols, 708
Correlative conjunction, **79**–80
Correspondence. *See* Letters
Critical reading, **645**–649
Critical thinking, 631–638
    language and, 636–637
    reasoning, forms of, 631–636
Cross-reference cards, 659

Dates
    abbreviations, **297**–298
    capitalization, 277–278
    commas with, **320**–321
Days and months
    capitalization, 277–278
    comma, **320**–321
Declarative sentence, **119**, 305
Definite article, **52**, 53–54
Definitions, 685
Degrees of comparison. *See* Comparative
    degree; Positive degree;
    Superlative degree
Demonstrative adjective, 59
Demonstrative pronoun, **32**–33, 59
Denotation, 647–648
Derivations, 686
Descriptive writing, 466–471
    impressions in, **467**–469
    suggestions, **470**–471
Details
    paragraph, 404–406
    sentence, **384**–386
Dewey Decimal System, 663–664
Diagraming
    appositives, 144–145
    basic sentence parts, 121–127
    clauses, 160–163
    phrases, 143–144
Dialogue, 338–339, 541–**542**
Dictionary, 679–687
    antonyms and synonyms in, 686
    definitions, 685
    derived words, 686
    etymologies, 686
    field labels, 686
    finding words in, 681–682

main entry, 683–687
    part-of-speech labels, 685
    pronunciation, 684
    specialized, **670**–672
    spelling aid, 600–**601**, **679**–680, 683
    syllabification, 684
    usage labels, 686
*Did, done,* **208**
*Different from, different than,* **264–265**
Direct object, **106**–111
    or adverb, 108
    diagraming, 125
    or object of preposition, 108
    in questions, **109**–110
Direct quotation
    with concluding expression, **333**–334
    with interrupting expression, **334**
    with introductory expression, **333**
    quotation marks with, 331–339
Directions
    giving, **692**–693
    understood subject in, **101**–102
Discussions. *See* Group discussions
Dividing words, **348–350**, 684
*Done, did,* **208**
Double negatives, 261–263
Draft (composition)
    first, **368**–369, **488**–489, **507**–508,
        **520, 543**
    paragraph, **440**–442
*Drowned, drownded,* **208**

*Each,* **231**
Editing, **370**–371
*Effect, affect,* **264**
*ei, ie,* words, **615**–616
Emotion
    exclamation mark to show, 307
    interjection to express, 81, 307
Encyclopedias, **666**–667, **672**
End marks, **174**–175, 304, **305**–308
    to correct run-on sentences, **174**
    *see also* Exclamation mark; Period;
        Question mark
English. *See* Informal English; Nonstandard
    English; Slang; Standard English
Envelope, **555**, **558**
Essay, 475–496
    first draft, **488**–489
    outline, **485**–488
    parts, **475**–479
    prewriting, **479**–488
    revising, **490**–493
    thesis statement, 483–485
Essential expressions
    adjective clauses, 319
    appositives, 318
    participial phrases, 319
Etymology
    coined words, **597**–598
    dictionary, 686
    loan words, **595**–596
    new meanings, 596–**597**
Events, capitalization, **277**–278
*Every,* **231**

**714**

**716**

**717**

# Acknowledgments

The authors and editors have made every effort to trace the ownership of all copyrighted selections found in this book and to make full acknowledgment for their use.

The dictionary of record for this book is *Webster's New World Dictionary*, Second College Edition, Revised School Printing, copyright © 1983 by Simon & Schuster, Inc. The basis for the selection of vocabulary words appropriate for this grade level is *Living Word Vocabulary: A 43,000 Word Vocabulary Inventory* by Edgar Dale and Joseph O'Rourke, copyright © 1979.

Citations follow, arranged by unit and page for easy reference.

**Composition: Forms and Process of Writing.** **Pages 402** (first item) Abby Rand. Adapted from an article in *Travel & Leisure Magazine* (December 1981). **402-403** (second item) Michael Frome. Adapted from an article in *Travel & Leisure Magazine* (December 1981). **403** Kathleen Cecil. Adapted from an article in *Travel & Leisure Magazine* (December 1981). **405** Evelyn Conti and William Lass, "The Homemaker's Guide to the Bathroom and Kitchen." (New York: American Standard, Inc., 1974). **406** (first item) Carla Hunt. From an article in *Travel & Leisure Magazine* (October 1980). **406** (second item) Paul Goldberger. Adapted from an article in *Travel & Leisure Magazine* (April 1981). **406** (third item) From A WIZARD OF EARTHSEA by Ursula LeGuin. Copyright © 1968 by Ursula K. LeGuin. Reprinted by permission of Houghton Mifflin Company. **408** (first item), **443** Elsa Pedersen, *Alaska* (New York: Coward, McCann & Geoghegan, Inc. © 1968). **408** (second item), **409** (second item) Adapted from the book *How to Live with a Neurotic Dog* by Stephen Baker © 1960 by Prentice-Hall, Inc. Published by Prentice-Hall, Inc., Englewood Cliffs, New Jersey 07632. **409** (first item) Adapted from Pat Rose, "Night Watch with Post 53," from *Exploring Magazine*, February 1978. **413** Adapted from the book *Concise Book of Astronomy* by Jacqueline and Simon Mitton © 1978 by Trewin Coppleston Publishing, Limited. Published by Prentice-Hall, Inc., Englewood Cliffs, New Jersey 07632. **419, 460** (second item) Excerpt from *The Complete Beginner's Guide to Skin Diving* by Shaney Frey. Copyright © 1965 by Shaney Frey. Reprinted by permission of Doubleday & Company, Inc. **460** (first item) From the book *Hawaii: A History*, Second Edition, by Ralph S. Kuykendall and A. Grove Day © 1961 by Ralph S. Kuykendall and A. Grove Day. Published by Prentice-Hall, Inc., Englewood Cliffs, New Jersey 07632. **470** Susan Cooper, *The Grey King*. Copyright © 1975 by Susan Cooper (New York: Atheneum Publishers). **478-479** Adapted from Dorothy Sara, *The Complete Book of Handwriting Analysis* (New York: Dell Publishing Co., Inc. 1967).

**Study and Research Skills.** **Pages 636** Anastasia Toufexis, "The Shape of the Nation" *Time Magazine* (October 1985). Copyright © 1985 Time Inc. All rights reserved. Reprinted by permission from Time. **638** Phillip Elmer-Dewitt, "Tools in the Hands of Kids" *Time Magazine* (September 1985). Copyright 1985 Time Inc. All rights reserved. Reprinted by permission from Time. **667** *The Encyclopedia Americana*. Reprinted with permission of the Encyclopedia Americana, copyright 1981, Grolier Inc. **668** (index entry, text entry) *The World Almanac and Book of Facts* 1984. Reprinted by permission of The World Almanac, Division of Newspaper Enterprise Association, New York. **669** (index entry, map) Reprinted by permission. Copyright by Rand McNally & Company, R.L.81-S-120. **671-672** Excerpt from *Roget's International Thesaurus*, Fourth Edition by Robert Chapman. Copyright © 1977 by Harper & Row, Publishers, Inc. Reprinted by permission of the publisher. **673-674** From *Current Biography* 1984. Copyright © 1984 by the H.W. Wilson Company. Material reproduced by permission of the publisher. **676, 678** *Readers' Guide to Periodical Literature* Copyright © 1984, 1985 by The H.W. Wilson Company. Material reproduced by permission of the publisher. **680** (chart) **683-687** With permission. From Webster's *New World Dictionary*. Students Edition, Copyright © 1981 by Simon & Schuster, Inc.

**Art Acknowledgments.** **Pages 373** Mark Boulton, Photo Researchers. **426** Hazel Hankin, Stock Boston. **427** United Feature Syndicate, Inc., © 1960. **428** Haeseler, Art Resource. **455** The Granger Collection. **457** NASA. **472** General Motors Corporation. **473** Bob S. Smith,

**719**

# GRAMMAR USAGE MECHANICS